EXPERT RESUMES for
Manufacturing Careers
Engineering, Management, Executive, Operations, Production, and Technology

Wendy S. Enelow and
Louise M. Kursmark

Expert Resumes for Manufacturing Careers

© 2002 by Wendy S. Enelow and Louise M. Kursmark

Published by JIST Works, an imprint of JIST Publishing, Inc.
8902 Otis Avenue
Indianapolis, IN 46216-1033
Phone: 1-800-648-JIST   Fax: 1-800-JIST-FAX   E-mail: info@jist.com

Visit our Web site at **www.jist.com** for information on JIST, free job search information, book chapters, and ordering information on our many products!

See the back of this book for additional JIST titles and ordering information. Quantity discounts are available for JIST books. Please call our Sales Department at 1-800-648-5478 for a free catalog and more information.

Acquisitions and Development Editor: Lori Cates Hand
Copy Editor: Mary Ellen Stephenson
Cover Designer: Katy Bodenmiller
Interior Designer and Page Layout: Trudy Coler
Proofreader: Jeanne Clark
Indexer: Larry Sweazy

Printed in the United States of America
06 05 04 03 02   9 8 7 6 5 4 3 2 1

Library of Congress Cataloging-in-Publication Data

Enelow, Wendy S.
   Expert resumes for manufacturing and industrial jobs/ Wendy S. Enelow and Louise M. Kursmark.
       p. cm.
     Includes index.
     ISBN 1-56370-858-2
       1. Résumés (Employment) 2. Manufacturing industries—Vocational guidance. I. Kursmark, Louise M., 1956- II. Title.

HF5383 .E4788 2002
650.14'2—dc21   2001038926

ISBN 1-56370-858-2

CONTENTS AT A GLANCE

TABLE OF CONTENTS

ABOUT THIS BOOK

There are more than 18 million individuals employed in manufacturing professions in the United States, and in 2000 the manufacturing industry as a whole boasted an unemployment rate of only 3.6 percent. Although the industry may not be growing at double-digit percentages as in years past, the industry continues to exist as a solid player in our economy.

What's more, manufacturing offers diverse career opportunities, including

- Production personnel, craftsmen, technicians, and supervisors
- Engineering, product development, and quality professionals
- Production planning, scheduling, and operations support personnel
- Materials, supply-chain, distribution, and logistics professionals
- Equipment and facilities design, construction, and maintenance personnel
- Manufacturing "business support" personnel across a wide range of technical, administrative, and management functions
- Plant, operations, general, and executive managers

And the list continues. In every city and every state, there are countless manufacturing opportunities. And that's great news for you!

To take advantage of all of these opportunities, you must first develop a powerful, performance-based resume. To be a savvy and successful job seeker, you must know how to communicate your qualifications in a strong and effective written presentation. Sure, it's important to let employers know essential details, but a resume is more than just your job history and academic credentials. A winning resume is a concise yet comprehensive document that gives you a competitive edge in the job market. Creating such a powerful document is what this book is all about.

We'll explore the changes in resume presentation that have arisen over the past decade. In the past, resumes were almost always printed on paper and mailed. Today, e-mail has become the chosen method for resume distribution in many industries. In turn, many of the traditional methods for "typing" and presenting resumes have changed dramatically. This book will instruct you in the methods for preparing resumes for e-mail, scanning, and Web site posting, as well as the traditional printed resume.

By using *Expert Resumes for Manufacturing Careers* as your professional guide, you will succeed in developing a powerful and effective resume that opens doors,

INTRODUCTION

gets interviews, and helps you land your next great opportunity!

Let's be honest: Opportunities in the manufacturing industry have spiraled downward over the past decade, but perhaps not as significantly as you might believe. According to the U.S. Department of Labor, Bureau of Labor Statistics, the number of manufacturing jobs declined from 19.1 million in 1990 to 18.4 million in 2000.

Now, if you happened to be one of those 700,000 workers who were displaced, finding a new position may have been difficult. In fact, you might still be actively engaged in a job search. However, remember this important fact: There were 18.4 million jobs in manufacturing in 2000. Despite what you might hear or read, opportunities exist in manufacturing, from the small plastics injection-molding company to the multinational high-tech and electronics manufacturing conglomerate.

Department of Labor statistics also indicate that

- Manufacturing is by far the largest of the goods-producing industries in terms of employment.

- Manufacturing employees outnumber their colleagues in construction and mining (the other two major goods-producing industries) by nearly three to one.

- Although unemployment rates in 1992 and 1993 hit a high of 7.8 percent, the manufacturing industry boasted an unemployment rate of only 3.6 percent in 2000.

- Hourly earnings in the manufacturing industry in 2000 were $14.38, compared to an average of $13.74 for all workers.

- Hourly earnings have, in fact, grown steadily since 1991, even during the years when unemployment was at its peak.

These facts and statistics clearly demonstrate that there are solid employment opportunities within the manufacturing industry. What's more, the U.S. economy has given birth to some of the largest and most successful manufacturing companies in the world and will continue to do so. Although the industry may not be growing at double-digit percentages as in years past, the industry continues to exist as a solid player in our economy.

What's more, the dramatic and rapid emergence of technology throughout all sectors of our lives has changed what we manufacture and how we manufacture it. In turn, technology has created a host of new professional opportunities. When we combine all options, you're presented with the following array of career opportunities:

- **Manufacturing workforce** (hourly workers, laborers, craftsmen, tradesmen, technicians, and production supervisors)

- **Manufacturing, general, and executive management** (plant managers, vice presidents of operations, general managers, manufacturing and production managers, directors of operations, project managers, chief financial officers, chief executive officers, and presidents)

- **Product development and management professionals** (multidisciplinary engineers, engineering technicians, quality assurance and quality control specialists, and product line managers)

- **Production operations and support personnel** (production planners and schedulers, production controllers, process engineers, and materials managers)

- **Product movement personnel** (warehouse managers, purchasing agents, distribution managers, transportation planners, drivers, and logistics managers)

- **Facilities personnel** (design engineers, construction managers, maintenance and repair managers, technicians, and safety and security personnel)

- **Manufacturing "business support" personnel** (labor-relations specialists, training and development professionals, plant controllers, accounting managers, technical project managers, cost accountants, and OSHA and regulatory compliance personnel)

To take advantage of these opportunities, you must be an educated job seeker. That means you must know what you want in your career, where the hiring action is, what qualifications and credentials you need to attain your desired career goals, and how best to market your qualifications. It is no longer enough to be a talented craftsman, production supervisor, plant manager, or labor-relations consultant. Now, you must be a strategic marketer, able to package and promote your experience to take advantage of the available employment opportunities.

There's no doubt that the employment market has changed dramatically from only a few years ago. According to the U.S. Department of Labor (2000), you should expect to hold between 10 and 20 different jobs during your career. No longer is stability the status quo. Today, the norm is movement in a fast-paced and intense employment market. And to stay on top of all the changes and opportunities, you must proactively control and manage your career.

Job Search Questions and Answers for the Manufacturing Industry

Whether you're currently employed in a manufacturing job, looking to enter the field for the first time, or a recent victim of downsizing or layoff, the following questions and answers provide some practical advice.

How Do You Enter the Manufacturing Professions?

As with any other industry or profession, your employment experience, education, and credentials are the keys to entry and long-term success. It is difficult to obtain a position in manufacturing without some related work experience, training, technical credentials, or relevant education. Here are a few pointers:

- **If you're just starting to plan and build your career,** consider a four-year degree in a manufacturing-related discipline, a technical certification program, or other "craft-related" training program. Once you've earned your initial degree or completed your training, you'll want to keep your sights focused on continuing your education as you move forward in your manufacturing career. In many organizations, it will be a prerequisite for long-term career advancement.

- **If you're an experienced craftsman, tradesman, operations supervisor, business professional, technologist, manager, administrator, or the like,** but have no manufacturing experience, focus your resume on your professional experiences and how they relate to the field of manufacturing and its allied professions. Who better to build and buy a product than someone who is perhaps familiar with the product from the buyer's side?

How Do You Change the Product or Industry Focus of Your Manufacturing Career?

- **If you've had a successful manufacturing career and want to change your product focus,** the best advice is to "leave the product behind" when writing your resume. Sell your achievements, highlight your notable projects, quantify your results, and share your knowledge on your resume. However, do it without mentioning the specific product(s). Tell your reader that you "increased WIP by 22%" and NOT that you "increased WIP by 22% on the main cereal manufacturing line." If the product becomes the main focus of your resume, you've most likely knocked yourself out of the running.

What Is the Best Resume Strategy If You're Already in the Manufacturing Sector?

If you're already employed in the manufacturing field but are interested in moving onward and upward, remember one critical fact:

> Your resume is a marketing tool written to sell YOU!

If you're a production supervisor, section leader, or department manager, *sell* the fact that you've increased product throughput and reduced processing time. If you're a quality assurance technician, *highlight* the percentage of increase in product performance and reliability or the percentage of reduction in failure rates. If you're a plant controller, *sell* the fact that you reduced production costs by a certain percentage and contributed a specific number of dollars to bottom-line profit contributions.

When writing your resume, your challenge is to create a picture of knowledge, action, and results. In essence, you're stating, "This is what I know, this is how I've used it, and this is how well I've performed." Success sells, so be sure to highlight yours. If you don't, no one else will.

This same advice applies to you if you're unemployed due to layoff or downsizing. The job market will be competitive as you vie with others from your previous employer who were also laid off. Be sure to sell your specific, unique accomplishments to set yourself apart from others and demonstrate the value you offer your next employer.

WHERE ARE THE JOBS?

The jobs are everywhere—from multinational manufacturing conglomerates to the small basket manufacturer down the street; from high-tech electronics firms in Silicon Valley to 100-year-old tire manufacturers in rural communities; and in virtually every town and city across the United States.

- The jobs are **on the production floor,** at all levels and in all types of manufacturing organizations. Skilled and unskilled labor is constantly in demand. Your challenge is to find the "right" opportunity.

- The jobs are in the **engineering, development, and commercialization** of new products and new technologies.

- The jobs are in the **design** of new manufacturing techniques, processes, systems, and operations to accelerate productivity, reduce costs, and improve profitability.

- The jobs are in the areas of **production support** including purchasing, materials management, logistics, distribution, transportation, and the other functions that get materials to a production facility and then coordinate the movement of finished products.

- The jobs are in the **workforce support** professions such as labor relations, safety, organizational development, employee relations, benefits design and administration, personnel training, and other employee-service functions.

- The jobs are in the **design, construction, and maintenance** of world-class manufacturing facilities.

- The jobs are in the **corporate offices,** at the highest levels, as the manufacturing industry continues to evolve and reinvent itself.

The jobs are everywhere.

HOW DO YOU GET THE JOBS?

To answer this question, we need to review the basic principle underlying job search:

> Job search is marketing!

You have a product to sell—yourself—and the best way to sell it is to use all appropriate *marketing channels* just as you would for any other product.

Suppose you wanted to sell televisions. What would you do? You'd market your products using newspaper, magazine, and radio advertisements. You might develop a company Web site to build your e-business, and perhaps you'd hire a field sales representative to market to major retail chains. Each of these is a different marketing channel through which you're attempting to reach your audience.

The same is true for a job search. You must use every marketing channel that's right for you. Unfortunately, there is no single formula. What's right for you depends on your specific career objectives—the type of position, type of industry, geographic restrictions, salary requirements, and more.

Following are the most valuable marketing channels for a successful job search within the manufacturing industry. These are ordered from most effective to least effective.

1. **Referrals.** There is nothing better than a personal referral to a company or institution, either in general or for a specific position. Referrals can open doors that, in most instances, would never be accessible any other way. If you know anyone who could possibly refer you to a specific organization, contact that person immediately and ask for his assistance.

2. **Networking.** Networking is the backbone of every successful job search. Although you may consider it a task, it is essential that you network effectively with your professional colleagues and associates, past employers, past co-workers, suppliers, neighbors, friends, and others who may know of opportunities that are right for you. Another good strategy is to attend meetings of trade or professional associations in your area to make new contacts and expand your network. And particularly in today's nomadic job market—where you're likely to change jobs every few years—the best strategy is to keep your network "alive" even when you're *not* searching for a new position.

3. **Responses to newspaper, magazine, and periodical advertisements.** Although, as you'll read later, the opportunity to post job opportunities online has reduced the overall number of print advertisements, they still abound. Do not forget about this "tried and true" marketing strategy. If an advertiser has the job you want and you have the qualifications, it's a perfect fit.

4. **Responses to online job postings.** One of the greatest advantages of the technology revolution is an employer's ability to post job announcements and a job seeker's ability to respond immediately via e-mail. It's a wonder! In most (but not all) instances, these are bona fide opportunities, and it's well worth your while to spend time searching for and responding to appropriate postings. However, don't make the mistake of devoting *too* much time to searching the Internet. It can consume a huge amount of your time that you should spend on other job search efforts.

   To expedite your search, here are the largest and most widely used online job posting sites—presented alphabetically, not necessarily in order of effectiveness or value (see the appendix for more job search sites):

www.careerbuilder.com

www.dice.com

www.flipdog.com

www.headhunter.net

www.hotjobs.com

www.monster.com

www.sixfigurejobs.com

5. **Targeted e-mail campaigns (resumes and cover letters) to recruiters.**
Recruiters have jobs, and you want one. It's pretty straightforward. The only
catch is to find the "right" recruiters who have the "right" jobs. Therefore,
you must devote the time and effort to preparing the "right" list of recruiters.
There are many resources on the Internet where you can access information
about recruiters (for a fee), sort that information by industry (manufacturing,
purchasing, logistics, engineering, and so on), and then cross-reference with
position specialization (management, technical, administration). This allows
you to identify just the "right" recruiters who would be interested in a candidate with your qualifications. What's more, because these campaigns are trans-
mitted electronically, they are easy and inexpensive to produce.

When working with recruiters, it's important to realize that they *do not* work
for you! Their clients are the hiring companies that pay their fees. They are not
in business to "find a job" for you, but rather to fill a specific position with a
qualified candidate, either you or someone else. To maximize your chances of
finding a position through a recruiter or agency, don't rely on just one or two,
but distribute your resume to many that meet your specific criteria.

6. **Online resume postings.** The Net is swarming with reasonably priced (if not
free) Web sites where you can post your resume. It's quick, easy, and the only
passive thing you should do in your search. All of the other marketing channels
require action on your part. With online resume postings, once you've posted,
you're done. You then just wait (and hope!) for some response.

7. **Targeted e-mail and print campaigns to employers.** Just as with campaigns
to recruiters (see item 5 above), you must be extremely careful to select just
the right employers that would be interested in a candidate with your qualifications. The closer you stick to "where you belong" in relation to your specific
experience, the better your response rate will be. If you are targeting companies that manufacture technology, you can also contact these employers via
e-mail. If you are looking at employers outside the technology manufacturing
industries, we believe that print campaigns (paper and envelopes mailed the
old-fashioned way) are a more suitable and effective presentation—particularly
if you are a management or executive candidate.

8. **In-person "cold calls" to companies and recruiters.** We consider this the
least effective and most time-consuming marketing strategy for manufacturing
jobs. It is extremely difficult to just walk in the door and get in front of the
right person, or any person who can take hiring action. You'll be much better
off focusing your time and energy on other, more productive channels.

WHAT ABOUT OPPORTUNITIES IN CONSULTING AND CONTRACTING IN THE MANUFACTURING INDUSTRY?

Are you familiar with the term "free agent"? It's the latest buzz word for an independent contractor or consultant who moves from project to project and company to company as the workload dictates. If you are in the manufacturing industry and have a particular expertise (for example, process redesign, change management, new product development, or operations turnaround), you might want to consider this avenue.

According to a recent article in *Quality Progress* magazine (November 2000), 10 years ago less than 10 percent of the U.S. workforce was employed as free agents. Currently, that number is greater than 20 percent and is expected to increase to 40 percent over the next 10 years. The demand for free agents is vast, and the market offers excellent career opportunities.

The reason for this growth is directly related to the manner in which companies are now hiring—or not hiring—their workforces. The opportunity now exists for companies to hire on a "per project" basis and avoid the costs associated with full-time, permanent employees. Companies hire the staff they need just when they need them—and when they no longer need them, the staff is gone.

The newest revolution in online job search has risen in response to this demand: job auction sites where employers bid on prospective employees. Individuals post their resumes and qualifications for review by prospective employers. The employers then competitively bid to hire or contract with each candidate. Two well-established job auction Web sites are www.freeagent.com and www.elance.com; you can also identify contract opportunities at many other sites, including www.dice.com. Check out these opportunities. They're quite interesting, particularly if you're pursuing a career in consulting or contracting within the manufacturing industry.

Conclusion

Career opportunities are prevalent within the manufacturing industries and professions today. What's more, it has never been easier to learn about and apply for jobs. Arm yourself with a powerful resume and cover letter, identify your most appropriate marketing channels, and start your search today. You're destined to reach the next rung on your career ladder.

PART I

Resume Writing, Strategy, and Formats

CHAPTER 1

Resume Writing Strategies for Manufacturing Careers

If you're reading this book, chances are you've decided to make a career move. It may be because

- You're graduating from college or technical school and are ready to launch your professional career.

- You've just earned your graduate degree and are ready to make a step up in your career.

- You're ready to leave your current position and move up the ladder to a higher-paying and more responsible position.

- You've decided on a career change and will be looking at opportunities in both the manufacturing industry and related professions.

- You're unhappy with your current employer or management team and have decided to pursue opportunities elsewhere.

- You've been laid off, downsized, or otherwise left your position, and you must find a new one.

- You've completed a contract assignment and are looking for a new "free agent" job or perhaps a permanent position.

- You're relocating to a new area and need to find a new job.

- You're returning to the workforce after several years of unemployment or retirement.

- You're simply ready for a change.

There may even be other reasons for your job search besides these. However, no matter the reason, a powerful resume is an essential component of your search campaign. In fact, it is virtually impossible to conduct a search without a resume. It is your calling card that briefly, yet powerfully, communicates the skills, qualifications, experience, and value you bring to a prospective employer. It is the document that will open doors and generate interviews. It is the first thing people will learn about you when you forward it in response to an advertisement, and it is the last thing they'll remember when they're reviewing your qualifications after an interview.

Your resume is a sales document, and you are the product! You must identify the *features (what you know* and *what you can do)* and *benefits (how you can help an employer)* of that product, then communicate them in a concise and hard-hitting written presentation. Remind yourself over and over, as you work your way through the resume process, that you are writing marketing literature designed to sell a new product—YOU—into a new position.

Your resume can have tremendous power and a phenomenal impact on your job search. So don't take it lightly. Rather, devote the time, energy, and resources that are essential to developing a resume that is well-written, visually attractive, and effective in communicating *who* you are and *how* you want to be perceived.

Resume Strategies

Following are the nine core strategies for writing effective and successful resumes.

RESUME STRATEGY #1: WHO ARE YOU, AND HOW DO YOU WANT TO BE PERCEIVED?

Now that you've decided to look for a new position, the very first step is to identify your career interests, goals, and objectives. *This task is critical* because it is the underlying foundation for *what* you include in your resume, *how* you include it, and *where* you include it. You cannot write an effective resume without knowing, at least to some degree, what type or types of positions you will be seeking.

There are two concepts to consider here:

- **Who you are:** This relates to what you have done professionally and/or academically. Are you a metal craftsman, electrical engineer, production planner, logistics specialist, or purchasing agent? Are you a facilities engineer, cost accountant, quality director, or vice president of manufacturing? Are you a recent graduate with an undergraduate degree in mechanical engineering, or have you just earned your MBA? Who are you?

- **How you want to be perceived:** This relates to your current career objectives. If you're an engineer looking for a position as an engineering manager or project manager, don't focus solely on your technical and design skills. Put an equal emphasis on your success in team building and leadership, project budgeting, project management, and new product development. If you're a production floor supervisor seeking a promotion to the next tier of management, highlight your accomplishments in reducing operating costs, improving productivity, streamlining operations, eliminating product defects, and contributing profits to the bottom line.

The strategy, then, is to connect these two concepts by using the *Who You Are* information that ties directly to the *How You Want to Be Perceived* message to determine what information to include in your resume. By following this strategy, you're painting a picture that allows a prospective employer to see you as you wish to be seen—as an individual with the qualifications for the type of position you are pursuing.

> **WARNING:** If you prepare a resume without first clearly identifying what your objectives are and how you want to be perceived, your resume will have no focus and no direction. Without the underlying knowledge of "This is what I want to be," you do not know what to highlight in your resume. In turn, the document becomes an historical overview of your career and not the sales document it is designed to be.

RESUME STRATEGY #2: SELL IT TO ME...DON'T TELL IT TO ME

We've already established the fact that resume writing is sales. You are the product, and you must create a document that powerfully communicates the value of that product. One particularly effective strategy for accomplishing this is the "Sell It to Me...Don't Tell It to Me" strategy, which impacts virtually every single word you write on your resume.

If you "tell it," you are simply stating facts. If you "sell it," you promote it, advertise it, and draw attention to it. Look at the difference in impact between these examples:

> *Tell It Strategy:* Supervised mechanical retrofit of 2-acre manufacturing facility.

> *Sell It Strategy:* Directed team of 12 responsible for $2.8 million mechanical retrofit of 2-acre manufacturing facility. Slashed project budget 20% and achieved all quality and safety objectives.

> *Tell It Strategy:* Participated in a large-scale reorganization of the entire manufacturing facility.

> *Sell It Strategy:* Spearheaded plant-wide reorganization impacting 1,000 employees and over $450 million in product throughput each year. Reduced operating costs 22%, reduced waste 18%, introduced lean manufacturing techniques, and added $14+ million to bottom-line profits.

> *Tell It Strategy:* Set up machines to manufacture chemicals and allied products.

> *Sell It Strategy:* Configured product equipment for the manufacture of chemicals and allied products for Fortune 500 customers worldwide. Initiated process improvements that saved $50,000/year.

What's the difference between "telling it" and "selling it"? In a nutshell…

Telling It	Selling It
Describes features.	Describes benefits.
Tells what and how.	Sells why the "what" and "how" are important.
Details activities.	Includes results.
Focuses on what you did.	Details how what you did benefited your employer, department, team members, students, and so on.

RESUME STRATEGY #3: USE KEY WORDS

No matter what you read or who you talk to about job search, the concept of key words is sure to come up. Key words (or, as they were previously known, *buzz words*) are words and phrases specific to a particular industry or profession. For example, key words for the manufacturing industry include *production planning and scheduling, production operations, inventory control, quality assurance, process engineering, robotics, systems automation, integrated logistics, product specifications, project management,* and many, many more.

Whenever you use these words and phrases—in your resume, in your cover letter, or during an interview—you are communicating a very specific message. For example, when you include the words "new product design" in your resume, your reader will most likely assume that you have experience in R&D, product engineering, specifications and documentation, product testing, failure analysis, performance analysis, product costing, new product manufacturing, and more. As you can see, people will make inferences about your skills based on the use of just one or two individual words.

Here are a few other examples:

- When you use the words **integrated logistics,** people will assume you have experience with supply-chain management, warehousing, distribution, purchasing, materials management, inventory control, and more.

- When you mention **preventive maintenance,** readers and listeners will infer that you have experience in scheduling and performing maintenance on plant equipment, troubleshooting system failures, designing regularly scheduled maintenance and repair programs, and more.

- By referencing **manufacturing technology** in your resume, you convey that you most likely have experience in systems design and automation, robotics, SAP (or other leading-edge systems), and more.

- When you use the word **hazmat,** most people will assume you are familiar with hazardous materials handling, storage, transportation, and destruction, along with state and federal regulations (including OSHA), risk assessment, and more.

Key words are also an integral component of the resume scanning process, whereby employers and recruiters electronically search resumes for specific terms to find candidates with the skills, qualifications, and credentials for their particular hiring needs. Although not as prevalent in "traditional" manufacturing as in other industries, particularly in technology-related industries and large corporations with significant hiring activity, key-word scanning is increasing in popularity because of its ease and efficiency. Just like any other job seekers, manufacturing professionals must stay on top of the latest trends in technology-based hiring and employment.

In organizations where it has been implemented, electronic scanning has replaced the more traditional method of an actual person reading your resume (at least initially). Therefore, to some degree, the *only* thing that matters in this instance is that you have included the "right" key words to match the company's or the recruiter's needs. Without them, you will most certainly be passed over.

Of course, in virtually every instance, your resume will be read at some point by human eyes. So it's not enough just to throw together a list of key words and leave it at that. In fact, it's not even necessary to include a separate "key-word summary" on your resume. A better strategy is to incorporate key words naturally into the text within the appropriate sections of your resume.

Keep in mind, too, that key words are arbitrary; there is no defined set of key words for a facilities engineer, metalworker, production supervisor, QA specialist, project manager, or vice president of operations. Employers searching to fill these positions develop a list of terms that reflect the specifics they desire in a qualified candidate. These might be a combination of professional qualifications, skills, education, length of experience, and other easily defined criteria along with "soft skills," such as leadership, problem-solving, and communication.

NOTE: Because of the complex and arbitrary nature of key-word selection, we cannot overemphasize how vital it is to be certain that *all* of the key words that represent your experience and knowledge are included in your resume!

How can you be sure that you are including all the key words, and the right key words? Just by describing your work experience, achievements, educational credentials, technical qualifications, and the like, you will naturally include most of the terms that are important in your field. To cross-check what you've written, review online or newspaper job postings for positions that are of interest to you. Look at the precise terms used in the ads and be sure you have included them in your resume (as appropriate to your skills and qualifications).

Another great benefit of today's technology revolution is the ability to find instant information, even information as specific as key words for the manufacturing industries. Refer to the appendix for Web sites that include thousands of key words. These are outstanding resources.

RESUME STRATEGY #4: USE THE "BIG" AND SAVE THE "LITTLE"

When deciding what you want to include in your resume, try to focus on the "big" things—new programs, special projects, cost savings, productivity and efficiency improvements, new products, technology implementations, and more. Give a good, broad-based picture of what you were responsible for and how well you did it. Here's an example:

> Managed daily operations of Production, Manpower, Maintenance Scheduling, Materials, and Safety departments, with a direct reporting staff of 8 and 43 hourly employees. In addition, controlled a $4.8 million annual operating budget and up to $10 million in annual project budgets each year. Consistently achieved/surpassed all operating, quality, and financial objectives.

Then, save the "little" stuff—the details—for the interview. With this strategy, you will accomplish two things: You'll keep your resume readable and of a reasonable length (while still selling your achievements), and you'll have new and interesting information to share during the interview, rather than merely repeating what is already on your resume. Using the above example, when discussing this experience during an interview, you could elaborate on your specific achievements; namely, improving productivity and efficiency ratings, reducing annual operating costs and annual purchasing costs, sourcing new vendors, streamlining the work force, and automating previously manual operations.

RESUME STRATEGY #5: MAKE YOUR RESUME "INTERVIEWABLE"

One of your greatest challenges is to make your resume a useful interview tool. Once the employer determines that you meet the primary qualifications for a position (you've passed the key-word scanning test or initial review) and you are contacted for a telephone or in-person interview, your resume becomes all-important in leading and prompting your interviewer during your conversation.

Your job, then, is to make sure the resume leads the reader where you want to go and presents just the right organization, content, and appearance to stimulate a productive discussion. To improve the "interviewability" of your resume, consider these tactics:

- Make good use of Resume Strategy #4 (Use the "Big" and Save the "Little") to invite further discussion about your experiences.

- Be sure your greatest "selling points" are featured prominently, not buried within the resume.

- Conversely, don't devote lots of space and attention to areas of your background that are irrelevant or about which you feel less than positive; you'll only invite questions about things you really don't want to discuss.

- Make sure your resume is highly readable—this means plenty of white space, an adequate font size, and a logical flow from start to finish.

RESUME STRATEGY #6: ELIMINATE CONFUSION WITH STRUCTURE AND CONTEXT

Keep in mind that your resume will be read *very quickly* by hiring authorities! You may agonize over every word and spend hours working on content and design, but the average reader will skim quickly through your masterpiece and expect to pick up important facts in just a few seconds. Try to make it as easy as possible for readers to grasp the essential facts:

- Be consistent—for example, put job titles, company names, and dates in the same place for each position.

- Make information easy to find by clearly defining different sections of your resume with large, highly visible headings.

- Define the context in which you worked (for example, the organization, your department, or the specific challenges you faced) before you start describing your activities and accomplishments.

RESUME STRATEGY #7: USE FUNCTION TO DEMONSTRATE ACHIEVEMENT

When you write a resume that focuses only on your job functions, it can be dry and uninteresting and will say very little about your unique activities and contributions. Consider the following example:

> Responsible for all aspects of electrical wiring needs of multiple-facility property.

Now, consider using that same function to demonstrate achievement and see what happens to the tone and energy of the sentence. It becomes alive and clearly communicates that you deliver results.

> Delivered $200,000 commercial electrical wiring project on time and within budget. Supervised field crew of 8 electricians and helpers, ordered all project supplies and materials, designed efficient scheduling system, and achieved all customer specifications.

Try to translate your functions into achievements and you'll create a more powerful resume presentation.

RESUME STRATEGY #8: REMAIN IN THE REALM OF REALITY

We've already established that resume writing is sales. And, as any good salesperson does, one feels somewhat inclined to stretch the truth, just a bit. However, be forewarned that you must stay within the realm of reality. Do not push your skills and qualifications outside the bounds of what is truthful. You never want to be in a position where you have to defend something that you've written on your resume. If that's the case, you'll lose the opportunity before you ever get started.

RESUME STRATEGY #9: BE CONFIDENT

You are unique. There is only one individual with the specific combination of employment experience, qualifications, achievements, education, and technical qualifications that you have. In turn, this positions you as a unique commodity within the competitive job search market. To succeed, you must prepare a resume that is written to sell *you*, and to highlight *your* qualifications and *your* success. If you can accomplish this, you will have won the job search game by generating interest, interviews, and offers.

There Are No Resume Writing Rules

One of the greatest challenges in resume writing is that there are no rules to the game. There are certain expectations about information that you will include: principally, your employment history and your educational qualifications. Beyond that, what you include is entirely up to you and what you have done in your career. What's more, you have tremendous flexibility in determining how to include the information you have selected. In chapter 2, you'll find a complete list of each possible category you might include in your resume, the type of information in each category, preferred formats for presentation, and sample text you can edit and use.

Although there are no rules, there are a few standards to live by as you write your resume. The following sections discuss these standards in detail.

CONTENT STANDARDS

Content is, of course, the text that goes into your resume. Content standards cover the writing style you should use, items you should be sure to include, items you should avoid including, and the order and format in which you list your qualifications.

Writing Style

Always write in the first person, dropping the word "I" from the front of each sentence. This style gives your resume a more aggressive and more professional tone than the passive third-person voice. Here are some examples:

First Person

> Manage 12-person team in the design and market commercialization of new plastics products for Allied's $200 million Consumer Division.

Third Person

> Ms. Lewis manages a 12-person team in the design and market commercialization of new plastics products for Allied's $200 million Consumer Division.

By using the first-person voice, you are assuming "ownership" of that statement. You did such-and-such. When you use the third-person voice, "someone else" did it. Can you see the difference?

Phrases to Stay Away From

Try *not* to use phrases such as "responsible for" or "duties included." These words create a passive tone and style. Instead, use active verbs to describe what you did.

Compare these two ways of conveying the same information:

> Duties included the coordination of all production planning and scheduling activities to support a multimillion-dollar technology manufacturing operation.

OR

> Managed 16-person production planning and scheduling organization supporting a $125 million technology manufacturing organization. Streamlined manpower planning and project assignment, reallocated technology resources, redesigned materials flow, and cut 12% from annual operating costs.

Resume Style

The traditional **chronological** resume lists work experience in reverse-chronological order (starting with your current or most recent position). The **functional** style de-emphasizes the "where" and "when" of your career and instead groups similar experience, talents, and qualifications regardless of when they occurred.

Today, however, most resumes follow neither a strictly chronological format nor a strictly functional format; rather, they are an effective mixture of the two styles, usually known as a "combination" or "hybrid" format.

Like the chronological format, the hybrid format includes specifics about where you worked, when you worked there, and what your job titles were. Like a functional resume, a hybrid emphasizes your most relevant qualifications—perhaps within chronological job descriptions, in an expanded summary section, in several "career highlights" bullet points at the top of your resume, or in project summaries. Most of the examples in this book are hybrids and show a wide diversity of organizational formats that you can use as inspiration for designing your own resume.

Resume Formats

Resumes, principally career summaries and job descriptions, are most often written in a paragraph format, a bulleted format, or a combination of both. Following are three job descriptions, all very similar in content, yet presented in each of the three different writing formats. The advantages and disadvantages of each format are also addressed.

Paragraph Format

WAREHOUSE MANAGER   1998 to 2001
Royalston Manufacturing Company, Lewiston, Maine

Managed a staff of 45 warehouse specialists and supervised hundreds of transportation specialists moving products between six manufacturing facilities throughout the Eastern U.S. Coordinated product flow to 315 retail outlets throughout North America. Controlled a $1.6 million annual operating budget.

Developed and monitored internal controls and implemented new processing procedures to streamline workflow. Facilitated a significant increase in the efficiency of product receipt, storage and issue procedures, resulting in a 42% reduction in inventory requirements.

Successfully resolved complex logistical issues involving the movement of more than $500 million in product each year. Worked cooperatively with cross-functional management teams to identify and resolve problems impacting product flow and profitability.

Advantages

Requires the least amount of space on the page. Brief, succinct, and to the point.

Disadvantages

Achievements get lost in the text of the second paragraph. They are not visually distinctive, nor do they stand alone to draw attention to them.

Bulleted Format

Warehouse Manager   1998 to 2001
ROYALSTON MANUFACTURING COMPANY, Lewiston, Maine

- Managed a staff of 45 warehouse specialists and supervised hundreds of transportation specialists moving products between six manufacturing facilities throughout the Eastern U.S.

- Coordinated product flow to 315 retail outlets throughout North America.

- Controlled a $1.6 million annual operating budget.

- Developed and monitored internal controls and implemented new processing procedures to streamline workflow.

- Facilitated a significant increase in the efficiency of product receipt, storage and issue procedures, resulting in a 42% reduction in inventory requirements.

- Successfully resolved complex logistical issues involving the movement of more than $500 million in product each year.

- Worked cooperatively with cross-functional management teams to identify and resolve problems impacting product flow and profitability.

Advantages

Quick and easy to peruse.

Disadvantages

Responsibilities and achievements are lumped together with everything of equal value. In turn, the achievements get lost farther down the list and are not immediately recognizable.

Combination Format

Warehouse Manager   1998 to 2001
Royalston Manufacturing Company, Lewiston, Maine

Managed a staff of 45 warehouse specialists and supervised hundreds of transportation specialists moving products between six manufacturing facilities throughout the Eastern U.S. Controlled a $1.6 million annual operating budget. Coordinated product flow to 315 retail outlets throughout North America.

- Developed and monitored internal controls and implemented new processing procedures to streamline workflow.

- Facilitated a significant increase in the efficiency of product receipt, storage and issue procedures, resulting in a 42% reduction in inventory requirements.

- Successfully resolved complex logistical issues involving the movement of more than $500 million in product each year.

- Worked cooperatively with cross-functional management teams to identify and resolve problems impacting product flow and profitability.

Advantages

Our recommended format. Clearly presents overall responsibilities in the introductory paragraph and then accentuates each achievement as a separate bullet.

Disadvantages

If you don't have clearly identifiable accomplishments, this format is not effective. It also may shine a glaring light on the positions where your accomplishments were less notable.

E-mail Address and URL

Be sure to include your e-mail address prominently at the top of your resume. As we all know, e-mail has become one of the most preferred methods of communication in job search.

We advise against using your employer's e-mail address on your resume. Not only does this present a negative impression to future employers, it will also become useless once you make your next career move. And since your resume may exist in cyberspace long after you've completed your job search, you don't want to direct interested parties to an obsolete e-mail address. Instead, obtain a private e-mail address that will be yours permanently. A free e-mail address from a provider such as Yahoo!, Hotmail, or NetZero is perfectly acceptable to use on your resume.

In addition to your e-mail address, if you have a URL (Web site) where you have posted your Web resume, be sure to also display that prominently at the top of your resume. For more information on Web resumes, refer to chapter 3.

To draw even more attention to your e-mail address, consider this format for the top of your resume:

JOHN L. GREEN

johngreen23938@aol.com

999 Old Mill Lane
Smithville, VA 22890

Phone: (888) 556-1238
Fax: (888) 556-1239

PRESENTATION STANDARDS

Presentation regards the way your resume looks. It regards the fonts you use, the paper you print it on, any graphics you might include, and how many pages your resume should be.

Typestyle

Use a typestyle (font) that is clean, conservative, and easy to read. Stay away from anything that is too fancy, glitzy, curly, and the like. Here are a few recommended typestyles:

Tahoma	Times New Roman
Arial	Bookman
Krone	Book Antiqua
Soutane	Garamond
CG Omega	Century Schoolbook
Century Gothic	Lucida Sans
Gill Sans	Verdana

Although it is extremely popular, Times New Roman is our least preferred typestyle simply because it is overused. More than 90 percent of the resumes we see are typed in Times New Roman. Your goal is to create a competitive-distinctive document, and, to achieve that, we recommend an alternative typestyle.

The content, format, and length of your resume should dictate your choice of typestyle. Some fonts look better than others at smaller or larger sizes; some have "bolder" boldface type; some require more white space to make them readable. Once you've written your resume, experiment with a few different typestyles to see which one best enhances your document.

Type Size

Readability is everything! If the type size is too small, your resume will be difficult to read and difficult to skim for essential information. Interestingly, a too-large type size, particularly for senior-level professionals, can also give a negative impression by conveying a juvenile or unprofessional image.

As a general rule, select type from 10 to 12 points in size. However, there's no hard-and-fast rule, and a lot depends on the typestyle you choose. Take a look at the following examples:

Very readable in 9-point Verdana:

Won the 1999 "Employee of the Year" award at Chrysler's Indianapolis plant. Honored for innovative contributions to the design and manufacturability of the Zodiac product line.

Difficult to read in too-small 9-point Gill Sans:

Won the 1999 "Employee of the Year" award at Chrysler's Indianapolis plant. Honored for innovative contributions to the design and manufacturability of the Zodiac product line.

Concise and readable in 12-point Times New Roman:

Training & Development Consultant specializing in the design, development, and presentation of multimedia training programs for hourly workers, skilled labor, and craftsmen.

A bit overwhelming in too-large 12-point Bookman Old Style:

Training & Development Consultant specializing in the design, development, and presentation of multimedia training programs for hourly workers, skilled labor, and craftsmen.

Type Enhancements

Bold, *italics*, underlining, and CAPITALIZATION are ideal to highlight certain words, phrases, achievements, projects, numbers, and other information that you want to draw special attention to. However, do not overuse these enhancements. If your resume becomes too cluttered, nothing stands out.

NOTE: Resumes intended for electronic transmission and computer scanning have specific restrictions on typestyle, type size, and type enhancements. We discuss these details in chapter 3.

Page Length

For most industries and professions, including many in the manufacturing professions, the "one- or two-page rule" for resume writing still holds true. Keep it short and succinct, giving just enough to entice your readers. However, there are many instances when a resume may be longer than two pages. For example:

- You have an extensive list of technical qualifications that are relevant to the position for which you are applying.

- You have extensive educational training and numerous credentials/certifications, all of which are important to include.

- You have an extensive list of special projects, task forces, and committees to include that are important to your current career objectives.

- You have an extensive list of professional honors, awards, and commendations. This list is tremendously valuable in validating your credibility and distinguishing you from the competition.

In all of these instances, rather than overwhelm the reader with detail, it might be better to produce a separate list of these extensive qualifications and include it as an addendum to your resume.

Regardless of the length of your resume, but especially if it's longer than two pages, make it more reader-friendly by carefully segmenting the information into separate sections. For instance, begin with your career summary and your work experience. Then follow with education, any professional or industry credentials, honors and awards, technology and equipment skills, publications, public speaking engagements, professional affiliations, civic affiliations, technology skills, volunteer experience, foreign-language skills, and other relevant information you want to include. Put each into a separate category so that your resume is easy to peruse, and your reader can quickly see the highlights. You'll read more about each of these sections in chapter 2.

Paper Color

Be conservative. White, ivory, and light gray are ideal. Other "flashier" colors are inappropriate for individuals in the manufacturing industry professions.

Graphics

An attractive, relevant graphic can really enhance your resume. A few of the sample resumes in chapters 4 through 11 use graphics to enhance their visual presentation. Just be sure not to get carried away. Be tasteful and relatively conservative.

White Space

We'll say it again: Readability is everything! If people have to struggle to read your resume, they simply won't make the effort. Therefore, be sure to leave plenty of white space. It really does make a difference.

ACCURACY AND PERFECTION

The very final step, and one of the most critical in resume writing, is the proof-reading stage. It is essential that your resume be well written, visually pleasing, and free of any errors, typographical mistakes, misspellings, and the like. We recommend that you carefully proofread your resume a minimum of three times, and then have two or three other people also proofread it. Consider your resume an example of the quality of work you will produce on a company's behalf. Is your work product going to have errors and inconsistencies? If your resume does, it communicates to a prospective employer that you are careless, and this is the "kiss of death" in a job search.

Take the time to make sure that your resume is perfect in all the little details that do, in fact, make a big difference to those who read it.

CHAPTER 2

Writing Your Resume

For many manufacturing industry professionals, resume writing is *not* at the top of their list of fun and exciting activities! How can it compare to developing a new product, designing a new production method, resolving a long-standing product defect, or eliminating potential safety risks from the workplace? In your perception, we're sure that it cannot.

However, resume writing can be an enjoyable and rewarding task. You can look at your resume proudly, reminding yourself of all that you have achieved. When you've completed this snapshot of your career and your success, we guarantee you'll look back with tremendous self-satisfaction as you launch and successfully manage your job search.

The very first step in finding a new position or advancing your career, resume writing can be the most daunting of all tasks in your job search. If your current job doesn't involve lots of writing, it may have been years since you've actually sat down and written anything other than notes to yourself. Even for people who write on a regular basis, resume writing is unique. It has its own style and a number of peculiarities, as with any specialty document.

Therefore, to make the writing process easier, more finite, and more efficient, we've consolidated it into four discrete sections:

- **Career Summary.** Think of your Career Summary as the *master production plan* of your resume. It is the accumulation of everything that allows the manufacturing plant, the production floor, the supply chain, the warehouse, and the entire operation to work. It is the backbone, the foundation of your resume.

- **Professional Experience.** Professional Experience resembles the *systems and conveyor belts* that move your products through the manufacturing process. This section describes the specifics that make up the larger master plan. Your professional experience demonstrates how you put all of your capabilities to work.

- **Education, Credentials, and Certifications.** Think of this section as your *accreditation,* the third-party validation of your qualifications, knowledge, and expertise.

- **The "Extras"** (Technology Qualifications, Equipment Skills, Training and Public Speaking, Publications, Honors and Awards, Professional Affiliations, Civic Affiliations, Foreign Languages, Personal Information, and so on). These make up the *product features* section of your resume, the "extra stuff" that helps distinguish you from others with similar qualifications.

Step-by-Step: Writing the Perfect Resume

In the preceding section, we outlined the four core resume sections. Now, we'll detail the particulars of each section—what to include, where to include it, and how to include it.

CONTACT INFORMATION

Before we start, let's briefly address the very top section of your resume: your name and contact information.

Name

You'd think this would be the easiest part of writing your resume…writing your name! But you might want to consider these factors:

- Although most people choose to use their full, formal name at the top of a resume, it has become increasingly more acceptable to use the name by which you prefer to be called.

- Bear in mind that it's to your advantage to have readers feel comfortable calling you for an interview. Their comfort level may decrease if your name is gender-neutral, difficult to pronounce, or very unusual; they don't know who they're calling (a man or a woman) or how to ask for you. You can make it easier for them by following these examples:

> Lynn T. Cowles (Mr.)
>
> (Ms.) Michael Murray
>
> Tzirina (Irene) Kahn
>
> Ndege "Nick" Vernon

Address

You should always include your home address on your resume. If you use a post office box for mail, include both your mailing address and your physical residence address.

Telephone Number(s)

Your home telephone number should be included. If you're at work during the day, when you can expect to receive most calls, consider including a work phone number (if it's a direct line, and you can receive calls discreetly). Or you can include a mobile phone number (refer to it as "mobile" rather than "cellular," to keep up with current terminology) or a pager number (however, this is less desirable because you must call back to speak to the person who called you). You can include a private home fax number (if it can be accessed automatically), but do not include your work fax number. NEVER include your employer's toll-free number. This communicates the message that you are using your employer's resources and budget to support your own personal job search campaign. Not a wise idea!

E-mail Address

Without question, if you have a private e-mail address, include it on your resume. E-mail is often the preferred method of communication in a job search, particularly in the early stages of each contact. Do not use your employer's e-mail address, even if you access e-mail through your work computer. Instead, obtain a free, accessible-anywhere address from a provider such as Yahoo!, Hotmail, or NetZero.

As you look through the samples in this book, you'll see how resume writers have arranged the many bits of contact information at the top of a resume. You can use these as models for presenting your own information. The point is to make it as easy as possible for employers to contact you!

Now, let's get into the nitty-gritty of the four core content sections of your resume.

CAREER SUMMARY

The Career Summary section at the top of your resume summarizes and highlights your knowledge and expertise.

You may be thinking, "But shouldn't my resume start with an Objective?" Although many job seekers still use Objective statements, we believe that a Career Summary provides a much more powerful introduction. Objectives are either too specific (limiting you to an "Electrical Engineering position") or too vague (doesn't everyone want "a challenging opportunity with a progressive organization offering the opportunity for growth and advancement"?). In addition, they can be read as self-serving, since they describe what *you* want, rather than suggesting what you have to offer an employer.

In contrast, an effective Career Summary allows you to position yourself as you wish to be perceived and immediately "paint a picture" of yourself in relation to your career goal. This section must focus on the specific skills, qualifications, and achievements of your career that are related to your current objectives. Your summary is *not* an historical overview of your career. Rather, it is a concise, well-written, and sharp presentation of information designed to *sell* you into your next position.

This section can have various titles, such as:

Career Summary	Management Profile
Career Achievements	Professional Qualifications
Career Highlights	Professional Summary
Career Synopsis	Profile
Executive Profile	Summary
Expertise	Summary of Achievements
Highlights of Experience	Summary of Qualifications

Or, as you will see in the first format example below (Headline Format), your summary does not have to have any title at all.

Five sample Career Summaries follow. Consider using one of these as the template for developing your Career Summary, or use them as the foundation to create your own presentation. You will also find some type of Career Summary in just about every resume included in this book.

Headline Format

MANUFACTURING OPERATIONS MANAGER / DIRECTOR
Production Planning / Logistics / Multi-Site Operations
MBA – Executive Management

MS – Manufacturing Systems & Technology

Paragraph Format

CAREER SUMMARY

SOLUTIONS-DRIVEN PRODUCTION MANAGER with experience leading high-quality, high-volume manufacturing operations. Track record of achievement for consistently increasing production volumes, quality ratings, efficiency, productivity, and bottom-line profitability. Strong, decisive, and team-driven leader with outstanding operational, analytical, organizational, and planning skills. Extensive technology and systems expertise.

Core Competencies Summary Format

QUALIFICATIONS SUMMARY

Project Engineer in Advanced Technology Industries

MS – Technology Design, Robotics & Automation

▶ New Product Design & Commercialization Systems	▶ Integration & Testing
▶ Project Design & Leadership	▶ Technical/Field Testing & Trials
▶ Program Budgeting & Resource Management	▶ Safety & Environmental Reviews
▶ Quality Control & Improvement	▶ Regulatory Compliance & Reporting
▶ Change Management & Revitalization	▶ Contract Negotiations & Reviews
▶ Business & Process Optimization	▶ Public Speaking & Executive Presentations

Guest Speaker, 2000 "Technology Innovations in Manufacturing" Conference
Winner, 1999 DuPont Award for Leadership Excellence

Bullet List Format

Professional Qualifications

- **Safety Engineer** with 10 years' professional experience.
- Expertise in **risk assessment, analysis, and control.**
- Extensive knowledge of OSHA, EPA, and other state and federal regulations governing workplace safety.
- **Award-winning** record of safety management and incident reduction at 3 multinational corporations.
- Two years' experience as a **Safety Trainer & Inspector.**
- Outstanding communication, organizational, and project management skills.

Category Format

PROFESSIONAL CAREER HIGHLIGHTS

Experience....... 12 years as a Maintenance Director and Manager for Dow Corning and its subsidiaries

Education .... Graduate Certificate in Facilities Maintenance and Engineering—University of Washington
BS—Operations Management—University of Oregon

Publications..... "Improving Workforce Productivity Through Maintenance Systems Design & Optimization," *American Manufacturing Association,* 2000
"Redesigning Maintenance Processes To Enhance Productivity," *National Facilities Maintenance Association*, 1999

Awards .... Employee of the Year, Dow Corning, 2000
Employee of the Year, Bell Laboratories, 1992

PROFESSIONAL EXPERIENCE

Your Professional Experience forms the meat of your resume—the "systems and conveyor belts," as we discussed before. It's what gives your resume substance, meaning, and depth. It is also the section that will take you the longest to write. If you've had the same position for 10 years, how can you consolidate all that you have done into one short section? If, on the opposite end of the spectrum, you have had your current position for only 11 months, how can you make it seem substantial and noteworthy? And, for all of you whose experience lies in between, what do you include, how, where, and why?

These are not easy questions to answer. In fact, the most truthful response to each question is, "It depends." It depends on you, your experience, your achievements and successes, and your current career objectives.

Five examples of Professional Experience sections appear below. Review how each individual's unique background is organized and emphasized, and consider your own background when using one of these as the template or foundation for developing your Professional Experience section.

Achievement Format

Emphasizes each position, overall scope of responsibility, and resulting achievements.

PROFESSIONAL EXPERIENCE

SURAMCO MANUFACTURING, INC., Bedford, VA
Materials Manager (1998 to Present)

Senior Business Unit Director with full responsibility for strategic planning, staffing, budgeting, and operations of the corporation's complete materials management function. Direct 11 hourly and professional staff in production planning and scheduling, purchasing, and stores. Turn $12.5 million annually in inventory, manage $400,000 annual operating budget, and direct $3+ million in annual purchasing expenditures.

Achievements

➤ Pioneered corporation's transition to World Class Manufacturing techniques. Efforts impacted all key operating departments and business units throughout the corporation.

➤ Designed and implemented first-ever production planning and master scheduling processes. Results included 32% reduction in inventory ($1.8 million), 13% improvement in on-time delivery, and 21% reduction in manpower requirements.

➤ Appointed Project Leader to facilitate the implementation of MAPICS / IBM AS360 manufacturing and business technology.

➤ Captured $180,000+ in annual cost savings through a series of internal design and process improvement initiatives.

➤ Sourced new vendors in Eastern Europe and reduced annual purchasing cost 18%.

Challenge, Action, and Results (CAR) Format

Emphasizes the challenge of each position, the action you took, and the results you delivered.

PROFESSIONAL EXPERIENCE

■ **Vice President of Operations** (1998 to Present)
■ **Plant Manager** (1994 to 1998)
WIP SYSTEMS INTERNATIONAL, Bulverde, Texas

Challenge:	Plan and direct the turnaround and return to profitability of $42 million technology systems manufacturer plagued with cost overrides, poor productivity, dissatisfied customers, and multimillion-dollar annual losses.
Action:	Rebuilt the entire management team, introduced advanced technologies and systems to expedite production flow, retrained all operators and supervisors, and implemented team-based work culture.
Results:	■ Achieved/surpassed all turnaround objectives and returned the operation to profitability in first year. Delivered strong and sustainable gains — 70% improvement in operating efficiency. — 250% reduction in cycle times. — 75% improvement in product quality ratings. — 100% on-time customer delivery. ■ Replaced obsolete equipment with state-of-the-art systems, redesigned and upgraded facility, introduced stringent standards to achieve OSHA compliance, and established in-house day-care facility (with dramatic reduction in absenteeism). ■ Restored credibility with a key customer generating over $30 million a year in revenues to WIP. Resolved long-standing quality and delivery issues, implemented key account management strategy, and revitalized business relationship.

- Achieved ISO 9000 certification and several other world-class credentials.
- Partnered with HP, IBM, and Dell to integrate their technologies into WIP's software applications. Received over $200,000 in technology resources at no cost to the company.
- Quoted in the National Manufacturing Association's annual publication as one of 1999's **"Leaders in Manufacturing."**

Functional Format

Emphasizes the functional areas of responsibility within the job and associated achievements.

Employment Experience

CORPORATE TRAINER   WILLIAMS-OWENS MANUFACTURING COMPANY, Duluth, MN   1998 to Present

Member of 6-person corporate training and development organization supporting 2000-person workforce at one of the world's largest gumball manufacturing facilities. Scope of training responsibility is extensive and includes:

Curriculum/Instruction
- Supervise development of training plans, programs, goals, and objectives; develop new course offerings in MAPICS technology, SAP technology, WIP techniques, and team-building for cooperation.
- Create multimedia instructional tools and programs to supplement classroom education; create self-paced programs to encourage the development of supervisory staff for both production and production support areas.
- Develop Master Schedule and direct the entire scheduling process.
- Recruit, interview, hire, and direct work performance of training support staff and administrators.

Staff Training & Development
- Orchestrate professional development opportunities for training staff across all technology, business, and operational areas.
- Introduce PC-based instructional tools and programs to enhance the development of the company's professional training staff.
- Conduct regularly scheduled performance reviews of training and support staff.
- Supervise and coordinate work of team leaders responsible for training craftspersons, laborers, and other production floor personnel.

Outreach & Communications
- Revitalized fledgling employee newspaper, recruited a talented team of volunteer writers and production personnel, and expanded distribution to include all employees.
- Write and publish press releases, flyers, and other promotional materials to encourage employee participation in work-sponsored training programs.
- Lead public speaking engagements at area vocational schools and technical colleges to recruit qualified personnel.

Project Highlights Format

Emphasizes the scope and outcomes of specific projects.

PROJECT MANAGER   December 1992 to Present
MOLTEN METAL TECHNOLOGY
($650 million metal products design & manufacturing company)

Travel to Molten facilities nationwide to orchestrate a series of special projects and assignments. Delivered all projects on time and within budget for 10 consecutive years. Recent projects include:

- **Recycling Facility Development & Construction** ($12.8 million). Co-led fast-track design and construction team bringing project from concept to completion in just 16 months.
  RESULT: Built an environmentally safe and regulatorily compliant facility at 12% under projected cost.

- **Capital Improvement Project** ($6.2 million). Led $50+ million in capital improvements with individual project costs at $50,000 to $750,000. *RESULT: Upgraded facilities, production lines, technical competencies, product staging, and distribution areas for a better than 22% increase in productivity.*

- **SAP Implementation Project** ($1.8 million). Led 12-person technology and support team in a massive SAP implementation project impacting virtually the entire facility and workforce.
  RESULT: Created a totally integrated technology environment linking inventory, production planning, quality, cost accounting, and other core manufacturing and support functions.

- **OSHA Compliance Project** ($500,000). Led year-long project to identify non-compliance issues and initiate appropriate remedial activity. *RESULT: Passed 2000 OSHA inspection with zero findings.*

- **Annual Shutdown & Maintenance Project** ($100,000). Planned, scheduled, and directed annual plant shutdown and maintenance programs for three facilities involving as many as 100 craftsmen. *RESULT: Restored all facilities to full operation within stringent time constraints.*

Experience Summary Format

Briefly emphasizes specific highlights of each position. Best used in conjunction with a detailed Career Summary.

EXPERIENCE SUMMARY

Purchasing & Sourcing Agent, Elm Manufacturing Systems, Lewisburg, TN — 2000 to Present
- Implemented cost savings that slashed 400% from annual purchasing costs.
- Established world-class supplier performance standards.
- Acquired and implemented Automated Purchasing System.

Facilities Purchasing Agent, Crestar Technologies, Knoxville, TN — 1997 to 2000
- Developed global buying strategy to maximize leverage, value, and efficiency.
- Implemented cost-avoidance program that saved over $200,000 in the first year.
- Directed several internal task forces — import/export business analysis, minority suppliers, office automation, and lease/buy analysis.

Production Control Coordinator, IMPX Production, Inc., Knoxville, TN — 1994 to 1997
- Ranked #1 for performance and achievement in materials planning and control.
- Established JIT replenishment system with key suppliers.
- Negotiated and executed multimillion-dollar contracts.

EDUCATION, CREDENTIALS, AND CERTIFICATIONS

Your Education section should include college, certifications, credentials, licenses, registrations, and continuing education. Highlight particularly notable achievements prominently in your Education section or bring them to the top in your Career Summary (as demonstrated by the Headline format in the previous section on writing career summaries).

The following sample Education sections illustrate a variety of ways to organize and format this information.

Academic Credentials Format

EDUCATION

M.S., Management Science, University of Colorado, 1996

B.S., Industrial Engineering, University of Nevada, 1992

Highlights of Continuing Professional Education:

- Organizational Management & Leadership, Colorado Leadership Association, 2001
- Industrial Engineering Technology in Today's Modern Manufacturing Organization, Purdue University, 2000
- SAP Implementation & Optimization, American Society for Quality Control, 1998
- Conflict Resolution & Violence Management in the Workplace, Institute for Workplace Safety, 1998

Wastewater Pre-Treatment Certification, State of Colorado, 1997

OSHA Certified Engineer, 1994

Executive Education Format

EDUCATION

Executive Development Program	STANFORD UNIVERSITY
Executive Development Program	UNIVERSITY OF CALIFORNIA AT LOS ANGELES
Master of Business Administration (MBA)	UNIVERSITY OF CALIFORNIA AT LOS ANGELES
Bachelor of Science Degree	UNIVERSITY OF CALIFORNIA AT IRVINE

Certifications Format

TECHNICAL CERTIFICATIONS & DEGREES

Certificate in Maintenance Management, DeVry Institute of Technology, 1999

Certificate in HVAC Systems Installation, Swinburne Institute of Technology, 1997

Certificate in Facilities Design & Maintenance, DeVry Institute of Technology, 1995

Certificate in Workplace Safety, American Safety Institute, 1995

B.S., General Studies, Iowa State University, 1992

Specialized Training Format

Technical Licenses & Certifications

- Rhode Island Journeyman License #67382
- Vermont Journeyman License #LK3223839
- Licensed Electrician #8737262
- Construction Supervisor #99089
- Impact Training, Motor Control Seminar, 2001
- CAT-5 Certification, 2000
- Variable Speed Drive Certification, 1999
- Soars Grounding of Electrical Systems For Safety Certification, 1998
- Graduate, Catonsville High School, Catonsville, Maryland, 1995

Non-Degree Format

Training and Education

UNIVERSITY OF TOLEDO, Toledo, Ohio
> **BS Candidate—Chemical Engineering** (Senior class status)

UNIVERSITY OF MICHIGAN, Ann Arbor, Michigan
> **Dual Majors in Chemical Engineering and Computer Science** (2 years)

GRADUATE, 100+ hours of continuing professional education through the University of Illinois, University of Michigan and University of Wisconsin.

THE "EXTRAS"

Your resume focuses primarily on information (most likely, your professional experience and academic credentials) that is directly related to your career goals. However, you also should include things that will distinguish you from other candidates and clearly demonstrate your value to a prospective employer. And, not too surprisingly, the "extras" often get you the interviews.

Following is a list of the other categories you might or might not include in your resume, depending on your particular experience and your current career objectives. Review the information. If it's pertinent to you, use the samples for formatting your own data. Remember, however, that if something is truly impressive, you may want to include it in your Career Summary at the beginning of your resume in order to draw even more attention to it. If you do this, you don't have to repeat the information at the end of your resume.

Technology Skills and Qualifications

Many manufacturing industry professionals will have a separate section on their resumes for technology skills and qualifications. Here, you will summarize all the hardware, software, operating systems, applications, networks, and more that you know, and that are relevant to your current career objectives.

You'll also have to consider placement of this section in your resume. If you are applying for positions that require strong technical skills, we recommend that you insert this section immediately after your Career Summary (or as a part thereof). If, on the other hand, your technical skills are more of a plus than a specific requirement, you should place them after your Education section.

Either way, technical skills are vital in virtually any career within manufacturing; and the fact that you can offer such skills is extremely important information to a prospective employer. Be sure to display technical skills prominently.

The following examples show different ways to format and present your technical qualifications.

TECHNOLOGY PROFILE

Operating Systems	Windows NT 4.0 Workstation/98/95/3.x; NetWare 6.x; MS-DOS 6.22
Manufacturing Systems	SAP R/3, MRP, DRP, APS
Protocols/Networks	TCP/IP, NetBEUI, IPX/SPX, Ethernet 10/100Base-T
Hardware	Hard drives, printers, scanners, fax/modems, CD-ROMs, Zip drives, Cat5 cables, hubs, NIC cards
Software	Microsoft Office Modules, FileMaker Pro, PC Anywhere, MS Exchange, ARCserve, Project Manager

TECHNOLOGY SKILLS SUMMARY

Windows NT 4.0 Workstation	SAP	TCP/IP
Windows 98/95/3.x	MRP	Ethernet 10
NetWare 6.x	DRP	IPX/SPX
Microsoft Office	MS Exchange	ARCserve
Project Manager	PC Anywhere	FileMaker Pro

Equipment Skills and Qualifications

Many people employed in the manufacturing industries will have a unique portfolio of equipment skills and knowledge. You must communicate this information in your resume, highlighting all the equipment with which you are proficient and/or familiar. This demonstrates that you have the knowledge and skills for a particular position. Consider this format for an individual with extensive experience in pharmaceutical product packaging:

Trained in and worked on diverse packaging equipment, materials, and technology, including R.A. Jones, Hoppmann, Syntron, Lakso, Scandia, Westbrook, Wexxar, and Edson:

Leaflet Inserters	Cappers	Bottle Cleaners & Elevators
Fillers	Desiccants	Neckbanders
Heat Tunnels	Labelers	Cartoners
Case Packers & Sealers	Hoppers	Bundlers
Sorters	Carousels	Cottoners

Honors and Awards

If you have won honors and awards, you can either include them in a separate section on your resume or integrate them into the Education or Professional Experience section, whichever is most appropriate. If you choose to include them in a separate section, consider this format:

❑ Winner, 2001 **"Recognition"** award from Cox Manufacturing, Inc.

❑ Winner, 1998 **"Innovation"** award for outstanding contributions to workplace safety and performance improvement from the National Association of Manufacturing Industry Professionals

❑ Named **"Employee of the Year,"** DeLeague Plastics, Inc., 1997

❑ **Summa Cum Laude Graduate**, Washington & Lee University, 1989

Public Speaking

People invited to give public presentations at conferences, seminars, workshops, training programs, symposia, and other events are usually considered experts in their fields. So, if you have public-speaking experience, be sure to include this very complimentary information in your resume. Here's one way to present it:

◆ *Keynote Speaker,* "Advancing Technology Innovation in the Industrial Workplace," 2000 National Association on Manufacturing Excellence Conference, New York

◆ *Panel Presenter,* "Chemical Engineering Techniques & Technologies," 1999 Chemical Engineering Association Annual Conference, Dallas

◆ *Session Leader,* "Optimizing Scheduling, Workflow, & Personnel," 1997 Chemical Engineering Association Annual Conference, Los Angeles

Publications

If you're published, you must be an expert (or at least most people will think so). Just as with your public-speaking engagements, be sure to include your publications. They validate your knowledge, qualifications, and credibility. Publications can include books, articles, online Web site content, manuals, and other written documents. Here's an example:

Co-Author, "Computer-Aided Design of Hybrid Microcircuits," National Electronic Packaging Conference, 2001.

Author, "Subtle Aspects of Micro-Packaging," Product Assurance Conference, 1998.

Author, "Micro-Packaging Practices, Policies, and Processes," IBM Training Manual, 1996.

Co-Author, "Advanced Packaging Technologies in the Workplace," IBM Training Manual, 1996.

Teaching and Training Experience

Many professionals in the manufacturing industry also teach or train at colleges, universities, technical schools, and other organizations, in addition to training that they may offer "on the job." If you've trained others, you will want to include that experience on your resume. If someone hires you (paid or unpaid) to speak to an audience, it communicates a strong message about your skills, qualifications, knowledge, and expertise. Here's a format you might use to present that information:

✓ **Adjunct Faculty,** Department of Electronics Engineering, Maryland State University, 1997 to Present. Teach Introductory and Advanced Electronics Engineering.

✓ **Guest Lecturer,** Department of Technology & Engineering, Rebec Community College, 1996 to Present. Provide semi-annual, daylong lecture series of the integration of engineering and technology in the workplace.

✓ **Trainer,** Chesapeake Institute of Technology, 1992 to Present. Teach "Engineering 101" to first-year students.

Committees and Task Forces

Many manufacturing industry professionals serve on committees, task forces, and other special project teams either as part of, or in addition to, their full-time responsibilities. Again, this type of information further strengthens your credibility, qualifications, and perceived value to a prospective employer. Consider a format such as the following:

- Member, 2000–01 Corporate Planning & Reorganization Task Force
- Member, 1999–00 Study Team on "Redesigning Corporate Training Systems to Maximum Employee Productivity"
- Chairperson, 1997–98 Committee on "Safety & Regulatory Compliance in the Workplace"

Professional Affiliations

Note your memberships in any educational, professional, or leadership associations on your resume. It communicates a message of professionalism, a desire to stay current with the industry, and a strong professional network. What's more, if you have held leadership positions within these organizations, be sure to include them. Here's an example:

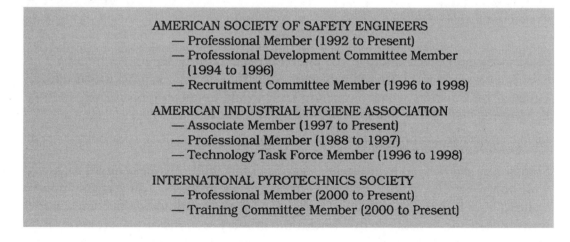

AMERICAN SOCIETY OF SAFETY ENGINEERS
— Professional Member (1992 to Present)
— Professional Development Committee Member (1994 to 1996)
— Recruitment Committee Member (1996 to 1998)

AMERICAN INDUSTRIAL HYGIENE ASSOCIATION
— Associate Member (1997 to Present)
— Professional Member (1988 to 1997)
— Technology Task Force Member (1996 to 1998)

INTERNATIONAL PYROTECHNICS SOCIETY
— Professional Member (2000 to Present)
— Training Committee Member (2000 to Present)

Civic Affiliations

Civic affiliations are fine to include if they

- Are with a notable organization.

- Demonstrate leadership experience.

- May be of interest to a prospective employer.

However, positions such as treasurer of your local condo association and singer with your church choir are not generally of value in marketing your qualifications. Here's an example of what to include:

- Volunteer Chairperson, United Way of America—Detroit Chapter, 1998 to Present

- President, Lambert Valley Conservation District, 1997 to Present

- Treasurer, Habitat for Humanity—Detroit Chapter, 1996 to 1997

Personal Information

We do not recommend that you include such personal information as birth date, marital status, number of children, and related data. However, sometimes, mentioning personal information is appropriate. If this information will give you a competitive advantage or answer unspoken questions about your background, then by all means include it. Here's an example:

- Born in Argentina. U.S. Permanent Residency Status since 1987.

- Fluent in English, Spanish, and Portuguese.

- Competitive Triathlete. Top-5 finish, 1987 Midwest Triathlon and 1992 Des Moines Triathlon.

Note in the above example that the job seeker speaks three languages fluently. This is a particularly critical selling point and, although this example lists it under Personal Information, we recommend that it would be more appropriately highlighted in a Career Summary.

Consolidating the Extras

Sometimes you have so many extra categories at the end of your resume, each with only a handful of lines, that spacing becomes a problem. You certainly don't want to have to make your resume a page longer to accommodate five lines, nor do you want the "extras" to overwhelm the primary sections of your resume. Yet you believe the information is important and should be included. Or perhaps you have a few small bits of information that you think are important but don't merit an entire section. In these situations, consider consolidating the information using one of the following formats. You'll save space, avoid over-emphasizing individual items, and present a professional, distinguished appearance.

PROFESSIONAL PROFILE

Technology	IBM & HP Platforms Microsoft Office Suite, SAP R/3, ProjectPlanner, MRP, DRP, LAN, WAN, KPM, Lotus, Lotus Notes, Novell Networks
Affiliations	International Association of Electrical Inspectors American Electrical Association Florida Association of Electrical & Electronic Engineers
Public Speaking	Speaker, IEEE Conference, Dallas, 2000 Presenter, AEA National Conference, San Diego, 1998 Panelist, APICS National Conference, Miami, 1996
Languages	Fluent in English, Spanish, and German

ADDITIONAL INFORMATION

- Co-Chair, Education Committee, Detroit Technology Association.
- PC literate with MRP, DRP, SAP, and Kaizen technologies.
- Available for relocation worldwide.
- Eagle Scout ... Boy Scout Troop Leader.

Writing Tips, Techniques, and Important Lessons

At this point, you've done a lot of reading, probably taken some notes, highlighted samples that appeal to you, and are ready to plunge into writing your resume. To make this task as easy as possible, we've compiled some "insider" techniques that we've used in our professional resume-writing practices. We learned these techniques the hard way through years of experience! We know they work; they will make the writing process easier, faster, and more enjoyable for you.

GET IT DOWN—THEN POLISH AND PERFECT IT

Don't be too concerned with making your resume "perfect" the first time around. It's far better to move fairly swiftly through the process, getting the basic information organized and on paper (or on screen), instead of agonizing about the perfect phrase or ideal formatting. Once you've completed a draft, we think you'll be surprised at how close to "final" the resume looks, and you'll be able to edit, tighten, and improve formatting fairly quickly.

WRITE YOUR RESUME FROM THE BOTTOM UP

Here's the system:

- **Start with the easy things**—Education, Technology, Professional Affiliations, Public Speaking, Publications, and any other extras you want to include. These items require little thought and can be completed in just a few minutes.

- **Write short job descriptions for your earlier positions, the ones you held years ago.** Be very brief and focus on highlights such as rapid promotion, achievements, innovations, professional honors, or employment with well-respected, well-known companies.

Once you've completed this, look at how much you've written in a short period of time! Then move on to the next step.

- **Write the job descriptions for your most recent positions.** This will take a bit longer than the other sections you have written. Remember to focus on the overall scope of your responsibility, major projects and initiatives, and significant achievements. Tell your reader what you did and how well you did it. You can use any of the formats recommended earlier in this chapter, or you can create something that is unique to you and your career.

Now, see how far along you are? You've completed 90 percent of your resume and there's only one small section left to do.

- **Write your Career Summary.** Before you start writing, remember your objective for this section. The summary should not simply rehash your experience. Rather, its design highlights the skills and qualifications you have that are most closely related to your current career objective(s). The summary should capture the reader's attention and "sell" your expertise.

That's it. You're done. We guarantee that the process of writing your resume will be much, much easier if you follow the "bottom-up" strategy. Now, on to the next tip.

INCLUDE NOTABLE OR PROMINENT "EXTRA" STUFF IN YOUR CAREER SUMMARY

Remember the "extra-credit sections" that normally appear at the bottom of your resume? If your extra information is particularly significant or prominent—you won a notable award, spoke at an international conference, developed a new engineering methodology, designed a new product that generated tens of millions of dollars in new revenues, or slashed 50 percent from production costs—you might want to include it at the top in your Career Summary.

Remember that the summary section should distinguish you from the crowd of other qualified candidates. As such, if you've accomplished anything that clearly demonstrates your knowledge, expertise, and credibility, consider moving it to your Career Summary for added attention. Refer to the sample Career Summaries earlier in the chapter for examples.

USE RESUME SAMPLES TO GET IDEAS FOR CONTENT, FORMAT, AND ORGANIZATION

This book is just one of many resources where you can review the resumes of other manufacturing industry professionals to help you formulate your strategy, write the text, and format your resume. What's more, publishers print and sell these books precisely for that reason. You don't have to struggle alone. Rather, use all the available resources at your disposal.

Be forewarned, however, that it's unlikely you will find a resume that fits your life and career to a "t." It's more likely that you will use "some of this sample" and "some of that sample" to create a resume that is uniquely "you."

INCLUDE DATES OR NOT?

Unless you are over age 50, we recommend that you date your work experience and your education. Without dates, your resume becomes vague and difficult for the typical hiring manager or recruiter to interpret. What's more, it often communicates the message that you are trying to hide something. Maybe you haven't worked in two years, maybe you were fired from each of your last three positions, or maybe you never graduated from college. Being vague and creating a resume that is difficult to read will, inevitably, lead to uncertainty and a quick toss into the "not interested" pile of candidates. By including the dates of your education and your experience, you create a clean and concise picture that one can easily follow to track your career progression.

An Individual Decision

If you are over age 50, dating your early positions must be an individual decision. On the one hand, you do not want to "date" yourself out of consideration by including dates from the 1960s and early 1970s. On the other hand, those positions might be worth including for a number of reasons. Further, if you omit those early dates, you may feel as though you are misrepresenting yourself (or lying) to a prospective employer.

The following strategy will overcome those concerns while still including your early experience: Create a separate entry for "Previous Professional Experience" in which you summarize your earliest employment. You can tailor this statement to emphasize just the most important parts of that experience.

If you want to focus on the reputation of your past employers, include a statement such as

- Previous experience includes supervisory positions with IBM, Dell, and Xerox.

If you want to focus on the rapid progression of your career, consider this example:

- Promoted rapidly through a series of increasingly responsible engineering and engineering-management positions with Zyler Form Molding, Inc.

If you want to focus on your early career achievements, include a statement such as

> • Member of 6-person task force credited with the design and rollout of Intel's first-generation microprocessing technology.

By including any one of the above paragraphs under the heading "Previous Professional Experience," you are clearly communicating to your reader that your employment history dates further back than the dates you have indicated on your resume. In turn, you are being 100 percent above-board and not misrepresenting yourself or your career. What's more, you're focusing on the success, achievement, and prominence of your earliest assignments.

Include Dates in the Education Section?

If you are over age 50, we generally do not recommend that you date your education or college degrees. Simply include the degree and the university with no date. Why exclude yourself from consideration by immediately presenting the fact that you earned your college degree in 1958, 1962, or 1966—about the time the hiring manager was probably born? Remember, the goal of your resume is to share the highlights of your career and open doors for interviews. It is *not* to give your entire life story. As such, dating your college degree isn't mandatory.

However, if you use this strategy, be aware that the reader will likely assume that there is *some* gap between when your education ended and your work experience started. Therefore, if you choose to begin your chronological work history with your first job out of college, omitting your graduation date could actually backfire, because the reader may assume you have experience that predates your first job. In this case, it's best either to *include your graduation date* or *omit dates of earliest experience,* using the summary strategy discussed above.

ALWAYS SEND A COVER LETTER WHEN YOU FORWARD YOUR RESUME

Employers expect to receive a cover letter with a resume, as part of appropriate job search etiquette. When you prepare a resume, you are writing a document that you can use for each and every position you apply for, assuming that the requirements for all of those positions will be similar. The cover letter, then, allows you to customize your presentation to each company or recruiter, addressing their specific hiring requirements. It is also the appropriate place to include any specific information that has been requested, such as salary history or salary requirements (see the following section for more on including salaries).

NEVER INCLUDE SALARY HISTORY OR SALARY REQUIREMENTS ON YOUR RESUME

Your resume is *not* the correct forum for a salary discussion. First of all, you should never provide salary information unless a company has requested that information and you choose to comply. (Studies show that employers will look at your resume anyway, so you may choose not to respond to this request, thereby avoiding pricing yourself out of the job or locking yourself into a lower salary than the job is worth.)

When contacting recruiters, however, we recommend that you do provide salary information, but again, only in your cover letter. With recruiters you want to "put all of your cards on the table" and help them make an appropriate placement by providing information about your current salary and salary objectives. For example, "Be advised that my current compensation is $55,000 annually and that I am interested in a position starting at a minimum of $65,000 per year." Or, if you would prefer to be a little less specific, you might write, "My annual compensation over the past three years has averaged $50,000."

ALWAYS REMEMBER THAT YOU ARE SELLING

As we have discussed over and over throughout this book, resume writing is sales. Understand and appreciate the value you bring to a prospective employer, and then communicate that value by focusing on your achievements. Companies don't want to hire just anyone; they want to hire "the" someone who will make a difference. Show them that you are that candidate.

CHAPTER 3

Printed, Scannable, Electronic, and Web Resumes

After you've worked so tirelessly to write a winning resume, your next challenge is the resume's design, layout, and presentation. It's not enough for it to read well; your resume must also have just the right look for the right audience. And, just as with everything else in a job search, no specific answers exist. You must make a few decisions about what your final resume presentation will look like.

The Four Types of Resumes

In today's employment market, job seekers use four types of resume presentations:

- Printed
- Scannable
- Electronic (e-mail attachments and ASCII text files)
- Web

The following sections give details on when you would need each type, as well as how to prepare these types of resumes.

THE PRINTED RESUME

We know the printed resume as the "traditional resume," the one that you mail to a recruiter, take to an interview, and forward by mail or fax in response to an advertisement. When preparing a printed resume, you want to create a sharp, professional, and visually attractive presentation. Remember, that piece of paper conveys the very first impression of you to a potential employer, and that first impression goes a long, long way. Never be fooled into thinking that just because you have the best qualifications in your industry, the visual presentation of your resume does not matter. It does, a great deal.

THE SCANNABLE RESUME

The scannable resume can be referred to as the "plain-Jane" or "plain-vanilla" resume. All of the things that you would normally do to make your printed resume look attractive—bold print, italics, multiple columns, sharp-looking type-style, and more—are stripped away in a scannable resume. You want to present a document that can be easily read and interpreted by scanning technology.

Although the technology continues to improve, and many scanning systems in fact can read a wide variety of type enhancements, it's sensible to appeal to the "lowest common denominator" when creating your scannable resume. Follow these formatting guidelines:

- Choose a commonly used, easily read font such as Arial or Times New Roman.

- Don't use bold, italic, or underlined type.

- Use a minimum of 11-point type size.

- Position your name, and nothing else, on the top line of the resume.

- Keep text left-justified, with a "ragged" right margin.

- It's okay to use common abbreviations (for instance, scanning software will recognize "B.S." as a Bachelor of Science degree). But, when in doubt, spell it out.

- Eliminate graphics, borders, and horizontal lines.

- Use plain, round bullets or asterisks.

- Avoid columns and tables, although a simple two-column listing can be read without difficulty.

- Spell out symbols such as % and &.

- If you divide words with slashes, add a space before and after the slash to be certain the scanner doesn't misread the letters.

- Print using a laser printer on smooth white paper.

- If your resume is longer than one page, be sure to print on only one side of the paper; put your name, telephone number, and e-mail address on the top of page two; and don't staple the pages together.

- For best possible results, mail your resume (don't fax it), and send it flat in a 9   12 envelope so that you won't have to fold it.

Of course, you can avoid scannability issues completely by sending your resume electronically, so that it will not have to pass through a scanner to enter the company's databank. Read the next section for electronic resume guidelines.

THE ELECTRONIC RESUME

Your electronic resume can take two forms: e-mail attachments and ASCII text files.

E-mail Attachments

When including your resume with an e-mail, simply attach the word-processing file of your printed resume. Because a vast majority of businesses use Microsoft Word, it is the most acceptable format and will present the fewest difficulties when attached.

However, given the tremendous variety in versions of software and operating systems, not to mention printer drivers, it's quite possible that your beautifully formatted resume will look quite different when viewed and printed at the other end. To minimize these glitches, use generous margins (at least 0.75 inch all around). Don't use unusual typefaces, and minimize fancy formatting effects.

Test your resume by e-mailing it to several friends or colleagues, then having them view and print it on their systems. If you use WordPerfect, Microsoft Works, or another word-processing program, consider saving your resume in a more universally accepted format such as RTF or PDF. Again, try it out on friends before sending it to a potential employer.

ASCII Text Files

You'll find many uses for an ASCII text version of your resume:

- To avoid formatting problems, you can paste the text into the body of an e-mail message rather than send an attachment. Many employers actually prefer this method. Pasting text into an e-mail message lets you send your resume without the possibility of also sending a virus.

- You can readily copy and paste the text version into online job application and resume bank forms, with no worries that formatting glitches will cause confusion.

- Although it's unattractive, the text version is 100 percent scannable.

To create a text version of your resume, follow these simple steps:

1. Create a new version of your resume using the Save As feature of your word-processing program. Select "text only" or "ASCII" in the Save As option box.

2. Close the new file.

3. Reopen the file, and you'll find that your word processor has automatically reformatted your resume into Courier font, removed all formatting, and left-justified the text.

4. To promote maximum readability when sending your resume electronically, reset the margins to 2 inches left and right, so that you have a narrow column of text rather than a full-page width. (This margin setting will not be retained when you close the file, but in the meantime you can adjust the text formatting for best screen appearance. For instance, if you choose to include a horizontal line (perhaps something like this: ++++++++++++++++++++++++++) to separate sections of the resume, by working with the narrow margins you won't make the mistake of creating a line that extends past the normal screen width. Plus, you won't add hard line breaks that create odd-length lines when seen at normal screen width.)

5. Review the resume and fix any "glitches" such as odd characters that may have been inserted to take the place of "curly" quotes, dashes, accents, or other nonstandard symbols.

6. If necessary, add extra blank lines to improve readability.

7. Consider adding horizontal dividers to break the resume into sections for improved skimmability. You can use any standard typewriter symbols such as *, -, (,), =, +, ^, or #.

To illustrate what you can expect when creating these versions of your resume, on the following pages are some examples of the same resume (top portion only) in traditional printed format, scannable version, and electronic (text) format.

THE WEB RESUME

This newest evolution in resumes combines the visually pleasing quality of the printed resume with the technological ease of the electronic resume. You host your Web resume on your own Web site (with your own URL), to which you refer prospective employers and recruiters. Now, instead of seeing just a "plain-Jane" version of your e-mailed resume, with just one click a viewer can access, download, and print your Web resume—an attractive, nicely formatted presentation of your qualifications.

What's more, because the Web resume is such an efficient and easy-to-manage tool, you can choose to include more information than you would in a printed, scannable, or electronic resume. Consider separate pages for achievements, technology qualifications, equipment skills, honors and awards, management skills, and more, if you believe they would improve your market position. Remember, you're working to sell yourself into your next job!

For those of you in technologically related manufacturing professions, you can take it one step further and create a virtual multimedia presentation that not only tells someone how talented you are, but also visually and technologically demonstrates it. Web resumes are an outstanding tool for people seeking jobs in technology-based manufacturing industries.

A simplified version of the Web resume is an online version of your Microsoft Word resume. Instead of attaching a file to an e-mail to an employer, you can include a link to the online version. This format is not as graphically dynamic as a full-fledged Web resume, but it can be a very useful tool for your job search. For instance, you can offer the simplicity of text in your e-mail, plus the instant availability of a printable, formatted word-processing document for the interested recruiter or hiring manager. For a demonstration of this format, go to www.e-resume-central.com and click on "SEE A SAMPLE."

JAMES L. BALDUFF

47 W. Oakcrest Lane
Elizabeth, New Jersey 07208
Email: jlbalduff@hotmail.com

Home: 908.587.3636

Office: 908.544.1147

QUALITY ASSURANCE MANAGER

Advanced Telecommunications Products, Systems & Technologies

17 Years' Experience in Engineering, Manufacturing, Quality & Performance Improvement

Member of 10-person Senior Management Team leading one of the most profitable manufacturing facilities of a worldwide leader in the telecommunications industry. Delivered double-digit gains in product quality and yield through combined expertise in:

- QA Planning & Organizational Leadership
- Process Design & Automation
- Productivity, Efficiency & Yield Improvement
- Project Planning, Budgeting & Leadership
- Budgeting & Resource Allocation

- Product Manufacturability & Optimization
- Systems Integration & Simplification
- Professional & Technical Staffing
- Cross-Functional Team Leadership
- Supplier Quality Assurance

PROFESSIONAL EXPERIENCE

ABC INC., Elizabeth, New Jersey	1993 to Present

- ◆ **QUALITY ASSURANCE MANAGER – MOBILE SYSTEMS DIVISION** (1998 to Present)
- ◆ **SENIOR QUALITY ENGINEER – MOBILE SYSTEMS DIVISION** (1995 to 1998)
- ◆ **QUALITY ENGINEER – PRIVATE RADIO SYSTEMS DIVISION** (1993 to 1995)

Lead the QA organization for the manufacturing group of ABC's $1 billion US Mobile Systems Division. Manage a team of 10 direct reports and oversee 25 QA inspectors. Control a $1 million annual operating budget allocated for staffing, training, consulting and project delivery.

Manage within an intensely fast-paced, high-growth organization that has doubled revenues consistently year-over-year for the past three years. Member of the Worldwide Mobile Systems Quality Management Council working with 12-person international quality management team to drive corporate-wide QA initiatives to maintain world class manufacturing. Extensive travel within Sweden. Limited travel to Brazil.

Project Highlights, Achievements & Performance Improvements

- Spearheaded initiative to expand quality commitment throughout the entire manufacturing organization, developed cross-functional quality teams, implemented real-time feedback for production operators and **reduced quality defects from 10% to less than 4%.**

- Led quality team that **reduced test failure rate from 25% to 15%** on the Division's largest transceiver product line (monthly production of 4000–6000 units).

- Led quality improvement team that introduced the Division's first fully integrated product (LRO-2000 PCS base station). Consulted with customers, design engineers and manufacturing teams to facilitate product development, reliability and quality. **Delivered 50%–75% increase in production yields.**

The print version of the resume section.

JAMES L. BALDUFF

47 W. Oakcrest Lane
Elizabeth, NJ 07208
Home: 908.587.3636   Office: 908.544.1147   Email: jlbalduff@hotmail.com

QUALITY ASSURANCE MANAGER

Advanced Telecommunications Products, Systems & Technologies
17 Years' Experience in Engineering, Manufacturing, Quality & Performance Improvement

Member of 10-person Senior Management Team leading one of the most profitable manufacturing facilities of a worldwide leader in the telecommunications industry. Delivered double-digit gains in product quality and yield through combined expertise in:

QA Planning & Organizational Leadership	Product Manufacturability & Optimization
Process Design & Automation	Systems Integration & Simplification
Productivity, Efficiency & Yield Improvement	Professional & Technical Staffing
Project Planning, Budgeting & Leadership	Cross-Functional Team Leadership
Budgeting & Resource Allocation	Supplier Quality Assurance

PROFESSIONAL EXPERIENCE

ABC INC., Elizabeth, New Jersey   1993 to Present

QUALITY ASSURANCE MANAGER – MOBILE SYSTEMS DIVISION (1998 to Present)
SENIOR QUALITY ENGINEER – MOBILE SYSTEMS DIVISION (1995 to 1998)
QUALITY ENGINEER – PRIVATE RADIO SYSTEMS DIVISION (1993 to 1995)

Lead the QA organization for the manufacturing group of ABC's $1 billion US Mobile Systems Division. Manage a team of 10 direct reports and oversee 25 QA inspectors. Control a $1 million annual operating budget allocated for staffing, training, consulting and project delivery.

Manage within an intensely fast-paced, high-growth organization that has doubled revenues consistently year-over-year for the past three years. Member of the Worldwide Mobile Systems Quality Management Council working with 12-person international quality management team to drive corporate-wide QA initiatives to maintain world class manufacturing. Extensive travel within Sweden. Limited travel to Brazil.

Project Highlights, Achievements & Performance Improvements

- Spearheaded initiative to expand quality commitment throughout the entire manufacturing organization, developed cross-functional quality teams, implemented real-time feedback for production operators and reduced quality defects from 10% to less than 4%.

- Led quality team that reduced test failure rate from 25% to 15% on the Division's largest transceiver product line (monthly production of 4000–6000 units).

- Led quality improvement team that introduced the Division's first fully integrated product (LRO-2000 PCS base station). Consulted with customers, design engineers and manufacturing teams to facilitate product development, reliability and quality. Delivered 50%–75% increase in production yields.

The scannable version of the resume section.

JAMES L. BALDUFF
47 W. Oakcrest Lane
Elizabeth, NJ 07208
Home: 908.587.3636
Office: 908.544.1147
Email: jlbalduff@hotmail.com

****
QUALITY ASSURANCE MANAGER
Advanced Telecommunications Products, Systems & Technologies
17 Years' Experience in Engineering, Manufacturing, Quality & Performance
Improvement

Member of 10-person Senior Management Team leading one of the most profitable
manufacturing facilities of a worldwide leader in the telecommunications industry.
Delivered double-digit gains in product quality and yield through combined
expertise in:
* QA Planning & Organizational Leadership
* Product Manufacturability & Optimization
* Process Design & Automation
* Systems Integration & Simplification
* Productivity, Efficiency & Yield Improvement
* Professional & Technical Staffing
* Project Planning, Budgeting & Leadership
* Cross-Functional Team Leadership
* Budgeting & Resource Allocation
* Supplier Quality Assurance

****
PROFESSIONAL EXPERIENCE
1993 to Present
ABC INC., Elizabeth, New Jersey

QUALITY ASSURANCE MANAGER — MOBILE SYSTEMS DIVISION (1998 to Present)
SENIOR QUALITY ENGINEER - MOBILE SYSTEMS DIVISION (1995 to 1998)
QUALITY ENGINEER - PRIVATE RADIO SYSTEMS DIVISION (1993 to 1995)

Lead the QA organization for the manufacturing group of ABC's $1 billion US Mobile
Systems Division. Manage a team of 10 direct reports and oversee 25 QA inspectors.
Control a $1 million annual operating budget allocated for staffing, training,
consulting and project delivery.

Manage within an intensely fast-paced, high-growth organization that has doubled
revenues consistently year-over-year for the past three years. Member of the
Worldwide Mobile Systems Quality Management Council working with 12-person
international quality management team to drive corporate-wide QA initiatives to
maintain world class manufacturing. Extensive travel within Sweden. Limited travel
to Brazil.

Project Highlights, Achievements & Performance Improvements
* Spearheaded initiative to expand quality commitment throughout the entire
manufacturing organization, developed cross-functional quality teams, implemented
real-time feedback for production operators and reduced quality defects from 10% to
less than 4%.
* Led quality team that reduced test failure rate from 25% to 15% on the Division's
largest transceiver product line (monthly production of 4000-6000 units).
* Led quality improvement team that introduced the Division's first fully
integrated product (LRO-2000 PCS base station). Consulted with customers, design
engineers and manufacturing teams to facilitate product development, reliability
and quality. Delivered 50%-75% increase in production yields.

The electronic/text version of the resume section.

The Four Resume Types Compared

This chart quickly compares the similarities and differences between the four types of resumes we've discussed in this chapter.

	PRINTED RESUMES	SCANNABLE RESUMES
TYPESTYLE/ FONT	Sharp, conservative, and distinctive (see our recommendations in chapter 1).	Clean, concise, and machine-readable: Times New Roman, Arial, Helvetica.
TYPESTYLE ENHANCEMENTS	**Bold,** *italics,* and <u>underlining</u> for emphasis.	CAPITALIZATION is the only type enhancement you can be certain will transmit.
TYPE SIZE	10-, 11-, or 12-point preferred... larger type sizes (14, 18, 20, 22, and even larger, depending on typestyle) will effectively enhance your name and section headers.	11- or 12-point, or larger.
TEXT FORMAT	Use centering and indentations to optimize the visual presentation.	Type all information flush left.
PREFERRED LENGTH	1 to 2 pages; 3 if essential.	1 to 2 pages preferred, although length is not as much of a concern as with printed resumes.
PREFERRED PAPER COLOR	White, Ivory, Light Gray, Light Blue, or other conservative background.	White or very light with no prints, flecks, or other shading that might affect scannability.
WHITE SPACE	Use appropriately for best readability.	Use generously to maximize scannability.

ELECTRONIC RESUMES	WEB RESUMES
Courier.	Sharp, conservative, and distinctive… attractive onscreen and when printed from an online document.
CAPITALIZATION is the only enhancement available to you.	**Bold,** *italics,* and <u>underlining</u>, and color for emphasis.
12-point.	10-, 11-, or 12-point preferred… larger type sizes (14, 18, 20, 22, even larger, depending on typestyle) will effectively enhance your name and section headers.
Type all information flush left.	Use centering and indentations to optimize the visual presentation.
Length is immaterial; almost definitely, converting your resume to text will make it longer.	Length is immaterial; just be sure your site is well organized so viewers can quickly find the material of greatest interest to them.
N/A.	Paper is not used, but do select your background carefully to maximize readability.
Use white space to break up dense text sections.	Use appropriately for best readability both onscreen and when printed.

Are You Ready to Write Your Resume?

To be sure that you're ready to write your resume, go through the following checklist. Each item is a critical step that you must take in the process of writing and designing your own winning resume.

❏ Clearly define "who you are" and how you want to be perceived.

❏ Document your key skills, qualifications, and knowledge.

❏ Document your notable career achievements and successes.

❏ Identify one or more specific job targets or positions.

❏ Identify one or more industries that you are targeting.

❏ Research and compile key words for your profession, industry, and specific job targets.

❏ Determine which resume format suits you and your career best.

❏ Select an attractive font.

❏ Determine whether you need a print resume, a scannable resume, an electronic resume, a Web resume, or all four.

❏ Secure a private e-mail address (not your employer's).

❏ Review resume samples for up-to-date ideas on resume styles, formats, organization, and language.

PART II

Sample Resumes for Manufacturing Careers

CHAPTER 4

Resumes for Production Personnel and Supervisors

- Hourly Workers and Laborers

- Craftsmen—Metalworkers, Ironworkers, and Assembly Personnel

- Tradesmen—Electricians, Mechanics, HVAC Technicians, and Machinists

- Production Supervisors/Production Line Supervisors

- Section Leaders

- Department Supervisors and Leaders

- Technicians

RESUME 1: ROSS MACPHERSON, MA, CPRW, JCTC, CEIP, CJST; PICKERING, ONTARIO

KATHY L. BONNELLY

10 Donald Court
Augusta, Ontario A2B 3C3
Phone: (905) 444-5566 ◆ Alternate: (905) 444-6789

Assembly / Factory Production / Light Industrial

➢ Ability to **quickly learn complex task**s and operate both **machinery and hand tools.**

➢ Extremely **dedicated** and **hardworking** with the ability to work in fast-paced environments under very tight deadlines.

➢ **Highly reliable**, **flexible**, and **focused** on achieving tasks to **highest standards.**

➢ Demonstrated ability to **exceed production quotas** while maintaining standards for **accuracy and safety.**

➢ Comfortable and proficient working in both a **team** and **team leader** capacity.

➢ Strong **problem solving** and **troubleshooting** skills.

WORK EXPERIENCE

Brake Line Operator   1997 – Present
STU LOGISTICS LIMITED (formerly Taiklor Transportation Ltd.)   Ajax, Ontario
Multi-million dollar outsource company providing pre-assembled parts for automobile industry. ISO 9002 certified.

• Accurately assembled brake lines as a batch commodity for Chevy, Lumina, and Buick automobiles.

• Organized components, assembled to exacting specifications, and packaged in plastic totes, racks, or 8x8 Zytechs.

• Consistently finished daily quota ahead of schedule and assisted assembly in other brake line areas.

• Successfully trained over 30 new employees on proper assembly sequence, procedures, and safety issues.

Achievements:

➢ **Consistently exceeded hourly quotas of 100 units by 50%.**

➢ **Twice awarded employee recognition for Perfect Attendance and Punctuality.**

Display Assembler   1995 – 1997
TOP STUDIOS LTD.   Scarborough, Ontario
Leading producer of display advertisements and flyers for major department stores and retailers across Canada.

• Working as part of a team, created a wide variety of promotional displays for companies such as Sears Canada, The Bay, Eatons, Zellers, and Kmart.

• Successfully created complex artistic media and structures according to exacting design specifications, requiring dexterity, ability to work with a variety of hand tools, accuracy, and attention to detail.

• Worked effectively in a very fast-paced environment, always meeting extremely demanding deadlines and working overtime as required.

• Personally selected to train new employees on proper procedures, safety, and production process.

Bold type in the attractively boxed summary ensures that key words and phrases stand out.
Measurable achievements are included to demonstrate this employee's value to the organization.

KATHY L. BONNELLY
Phone: (905) 444-5566 ◆ Alternate: (905) 444-6789   2

WORK EXPERIENCE, continued...

Professional Small Animal Groomer   1994 – 1995
PETSOURCE INC.   Augusta, Ontario
Local company specializing in animal grooming and care.

- ◆ Provided high quality grooming service, booked all appointments, and answered customer inquiries as required.
- ◆ Completed all grooming orders according to customer request, including preparation, trim, bath, shampoo, and dry.
- ◆ Supervised 3 other employees (2 groomers, 1 apprentice), including all daily scheduling, delegation, and on-the-job coaching.

Professional Small Animal Groomer / Veterinary Assistant / Receptionist   1986 – 1994
SUNNYDALE VETERINARY SERVICES   Toronto, Ontario
Full-service veterinary clinic with locations throughout Greater Toronto.

- ◆ Opened clinic daily, retrieving files for morning appointments, admitting grooming clients and hospital patients, and handling customer inquiries with respect to veterinary care and pet grooming.
- ◆ Effectively fulfilled all client grooming orders, including preparation, trim, bath, shampoo, and dry.
- ◆ Additionally called upon to maintain exercise and water intake for animals as well as prep animals for surgery as required.
- ◆ Demonstrated excellent organizational and communication skills.

Achievements:

- ➢ **Award winner in inaugural Metro East Groom-a-Ganza (1992), successfully placing 4th out of 64 entrants.**

EDUCATION

Apprentice Small Animal Groomer – PARKER PET CARE LTD., Scarborough, Ontario   1986

Graduate – OSHAWA CENTRAL COLLEGIATE, Oshawa, Ontario   1985

REFERENCES

Available upon request.

RESUME 2: PATTI CASH, CPRW, CEIP; PRESCOTT, AZ

ALAN J. FISCHER

116 Quiet Cove
Cedar Rapids, Iowa 56830
319.444.5565

PROFILE

Experience and practical knowledge of *Thermal Arc Plasma* welding in a high-volume manufacturing operation with strong quality control abilities. Thorough understanding of equipment, its performance, and operation. Self-motivated individual, but also able to function effectively as a member of a results-oriented team.

"Alan has progressed very well — 100% production with an extremely low reject rate."
Employee Action Form - 1998

QUALIFICATIONS

➤ Consistent merit pay increases resulting from achieving 100% production goals.
➤ Maintain low reject rate - *below 1%* - company standard is 5%.
➤ Skilled as welder; ability to comprehend specifications, lay out material, set up machinery, operate welding apparatus, torches, and other attendant equipment.
➤ Perform effectively despite sudden deadlines and changing priorities.
➤ Highly reliable self-starter; can be counted on to complete assignments with little or no supervision.
➤ Possess good communication and interpersonal skills.
➤ Troubleshoot utilizing solid problem-solving capabilities.
➤ Experienced in tig welding. Performed complex fabrications utilizing Carbon-Arc, Gas-Metal Arc, Gas-Tungsten Arc, Submerged Arc, and Plasma-Arc equipment.

"Alan Fischer has demonstrated excellent working skills. He has consistently run over 50% on plasma weld production."
Employee Action Form - 1998

EMPLOYMENT SUMMARY

LCM INVESTMENT CASTING   *($100M Manufacturer of Playboy Titanium Golf Clubs)*   Cedar Rapids, IA
PLASMA WELDER, 1997 to current
• Selected to enter specialized training for titanium welding.
• Responsible for outgoing quality control, maintaining a reject rate below company standard.

ARROWSMITH CUSTOM WELDING   *($5M national manufacturer of custom metal works)*   Des Moines, IA
ARC WELDER, 1993 to 1996
• Fabricated custom metal staircases, intricate wrought iron railings, and entry gates according to architect's drawings, layout, and specifications.

CONSTRUCTION
INDEPENDENT MASONRY CONTRACTOR, 1987 to 1993
• Performed varied custom designs encompassing block masonry foundation walls, fireplaces and chimneys, and intricate tile, marble, and granite installations.

Including effective quotes lends an outside perspective to this employee's statement of his qualifications.

Donald Keller

P.O. Box 897
Jackson, WA 98293
(306) 777-8866

Ironworker / Millwright

Take pride in doing quality work—can be depended upon to complete the job with flexibility and resourcefulness. Adaptable; adept at learning and understanding new procedures and techniques. Team player who gets along well with everyone. Great sense of humor—speaks "ironworker" as second language! Willing to relocate.

QUALIFICATIONS

- Over 20 years' experience in oil refineries, sawmills, asphalt shingle mills, and boat yards.
- Strong mechanical aptitude with demonstrated ability to operate, repair, and maintain heavy equipment and machinery, mounted motors, and motor bases.
- Ability to read and comprehend blueprints and job specifications.
- Knowledge of safety procedures and regulations—safe work record.
- AWS, ASME, WABO, 1" plate steel; Pipe 2", Scheduled 80 carbon steel and API 6G 6" Scheduled 40 pipe, and C-Stop Certifications—current.
- Member, Local Association of Building Officials.

Areas of Expertise

- Metal Fabrication / Structural Steel Construction.
- Welding—SMAW, wire, and TIG; plasma arc cutting; oxy-fuel cutting and welding; carbon arc.

Exemplary Projects

- Refit of *Berg Star* and *Berg Sea* icebreakers.
- Construction of IKO Pacific.
- Construction of Selco Mill dry kiln.
- Pasquah Forest sawmill construction and maintenance.
- Reconstruction and structural welding of fuel storage tanks at ARCO Oil Refinery.

WORK HISTORY

Millwright / Ironworker / Structural Welder / Mechanic
PM CONTRACTORS, INC., Jackson, WA, 1996–present

Previous 16+ years—details available:

Halton Construction, Jackson. WA	AM Southland, Mount Ashton, Washington
South Jackson Lumber Company, Jackson, WA	Marina Contractors, Seattle, Washington
Homebuilders Incorporated, Ballard, Oregon	Capertown Logging, Capertown, Alaska
Chaqach Forest Products, Seward, Alaska	F/V *Pacific Hunter* (105' bottom fisher), Angler, Alaska

SPECIAL INTERESTS

Avid Skier (35 years—Mt. Bachelor Ski Area)
Knowledgeable in the use and maintenance of ski lifts;
early experience as apprentice chair-lift mechanic.

EDUCATION

Diesel Hydraulics, Jackson Technical College, Jackson, Washington
Welding, Angler Community College, Angler, Alaska

This resume covers a lot of ground for this semi-retired ironworker/millwright. He wants to work servicing ski chair lifts in an area closer to grandchildren yet also would consider ironworker/millwright positions.

RICHARD GORNITZKY

3 Noah Drive, Brick, New Jersey 08723   (732) 920-9330

CODEABLE WELDER / FABRICATOR

Robotics, pressure equipment, and purge welding experienced and expert in working with hardened, stainless and carbon steel; aluminum; corrugated metals; castings; and anti-vortex fabrications. Work history reflects consistency, leadership, and acute attention to detail in performing intricate work. Solid written and verbal communications skills. Able to work from blueprints. Passed American Society of Mechanical Engineers (ASME) plate and pipe tests. UL certified for marine applications.

CORE COMPETENCIES

❑ Proven track record in capturing company revenues by re-fabricating tools and equipment, thereby eliminating the need to buy new, costly apparatus.

❑ Worked in a methanol manufacturing plant and an outage management environment. Demonstrated ability to work safely and responsibly in areas that are potentially life threatening. Fully cognizant of the critical need for performing perfect, mistake-proof work.

❑ Solid work ethic, with proven ability to render decisions based on sound judgment.

CAREER HISTORY

Lead Welder: SOUTH JERSEY CONTRACTORS (SJP), Cliffwood, NJ (10/97–Present)

❑ Manage a welding shop for one of New Jersey's largest contractors and builders of multimillion-dollar homes and upscale closed communities throughout the state.

❑ Utilize steel and corrugated metal in the repair and maintenance of 500+ pieces of equipment, encompassing buckets, bulldozers, loaders, backhoes, trucks, and excavating / rock-crushing equipment. Perform both shop and site work.

❑ Direct and monitor the activities of a staff of welders. Train tradesmen in all facets of welding, including blueprint reading.

❑ Work hand-in-hand with the engineering department to fabricate pipe for pumping stations.

❑ Create anti-vortex fabrications on large diameter pipes.

❑ Work with aluminum and stainless steel to create Cagges-Framework pipe rails.

❑ Read and comply with blueprints.

Welder / Fabricator: T.W. DELISA, INC., Neptune City, NJ (10/95–10/97)

❑ Performed management functions at this leading recycling center, such as inventory control processes that reduced on-hand inventory assets and purchasing all steel and raw materials for annual cost savings.

❑ Repaired, rebuilt, and maintained in-house apparatus such as tables, racks, beams, flooring and overhead stations, and on-site equipment such as heavy machinery buckets, company trucks, blades, carriers, sweepers, and aprons.

Welder / Fabricator: GETINGE INTERNATIONAL, INC., Lakewood, NJ (8/93–10/95)

❑ Performed intricate stainless steel work in the manufacture of products serving the health care industry, including the world's major pharmaceutical corporations.

❑ Manufactured sterilization chambers, apparatus requiring sterilization, stainless steel and aluminum fascia panels, hospital carts and carriages, and piping skids.

(Page 1 of 2)

Notice how the first of the "core competencies" mentions "capturing company revenues"; this kind of statement shows that the employee clearly understands why his work as a welder is important.

RICHARD GORNITZKY   **Page 2**

CAREER HISTORY (Continued)

Maintenance Welder: C.P.S. CHEMICAL CORPORATION, Oldbridge, NJ (8/92–3/93)
- Performed pipefitting work throughout this methanol-producing chemical plant.
- Instituted a safety protocol that was implemented on an organization-wide basis.

Lead Welder / Fabricator: NATIONAL WASTE DISPOSAL, Jackson, NJ (1/86–10/91)
- Managed and delegated routine and welding department activities.
- Managed inventory and purchased steel and all raw materials. Sourced vendors for cost-competitive pricing of materials.
- Performed preventative maintenance and repair of all company trucks.

Custom Marine Fabricator: ALUMAFAB, Brick, NJ (7/84–1/86)
- Worked within a two-person operation to build tuna towers and fuel tanks for boats.
- Drove forward customer management initiatives that contributed to a better than 20 percent gain in long-term client relationships.

Apprentice Millwright Welder: GENERAL MOTORS CORP., Linden, NJ (3/79–6/84)
- Gained critical skills and field-related experience.

Welder: ESTEY METAL PRODUCTS, Eatontown, NJ (7/77–3/79)
- Constructed staircases, libraries, and assorted library equipment.

CERTIFICATIONS

- **AMERICAN SOCIETY OF MECHANICAL ENGINEERS (ASME)**
- **UL CERTIFIED**

EDUCATION

- **GENERAL MOTORS TECHNICAL INSTITUTE,** Woodbridge, NJ
  Millwright Welder Apprenticeship Course Completed, 1982–1984

- **TOMS RIVER VO-TECH,** Toms River, NJ
  Certificate of Welding and Blueprints, 1979–1981

- High School Graduate

Thomas Martin, Jr.

498 West 10th Street
Elmira, New York 14901

Home: (607) 491-8857
Cellular: (607) 851-4466

Professional Goal

Career opportunity in quality control where my training in industrial technology and extensive experience in the operation, troubleshooting, repair, and calibration of equipment will be of benefit.

Areas of Expertise

▸ Extensive hands-on experience in the set up and operation of machine tools and broad understanding of preventative maintenance procedures.

▸ Thorough knowledge of numerous electrical, electronic, and mechanical systems.

▸ Strong analytical, diagnostic, and troubleshooting skills; able to identify complex problems and implement successful solutions.

▸ Function effectively as an autonomous, self-motivated individual and as an active, contributing team member.

▸ Demonstrate high level of interest in developing and enhancing knowledge of processes, products, and technology.

Professional Experience

MICROTECH, INC., Dade, New York   1979 to Present
Class A Precision Machinist
Perform initial set up, operation, programming, inspection, and preventative maintenance on the following equipment: Kellenberger and Kel-Varia CNC Cylindrical Grinders (Kelco 90 Control); Hardinge Kel-Vision CNC Cylindrical Grinder (GE Fanuc 18-T Control); Blohm Profimat CNC Surface Grinder (GE Fanuc 15-M Control); Hardinge Vertical CNC (GE Fanuc 18-T Control) and Conquest CNC 65 Turning Lathes; Cincinnati T-10 Milling Center, Favretto Surface and Dovetail Grinders; Thompson Surface Grinder; Brown & Sharpe Universal Grinder; Technica 25M 5100 Center Grinder.

▸ Perform multiple tasks simultaneously in cell work and machining centers.

▸ Experience working within close tolerances (.0002) on finished parts, and maintaining low micro finish on finished products.

▸ Proficient in modifying, writing, and troubleshooting programs for Kellenberger Grinders.

▸ Utilize blueprints, job parts routings, engineering specifications, and MRP dispatch sheets.

▸ Train, orient, and assist new staff in the operation of surface and cylindrical grinders.

▸ Recipient of several Level III Total Quality Awards for improving machine efficiency and reducing job unit times.

▸ Initiated installation of state-of-the-art lighting system throughout the shop floor, significantly reducing time in locating truckers.

▸ Solved major problem of the Blohm Surface Grinder through implementation of coolant chiller to maintain temperature control.

▸ Successfully collaborate with engineers and programmers on production processes and development of prototype parts.

Education

Industrial Technology Program, 1993 to 1997 — Dade Community College
<u>Field of Study</u>: Micro Operating Systems, Manufacturing Methods, NC Programming, Industrial Organization, Production Control, Word Processing, Algebra & Trigonometry I & II.
General Studies Diploma, 1978 — Dade Senior High School
Professional Development (Microtech, Inc.) — Total Quality Seminars, Geometrical Tolerancing and Dimensioning.

Before launching into a detailed summary of experience and equipment knowledge, this resume starts with a clearly stated goal and a concise listing of "areas of expertise."

Mary Grandy

230 Kennsington Drive — Minneapolis, MN 55402 — 612.555.0101

TEXTILE INDUSTRY PROFESSIONAL

HIRING ASSETS

- More than 20 years' experience in textile production, from initial design, to measurement, fitting, dimensions, fabric, through creation of finished product. Have created textile products for **large corporate to small markets.**
- Able to rapidly and economically produce **large or small quantities of world-class products in response to market demand.** Proven success at developing new products with broad market appeal.
- **Environmental steward;** strive to minimize use of natural resources and discharge of net waste to environment.
- Strong work ethic and record of impeccable reliability, flexibility, and willingness to learn (learn quickly!).
- Sharp, well organized, hard working; able to meet deadlines and produce highest **quality** work with **precision.**
- Enthusiastic team member whose **participation brings out the best in others. Resourceful** problem solver.

SKILLS: **Computerized/Industrial** sewing machines, including single and double needle lockstitch, automatic hemmers, blind stitch machines, high-speed sergers, and various taping machines. Also proficient with industrial cutting knife/blade, air tools, power screwdrivers, hammers, skill saw, ban saw, tape measures, patterns. **Skilled at using technologies that enable production of small quantities of textile goods at the cost of bulk-produced items.**

CAREER SUCCESSES

- Gained exposure to production of a **broad textile product line** at American Textile: exercise mats, briefcases, camera cases, bedding, etc. **Became staff expert** in sewing duck blinds for commercial client.
- Received **performance-based pay raises** at Premium Comfort, sewing air beds on a certification process system.
- **Established Duluth Marine's Upholstery Department.** Researched, analyzed, and purchased industrial machines. Designed worktables for both cutting and sewing areas, maximizing attic space to cut costs. **Sought out distributors/vendors and established professional relationships with them** to secure best pricing/terms available. Subsequently **worked independently to maintain a highly profitable upholstery department.** Produced mooring covers, sun tops, cockpit covers, paddleboat covers, boat lift tarps, snowmobile covers, and numerous smaller items. Extensive communications with customers on site and via telephone.
- Enjoyed **progressive experience with Allen Boats,** one of the leading boat producers in the world. Received **consecutive promotions:** from hire to sew sun top sets for Lund America, to stapling, sewing, and assembling fish boat seats for Lund, to sewing and stapling board work for Larson/Glastron boat interiors.
  - **Promoted to Engineering,** becoming skilled in pattern work for boat interiors and sun tops. Gained proficiency with using machinery to make actual patterns from Masonite. Became expert at putting any aspect of a boat interior, cover, etc. onto a production line.
  - Learned a highly skilled craft from supervisor – who could not speak or hear – through sign language.
- **Successfully produced piece-rate garments for Munsingwear,** demonstrating my ability to maintain intense focus and concentration for 8-hour shifts, while coordinating hand movement, piecework, and diverse equipment.
- **Operated industrial machinery** to produce snowmobile suits, jackets, and ski pants for men and women.

TEXTILE INDUSTRY EXPERIENCE

Sewing Production: Duck Blinds	American Textile Products – Minneapolis, MN	2000
Certification Sewing: Air Beds	Premium Comfort Corporation – Minneapolis, MN	1997 – 2000
Upholstery Manager/Specialist	Duluth Marine – Duluth, MN	1992 – 1996
Engineering/Sewing/Production	Allen Boats – Duluth, MN	1981 – 1989
Garment Piecework Production	Munsingwear – Minneapolis, MN	1976 – 1978; 1979 – 1981
Apparel Production	Silverline/Arctic Cat – St. Paul, MN	1978 – 1979

OTHER PRODUCTION EMPLOYMENT

- PROSTAFF, 2000 – Present: Production with Acumed – St. Paul, manufacturer of medical supplies.
- KELLY SERVICES PRODUCTION WORK: 1997: Westinghouse, Emerald Plastics, Goldleaf Plastics, National Linen, ABC Printing, and Kraft. Production with Ultra Pac (2000) and Gold 'N Plump Poultry (1996-1997).

EDUCATION

- PROFESSIONAL DEVELOPMENT: Communications, Problem Solving, Quality, Team Work, Workforce Issues.
- Honors Graduate (top 100 of +450 students), Monroe High School – Minneapolis, MN

Appropriate graphics liven up this resume. Bold type is used throughout to make sure that key words stand out on a rather text-dense page.

Jesse Allen

977 East Virginia Road
Imperial, California 92251

home: 760 923-1753
mobile: 805 207-7396
email: jallen1@earthlink.com

Rig Supervisor / Manager / Consultant
Drilling / Workover / Well Field Service Operations
Preference: Overseas rotational job in Asia, South America, and the former Soviet Union.

SUMMARY OF QUALIFICATIONS

26+ years of broad-based knowledge and hands-on, industry-related experience encompassing a wide range of equipment and procedures used in the drilling, production, and maintenance of **oil, gas,** and **geothermal production and injection wells,** human resources, and field administration, including 17 years of supervision and management. A team leader, highly adaptable to varying environments across the globe (hostile environments, environmentally sensitive areas). Analytical thinker recognized for fast problem-solving actions and strong interpersonal skills. Basic conversational Spanish.

Solid experience in all phases of well operations and rig processes. Committed to leading a lean, efficient, empowered work force to achieve quality and excellence with integrity.

Proven ability to improve production efficiency, analyze and implement new processes, and achieve buy-in by production, management, and administrative staff.

- Detail-oriented, meticulous, conscientious, and results-driven; able to identify, analyze, and troubleshoot highly complex problems.
- Quick and effective problem-solver; know when individual action is required.
- Flexible and adaptive to change; resourceful in getting the job done.
- Job completion always within budget and on time despite sudden setbacks and changing priorities.
- Strong planning, organizational, and estimating skills with long-term focus on the bottom line.

Technical Skills
Extremely knowledgeable in remedial and production rig work. Supervision and hands-on experience with:
- Coil tubing—**large diameter units (2 3/8"-32")**—on well cleanouts, cementing operations, plug and abandonments, stimulation and acid work, cleaning slotted liners, hydra-blasting/acid washing liner, perforations, and N2 operations
- Wireline and slickline operations
    running and setting all types of production, testing, and well service tools as well as perforating and running various types of logs and surveys
- Repair and maintenance of surface production equipment
    well heads, xmas trees, flowlines, scrubbers, separators, and related production facility equipment.
- Oil and water based drilling and workover fluids
    foam, aerated mud, drilling with aerated drilling fluids

Supervision of drilling and workover operations in situations of
- Overbalance
- Lost circulation
- Underbalance
- High deviation
- Extremely hazardous conditions due to extreme bottom hole temperature or pressure, lethally high concentrations of H2S, or remote location of the job site

The functional style of this resume allows a strong page-1 presentation of skills and knowledge related to the energy industry.

Jesse Allen

Key Accomplishments

- Implemented lead man position to replace traditional supervisor role. Allows workers to develop "ownership" and provide more input into the production process—scheduling tasks, completing jobs, using their experience and intelligence to perform their jobs at a higher level.
- As key member of TQM team, instrumental in creating a quality assurance manual and training shop employees in its use.

Leadership Abilities

- Act as liaison between contractor and contractee as well as with local, state, and federal agencies; familiar with U.S. and Mexico. Ensure work is carried out within specifications of company safety guidelines in a safe, environmentally responsible, and cost-effective manner.
- Implement safety and hazardous response programs.
- Manage logistical requirements and daily operations of rig area.
- Work in coordination with engineers and company representatives to write programs and design workflow.
- Supervise maintenance management program to include scheduling, equipment outage, readiness, dispatching, and inventory reporting.
- Complete daily job reports detailing job descriptions, number of hours worked, tools and equipment utilized, daily costs of operations, and cumulative job cost.

WORK EXPERIENCE — Highlights

Rig Supervisor	Key Energy Services, Santa Paula, CA	2000
Well Field Operations Supervisor	M and D Enterprises, Holtville, CA	1998 – 2000
Rig Supervisor	Parker Drilling Company, Tulsa, OK	1997 – 1998
Consultant (Drilling, Workover, and Well Field Operations)	Independent Consultant, Imperial, CA	1991 – 1997

As Rig Supervisor for Parker Drilling Company, work required a strong hands-on approach because of the extensive use of SABA (Supplied Air Breathing Apparatus) and SCBA (Self Contained Breathing Apparatus) and the hazards involved in moving and supplying rigs by helicopter due to extremely remote "fly-in" locations in Indonesia and South America.

EDUCATION / TRAINING / CERTIFICATIONS

Certified I.A.D.C. and **M.M.S. Well Control, Supervisor's Level**	Parker Drilling Well Control School, 1997
Cementing School for Service Supervisors	Dowell Schlumberger Tech, Tulsa, OK, 1987
Coiled Tubing and Nitrogen Training for Service Supervisors	Dowell Schlumberger Tech, Tulsa, OK, 1987
Personnel - Time Management	Pageant-Thompson, Anaheim, CA, 1985
Welex Perforating and Wireline	Training School, Ventura, CA, 1984
Well Control	Ventura College, Ventura, CA, 1981

PROFESSIONAL AFFILIATION

International Association of Drilling Contractors

MARK E. KELLY

526 Altamont Avenue, Schenectady, NY 12306 • Phone: (518) 222-5666 • kellymark@yahoo.com

PLANT MANUFACTURING MANAGER / PRODUCTION MANAGER
Technology Management with focus in Cabinetry

KEY MANAGEMENT STRENGTHS

• Quality Control Management	• Team Leadership	• Personnel Training & Development
• Production Planning & Scheduling	• Safety Compliance	• Manufacturing & Information Technology

PROFILE

RESULTS-ORIENTED, hard-working manufacturing supervisor with excellent analytical, organizational, team building, and strategic planning skills. Detail oriented with strong technical and mechanical ability; background in manufacturing cabinetry. Outstanding knowledge of woodworking and demonstrated high-quality building skills. Able to learn new tasks quickly. Strong performance in both independent and team settings. Superior interpersonal skills with an innate ability to get along with diverse groups of people. Deep knowledge of OSHA, EPA, and regulatory compliance. Fluent in conversational German and Spanish. Willing to relocate.

EDUCATION

Bachelor of Science (Technology Management), GPA: 3.8 Union College – 1998
Coursework included:
>   Technology and Operations Management, Small Business Management, Managing Organizations, Product Innovation, Safety and Environment, Material in Technology

Associate of Applied Science in Cabinetry and Architectural Woodworking, GPA: 3.7
Schenectady Community College – 1993
>   **Phi Theta Kappa International Honor Society of Colleges – 1992**

Various additional workshops related to special cabinetry techniques of tools of the trade

SELECTED ACHIEVEMENTS

- Streamlined chip-disposal process by implementing chipper-shredder machine to create sawdust, eliminating cost of chip removal. **Achieved savings of $125,535 over a 2-year period.**
- Wrote and implemented safety and operations manual for Cabinetworks Technology.
- Instrumental in implementing Windows Manufacturing program, which allows for scheduling and tracking of production jobs. **Total efficiency significantly enhanced by lower incidence of "down time."**

PROFESSIONAL EXPERIENCE

Apple Barrel Mill, Schoharie, New York   1992–present
ASSISTANT FOREMAN – Graveyard Shift (1996–present)
- Manage and direct all aspects of plant operation, including coordinating work schedules, instituting policies and procedures, and conducting evaluations and disciplinary measures.
- Direct and supervise 25 assembly team members to ensure quality and timely completion of work orders, delegating corrections as necessary; conduct TQM inspections.
- Coordinate and conduct training of staff to ensure efficient equipment operation.
- Accountable for maintaining compliances with safety standards and EPA regulations.
- Consistently achieve and surpass performance objectives.

LEADMAN – Swing Shift (1992–1995)
- Directed and supervised assembly workers including maintenance of safety requirements and production levels.
- Implemented and maintained updated training in production, tools, safety, and policy and procedures.

AWARDS

- New York State Vocational Industrial Club of America – VICA Cabinetry and Millwork, 1989
- Employee of Quarter at Victory Stores (a.k.a. Apple Barrel Mill)

This individual's recent bachelor's degree (completed while he worked nights as an Assistant Foreman) is a strong qualification for his current goal of a management position. Therefore, it is placed prominently toward the top of this resume.

JOHN A. LUCAS
810 New Hope Court
Lodi, California 95624
(209) 334-9903

MANUFACTURING DEPARTMENT MANAGER

15+ years of cross-functional production management experience. Proven ability to discover and eliminate scheduling production bottlenecks and measurably increase output and profits. Strong track record in managing complex projects, keeping on schedule, and maintaining high quality standards. Well-qualified in estimating materials/labor planning and specifications. Effective in getting cooperation of staff.

DEMONSTRATED STRENGTHS

Reliability • Priority-Setting • Organization • Communication • Staff Training • Workflow Optimization
Work Ethic • Team Building • Leadership • Safety Conscious • Cross-Culturally Sensitive

MAINTENANCE AND MECHANICAL SKILLS

Equipment Maintenance • Electrical • Plumbing • Pipe Fitting • I-P Repairs
Moore 352 Controller Programming • Scrolls • Rotary Vacuum Filter Maintenance
Conduit Installation, Cutting, Welding • Auto Control Valves • Pneumatic Controllers

EMPLOYMENT HIGHLIGHTS

BBD PRODUCTS, INC., Tracy, CA   February–May 2001
Production Supervisor — Recruited to revitalize production management for a crew of 40+ of this high-speed manufacturer of fiberglass conducting with 5 plants in Richmond. Generated up to $4 million in sales volume until down-trending market resulted in massive downsizing.

- Directed an environment to accelerate production output and strengthen quality performance.
- Participated in strategy planning and consensus building for favorable union relations.
- Emphasized cooperation and team building to improve production output and workforce management.

APPLEBEE CO., Tracy, CA *(subsidiary of Imperial Apple)*   1985–2001
Shift Superintendent *(1997–2001)*
Production Supervisor *(1987–1997)*
Labor, Operator, Loader, Instrument Technician *(1985–1987)*
Achieved fast-track promotions in recognition of superior performance of this high-volume sugar processing and packaging manufacturer with 350+ employees.

- Recognized as company's most notable troubleshooter: Provided leadership, labor resources, cross-training, and supported efforts in enhancing production, safety, sanitation, and quality control.
- Assumed responsibility for a manufacturing operation with low production yields and a stagnant workforce. Within one year, improved productivity on all shifts due to effective team building.
- Spearheaded cross-functional training to educate, develop, and motivate staff (operators, technicians, electricians, mechanics, and lab personnel) to achieve required production results.
- As Production Supervisor, credited with the implementation of a fully-integrated TQM program that eliminated obstacles to quality control and improved overall performance of operation.
- Directed collaborative efforts for continuous improvement including control systems, design, and workflow optimization processes, resulting in significant costs savings and profitability.
- Devised computer-generated training procedures with measurable labor efficiency results.
- Launched start-up of new juice-softening process, providing an uninterrupted high-quality product through effective problem-solving skills. Trained staff to gain a better understanding of the process.

This resume is replete with strong, meaningful language—note the phrases "eliminate scheduling production bottlenecks" and "increase output and profits" in the summary.

JOHN A. LUCAS   Page two

KEY SUCCESS FACTORS

Production Management

- Focused efforts on performance improvements processes, operations design, and cross-training/coaching, which created a positive working environment and strengthened labor efficiency.
- Demonstrated leadership and production management competencies during a period of transition and change management.
- Guided a series of efficiency improvement initiatives throughout all core production planning, production scheduling, and manufacturing operations with successful cost savings.
- Maintained and reduced costs through effective price negotiations with vendors and through disposition of on-hand materials for varied maintenance projects.
- Forged strategies and managed sensitive labor relations issues in cooperation with management teams, union officials, and hourly union staff.

Training and Development

- Devised innovative training and performance development programs resulting in motivating staff to achieve maximum productivity.
- Established a conscientious effort to maintain open communications to ensure effective interchange of information between work groups and support resources within the organization.
- Monitored workforce performance against strategy plans and implemented corrective action for standards of quality, sanitation, and safety.

Safety Management

- Structured safety training and chaired meetings to create safety awareness, delivering a reduction in lost time accidents and improving labor efficiency ratings.
- Acquired extensive training and hands-on experience in hazardous material handling procedures, safety and loss issues, control issues, and regulatory compliance standards.

PROFESSIONAL DEVELOPMENT

CPR and First Aid Certified 2000

Hazardous Waste Operations and Emergency Response, Safety Training Institute 2000

Respirator Training, 3M Innovation 2000

Beet End Operations/Beet Sugar Technology, Colorado State University 1995

Sugar End Operations/Beet Sugar Technology, Colorado State University 1994

Supervisor Development, Safety Center Incorporated 1993

Statistical Process Control, Qualpro 1993

How to Communicate with Confidence, Clarity and Credibility, National Seminars 1992

TERESA ANDERSON
718 Two Pond Road
Middle, SC 29002
(876) 723-5512

OBJECTIVE	A supervisory position that will benefit from my experience, loyalty, and ability to motivate others.
PROFILE	• Excellent written and verbal communication skills. • Comfortable with culturally diverse groups. • Very organized as relates to time and project. • Strong work ethic; loyal.
EXPERIENCE	**1981-Present** **WestPoint Stevens, Division of WestPoint Pepperell**, Middle, SC *Supervisor — Pillowcase Department*, 1995-Present • Supervise 33 employees. • Interview, hire, and terminate employees. • Train employees on plant computer system to record machine production. • Conduct safety meetings and encourage continual safety awareness — department had 2 million accident-free hours. • Meet daily with quality assurance manager to ensure high quality product. • Assist in quarterly plant-wide inventory. **Department consistently meets or exceeds company-set production goals.** *Management Trainee Program* • Rotated through all departments of plant. • Filled in on as-needed basis for supervisors in all departments. *Training Instructor* • Provided formal computer and machine-operation training to approximately 500 employees. *Data Entry Clerk* *Automatic Pillowcase Machine Operator*
EDUCATION	**Associate's Degree**, Business Management, 1995 Tri-County Technical College, Greenville, SC Dean's List — GPA 3.1 **Continuing Education** — WestPoint Stevens • Management Development • Managing Without Interference • Analytical Methods Training • Excelling as a First-Time Supervisor • PLATO 2000 software • CPR and First Aid

In a brief, one-page presentation, this resume clearly shows career progression and ability to meet business goals.

Tom Farmer

45 Horse Trail Drive, Ottawa, Ontario K1P 6E2
(613) 234-4174   tom_farmer@hotmail.com

PRODUCTION SUPERVISOR

Team Leader ◆ Technical Trainer ◆ Schedule Coordinator

PROFILE

EXCEL FIBREOPTICS EMPLOYEE

Experienced Supervisor of a work-cell production environment for a rapid-growth company and world leader in fibre optics manufacturing. Committed to meeting production deadlines and targets. Proven experience in quality control of manufacturing procedures and practices. Strong personnel management skills in dealing with difficult situations. Technical training in leading-edge computerized manufacturing techniques. Shop floor experience.

PRODUCTION EXPERIENCE

Production Supervisor/Team Leader
EXCEL FIBREOPTICS, Ottawa, October 2000-August 2001

ENVIRONMENT
- Rapid-growth 24/7 production unit involving the assembly of DWSN passive optical components.

PERSONNEL MANAGEMENT
- Supervised 4 Work Cell Coordinators and 75 assemblers, involving $100K work stations per assembler. Approximately 75% of job time spent on people issues — e.g., low productivity. Implemented corrective action and continuously improved performance of the manufacturing team through training, teamwork, disciplinary action, motivation enhancement, information sessions, and performance review. Reduced absenteeism to less than 2% on a regular basis.
- Constantly monitored production reports to maintain targets. Improved input/feedback process with assemblers, thereby improving productivity.
- Facilitated training of new employees in cell groups to achieve production targets within 4-6 weeks.
- Completed leadership training in coaching, communication and listening, dealing with difficult situations, managing multiple priorities, diversity and harassment, and performance management.
- Fostered and maintained harmonious relations within the work group. Managed employee relations within department.

OPERATIONS & QUALITY CONTROL
- Coordinated production workflow in a manufacturing environment involving significant changes every month.
- Developed customized formats on a database using Excel to improve reporting procedures.
- Maintained accurate data records for production and updated managers.
- Implemented and monitored ISO 9001 standards.
- Consistently met targets from planning department at 80% of predictability under difficult production circumstances.

TROUBLESHOOTING
- Supported production activities in a hands-on manner.
- Troubleshot product lines and tests to achieve performance objectives.
- Read blueprint plans, then talked assembler through a process.

Breaking down an extensive qualifications/accomplishments list using appropriate subheadings makes this material more comprehensible to the reader. Note the "Profile" section that briefly summarizes this individual's career experience.

Tom Farmer
Page 2

(613) 234-4174
tom_farmer@hotmail.com

PRODUCTION EXPERIENCE, continued

EXCEL FIBREOPTICS, Ottawa, 1997-2001
Technical Trainer, 1999-2001

- Trained new employees in production assembly processes.
- Developed and reviewed training procedures and processes. Evaluated trainee performance on fibre handling, mechanical splice, connector cleaning and inspection, and DWDM device assembly.
- Ensured trainees were aware of specific and company-wide policies, procedures, goals, and objectives. Delivered non-production courses such as WHMIS, QA awareness, Health & Safety, Crisis Management, etc.

Field Trainer/Intermediate Assembler, 1997-1999

- Performed intermediate mechanical, electrical, and optical operations with defined procedures, drawing, and operating standards.
- Coordinated product inspection and product documentation before shipping.

RELATED EMPLOYMENT

Parts Person & Shipper/Receiver
Northern Auto Transmission, Ottawa, 1994-1997

- Performed inspection of used parts, inventory control, order-filling, shop supply ordering, shipping/receiving, quality inspection of transmissions, supervision and training of employees.

PERSONALITY TRAITS

- Get along easily with people. Patient with trainees. Open minded. Optimistic. Very keen to do a good job. Enjoy multi-tasking.

TRAINING, COURSES, AWARDS

- Certified as a Technical Trainer and Team Leader
- Certified as a Welder/Fitter and Forklift Operator
- Canadian Oxygen LTD Award in Excellence in Welding
- High school diploma

HOBBIES

- Woodworking, Furniture Refinishing, Electronic Repairs

REFERENCES available on request

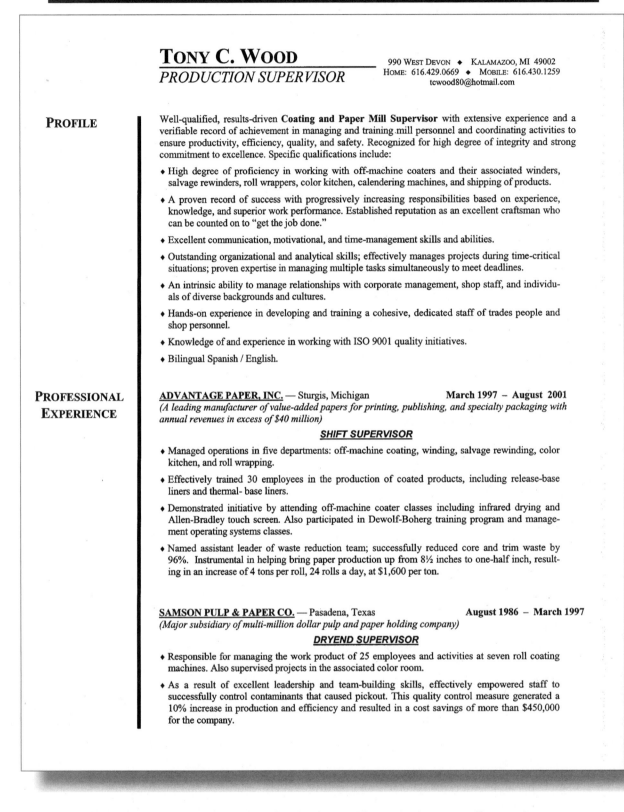

TONY C. WOOD
PRODUCTION SUPERVISOR

990 WEST DEVON ◆ KALAMAZOO, MI 49002
HOME: 616.429.0669 ◆ MOBILE: 616.430.1259
tcwood80@hotmail.com

PROFILE

Well-qualified, results-driven **Coating and Paper Mill Supervisor** with extensive experience and a verifiable record of achievement in managing and training mill personnel and coordinating activities to ensure productivity, efficiency, quality, and safety. Recognized for high degree of integrity and strong commitment to excellence. Specific qualifications include:

♦ High degree of proficiency in working with off-machine coaters and their associated winders, salvage rewinders, roll wrappers, color kitchen, calendering machines, and shipping of products.

♦ A proven record of success with progressively increasing responsibilities based on experience, knowledge, and superior work performance. Established reputation as an excellent craftsman who can be counted on to "get the job done."

♦ Excellent communication, motivational, and time-management skills and abilities.

♦ Outstanding organizational and analytical skills; effectively manages projects during time-critical situations; proven expertise in managing multiple tasks simultaneously to meet deadlines.

♦ An intrinsic ability to manage relationships with corporate management, shop staff, and individuals of diverse backgrounds and cultures.

♦ Hands-on experience in developing and training a cohesive, dedicated staff of trades people and shop personnel.

♦ Knowledge of and experience in working with ISO 9001 quality initiatives.

♦ Bilingual Spanish / English.

PROFESSIONAL EXPERIENCE

ADVANTAGE PAPER, INC. — Sturgis, Michigan   **March 1997 – August 2001**
(A leading manufacturer of value-added papers for printing, publishing, and specialty packaging with annual revenues in excess of $40 million)

SHIFT SUPERVISOR

♦ Managed operations in five departments: off-machine coating, winding, salvage rewinding, color kitchen, and roll wrapping.

♦ Effectively trained 30 employees in the production of coated products, including release-base liners and thermal- base liners.

♦ Demonstrated initiative by attending off-machine coater classes including infrared drying and Allen-Bradley touch screen. Also participated in Dewolf-Boherg training program and management operating systems classes.

♦ Named assistant leader of waste reduction team; successfully reduced core and trim waste by 96%. Instrumental in helping bring paper production up from 8½ inches to one-half inch, resulting in an increase of 4 tons per roll, 24 rolls a day, at $1,600 per ton.

SAMSON PULP & PAPER CO. — Pasadena, Texas   **August 1986 – March 1997**
(Major subsidiary of multi-million dollar pulp and paper holding company)

DRYEND SUPERVISOR

♦ Responsible for managing the work product of 25 employees and activities at seven roll coating machines. Also supervised projects in the associated color room.

♦ As a result of excellent leadership and team-building skills, effectively empowered staff to successfully control contaminants that caused pickout. This quality control measure generated a 10% increase in production and efficiency and resulted in a cost savings of more than $450,000 for the company.

With a job-title headline highly visible under the name, this resume starts off strongly. It continues with good organization and formatting that create a clear, easily skimmed document.

TONY C. WOOD   *Page 2*

PROFESSIONAL EXPERIENCE (CONT.)

CHANEY PULP & PAPER – Pasadena, Texas   October 1975 – August 1986
(A leading producer and distributor of coated and uncoated papers with $200 million annual revenue)

OPERATOR / SUPERVISOR

♦ Exceptional hands-on experience with No. 22 Rice Barton Blade Trailing, No. 27 Flooded Nip Coaters, rod blade coater, and Deckle increase, and the subsequent supervision of employees working with these machines. Ensured maximum safety of employees and allowed timely production of quality product.

♦ Effectively supervised a team of 25 individuals. Promoted team building and collaboration to ensure efficiency and work quality.

EDUCATION

BACHELOR OF ARTS, BIBLE STUDIES / THEOLOGY
UNIVERSITY OF OKLAHOMA — Tulsa, 1984

ADDITIONAL TRAINING

First Responder Training	1999
Confined Space Entry	1999
Accident Reduction	1997 – 2000
Fork Truck Operation and Safety	1999

COMMUNITY/ VOLUNTEER ACTIVITIES

Frequent guest speaker on topics related to drug and alcohol abuse
for Alcoholics Anonymous meetings, 1991 – Present

Member Board of Trustees, New Beginnings Women's Center, 1981 – 1999

Chairman of the Board, Mediation Committee, House Improvement and Community Service,
New Beginnings Women's Center, 1981 – 1999

♦ ♦ ♦

Art Klass

2717 West Paul Street   Clinton, IL 57843   (303) 382-1230   E-mail: artkl@hotmail.com

Operations / Manufacturing / Facilities Management

My career reflects 30 years' experience in supervision, operations, and management in the highly competitive and diligently regulated industries of chemical/paper/plastics manufacturing. Responsible for multiple divisions which included 200 personnel, budgetary oversight of $1.8M/year, and an $8M special installation project as part of capital improvement campaign.

Awarded a **Bachelor of Science** degree in Instrument and Process Control Technology from Illinois State University. Hold additional certifications in Plant Engineering and Welding. Received on-going training through DCS Phase One of Reliance Automation, as well as Phase One/Advance Design of the Allen & Bradley PLC 5. Have enhanced academic and professional experience with additional training in negotiations, risk management, human resources, finance, quality/safety, and regulatory compliance.

Professional Objective:

These skills and abilities could be utilized in a variety of leadership capacities within your organization. I believe the strengths of my background could be maximized as **Chief Operating Officer, Plant Manager, Facilities Manager,** or **Director of Quality Control & Risk Management.**

Career History:

Electrical/Instrument Superintendent   **Perfection Paper Carlisle Mill**   **1996-present**
- Responsible for all instrumentation and electrical equipment in mill producing 600 tons per day.
- Supervised technicians and panel of environment, health, and safety professionals as EHS Coordinator.
- Wrote and coordinated all new safety, health, and environmental procedures and programs.
- Took risk-management initiatives to reduce failures by 31%.
- Sought by corporate executives to serve as Project Leader of major (RTO) system design & installation.
- Led team to bring Perfection Paper Mill 2 into compliance with MACT I guidelines.
- Project supervisor of over 200 people – skillfully negotiated union grievances and non-union contracts while maintaining positive internal and external relationships.

Electrical/Instrumentation Superintendent   **ChampPrint Manufacturing Inc.**   **1984-1995**
- Responsible for all electrical and instrumentation in the mill.
- Designed and purchased electrical/mechanical equipment for $30M capital improvement project.
- Served as Safety Chairperson to reduce workman's compensation costs by 43%.
- Reduced Total Incident Ratio and Lost Time Incidents by 66%.
- Preventative maintenance increased productivity by 50 feet per minute.
- Efforts reduced down time by 40% for an annual savings of $200K.
- Point person in all safety, quality, and regulatory compliance issues.
- Interim Human Resources Coordinator responsible for interviewing, hiring, union grievances, record keeping, policy development, and clear articulation of mill management goals and objectives.

Electrical Maintenance   **PitMoore-MC, Inc.**   **1970-1983**
- Oversaw 5 technicians in the areas of troubleshooting, systems design, and equipment upgrade.
- Supervised concept-to-completion installation of two full chemical processes.

References Available upon Establishment of Mutual Interest

The narrative style used in the introduction and objective makes this resume highly personal. Then, within the career history section, briefer, harder-hitting statements convey essential information.

GEOFFREY C. HOWARD

16 Chestnut Hill Drive, Lexington, MA 02167, (617) 541-8286, Office: (617) 424-6400

OBJECTIVE: To improve the profitability and productivity of a progressive organization.

SUMMARY OF QUALIFICATIONS:
- Over 6 years of increasingly responsible experience in the pharmaceutical, food processing, and manufacturing industries.
- Proven record of management skills; reference states "flexible in his solutions....commanded authority with subordinate employees."
- Work well independently or as a team member; "able to master difficult situations."
- Bilingual German/English; excellent communication skills.

RELEVANT EXPERIENCE:

Leiner Health Products, Largo, Florida   1997 to Present
Packaging Supervisor 5/99 to Present
- Supervise 28 machine operators, assemblers, and packagers.
- Coordinate workload and manpower availability to optimize production and efficiency. Accordingly, administer performance measurements, ensure paper flow continuity, and monitor production floor.
- Train and orient all new employees.

Production Scheduler, 12/98 to 5/99
- Ensured products are manufactured on time to meet customer orders. Prepared production documentation for all departments to guide their operations in order to fill inventory needs.

Materials Clerk/Quality Control Inspector 9/98 to 12/98
- Processed materials documentation on the movement of all raw materials and finished products.
- Responsible for performing in-process checks of OTC pharmaceutical packaging. Performed incoming inspection of all materials and final inspections of materials; completed all documentation of batch productions.

Toni Zurich Corporation, Zurich, Switzerland   1989 to 1996
Group Manager 1991 to 1996
- Responsible for ensuring quality standards during the production of ice cream and the direction of personnel in various functions of line work and machine operations.
- Performed inspections of all cleaning processes in the production department including freezers and filling facilities.
- Enforced all safety regulations, internal orders, and legal requirements of the production process; also trained apprentices.

Machine Operator 1989 to 1991
- Major focus of this position was the control of filling machines, freezers, fruit-mixing machines, and exterior packaging machines. Maintained replenishment of packaging materials and ensured all cleaning was completed.

Jowa AG, Zurich, Switzerland   1984 to 1987
Apprentice/Production Supervisor/Quality Control
- Completed 3-year apprenticeship and was hired to head the plant in the preparation of sweet short-crust and puff pastry for baked goods. Also supervised the production of filling and baking of non-cream cakes.

EDUCATION:
- Bachelor of Science, University of Zurich, Zurich, Switzerland, 1987
- Computer Skills: Novell, Excel, and MS Word
- Apprenticeship: Jowa AG, Zurich, Switzerland (Food Technician)

INTERESTS:
Sports, Family Activities

Rather than a bland or "me"-focused objective, this resume starts with a brief objective that will certainly catch the eye of hiring authorities.

VINCENT L. DINATA

1976 Sixers Boulevard
Philadelphia, PA 19114
(215) 907-1912

OBJECTIVE   A motivating, challenging, and rewarding position as a **Production Supervisor** where education and experience can be effectively utilized.

PROFESSIONAL HIGHLIGHTS

8/92-
present

Padrone Industries, Philadelphia, PA
MANUFACTURING LEADER — 2/95-present
Hire, train, motivate, and dismiss personnel. Coordinate, plan, and directly supervise the activities of 115 subordinates engaged in producing 3,000 pieces per day. Utilize knowledge of manufacturing technology, methods, and procedures to direct industry with procurement maintenance and quality control action to obtain optimum manufacturing and use of manpower, machines, and equipment. Coordinate the preparation of manufactured products to develop new markets, increase share of market, and obtain a competitive position within the industry. Inspect completed work to locate errors. Send back damaged goods. Establish priorities and expedite workflow. Resolve staff grievances. Schedule staff and production. Handle difficult situations using tact, discretion, and excellent judgment. Troubleshoot and communicate.

ACHIEVEMENTS: **Consistently surpass manufacturing goal by 100%. Meet all deadlines on time for the manufacturing of 3,000 pieces.**

PRODUCTION CONTROL COORDINATOR — 8/92-2/95
Reported directly to Manufacturing Leader. Conferred with management to ascertain employee's ability to surpass the production of 60,000 pieces daily. Ensured that continuous production of 60,000 pieces complied with established company standards. Compared product numbers to invoice numbers to ensure that they correlated. Prepared and submitted daily report to Manufacturing Leader. Remained calm in a crisis situation and made logical decisions under immense pressure. Met all deadlines on time.

2/89-
8/92

Eagles Industries, Philadelphia, PA
ASSEMBLY LINE WORKER

EDUCATION   **THE PENNSYLVANIA STATE UNIVERSITY,** State College, PA
B. S. DEGREE IN ELECTRICAL ENGINEERING, 1990

COURSES: QS 9000, Quality Performance, Leadership, Time & Stress Management, Quality Control

COMPUTERS: Windows NT, Windows 95, Lotus 1-2-3, Word

The Career Experience section focuses on the variety of activities this individual performs in his job as Manufacturing Leader. It then effectively highlights strong and relevant achievements.

RESUME 16: DAYNA FEIST, CPRW, JCTC, CEIP; ASHEVILLE, NC

Dawn L. Freeman

265 Charlotte Street • Asheville, NC 28801

gatehous@aol.com

(828) 254-7893

Target: First-Line Supervision in production environment, with freedom to make changes and teach in a company that values performance. Aspire to earn a reputation for fairness, to inspire loyalty and teamwork, and to help others and the company grow. Willing to travel and/or relocate.

Selected Achievements

- **Boosted efficiency of Cincinnati lab from 79% to 104% within 4 months** by collaborating with warehouse to reorganize supplies for simpler restocking; communicating high expectations regularly; emphasizing accountability; listening, coaching, and developing trust; working closely with other departmental supervisors to reduce waste, time, and materials; and terminating the (very) few employees incapable of improving performance. *Results*—Built strongest, best trained, most knowledgeable team in plant, successfully meeting department goals with fewer staff.

- **Challenged to prepare facility for impending lab closure** due to astronomical transportation costs out of our control. Evaluated and made all decisions to impact bottom line; worked even closer with purchasing agent to keep minimal inventory, and met and exceeded quality guidelines. *Results*—Lab stayed open 2 years longer than anticipated (till 1995), allowing employees time to prepare as best as possible.

- **Youngest, and only the second female,** to become a supervisor in plant history (1985).

Durable, high-energy multi-tasker with outstanding desire to excel . . .
Exemplary organizational skills . . . Adaptable . . . Ethical

---

CORELEX INC., a Wholly Owned Subsidiary of RUSTON MOSS CO.
Photofinishing for mass retailers (e.g., Kmart, Wal-Mart), with 52 labs nationally

Production Supervisor 3 • Toledo, Ohio • 1995–2001

Packaging & Billing accountability for "next day or free" 7-day operation handling 12,000–25,000 rolls of film daily with turnaround necessary within one shift. Quality assurance, analysis, and reporting; performance appraisal, coaching, and operator certification. First-line supervision of 25–30 operators in packaging and 7–8 in billing.

- Standardized intra-department communications with a "huddle" board to increase information speed and accuracy that became mandatory for all departments.

- Instituted "field trips" to other departments to bring visual impact and reality to department policies and problem-solving.

Production Supervisor 2 • Dayton, Ohio • 1992–1995
Budget of $12 million; 100–200 employees.

Led and mentored a team of 5 first-line supervisors and an hourly production staff of up to 200, managed a direct labor/materials operating budget of $5,400,000, and directed all production functions (transportation schedules, operator schedules, quality, efficiency, service time). Reported directly to operations manager.

- Challenged to achieve overnight enlargement service (from previous 2- to 5-day turnaround). Analyzed current service, educated operators, enlisted operator and supervisor support, and maintained consistent, daily communication on progress. *Results*—Service commitments were met; I received a formal thank-you from the operations manager, a recognition letter from the regional quality manager, and personal satisfaction.

- Transitioned lab from 5- to 7-day operation. Analyzed volume spread and productivity-to-volume to schedule minimum number of employees on weekend; personally explained changes to each employee; and hired for the weekends. *Results*—A successful, smooth transition within a month with new hires who wanted weekend work and which painfully impacted as few employees as possible.

- Restructured labor reporting to rectify computer-generated report that was virtually useless. Designed user-friendly coding system tying tasks to 1 of 3 product lines, allowing labor, volume, and budget comparisons pinpointing areas of greatest improvement opportunities.

This resume was written for a production supervisor who was looking for a first-line position because she really liked the training aspect of her job.

(828) 254-7893   gatehous@aol.com   *Dawn L. Freeman*

2

Production Supervisor 2 & 3 • Dayton, Ohio • 1985–1992

One of 3 supervisors on a 4-week shift rotation and department rotation; reported to production manager. Supervised an average of 60 personnel (an entire shift, not just a department). *Challenge*—To supervise and positively impact a different group of people, different departments, and different product mix amidst total changes in focus. *Result*—Successfully managed workflow, service commitments, quality assurance, productivity, and documentation/administrative functions while learning all lab functions, befriending all lab personnel, and mastering in-depth workflow knowledge.

- Selected in 1990 to assist 9-week California start-up of premiere Rustonex line.
- Given authority to test, analyze, and document equipment as decision maker for potential purchase by plant.
- Initiated daily review of quality returns by packaging supervisor, increasing training results with excellent show-and-tell examples.
- Consolidated funneling of information to print inspectors through one person, for increased uniformity.

Instructor / Ruston Moss • Dayton, Ohio • 1980 – 1985

Trained new-hire and cross-training employees. Ensured uniform following of established procedures; audited product; evaluated and resolved quality issues; eliminated, modified, and/or developed handling procedures as needed. Close collaboration with shift supervisor.

- Outperformed 200 employees as one of 5 selected for specialized training as part of launch of radically new (for plant) product line.

Prior Production Positions, Dayton, Ohio (1969–1980), include quality auditor, data entry operator, and packaging operator.

Professional Training
Dale Carnegie Course
Women's Leadership Forum
Statistical Process Control Seminar
Harassment/Sensitivity Training Seminars
Hazardous Materials Handling/Bloodborne Pathogen Precautions
Directions International Seminar (Quality Improvement)

Certified Instructor, Development Dimensions International Leadership Skills Course

PC experience with Excel, Word, Lotus 1-2-3

Gary A. Samson

3841 McDonnell Court   Coralville, IA 52242   319-555-2913

Profile

Successful, experienced manager earning fast-track promotions. Proven record of improving and maintaining profitable operations. Skilled in approaching processes and problems from different perspectives, resulting in creative and innovative solutions. Ability to build rapport with employees by creating upbeat working environment and leading by example.

Highlights of Achievements

▶▶   Initiated scrap-tracking program that significantly reduced losses due to scrap; program was ultimately adopted by other departments.

▶▶   Turned around lowest- to highest-volume shift in two production areas.

▶▶   Earned promotion to Managing Partner (a more independent, autonomous capacity than Restaurant Manager), one of only seven in Iowa.

▶▶   Consistently maintained sales volume ranking in Top 5 in the state.

▶▶   Improved employee satisfaction with their jobs by 16% within one year.

▶▶   Named *Outstanding Restaurant Manager in Iowa Region* (1996).

▶▶   Named *Outstanding 1st Assistant Manager in Iowa Region* (1993).

▶▶   Named *Outstanding 2nd Assistant Manager in Iowa Region* (1990).

Professional Experience

JOHN DEERE TRACTORS • Cedar Rapids, Iowa   1998-Present
Manufacturing Supervisor
- Supervise, motivate, and schedule overtime for 40+ hourly employees assembling circuit boards for instrument-panel clusters.
- Schedule building of parts in collaboration with final assembly departments.
- Collaborate with union representatives in matters relating to discipline and grievances.
- Make presentations to employees regarding safety, product, and line changes.
- Process payroll utilizing John Deere's TA system.
- Participate in QS 9000 recertification audits.

— continued —

After transitioning from the restaurant industry to manufacturing, this individual updated his resume to apply for a similar position with a larger company. His earlier accomplishments remain in the resume

Gary A. Samson   319-555-2193

Professional Experience
— continued —

MCDONALD'S CORP. • Johnson County, Iowa   1987-1998
Managing Partner (1996-1998) — **Restaurant Manager** (1995-1996) — **1st Assistant Manager** (1991-1995) — **2nd Assistant Manager** (1987-1991) — **Manager Trainee** (1987)
- Hired, trained, and managed 8 management-level, 65 hourly, and 3 maintenance employees.
- Developed annual budgets and sales goals; collaborated with regional operations manager to create store's financial plan.
- Ensured safety and security of employees, customers, and physical plant.
- Simultaneously managed traditional store and SPOD (special points of distribution) outlet located nearby main store; used as training site for managers.
- Implemented creative strategies to increase sales, lower food costs, and retain quality team members.
- Acted as mentor to management-track employees, supplying the corporation's system with many promotable leaders.
- Taught management classes to prepare employees for success in corporate-offered courses.
- Monitored adherence to corporation's exacting standards regarding products and service.
- Performed Human Resources functions including performance reviews, payroll, benefits, employee counseling.
- Planned and implemented promotions, advertising, and marketing efforts.
- Monitored inventory and ordered supplies.

Education

UNIVERSITY OF IOWA • Iowa City, Iowa
Bachelor of Arts   1986
    Major: Mass Communications   *Minor:* Physical Education

KIRKWOOD COMMUNITY COLLEGE • Cedar Rapids, Iowa
Coursework in **Mechanical Engineering**   1979-1982

Training

▶ John Deere Management Training
▶ Lean Manufacturing
▶ Diversity
▶ Job-related Technical Training

▶ McDonald's University
▶ Managing the Changing Workforce
▶ Seven Habits of Highly Effective People (taught by author Stephen Covey)

— References available on request —

because they demonstrate his track record of supervisory achievements, although in a different industry.

CHAPTER 5

Resumes for Engineering, Product Development, and Quality Professionals

- Engineers—Electrical, Electronic, Mechanical, Chemical, R&D, and Quality
- Product Testing and Analysis Personnel
- Quality Assurance and Quality Control Personnel
- Quality Control Chemists and Lab Personnel
- TQM and ISO Project Managers

SHELLEY LYNN CROW

116 Park Ave. • New York, NY 12589 • (350)254-6891 • slcrowbird@yahoo.com

OBJECTIVE	To obtain a full-time position with a growing company that will offer diverse experience in the field of chemical engineering and utilize my strong work ethic and ambition.
EDUCATION	**New York University, New York, NY, May 2002** B.S. Candidate, Chemical Engineering GPA: 3.1

EXPERIENCE

Jan. 2000 –
May 2000

Product Development Intern — Clark-Johnston Corporation, Manhattan, NY
- Gained full understanding of product specifications and materials for current Pull-Ups® training pants.
- Planned and implemented clinical studies to monitor effects of changes in child care product designs and developed raw materials for optimal product performance.
- Recommended changes for future large-scale testing based on product performance and participants' responses from small-scale studies.
- Facilitated bench testing to predict and explain failures in product design changes.
- Supported product, materials, and process teams with their project activities in order to meet crucial timing for small- and large-scale use studies.
- Compiled study results which were presented to the Product Review Board to obtain product safety clearance.
- Conducted meetings, presentations, and wrote technical reports to document research and development findings.

May 1998 –
Aug. 1998

Corporate Intern — Caterpillar, Inc., Brownsfield, CT
- Coordinated an Illinois Environmental Protection Agency (IEPA) TV shoot that highlighted pollution prevention stories which aired on the Public Broadcasting System.
- Worked on the development of an interactive environmental awareness program between Caterpillar and the community.
- Gained understanding of the theory and operation of a distillation unit and was responsible for troubleshooting any problems.
- Calculated the return on investment (ROI) for the distillation unit to verify that it was a cost savings for the company.
- Organized the purchase of a used gas chromatograph and ordered all necessary lab supplies that would eventually be shipped to an undercarriage facility in China.

June 1992 –
Aug. 1997

Office Assistant — Crow Sheet Metal, Inc., Crow's Cellular & Paging, Mt. Vernon, IL
- Assisted with the monthly billing and helped train others to use the billing program.
- Provided assistance to customers in the sales office.
- Served as a receptionist, typist, and filing clerk.
- Performed data entry and accounting assistant services.

HONORS

New York University Dean's List
Omega Chi Epsilon Fraternity – Chemical Engineering Honor Society
Phi Eta Sigma — Honor Society
New York University Scholarship

ACTIVITIES

Society of Women Engineers
American Institute of Chemical Engineers
Alpha Chi Omega Sorority
Participant — Campus Crusade

REFERENCES Available Upon Request

This soon-to-graduate engineer positions herself well through a combination of educational qualifications and relevant internships.

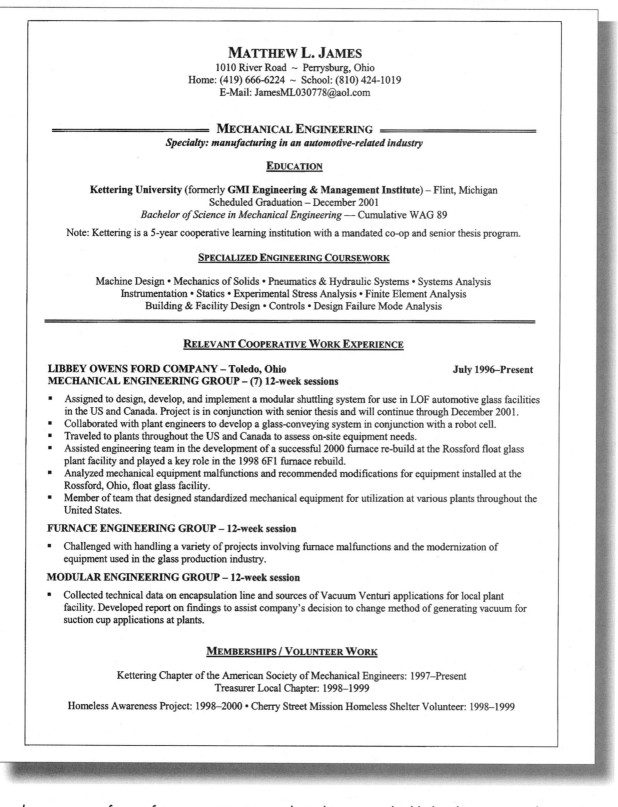

MATTHEW L. JAMES
1010 River Road ~ Perrysburg, Ohio
Home: (419) 666-6224 ~ School: (810) 424-1019
E-Mail: JamesML030778@aol.com

MECHANICAL ENGINEERING
Specialty: manufacturing in an automotive-related industry

EDUCATION

Kettering University (formerly **GMI Engineering & Management Institute**) – Flint, Michigan
Scheduled Graduation – December 2001
Bachelor of Science in Mechanical Engineering — Cumulative WAG 89

Note: Kettering is a 5-year cooperative learning institution with a mandated co-op and senior thesis program.

SPECIALIZED ENGINEERING COURSEWORK

Machine Design • Mechanics of Solids • Pneumatics & Hydraulic Systems • Systems Analysis
Instrumentation • Statics • Experimental Stress Analysis • Finite Element Analysis
Building & Facility Design • Controls • Design Failure Mode Analysis

RELEVANT COOPERATIVE WORK EXPERIENCE

LIBBEY OWENS FORD COMPANY – Toledo, Ohio   July 1996–Present
MECHANICAL ENGINEERING GROUP – (7) 12-week sessions

- Assigned to design, develop, and implement a modular shuttling system for use in LOF automotive glass facilities in the US and Canada. Project is in conjunction with senior thesis and will continue through December 2001.
- Collaborated with plant engineers to develop a glass-conveying system in conjunction with a robot cell.
- Traveled to plants throughout the US and Canada to assess on-site equipment needs.
- Assisted engineering team in the development of a successful 2000 furnace re-build at the Rossford float glass plant facility and played a key role in the 1998 6F1 furnace rebuild.
- Analyzed mechanical equipment malfunctions and recommended modifications for equipment installed at the Rossford, Ohio, float glass facility.
- Member of team that designed standardized mechanical equipment for utilization at various plants throughout the United States.

FURNACE ENGINEERING GROUP – 12-week session

- Challenged with handling a variety of projects involving furnace malfunctions and the modernization of equipment used in the glass production industry.

MODULAR ENGINEERING GROUP – 12-week session

- Collected technical data on encapsulation line and sources of Vacuum Venturi applications for local plant facility. Developed report on findings to assist company's decision to change method of generating vacuum for suction cup applications at plants.

MEMBERSHIPS / VOLUNTEER WORK

Kettering Chapter of the American Society of Mechanical Engineers: 1997–Present
Treasurer Local Chapter: 1998–1999

Homeless Awareness Project: 1998–2000 • Cherry Street Mission Homeless Shelter Volunteer: 1998–1999

Another one-page format for an engineering student, this resume highlights the co-op work experience that was an essential component of his undergraduate education.

MARK P. WILLIAMS

11044 RED LANE, APT. 33131 • BELLEVILLE, WASHINGTON 41111
(734) 555-1212

ELECTRO-MECHANICAL & PROJECT ENGINEER

Versatile and dedicated engineering professional with a proven track record of success in the aerospace and automotive industries. Creative problem-solver who thrives on challenges and gets the job done. Diligent, analytical team player with a talent for cost reductions, quality improvement, and creative solutions. Key areas of expertise include:

Engineering Processes: Failure analysis investigation, trend analysis and reporting, aerospace quality assurance, extrusion and cold-forming operations, plastic molding / transfer and compression molding. Excellent technical writing skills including specification control drawings, engineering change notices, and management reporting. Review and maintain OIAs, process sheets, and control plans.

Project Management: Hands-on manager with superb interpersonal and communication skills utilized to select talent, resolve conflict, and build successful teams. Outstanding ability to define and design programs, schedule deliverables, track, implement, and document project progress. Provide support and knowledge to Material Review Boards, control product assurance, and continuously meet and exceed deadlines.

Product Assurance: Serve as QS/ISO Internal Auditor. Perform and maintain statistical process control, quality assurance manual implementation, Taguchi methods of design, and internal consulting with electrical and mechanical design engineering/procurement/manufacturing/test engineering/incoming inspection/vendor surveillance. Review and rewrite QTPs and ATPs.

AWARDS & HONORS

Employee of the Month: Nominated by colleagues and selected by a cross-functional committee including superiors, human resources, and peers for solid results achieved and contributions made in conjunction with Noise Abatement Program, Cracking Commutator Warranty Investigation Team, representation in Plant Controller/financial analysis meetings, and saving company over $160,000 in capital expenditures.

Employee of the Quarter: Awarded for valuable contributions and accomplishments on behalf of the company.

Certificate of Appreciation: Recognized by Craig Mulhauser, President of Visteon Automotive Systems (Ford Motor Co.), for efforts in reducing capital expenditures on needed critical processing equipment in record time.

EMPLOYMENT HISTORY

FORD MOTOR COMPANY, Energy Transformation Systems Division, Belleville, WA   1992–Present
Troubleshoot mechanical failures and problems. Serve as point-of-contact to approve repairs and service to manufacturing equipment. Sustain and improve manufacturing equipment for optimal performance. Maintain operator instruction aids, process control sheets, and troubleshooting reaction plans.
- Serve as ISO 9000 Internal Auditor. Monitor testing and controls. Investigate other departments to assure documentation and maintenance of ISO 9000 requirements.
- Implemented reduction of varnishing process maintenance through use of magnetic collets. Saved company about 8 hours per month in maintenance and $24,000–$36,000 per year in materials.
- Increased production of armature coil winding machine 8% by adding lubrication and optimizing adjustments done in conjunction with maintenance.
- Reduced cost of armature thermal fusion process by redesigning fixture electrodes for 3x life.

<u>Manufacturing Engineer</u>

Challenge: Reduce $2 million warranty on cracking commutator to zero.

Action: Analyzed process issues and identified contributing factors. Addressed processing issues that form the commutator.

Result: Resourced the plastic resin supplier and initiated efforts to monitor and contain out-of-control process conditions.

Note how this resume highlights three core skills areas (engineering, project management, and product assurance) up front. It also emphasizes important awards and honors before segueing into a traditional chronological format.

MARK P. WILLIAMS

EMPLOYMENT HISTORY (continued)

GENERAL ELECTRIC ASTRO SPACE, East Windsor, NJ   1990–1991
Generated Engineering Change Notices (ECNs) for passive components across all program offices within program guidelines. Participated in Materials Review Boards and regularly interfaced with vendors to reduce fabrication delays. Wrote technical reports for review by project management and customers. Responsible for quality related SCDs (spec control drawings) and NSPARs (non-standard part acceptance requests) for electrical components on satellite flight equipment.
- Reviewed, analyzed, corrected, and processed 458 NSPARs for Mars Observer Program within a 3-month period.
- Updated source control drawings and interfaced with vendor to maintain program schedule for magnetic devices. Dedication resulted in avoidance of fabrication delays, cash penalties, and launch delays.

Electronic and Mechanical Component Specialist

Challenge: As a member of the Tiger Team, liaisoned between Parts Engineering and Failure Analysis Team in an effort to determine why a satellite thruster failed to fire.

Action: Analyzed and verified the fuse-derating criteria. Designed and developed testing procedure for components for quality assurance checks.

Result: Proved components were not at fault and derating criteria were adequate.

ITT AVIONICS, Clifton, New Jersey   1985–1990
Conducted component and module in-process testing, final test and reliability qualification tests, and critical component testing. Performed failure analysis of electrical components with mechanical damage. Liaison with vendors and engineering in coordination of project completion.
- Served as Materials Review Board member for dispositioning failed hardware for radar-jamming equipment.
- Selected as a member of Tiger Team for the analysis of mechanical damage to electrical components.

Associate Member, Product Assurance (1988–1990)

Challenge: Revise vibration portion of the sample testing program. Project was 24 months behind schedule.

Action: Researched and analyzed test profiles. Identified destructive vibrations level and rewrote sections of sample test program.

Result: Strengthened monitoring documentation for failed parts. Completed project only 1 month behind schedule despite previous delay.

Quality Control Engineer (1985–1988)

Challenge: Enhance accuracy of the Failure Reporting Database.

Action: Analyzed reports and weaknesses and omissions. Interviewed test personnel. Revised and clarified reporting procedures.

Result: Reduced failed component replacement time from 4 hours to 1 hour.

EDUCATION & TRAINING

BS / Mechanical Engineering, New Jersey Institute of Technology   1983

Additional Training:
- Introductory Auto CAD
- Design of Experiments—Taguchi
- Reliability / Availability and Maintainability Engineering
- Statistical Process Controls
- Active and Passive Network Analysis

Allan Chapman, M.S., Ch.E.

8888 Williamsburg Street ▪ Longview, TX 756002
(903) 757-6987 ▪ achapman@earthlink.net

Senior Chemical Engineer

Proven multifaceted knowledge and expertise in production, process, and project engineering
Mastery in chemistry and engineering provides unique added-value for chemical engineering
Build productive, committed teams through strategic motivation and hands-on management approach

Areas of Expertise

Chemical Production & Process Engineering	Environmental & Safety Chemical Engineering
Strategic Problem & Conflict Resolution	Hazardous Materials Handling & Logistics
New Product / Process Development	Process Analysis, Optimization, & Control
PLC / PHA / SPC / TQM / OSHA	Operations & Project Management
Team Development & Motivation	Condensation Process Chemistry
Supply Chain Management	Synthetic Organic Chemistry

Employment Chronicle

EASTMAN CHEMICAL COMPANY – TEXAS EASTMAN DIVISION (www.eastman.com) – Longview, TX (1980–2000)
(Texas Eastman is a division of Eastman Chemical, a leading international chemical company employing 15,000 in 30 countries, producing more than 400 chemicals, fibers, and plastics, and generating $4.59 billion in annual sales.)

Senior Chemical Engineer – Pilot Plant Operations (1992–2000)

As key contributor on Multi-Product Chemical Semiworks (MPCSW) management team, assumed full accountability for developing two core processes, operating and maintaining MPCSW to produce new products, and spearheading process improvements, and new process designs. Directed product storage, packaging, and shipping processes. Authored operating procedures manual. Led new unit operations installations, existing unit operations modifications, and multiple hazardous material projects. Resolved technical and chemical process/production issues, implementing innovative strategies. Initiated MOC and regulatory programs to ensure regulatory compliance.

Advanced Research Engineer – New Product Development (1989–1992)

Developed new products for commercial plants and Chemical Semiworks (CSW). Facilitated bench-scale testing of new processes. Collected and analyzed data for future scaleups. Prepared sample quantities of new products and submitted materials for fitness-for-use testing. Evaluated economics for manufacturing new products.

Advanced Chemical Engineer – Pilot Plant (1988–1989)

Selected as key contributor on Animal Nutrition Semiworks (ANSW) operations team. Operated and maintained animal nutrition product semiworks unit; supervised six operators. Orchestrated all packaging and storage activities, feedstock ordering/ receipts, shipping, and records management systems.

Advanced Process Improvement Engineer – Process Improvement Division (1982–1987)

Executed assigned process improvement projects and generated new projects in commercial plants. Collected and analyzed process data; analyzed collected samples in lab. Constructed and operated bench-scale models of whole and partial processes. Installed, monitored, and analyzed process experiments; developed proposals for permanent process improvements.

Process Improvement Engineer (1980–1982)

Completed orientation and required training courses and seminars. Performed assigned process improvement projects. Collected and analyzed process data, conducted laboratory analyses of samples, and provided detailed process performance data to management.

~ ~ ~Continued on Page Two ~ ~ ~

Written for an experienced engineer, this three-page resume is well organized and easy to skim to pick up essential information. Noteworthy results are highlighted in the Selected Projects section on page 2.

Allan Chapman, M.S., Ch.E.

Page Two

Selected Projects & Accomplishments

PRODUCTION ENGINEERING

- Identified malfunction of new vapor phase, fixed bed reactor, which had unstable operation and design capacity flaw. Stabilized reactor operations by modifying cooling systems and increased capacity from 50% to 100% of design configuration (1.5MPY).
- Analyzed high-temperature reactor operating at 65% of design. Identified quench tank flooding issue and changed out quench tank internals (packing and distributors); doubled quench circulation rate, bringing capacity to near design level. **Saved six days downtime** annually.
- Challenged to reduce downtime and potential exposure to catastrophic events from a fired-process heater. Installed supports for thermal expansion and minimized leaking fittings and flanges with the installation of new, all-welded fittings. **Successfully eliminated downtime and hazard risks.**
- Identified cause of Inconel 625 gate valves galling and freezing open in high-temperature process. Implemented dry, perflouoro elastomer free stem packing during reconstruction, **saving the company $30,000 annually** in valve replacements.

PROCESS ENGINEERING

- Discovered catalyst poison in the feed to a fixed bed palladium catalyst during laboratory analyses. Developed distillation step in the process during production to protect the catalyst. This step **increased catalyst life** and resulted in **annual savings in excess of $100,000.**
- **Reordered and combined existing unit operations** to create customized processes for new products and establish onsite manufacturing capacity. **Eliminated toll conversion and/or distillation costs.**
- **Enhanced distillation capacity by more than 150Klb/year** and **decreased byproduct formation by 50Klb/year** by optimizing fixed-bed reactor operation to achieve design capacity.
- **Met sales demands for proprietary solid glycol products** by designing and installing improved cooling system in a melt crystallization process. **Escalated capacity by 900Klb/year.**
- Conceptualized, designed, and created PLC-controlled crushing and bagging process, which **increased bagged capacity by 1.4MPY, thus meeting demand.**
- Developed innovative chemical process, which selectively produced desired product among three co-products. **Minimized capital costs by using existing equipment and elevated capacity by 5MPY.**
- Identified and evaluated a new, high-value product to be produced in a commercial plant operating at only 200 days/year. **Improved plant utilization 75%** (to 350 days/year) and **increased new product availability 1MPY.**
- Served as vital participant in revitalizing existing high-volume product process. **Newly developed catalyst reduced wastewater treatment load by 90%, thus saving approximately $1 million annually.**
- **Minimized operator exposure to toxic/hazardous materials** by designing and installing process samplers, which reduced exposure from sampling. Designed and fabricated railcar/truck loading systems to reduce exposure to loading operators.
- **Eliminated toll drumming, increased sales of molten glycol product, and generated $25,000 in revenues annually** by creating drum-filling process.

PROJECT MANAGEMENT

- **Spearheaded $750,000 project** encompassing installation of two-stage, fixed bed, high-pressure reactor. **Completed in half the estimated time and $100,000 under budget.**
- **Directed $300,000 project** consisting of fabricating railcar loading rack for flammable liquids. **Reduced manufacturing costs $50,000** by shipping via railcar, opposed to truck or drum shipments.
- **Co-managed $500,000 onsite product distillation project at half the anticipated cost ($250,000).**
- **Orchestrated $100,000 drum-filling process upgrade** for improved hazardous materials handling.
- **Designated as company expert for R&D and SAP implementation process issues** because of broad-based knowledge and proven expertise in these areas.

~ ~ ~Continued on Page Three ~ ~ ~

Allan Chapman, M.S., Ch.E.
Page Three

Selected Projects & Accomplishments (Continued)

SAFETY PROCESS

- **Conducted process hazard analyses** for myriad products and processes. Ensured process installations incorporated all PHA review recommendations.
- Led multinational team composed of U.S. and European safety, logistics, and operations specialists involved in investigation of hazardous material leaks. **Identified and repaired leak source.**
- **Facilitated/managed program to measure properties of new hazardous materials.** Published accumulated data and in-house testing results for use in MSDSs and safety protocols. Designated proprietary epoxide as highly hazardous material.

Patents

	Patent Description	Patent Number
1.	Continuous process for the preparation of 2-ethyl-2 (hydroxymethyl) hexenal and 2-butyl-2ethyl-1,3-propanediol.	5,146,004
2.	Continuous process for the recovery of 2 ethyl-hexenal and a tertiary amine from a mixture comprising 2-ethylhexanal, 2-ethyl-2 (hydroxymethyl), a tertiary amine, and water.	5,177,267
3.	Continuous process for the preparation of 2-ethyl-2 (hydroxymethyl)hexenal and 2-butyl-2-ethyl-1,3-propanediol.	5,235,118
4.	Isomerization of dimethylcyclohexane dicarboxylate.	5,231,218; W09410124; EP0665821

Education/Certifications

MISSISSIPPI STATE UNIVERSITY – Starkville, MS
ABD Ph.D., Chemistry
M.S. Ch.E.

TROY STATE UNIVERSITY – Troy, AL
M.S., Education

UNITED STATES AIR FORCE
Registered Radiology Technologist

Professional Development

Statistical Process Control (SPC) ■ Kepner-Tregoe Problem Solving
Total Quality Management (TQM) ■ Strategic Negotiations
Distillation Symposium ■ Innovation ■ DOT Training
Heat Exchanger Symposium ■ OSHA PSM
OSHA Management of Change

■ ■ ■

WILLIAM J. TROISE

800 Pike Lane • Cameron, New York 14800
Phone: (607) 772-1234 • Email: williamjtroise@cs.com

INDUSTRIAL / DESIGN ENGINEER

Accomplished professional with an impressive career in the design and development of manufacturing processes and systems for a wide range of industries. Strong analytical, technical, and engineering expertise in combination with accomplishments in process/quality improvement, documentation, and project management. Proficient in the creation and execution of training programs. Well versed in a variety of software applications, including CAD, CAM, and SPC.

PROFESSIONAL EXPERIENCE

EXECUTONE COMPANY, Power Tool Division, Tyson, PA   1988 to Present
(Manufacturer of pneumatic tools and custom air motors.)

Senior Computer-Aided Manufacturing Engineer (1996–Present)
Computer-Aided Manufacturing Engineer (1988–1996)
Evaluate, design, justify, and implement computer-aided manufacturing engineering systems. Manage computer-aided process planning system to facilitate development of manufacturing processes and shop floor documentation. Provide CAM support, including end-user training in Unigraphics and Numerical Control Post-Processor development. Conduct methodical engineering studies to reduce costs and improve quality using SPC, DOE, FMEA, and computer-simulation techniques. Collaborate with engineering and critical vendors throughout pre- and established production phases; convey and follow-up on corrective action. Define and coordinate the procurement of new tools.

- Designed and implemented online documentation system that provides access to over 150,000 engineering documents and drawings. Annual savings of $400,000.
- Advanced Technology Group member; implemented $30 million capital improvement "Master Plan" resulting in reduced costs and shorter lead times.
- Developed new methods and technology to reduce costs and improve quality for both new and existing products.
- Instrumental in implementation team's efforts to achieve ISO 9002 certification.

GENERAL ENGINEERING, Land System Division, Tyson, PA   1987 to 1988
(Manufacturer of machined components and sub-assemblies for the Defense Department.)

CAD/CAM Site Support Engineer
Provided site support for Unigraphics CAD/CAM system, IBM mainframe APT NC programming system, and PC applications. Ensured compliance with corporate and division audit standards. Trained end-users.

- Developed new applications resulting in productivity improvements.

CORNING INCORPORATED, Corning, NY   1984 to 1987
(Manufacturer of custom molds, production machine parts, specialty production machinery.)

Numerical Control Engineer - Precision Mold & Machining
Programmed Numerical Control machining centers and lathes using APT and CAD/CAM methods. Responsible for cost estimating and process planning. Determined manufacturing methods and procedures to efficiently utilize labor and capital equipment.

KELSEY AIR BRAKE, Dynapower Division, Kelsey, NY   1983 to 1984
(Manufacturer of hydraulic motor and pumps for aerospace and military applications.)

Process Engineer
Initiated and evaluated alternate methods and technology for process improvements. Performed value engineering on new and existing products, and Numerical Control programming.

This resume uses a clean sans-serif font for maximum clarity of text. Note how the first two position descriptions are combined to avoid repetitious details and to enable more prominent placement of key accomplishments.

WILLIAM J. TROISE   **Page Two**

DURIGON INDUSTRIES LIMITED, Fort Hood, Ontario   1979 to 1983
(Diverse subcontractor for the aerospace industry.)

    Numerical Control Programmer (1981–1983)
    Process Engineer (1979–1981)
    Responsible for Numerical Control programming, related tool design, tool proving, methods, estimating, and floor support. Determined manufacturing methods and tooling requirements. Provided engineering support and integration with customers through pre- and established production cycles.

FASCO PRODUCTS, Fort Hood, Ontario   1977 to 1979

    Owner/Manager
    Machining job shop with emphasis on hydraulic cylinder repair. Employed two part-time staff. Administrative and operational responsibility including P&L, budgeting, sales, production, and engineering.

DYNO PRODUCTS, LTD., Fort Hood, Ontario   1972 to 1977
(Designer and manufacturer of agriculture implements and hydraulic cylinders.)

    Product Coordinator
    Oversaw the hydraulic cylinder department, including design, production, and manufacturing engineering. Supervised 12–15 union employees.

CHEVROLET MOTOR DIVISION, GENERAL MOTORS, Kelsey, NY   1971 to 1972

    Production Worker
    Assisted on engine machining and assembly lines.

EDUCATION

    KELSEY STATE UNIVERSITY, Kelsey, NY
    M.S. in Industrial Engineering, 1995

    STATE UNIVERSITY COLLEGE AT BUFFALO, Buffalo, NY
    B.S. in Industrial Technology, 1978

    ERIE COMMUNITY COLLEGE, Buffalo, NY
    A.A.S in Management Engineering Technology, 1971

MICHAEL A. THOMPSON

mathompson@hotmail.com

12356 North 124th Street
Brookfield, Wisconsin 53049

Office: (414) 466-6098
Residence: (262) 784-6524

SENIOR PROJECT ENGINEER PROFILE
Design, Engineering, and Manufacturing Management

Fifteen years of progressively responsible experience in engineering design and project management for domestic and international automotive and heavy equipment manufacturers. Combine excellent technical, analytical, and engineering qualifications with demonstrated achievement delivering multi-million dollar projects on time and within budget. Master of Business Administration with undergraduate degrees in Mechanical Engineering and Machine Design. Strong leadership, team building, and problem solving skills. Qualifications include:

- Project Design & Management
- Multi-Site/Multi-Project Management
- Cross-Functional Team Leadership
- Continuous Improvement Processes
- Field Installation Management
- Client Presentations & Negotiations

- Process & Technologies Development
- Estimating, Budgeting, & P&L
- Cost Reduction, Profit Growth, & EVA
- Material & Supply Chain Management
- Vendor Selection & Negotiation
- Product & Technology R&D

PROFESSIONAL EXPERIENCE

MAJOR MIDWEST AUTOMOTIVE — MILWAUKEE, WI   Jan. 1995 to Present
(Design, engineering, and project management for production of upper & lower body structures, chassis and suspension stampings, assemblies, and modules for domestic & international automotive manufacturers.)

PROGRAM MANAGER — Milwaukee, WI (May 1996 to Present)
Fast-track promotion through a series of increasingly responsible engineering and project management positions. Oversee design, costing, testing, validation, prototyping, and development of manufacturing process to meet manufacturer's cycle times and just-in-time delivery requirements. Directly supervise 2 Project Managers and an extended team of 90+.

PLANT MANAGER — Rockford, IL (Jan. 1996 to May 1996)
Managed the financial performance for an assembly plant producing 195,000 light truck frames annually. Ensured conformance with plan and prepared monthly financials. Successfully negotiated Level 3 grievances with UAW union.

MANAGER, ENGINEERING & TECHNICAL RESOURCES — Rockford, IL (Jan. 1995 to Jan. 1996)
Directed a staff of 40+ engineers, robotics technicians, and tooling & maintenance workers. Developed and implemented capital expenditure plan for a 140,000-square-foot plant. Oversaw continuous improvement studies resulting in annual costs saving and increased line uptime from 62% to 74%. Drove ergonomic solutions resulting in 10% lower worker's compensation claims. Assisted in generating the plant's QS 9000 policies and procedures.

After activities and accomplishments are listed under each position on page 1, page 2 begins with a strong list of project results.

MICHAEL A. THOMPSON	mathompson@hotmail.com	Office: (414) 466-6098	Page 2 of 2

Selected Projects (Tower Automotive)

- Current project(s) in process—R472-P. Manage design, testing, prototype, 2 assembly lines, e-coat facility, building addition, frames, control arm, and detail parts. Annual sales $143.5 million, Capital $63.3 million, Tooling $35.8 million.
- Current project in process—Co-lead continuous improvement activities to globalize platform leadership at 49 business units. Goal is to benchmark internally as well as externally.
- Simplex project. Challenged to complete line modifications in two 3-week periods so OEM would not have to shut down operations. Annual sales $35.8 million, Capital $18.5 million, Tooling $10.6 million.
- Retrofit project. Brought in as the 5th project manager and challenged to minimize losses and deliver product/process on time. Installed two new assembly lines and a wax facility, trained work crews, and delivered product at cycle time. Annual sales $116.2 million, Capital $57.4 million, Tooling $38.7 million.

MAJOR AUTOMOTIVE SUPPLIER—MILWAUKEE, WI   Aug. 1985 to Dec. 1994
(Design & integration of engine systems/subsystems including supply chain management and test qualification.)

SENIOR PROJECT ENGINEER II (Nov. 1990 to Dec. 1994)
SENIOR PROJECT ENGINEER I (Nov. 1988 to Nov. 1990)
PROJECT ENGINEER II (Nov. 1986 to Nov. 1988)
PROJECT ENGINEER I (Aug. 1985 to Nov. 1986)

Rapid promotion through increasingly responsible engineering duties including project management. Directed centrifugal main fuel pump projects from proposal through development and into production. Ensured sound design by overseeing completion of supplier components through generation of statements of work, design specifications, and reviews. Performed trade studies to achieve lowest cost while maintaining specified requirements.

EDUCATION

MBA, Marquette University—Milwaukee, Wisconsin, 1994
BSME, University of Wisconsin—Madison, Wisconsin, 1985
AAS Machine Design, Milwaukee Technical College—Milwaukee, Wisconsin, 1985

AFFILIATIONS

Society of Automotive Engineers
Program Management Institute

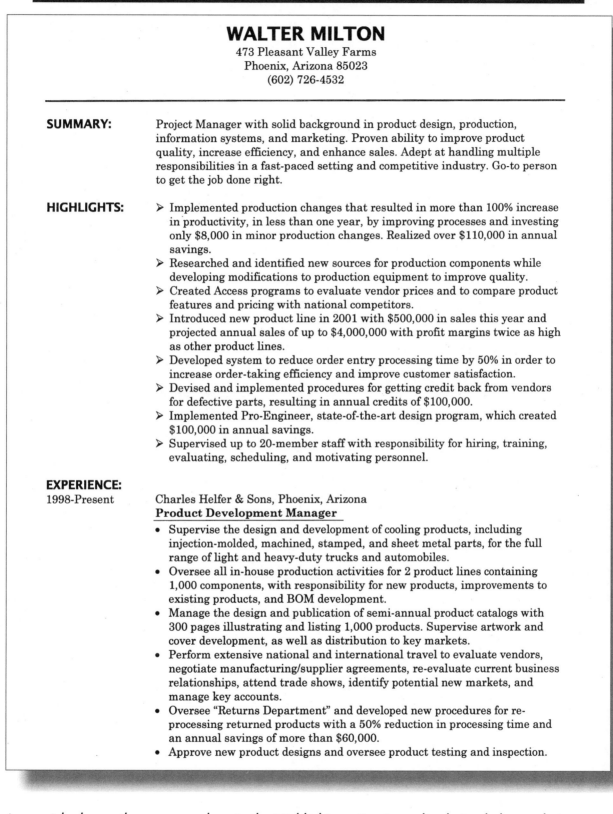

WALTER MILTON
473 Pleasant Valley Farms
Phoenix, Arizona 85023
(602) 726-4532

SUMMARY: Project Manager with solid background in product design, production, information systems, and marketing. Proven ability to improve product quality, increase efficiency, and enhance sales. Adept at handling multiple responsibilities in a fast-paced setting and competitive industry. Go-to person to get the job done right.

HIGHLIGHTS:

➢ Implemented production changes that resulted in more than 100% increase in productivity, in less than one year, by improving processes and investing only $8,000 in minor production changes. Realized over $110,000 in annual savings.

➢ Researched and identified new sources for production components while developing modifications to production equipment to improve quality.

➢ Created Access programs to evaluate vendor prices and to compare product features and pricing with national competitors.

➢ Introduced new product line in 2001 with $500,000 in sales this year and projected annual sales of up to $4,000,000 with profit margins twice as high as other product lines.

➢ Developed system to reduce order entry processing time by 50% in order to increase order-taking efficiency and improve customer satisfaction.

➢ Devised and implemented procedures for getting credit back from vendors for defective parts, resulting in annual credits of $100,000.

➢ Implemented Pro-Engineer, state-of-the-art design program, which created $100,000 in annual savings.

➢ Supervised up to 20-member staff with responsibility for hiring, training, evaluating, scheduling, and motivating personnel.

EXPERIENCE:
1998-Present

Charles Helfer & Sons, Phoenix, Arizona
Product Development Manager

• Supervise the design and development of cooling products, including injection-molded, machined, stamped, and sheet metal parts, for the full range of light and heavy-duty trucks and automobiles.

• Oversee all in-house production activities for 2 product lines containing 1,000 components, with responsibility for new products, improvements to existing products, and BOM development.

• Manage the design and publication of semi-annual product catalogs with 300 pages illustrating and listing 1,000 products. Supervise artwork and cover development, as well as distribution to key markets.

• Perform extensive national and international travel to evaluate vendors, negotiate manufacturing/supplier agreements, re-evaluate current business relationships, attend trade shows, identify potential new markets, and manage key accounts.

• Oversee "Returns Department" and developed new procedures for re-processing returned products with a 50% reduction in processing time and an annual savings of more than $60,000.

• Approve new product designs and oversee product testing and inspection.

In a quick glance, the many numbers in the Highlights section immediately catch the reader's eye.

WALTER MILTON   Page Two

1990-1998	FSC, Inc., Hartford, Connecticut

Engineering Analyst (1997-1998)
- Designed automotive cooling products, including radiators and condensers.
- Managed all aspects of Design Department budget, including training, hardware, software, and system maintenance costs.
- Served as Project Manager for implementation of information management system with annual savings of more than $120,000.
- Supervised international vendor relationships and developed product, tooling, and quality improvements.
- Implemented document management system to increase efficiency and access.

Associate Product Engineer (1994-1997)
Product Designer/Drafter (1990-1994)

EDUCATION: University of Hartford, West Hartford, Connecticut
Bachelor of Science – Business Management, 1997

Professional development training in:
Corporate Brand Positioning – American Management Association
Management Skills for the New or Prospective Manager
Quality Education System Training
Managing Multiple Projects, Objectives, and Deadlines
Pro-Engineer: Basic Design, Surface Design, Advanced Part Design, Advanced
   Assembly Design
Mission: Continuous Improvement
Fundamentals of Plastic Materials
A Designer's Guide to Part Design

COMPUTERS: Microsoft Office (Access, Excel, PowerPoint, Word and Outlook), Mas90, CADKey, Pro-Engineer, and Corel Draw

ACTIVITIES: American Association of Individual Investors, woodworking, backpacking, and snowboarding

REFERENCES: Furnished upon request.

Sharon M. Cihlar

17 Sidney Court, Mercerville, NJ 08550
609-586-5555 (H) ▪ 732-726-5555 (W) ▪ scihlar@net.com

Senior Science & Technology Director

Research & Technology Project Management – Packaging Technology – Fortune 500 Companies

Fifteen years' project management experience with 2 leading global consumer products companies. A catalyst for technological innovation, global teaming, product delivery, and commercialization. Combine strategic vision and leadership with a keen sense and ability to troubleshoot product and packaging problems. Strong team-building experience with cross-functional teams – instill in others a sense of urgency regarding project deadlines and quality issues. Well-developed skills in:

☑ Innovative Packaging Design	☑ Cost / Quality Improvement	☑ Problem Solving
☑ Global Packaging Strategies	☑ Project Management	☑ Team Leadership

Professional Experience

Personal Care Products, Inc., Woodbridge, NJ   1997 – 2001
Director, Packaging Development (2000 – 2001)
Personal Products Worldwide Division

Selected to rebuild department and spearhead new packaging development initiatives for global and regional distribution. Managed expense budget of $1 million and supervised 4 engineers.

- Revitalized department, infused new direction and vision, and re-built entire packaging development team. Focused team on marketplace-driven growth, technology, and commercialization while utilizing interdepartmental partnering to support initiatives.

- Strategically managed 4 personal products businesses launching 15 new consumer products within one year and developing 2 patentable technologies.

- Ensured successful launch of 3 global new products with unique packaging, each in 3 months, despite limited resources and high technical risk, through careful analysis and troubleshooting.

- Key player leading interdepartmental worldwide new package development initiative ($100K project). Team designed patentable carton while under budgetary and equipment limitations. Collaborated closely with marketing research and consumer focus groups.

- Recruited to 6-member interdepartmental Guidance Team of senior managers. Developed strategic vision and goals, and chartered 4 interdisciplinary teams for change management.

Director, Package Development (1997 – 2000)
Consumer Products Worldwide Division

Promoted to lead a staff of 3 packaging engineers to develop regional and global new package applications for personal hygiene products. Oversaw an expense budget of $1.5 million.

- Spearheaded the launches of 30 new products, personally developing the packaging design and materials for 10 new product launches.

- Led consumer products worldwide cross-functional team in $100K design project, which developed a new packaging carton design (patent pending).

- Saved more than $1 million over 3 years by initiating innovative cost improvement programs (CIP).

continued

The introduction to this resume conveys important leadership skills along with practical experience. The checkmark boxes give positive visual cues to the reader.

Sharon M. Cihlar
609-586-5555 (H) ▪ 732-726-5555 (W) ▪ scihlar@net.com   **Page 2**

Professional Experience

National Foods Company — WHQ, Newark, NJ   1986 – 1997

Packaging Engineer II, Frozen Food Sector (1993 – 1997)
Packaging development and design with Fortune 500 company. Ensured packaging materials and designs met cost, quality, productivity, customer service, and safety objectives. Led packaging project activities including the development of packaging performance enhancements.

- Saved $1 million annually by initiating cost-savings programs across broad packaging spectrum.
- Led packaging component simplification programs yielding cost savings of $800K annually.
- Team leader of next-generation packaging options for frozen food market, and provided technical assistance and troubleshooting for the domestic frozen food plants.

Packaging Engineer I, Food Service Sector (1991 – 1993)
- Led technical effort in innovative machine development for delivering single-serve frozen soup at convenience stores and quick service restaurants.
- Spearheaded cost savings of $80K annually and materials savings of 20% during the relaunch of entrees by identifying and implementing a shallower food-service tray.
- Sparked increase in line efficiencies (saving $60K) by recommending a change in bag material.
- Gained expertise in wide array of packaging materials: paper (carton), corrugate, aluminum, plastic (CPET, APET, PE, PP, PS, HDPE), and flexible films.

Research Chemist II, Packaging Technology (1988 – 1991)
- Implemented testing instrumental in cost-improvement programs, saving $1 million annually.
- Key laboratory resource in successful effort to improve resin systems used in thermoset plates.

Research Chemist I, Container Research (1986 – 1988)
Tested and evaluated packaging materials, assisted in quality control during plant trials, and troubleshot production problems. Trained lab technicians and coordinated scheduling of projects.

Education & Training

Master of Science, Chemistry, Rutgers University, New Brunswick, NJ	1990
Bachelor of Science, Chemistry, Susquehanna University, Selinsgrove, PA	1988

Continuing Professional Development

Kepnor Tregoe Project Management Training	2000
Harrisburg Center Invention Training	2000
Negotiations — Dr. Thomas Sellers, Yale University	2000
Management courses — American Management Association	1997
Molding Technology — Society of Manufacturing Engineers	1996

Computer Skills

Windows NT / 98, MS Office 2000 – Word, Excel, PowerPoint, MS Outlook, MS Project, IE

Professional Association

Institute of Packaging Professionals

DONALD P. HAWTHORN

2483 15th Avenue • Toledo, IA 50627 • Phone (641) 999-2444

**ENGINEERING MANAGEMENT • MANUFACTURING ENGINEERING
PROCESS IMPROVEMENT • QUALITY ASSURANCE**

Strategic thinker who plans for the end result and avoids unattended consequences. Effective package of skills spanning engineering, estimating/budgeting/finance, business planning, and ability to manage varied, simultaneous, and critical responsibilities. Diversified background features troubleshooting experience, significant international experience, and project management assignments. Eager for new challenges; willing to relocate. Areas of expertise:

- Engineering Systems
- Quality Systems/ISO
- Manufacturing Capacity Analysis
- Product Cost Accounting/Estimating
- Japanese Production Methods
- MRP Systems

"If something goes off with perfection, no one will know I have been there – my signature is invisible."

PROFESSIONAL EXPERIENCE

DAYCO PRODUCTS INC., TOLEDO, IA 1995 – PRESENT

Manufacturing Engineering Manager
Lead six-person engineering department for a $15 million manufacturing facility. Analyze and recommend monthly capacity planning including units produced, value of units, and production labor requirements. Develop up to 10 projects yearly and **manage prioritization and accountability for $1 million annual budget.**

Accomplishments:

- Guided efficiency improvement initiative by facilitating $250,000 project budget to upgrade and repower facility.
- Developed ground-floor formation of well-rounded Manufacturing Engineering Department to unify and centralize various functions that were previously done part-time or ignored.
- Updated and maximized IT procedures; created new position to fulfill duties.
- Reorganized entire engineering authority print files in order to re-establish working sync with masters and optimize performance.
- Wrote engineering procedures and input into ISO 9002 initiative — received certification in 1998; currently serve as Alternate Management Representative.
- Worked extensively with MRP system to transfer inputs from current system and avoid time-consuming hand inputs.

SAUER-SUNDSTRAND, AMES, IA 1973 – 1993

Senior Reliability Engineer
New-product troubleshooter and problem solver; independently tested new products to specification. Held various positions as Quality Assurance Engineer, Senior Buyer, Reliability Engineer, and Senior Reliability Engineer. Recruited to each successive position based on consistent contributions to productivity, quality, and efficiency improvement.

Continued on Page Two

This individual had been downsized and needed to move quickly into a new position. He had a lot of valuable experience he had overlooked before working with a professional resume writer, who was able to present his experience and accomplishments in a way that helped him quickly land a new job.

DONALD P. HAWTHORN

Page Two

SAUER-SUNDSTRAND (continued)

Accomplishments:

- Played instrumental role in developing innovative new product implementation system that never experienced a product recall for quality of manufacture.
- Provided critical interface as Quality Control expert between German company and Sauer-Sundstrand to achieve company objectives. Spent two months over three-year period developing a relationship and opening doors for communication.
- Acted as liaison with plants in Sweden, England, and Japan.
- Participated in startup of MRP system for purchasing department. Sent to troubleshoot rework credit discrepancies and correct purchasing and receiving errors made with Japanese and Italian products. Resolved 98% of disparities.

TECHNOLOGY SKILLS

Microsoft Word, Excel, WordPerfect, Lotus 1-2-3, Internet, e-mail

EDUCATION & PROFESSIONAL AFFILIATIONS

Bachelor of Science, **Metallurgical Engineering,** Iowa State University, Ames, IA
Bachelor of Science, **Agricultural Engineering,** University of Illinois at Urbana-Champaign

American Society for Quality (ASQ)
American Institute for Metallurgical Engineers (AIME)

C. EVAN WESTPHAL

1208 Clayton Avenue
Nashville, Tennessee 37221

e-t.wphal@worldnet.att.net

Home (615) 266-8601
Office (615) 653-5280

MANAGE BUSINESS DEVELOPMENT, PRODUCT, AND TECHNOLOGY PROJECTS
WITHIN INDUSTRIAL AND MANUFACTURING ENVIRONMENTS

Twenty years of combined experience in technology management, engineering, and operations. Blend expertise in business development, product development, and budget management with equally strong technical and project management qualifications. Develop effective information/database systems, upgrade analytical capabilities, and standardize and improve analytical methods and procedures. Strong PC experience with statistical analysis, spreadsheet, and word processing applications. Hold dual B.Sc. degrees in Applied Physics and Mathematics.

MANAGEMENT SKILLS PROFILE	TECHNICAL SKILLS PROFILE
• Project Planning, Scheduling, & Management	• Physical, Chemical, & Mineral Analysis
• Contract Development & Financial Analysis	• Statistical Analysis & Evaluation
• Lab Design, Development, & Organization	• Patent Applications / Legal Liability
• New Business Development	• Chemical Process Engineering
• Team Leadership & Group Management	• Field & Materials Engineering
• Goal Setting & Prioritization	• Industrial Mineral Processing

---

TECHNOLOGY MANAGEMENT EXPERIENCE

MIDDLE TENNESSEE CLAY COMPANY – Nashville, Tennessee   1993 – Present

Mines and processes minerals for a wide range of products including Sanitaryware, Ceramic Tile, Dinnerware, Refractories, Ceramics, and Fillers. A wholly-owned subsidiary of Hecla Mining Company.

CORPORATE TECHNICAL DIRECTOR – Recruited to provide technical leadership for corporate application and implementation of analytical methods and technology development, with a primary focus on business development through technology, both analytical and applied.

- Formulated intensive development efforts involving high-purity quartz (HPQ) for quartz lighting and electronics industries. Scope of project has evolved to include building and designing laboratory facilities, developing bench-scale process simulation and evaluation, pilot-scale development and production, and plant-scale evaluation at the customer's operation. Scope also includes financial business analysis and serving as primary customer liaison (both domestic and international).
- Spearheaded in-house development of unique SQC information system for major customer, Armstrong World Industries, that became a model by which customer judged all other suppliers. Became first bulk supplier to be awarded Armstrong's top supplier rating.
- Have two patent applications pending. Gained significant experience in collaborating with patent attorneys regarding liability and infringement issues, and making appropriate recommendations on technical issues.

WESTERN INDUSTRIAL MINERALS – Nashville, Tennessee   1990 – 1993

A mineral and mining processing operation with locations across the southeastern and southwestern US. Principally known as a major supplier of chemical-grade, high-purity limestone for customers in industrial and agricultural markets. A division of Western Industries, Inc.

CORPORATE TECHNICAL DIRECTOR – Senior technical manager and advisor responsible for quality control, product development, and technical services for limestone, mica, and gypsum processing. Led well-focused teams involved with quality control reporting and data storage projects that were innovative and cost effective.

- Programmed completed SQC data storage and reporting system tailored to each plant facility and provided statistical feedback of parameters for all products at each location.
- Granted a patent for chemical development enabling calcium sulfate (gypsum) to be incorporated in SBR latex.

The resume writer had to take the candidate's original seven-page resume and edit it down to two pages—no small feat! The candidate also wanted to make a distinction between his management and engineering/operations areas of expertise.

RESUME 27, CONTINUED

C. EVAN WESTPHAL – PAGE 2

TECHNOLOGY MANAGEMENT EXPERIENCE (CONTINUED)

THURSTON KAOLIN COMPANY – Sandersville, Georgia   1986 – 1989

One of the world's leading sources for processed kaolin clay, with facilities in North America and Europe. Thurston mines, processes, blends, and delivers a full spectrum of kaolin coating and filler pigments.

HEAD OF PROCESS ENGINEERING – Challenged to provide technical direction and involvement with all processing and mining operations. Evaluated, applied, and further developed R&D technology concepts, including analytical and evaluation procedures, bench and pilot testing, and commercial application. Managed process engineering projects that addressed quality issues, improved manufacturing yield, and enhanced environmental management. Specialized in washer mill degritting, centrifugal classification and desliming, and high-temperature kaolin calcining.

- Developed initial calcined kaolin product, Kaocal. Led this 20-month project involving engineering of the production process (extensive bench-scale work), proving the product via pilot production, and equipment evaluation and start-up.
- Designed and built new laboratory facilities; upgraded and acquired new equipment.

ENGINEERING & OPERATIONS EXPERIENCE

US AIR FORCE – Warner Robins AFB, Georgia   1985 – 1986

Corrosion Prevention and Control Office – Ensures that the Air Force has a viable program to prevent, detect, and control corrosion and minimize the impact of corrosion on Air Force systems.

MATERIALS ENGINEER – Evaluated and improved corrosion prevention technology and procedures employed with cargo and fighter aircraft for the Corrosion Prevention and Control Office of the USAF. Served on the Corrosion Prevention Advisory Board for the C-5A, the world's largest cargo-transport plane.

ENGELMANN CORPORATION – McIntyre, Georgia   1981 – 1984

A world-leading supplier of environmental technologies, specialty chemical and performance products, and related services.

WET PROCESS SUPERVISOR – Supervised all aspects of water-washed kaolin processing for the kaolin division. Executed process engineering projects (ozone generation and application, classification recovery) and developed plant operation information system.

GENERAL CORROSION SERVICES – Atlanta, Georgia   1980

An engineering firm specializing in corrosion engineering services for natural gas pipelines, cross-country and city distribution systems.

CORROSION FIELD ENGINEER / CREW CHIEF – Managed field crews of 2 to 5 conducting corrosion engineering surveys for natural gas transmission pipelines. Provided primary engineering support to client.

EDUCATION
BACHELOR OF SCIENCE IN MATHEMATICS – Georgia College – Milledgeville   1980
BACHELOR OF SCIENCE IN APPLIED PHYSICS – Georgia Institute of Technology – Atlanta   1980

ADDITIONAL INFORMATION
- Highly regarded by both corporate management and customers for ability to complete projects on time and under budget.
- Creative and innovative problem solver who perseveres in finding alternative methods to not only "get the job done" but get it done correctly and efficiently.

BILL H. POWERS, JR.
103 Wetherborne Court
Danville, Illinois 60414
Home (859) 239-9473
Mobile (859) 516-5225
wppjr@mis.net

QUALITY CONTROL / SENIOR PLANT AND OPERATIONS MANAGEMENT
Delivering strong operating and financial results in global manufacturing operations.

Strategic & Business Planning	QS 9000, ISO 9001, SPC Processes	Budget / Capital Planning
Productivity Improvement	Production Planning & Management	Quality Improvement
Distribution Management	Warehouse Management	Customer Retention
Production Processes & Standards	Human Resource Administration	Cost Avoidance

PROFESSIONAL PROFILE

Astute, confident management professional attuned to the changing needs of business. Special ability to identify and modify areas in need of improvement. Possess the vision necessary to develop and implement successful action plans, the experience to build and lead an effective team, and the drive and dedication to follow-through to a successful conclusion. Demonstrated proficiency across diverse products and organizations; characterized as a strong and decisive leader with excellent problem-solving, communication, negotiation, and team-building abilities. Personal and professional strengths include:

- Over 25 years of manufacturing management experience with steadily increasing levels of responsibility.
- Entrepreneurial minded with successful experience in P/L, setting and regulating policy and procedures, and facility operations.
- Proven ability to develop and implement structures and programs to improve process quality and efficiency.
- Verifiable record for cost reduction, expense control, and increased customer satisfaction.
- Recognized for delivering strong and sustainable gains in production, effective organizational leadership, and a decisive, empowering management style.
- Effective in the interpretation and application of balance sheet information.
- Recognized for the ability to develop and implement effective ideas.
- Thorough working knowledge of current international standards and customer requirements.
- Articulate and effective public speaker, able to motivate others to appropriate action.
- Specialized in quality employee training programs, including performance review and improvement.
- Effective team builder; able to identify and develop promotable candidates.

CAREER PROGRESSION

DANA CORPORATION   1973 – Present
US Fortune 100, tier-one manufacturer and supplier of original equipment and after-market automotive components. Employs over 80,000 globally. Annual sales $12B.

1996 – Present   **VICTOR REINZ DIVISION**   Danville, IL
<u>Vice President, Quality Control</u>. Direct division's ongoing QS 9000 / ISO 9001 implementation efforts and QC Department personnel. Deliver continuous customer support and maintain and correct product-quality issues for General Motors, Ford, Chrysler, Nissan, Honda, and Subaru-Isuzu. **Highlights:**

- Developed and orchestrated innovative scrap reduction process, resulting in over $500K annual cost reduction.
- Reduced customer defects from 4000 to 2 ppm within first 24 months of tenure.
- Championed superior customer relationship management responsible for a 20% reduction in formal complaints.
- Earned ISO 9001 / QS 9000 registration, Chrysler Gold Pentastar, and Subaru-Isuzu Quality awards.
- Awarded GM Supplier of the Year.
- First in state to receive Illinois Gold Award.

The three-column listing of expertise at the top of this resume is a strong key-word summary.

RESUME 28, CONTINUED

Confidential résumé of Bill H. Powers, Jr.   Page 2

CAREER PROGRESSION (Continued)

1995 – 1996   **DRIVESHAFT DIVISION**   Toledo, OH
<u>**Quality Director.**</u> Recruited to direct initial efforts to achieve and maintain ISO and QS 9000 certification for the facility. Encouraged and maintained quality in production; supplied continuing and aggressive customer service and support. Managed Quality Department staff. Products manufactured: Drivetrain components for use in the Custom Coach Building Industry with applications in heavy fire-fighting vehicles, luxury recreational vehicles, and earth-moving equipment. **Highlights:**

- Recognized for attaining and maintaining Malcolm Baldridge operational and quality standards.
- Participated in guaranteeing compliance with all state and federal regulations to ensure continued government contracts.

1993 – 1995   **MOBILE FLUID PRODUCTS DIVISION**   Greenville, SC
<u>**Plant Manager.**</u> Directed 630 employees in the 200,000 square feet facility. P/L responsibility for $80M annual sales servicing 500+ "ship-to" locations. Superintendent over all plant operations including strategic, budget, and production planning, forecasting, engineering, sales, customer service, and manpower. Customers: Caterpillar, VME, Clark, Komatsu Leach, Terex, John Deere, and Blount. **Highlights:**

- Reduced past-due deliveries by 90% during tenure.
- Maintained profitability and increased plant morale in the face of shrinking customer base and significant management restructure.

1992 – 1993   **SPICER CLUTCH DIVISION**   Auburn, IN
<u>**Medium Duty Product Leader.**</u> Coordinated product and process engineering efforts for entire product family. Directed manpower planning and manufacturing to support customer schedules. **Highlights:**

- Integrated process and application engineering groups to improve efficiencies.
- Coordinated sales and manufacturing groups to improve communication.
- Credited with the significant improvement in customer request compliance time due to innovative reorganization efforts.

1989 – 1992	**Manufacturing Manager, Clutch Division — Colorado Springs, CO**
1985 – 1989	**Quality Manager, Driveshaft Division — Gordonsville, TN**
1980 – 1985	**Test Engineer, Driveshaft Division — Toledo, OH**
1978 – 1980	**Supervisor, Heat Treat / Met Lab — Pottstown, PA**
1973 – 1978	**Lab Technician, Driveshaft Division — Toledo, OH**

EDUCATION

Bowling Green State University — Bowling Green, OH
Master of Business Administration

Ohio University — Athens, OH
Bachelor of Arts, Psychology

PROFESSIONAL AFFILIATIONS AND SPECIAL CERTIFICATIONS

Awarded US patent for balancing method (#4.998,448)
Member, American Society for Quality, 1985 – Present
ASQ Certified Quality Engineer, 1985 – Present
Member, American Management Association, 1980 – Present
Certified Supervisor, Dana University
Design and Analysis of Engineering Experiments — University of Michigan, Ann Arbor, MI

VICTOR B. HASSAN

318 Lowell Drive
New Haven, CT 06512

203-870-1294
VBHassan@att.net

SUMMARY

Accomplished professional with demonstrated success managing quality, productivity improvement, product development, and asset recovery programs. Experience spearheading ISO 9000 and ISO 14001 certification initiatives and introducing customer satisfaction and quality programs to manufacturing facilities in emerging markets worldwide. Excellent team building and leadership capabilities, with superb communication skills. Multilingual; Arabic / Spanish / English fluency and knowledge of Portuguese and Japanese.

PROFESSIONAL EXPERIENCE

DELTA FABRICATION INTERNATIONAL, LLC (1976-Present)

Quality & Knowledge Sharing Manager   Feb. 2000 - Present
Developing Markets Manufacturing & Supply Chain; New Haven, Connecticut
Design and implement Total Quality Management and productivity strategies for markets outside the US. Accountable for Mexico, Caribbean, Central and South America, China, India, and Egypt markets.

— Establish unified vision and foster cooperation among business units worldwide.
— Create multinational Quality Sharing Council to facilitate communication among business units.
— Spearhead ISO 9000-2000 and ISO 14001 certification initiatives in each country and ensure that operating standards are maintained.
— Promote "Customer First" initiatives in developing markets.
— Monitor performance and visit plant facilities worldwide to further quality and productivity goals.

Quality & Productivity Manager   June 1999 - Jan. 2000
Multinational Manufacturing Support; New Haven, Connecticut
Accountable for communicating quality and productivity objectives to manufacturing facilities worldwide, including Canada and US.

— Identified critical processes and shared knowledge worldwide to improve productivity.
— Developed and implemented "Customer First" and other quality initiatives.
— Established performance measurements and objectives; monitored results.
• **Recognized for successful implementation and management of Business Assessment process.**

Plant Quality Manager, Delta de Mexico; Cuernavaca, Mexico   Feb. 1997 - Apr. 1999
Managed quality assurance programs for this manufacturing facility.

— Created and implemented strategies that led to 30% increase in quality performance in first year.
— Instituted customer satisfaction and loyalty programs.
— Administered $500,000 budget and supervised a total of 38 people responsible for product quality.
— Promoted TQM initiatives and drove quality processes down to manufacturing floor.
• **Received Special Recognition for leading successful ISO 14001 certification efforts. This plant was first Delta Fabrication facility in the Western Hemisphere to achieve this certification.**
• **Recognized with Customer First Total Quality Champion Award.**

New Programs Manager, Delta de Mexico; Cuernavaca, Mexico   July 1995 - Jan. 1997
Directed new program implementation teams that adapted manufacturing processes to this plant facility.

— Reviewed US and Japanese techniques and processes for implementation by Delta de Mexico manufacturing operations.
— Assessed business issues related to transfer of technology from other manufacturing plants.
— Instituted "build to order" manufacturing practices.
• **Created and implemented workflow management system that allowed for tracking production to the minute on the manufacturing floor. (System still in use and known as the HASSAN.)**
• **Developed and introduced raw materials recycling concepts that yielded significant cost savings.**
• **Instituted Long-Term Incentive Plan (1996).**

The candidate had a large dossier of information about each job that he held. The writer succeeded in distilling all the data into a two-page resume without shortchanging some really strong achievements.

Victor B. Hassan	Résumé - Page Two

PROFESSIONAL EXPERIENCE

DELTA FABRICATION INTERNATIONAL, LLC (continued)

Asset Recovery Center Manager, Delta de Mexico; Cuernavaca, Mexico　　　Aug. 1993 - July 1995

Implemented asset recovery programs that delivered cost savings of $30 million annually to manufacturing operations. This initiative created new jobs, while improving Unit Manufacturing Cost, and was ultimately rolled out to manufacturing plants worldwide.

Product Engineering & Labs Manager　　　May 1989 - Aug. 1993
Delta de Mexico; Cuernavaca, Mexico

Managed product development and co-design activities, as well as overseeing Research and Development Laboratory operations. Achieved laboratory accreditation by Mexican government.

Supplier Quality Assurance Manager / Quality Assurance Engineer　　　Sept. 1983 - May 1989
Delta de Mexico; Mexico City, Mexico

Managed vendor relationships for manufacturing plants. Sourced and validated suppliers and monitored quality of materials/components delivered.

Manufacturing Engineer, Delta de Mexico; Mexico City, Mexico　　　Aug. 1982 - Sept. 1983

Developed plant layouts and designed manufacturing processes.

MICRO SYSTEMS, INC.; Cairo, Egypt
Hardware & Software Service Manager　　　1980 - 1982

Supervised field technicians providing preventative and corrective maintenance for computer systems.

DELTA FABRICATION INTERNATIONAL MEXICANA; Guadalajara, Mexico
Customer Service Technician　　　1976 - 1980

Serviced the needs of 120 customers for copier maintenance and repair.

SUPERIOR SEMICONDUCTORS; Guadalajara, Mexico
Semiconductors Quality Testing Foreman　　　1971 - 1975

Supervised 30 people accountable for quality inspection of electronic parts. Received eight months of training in Phoenix, Arizona, and developed first quality manual in the Spanish language.

EDUCATION

Bachelor of Science, Industrial Electronics & Communication
Cairo University; Cairo, Egypt

PROFESSIONAL ENRICHMENT

Management Certification Program (1997 - 1998)
University of Hartford; Hartford, Connecticut

Delta Fabrication International Corporate Training Programs

Advanced Management School	Inspecting for Quality
Leading the Enterprise	Problem Solving Process
Managing People & Processes	Quality Improvement Process
Operational Quality (Black Belt) Coach	Financing for Non-Financials
Operational Quality Leadership	International Supplier Quality Assurance
Management By Fact	Statistical Methods for Improving Performance
Just-In-Time Principles	A Delta T / Taguchi

SPECIAL SKILLS / PERSONAL

Microsoft Office; MS Project; Outlook.
Dual Citizenship: Egypt and Mexico; eligible to work in US (Non-Immigrant Status).

Walter M. Johnson

2405 Marydell Drive • Fairborn, OH 45324 • 937-855-9448

QUALITY ASSURANCE MANAGER

Experienced Quality Assurance Manager successful in positioning quality as a primary component of manufacturing, production, and customer service processes. Over 20 years of experience leading quality control functions to ensure that vendors, suppliers, and manufacturers perform to strict compliance regulations. Recognized among associates as a subject matter expert. Attentive to detail. Thorough, with meticulous follow-through. Effective working with domestic and international companies. Certified ISO 9000 registered auditor/lead auditor. Will travel as required.

PROFESSIONAL EXPERIENCE

Wright-Patterson AFB, OH   1978 - Present

Quality Assurance Manager accepting increasing levels of responsibility to ensure that vendors, suppliers, and manufacturers meet regulatory compliance of OSHA, DOT, and other state and federal agencies. Chosen to lead teams and serve as focal point for major projects involving the production and maintenance of highly technical avionics equipment and systems.

- Developed total task order package for Government Furnished Property (GFP) Contractor; directed all quality aspects of the contract.
- Chosen QA/MFG Team Leader for Training System Acquisition Source Selection Field Team; selected as team leader for numerous other projects.
- Evaluated 11 contractors to ensure their ability to support program office business over a 5-year period.
- Formulated QA/MFG assessment guidelines and conducted quality assurance on-site facility inspections stressing ISO 9000 conformance.
- Supported AC-130-U Gunship Program functional/physical configuration audit, ensuring that produced units matched specifications and proper testing was completed as ordered.
- Consistently reassessed contractors' capabilities, conducted in-depth QA audits, and examined critical purchase orders to ensure their correctness.
- Analyzed applicability of FAA quality assurance requirements, and recommended changes to ensure that all contracts met product quality standards.
- Assessed QA aspects of engineering change proposals, contract change proposals, advance change study notices, and service reports.
- Managed quality assurance for more than 20 Aeronautical Equipment System Office programs, providing input to acquisition plans and source selection.
- Consulted with other team leaders from manufacturing, engineering, contracting, logistics, configuration control, and program management.
- Hand-picked as Quality Assurance Team Chief for division's largest and highest-priority program.
- Ensured contractors' compliance with military and Department of Defense standards that included MIL-Q-9858A, MIL-STD-1520C, MIL-STD-1535A, and DOD-STD-2168.
- Directed over 15 in-house Simulator System Office programs in various stages of acquisition cycle; prepared QA requirements for source selection.

The challenge of marketing this candidate was to position him strongly for a quality assurance management position without revealing that all of his experience was with the U.S. Air Force.

Walter M. Johnson • Page 2 • 937-855-9448

EDUCATION / TRAINING

- Master of Arts, Management, Central Michigan University, Mt. Pleasant, MI
- Bachelor of Science, Business/Industrial Management, California Polytechnic University, Pomona, CA
- Associate of Applied Arts, Business Administration, Chaffey College, Alta Loma, CA
- Numerous professional training courses & seminars; complete list provided upon request.

CERTIFICATION

- Certified Program & Acquisitions Manager, Level III
- Certified Manufacturing & Production Manager, Level I
- Certified ISO 9000 Registered Auditor/Lead Auditor
- Certified Quality Assurance Professional
- Certified Professional Designation in Contract Management

MILITARY SERVICE

US Air Force — Honorable Discharge
Served in positions of production and quality assurance.

References will be provided when requested.

(Sometimes, employers are less eager to hire candidates who have no exposure to private industry.) The writer stressed his high level of responsibilities, achievements, and recognition.

MARK TILLEY

6815 Smith Passage
Stafford, TX 77477
Email: quality1@tmcc.net

Residence: (281) 665-8200
Cellular: (713) 544-3073
Fax: (281) 665-8201

QUALITY ASSURANCE EXECUTIVE

Top-performing Quality Assurance Executive with a track record of success in diverse manufacturing environments. Delivered millions of dollars in cost savings, profit gains, and new market opportunities by developing and implementing comprehensive quality programs. A hands-on, results-oriented manager with a strong focus on meeting customer needs and expanding market share. Completed 3 consecutive certification audits and subsequent surveillance audits with zero findings or observations. Expertise includes:

- **Quality Control / Management**
- **Multi-Site Quality Management**
- **ISO-9001 / QS-9000 / ISO-9002**
- **Quality & Performance Improvement**
- **Internal Quality Audits**

- **Quality System Certification Compliance**
- **Documentation & Technical Writing**
- **Customer Satisfaction & Retention**
- **Supplier Programs**
- **Staff Hiring, Supervision & Training**

PROFESSIONAL EXPERIENCE

ADVANCED MANUFACTURING CORPORATION – Stafford, TX, and Chicago, IL   1995 to Present

Director of Corporate Quality / Vice President, Sales

Hold concurrent roles as Senior Quality Assurance and Sales Executive for this $20 million metal stamping manufacturer of components for the automotive, computer, telecommunications, and appliance industries. Major customers include Compaq, General Motors, 3-Com, and Delphi Automotive Systems.

Broad scope of responsibility encompasses overall quality program management, budget control, sales, marketing, customer satisfaction, and management of manufacturers' representatives. Hire and direct a staff of 15 quality inspectors, quality managers, and administrative personnel at 2 manufacturing facilities, as well as 30 manufacturers' representatives across the U.S.

Quality Assurance responsibilities and accomplishments:
Challenged to develop and execute quality control strategies that would support growth and allow for expansion of customer base to include the automotive industry. Manage supplier program, internal quality audits, internal training, continuous improvement program, and documentation to support the quality assurance program for 2 facilities in accordance with ISO-9001 and QS-9000 / ISO-9002 guidelines.

- **Structured entire quality department, performed gap analysis, established quality program from the ground up, and wrote quality procedure manuals.**
- **Created and executed top-flight quality program leading to ISO-9001 and QS-9000 / ISO-9002 certification. Achieved all certifications several months ahead of schedule with no findings or observations.**
- **Reduced defective PPMs from 800 to zero and increased on-time delivery performance to 99.8% by instituting operator quality accountability incentives.**
- **Saved over $500,000 in annual operating costs by implementing cycle time reduction initiatives. Surplus savings were used to fund profit-sharing program.**
- **Implemented a manager bonus incentive that resulted in a 35% reduction in overtime.**

Sales and Marketing responsibilities and accomplishments:
After establishing a top-performing quality department, proposed and accepted newly created position as Vice President of Sales in addition to Corporate Quality responsibilities. Established a network of manufacturers' representatives and currently manage all manufacturers' representative affairs, including recruitment, administrative guidance, technical expertise, contract negotiation and drafting, and dispute resolution regarding account ownership and customer complaints. Develop marketing strategies, maintain trade show presence, and supervise 3 outside sales representatives.

Accomplishments, set off by bullets and emphasized with bold type, are the focal point of this resume for an experienced QA executive.

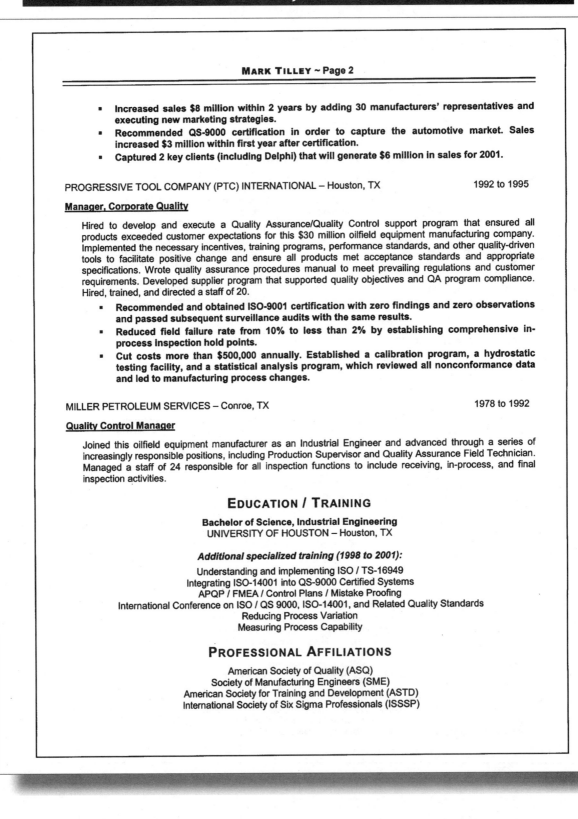

MARK TILLEY ~ Page 2

- Increased sales $8 million within 2 years by adding 30 manufacturers' representatives and executing new marketing strategies.
- Recommended QS-9000 certification in order to capture the automotive market. Sales increased $3 million within first year after certification.
- Captured 2 key clients (including Delphi) that will generate $6 million in sales for 2001.

PROGRESSIVE TOOL COMPANY (PTC) INTERNATIONAL – Houston, TX   1992 to 1995

Manager, Corporate Quality

Hired to develop and execute a Quality Assurance/Quality Control support program that ensured all products exceeded customer expectations for this $30 million oilfield equipment manufacturing company. Implemented the necessary incentives, training programs, performance standards, and other quality-driven tools to facilitate positive change and ensure all products met acceptance standards and appropriate specifications. Wrote quality assurance procedures manual to meet prevailing regulations and customer requirements. Developed supplier program that supported quality objectives and QA program compliance. Hired, trained, and directed a staff of 20.

- Recommended and obtained ISO-9001 certification with zero findings and zero observations and passed subsequent surveillance audits with the same results.
- Reduced field failure rate from 10% to less than 2% by establishing comprehensive in-process inspection hold points.
- Cut costs more than $500,000 annually. Established a calibration program, a hydrostatic testing facility, and a statistical analysis program, which reviewed all nonconformance data and led to manufacturing process changes.

MILLER PETROLEUM SERVICES – Conroe, TX   1978 to 1992

Quality Control Manager

Joined this oilfield equipment manufacturer as an Industrial Engineer and advanced through a series of increasingly responsible positions, including Production Supervisor and Quality Assurance Field Technician. Managed a staff of 24 responsible for all inspection functions to include receiving, in-process, and final inspection activities.

EDUCATION / TRAINING

Bachelor of Science, Industrial Engineering
UNIVERSITY OF HOUSTON – Houston, TX

Additional specialized training (1998 to 2001):
Understanding and implementing ISO / TS-16949
Integrating ISO-14001 into QS-9000 Certified Systems
APQP / FMEA / Control Plans / Mistake Proofing
International Conference on ISO / QS 9000, ISO-14001, and Related Quality Standards
Reducing Process Variation
Measuring Process Capability

PROFESSIONAL AFFILIATIONS

American Society of Quality (ASQ)
Society of Manufacturing Engineers (SME)
American Society for Training and Development (ASTD)
International Society of Six Sigma Professionals (ISSSP)

MICHAEL R. HART

309 Martell Drive — Birmingham, MI 48444
313–754–9247 — michael84@yahoo.com

SENIOR OPERATIONS AND MANAGEMENT EXECUTIVE

R&D — Testing — Product Development — Project Management — Training

Award-winning management career in the delivery of complicated technologies to build market share, drive revenue growth, and outperform competition. Strong management and contract negotiation experience. Thorough knowledge of manufacturing and business management quality-improvement principles including Six Sigma, TOC, and ISO 9001. Develop employees to ensure achievement of potential and allow for succession planning. Master's degree in Management.

AREAS OF EXPERTISE

- Six Sigma
- Resource Management
- Strategic Planning
- Leadership
- Program Management
- Engineering
- Team Building
- Communications
- Contract Management

SELECTED RECENT ACHIEVEMENTS

- Reduced original 2001 budget 45% ($1,200,000) with projected follow-on annual savings of $765,000 through effective Six Sigma project management that realigned resources and marketing activity for the commercial business sector.

- Contributed to bottom-line improvement in 2000 through cost avoidance of $480,000 by handling IT software design in-house rather than outsourcing.

- Decreased bid and order process time 42% for domestic bids and orders and 66% for international bids and orders.

- Achieved 35% savings for 2001 through organizational realignment and manpower efficiencies identified through the Order Management Process Improvement project.

- Completed analysis of rising costs of warranty using Six Sigma project tools with estimated annual savings of 20% beginning in 2001. Achieved more than 19% first quarter.

- Delivered major contract modification of $15,000,000 achieved by working with customer to define systems to be used by Army pilots in 1997.

- Lowered material overhead costs more than 25% by reducing manpower and improving dock-to-stock parts flow through development and implementation of quality-based Supplier Certification Program in 1995.

Using a three-page format allowed the resume writer to present a strong achievement summary on page 1, then go into chronological experience beginning on page 2.

MICHAEL R. HART – Page Two

CAREER HISTORY

ALLIED INDUSTRIES, Silver Spring, MD, 1990–Present
World's largest developer and manufacturer of systems sold to military and commercial (medical operations, communication media, tourist industry, and law enforcement) customers with annual sales of $300 million and 2,000 employees at two facilities.

Six Sigma Black Belt — Program Management, 1998–Present

Provide expertise in division management, sales, and engineering regarding production capabilities and methods. Utilize Value-Based Six Sigma Black Belt methodologies. Integrating two business databases into one system to improve efficiencies of financial reporting, MIS/IT maintenance time, inventory management, bid and order management for commercial sales, and manpower. Conducting in-house training seminars on Theory Of Constraints. Implementing critical-chain training for Six Sigma Black Belts, program managers, and key engineers. Guiding staff in development of project plans for R&D. Report to Director of Value Based Six Sigma and work with 6 indirect reports.

◆ Realized savings of 38% in 2000 and projected savings of 76% commencing in 2001 by implementing process and organizational changes identified through Six Sigma projects.

◆ Aligned organizational requirements and established additional manpower efficiencies with projected savings of 45% annually.

◆ Reduced warranty costs 6%, initially, by identifying and correcting weaknesses in new product development process that ensured reduced costs of customer service. Project annual savings of 15% with strong potential for increase.

◆ Winner of coveted "Best Practice" Award 2000 for Six Sigma Order Management Process Improvement project.

Senior Program Manager, 1990–1998

Managed asset coordination, production and delivery schedules, report development, and customer relations, including customer product improvement modifications. Directed $6 million research and development program that led to next-generation systems. Evaluated proposals. Delivered presentations to potential clients. Trained employees in sound business practices. Generated Army interest in upgrading aviation systems that contributed to future revenue growth. Achieved ISO-9001 quality program certification by developing processes to provide standards of business management in advertising contracts, bid and order procedures, and product development.

◆ Brought in major $15,000,000 contract modification by working with customer to define new system for use by Army pilots.

◆ Awarded additional $20,000,000 Army contract with potential options to grow the contract to $75,000,000 over three years.

◆ Pioneered benchmarking "Supplier Certification" Program that reduced material overhead costs 25% through reduced inventory, improved "dock-to-stock" cycle time, and reduced manpower requirements in receiving and inspection area. Program now used by other divisions.

◆ Spearheaded revolutionary depot-level maintenance and logistics support program for U.S. Army systems with projected annual sales of more than $8,000,000.

◆ Enhanced a $15,000,000 current contract by negotiating add-on modifications for additional $16,000,000 by responding to concerns of Army, Navy, and Marine helicopter pilots.

MICHAEL R. HART – Page Three

UNITED STATES ARMY, Various national and international locations, 1965–1990

Colonel (06), Honorable Retirement, 1990

Operations Director (Assistant Chief of Staff, Operations), Ft. Sill, OK, 1985–1990
Served as Third Army Operations Officer. Maintained effective communications. Developed long- and short-range goals. Conducted planned and unplanned situation management for 55 operating units while ensuring daily support for unit operational and training readiness. Reported to Commander, Third Army. Twelve direct and 25 indirect reports, including 6 foreign army officers.

♦ Awarded LEGION OF MERIT for "exceptional meritorious performance of duty demonstrated through superb leadership, effective management of resources, and unparalleled operational planning expertise reflected by greatly improved Third Army Battle Group and Amphibious Ready Group Readiness."

Chief Executive (Commanded Army Infantry Regiment), Ft. Benning, GA, 1983–1985. Oversaw $250 million in assets and 1,500 officers and men with a $10 million annual operating budget.

♦ Recognized for professional performance by winning all unit awards in 1984.

Program Manager and Teacher (Battalion Officer), United States Military Academy, West Point, NY, 1978–1983
Provided leadership and direction to all aspects of daily life from academic and military performance to habitability and well-being of 750 students and 6 commissioned officers. Taught leadership courses. Reported to Commandant of Cadets. Eight direct and 12 indirect reports.

♦ Appointed Chair of Tactics and Leadership Department, 1982.

CERTIFICATIONS AND CLEARANCES

Six Sigma Black Belt
Security Clearances: Army – Top Secret, SCI; A1 Secret (highest available)

EDUCATION AND PROFESSIONAL DEVELOPMENT

MS in Management
U.S. Army War College, Gettysburg, PA, 1977

BS in Engineering
U.S. Military Academy, West Point, NY, 1965

Seminars and Workshops   Six Sigma Statistical Tools and Analysis Techniques
Total Quality Management (TQM) and ISO-9000
Waste Management
Theory of Constraints (TOC) and Critical Chain for Program Managers
American Graduate Institute – Program Management: Lean Manufacturing;
JIT Delivery; Quality Function Deployment; Initial Product Development (IPD)

CHAPTER 6

Resumes for Production Planning, Scheduling, and Operations Support Personnel

- Production Planners, Schedulers, Analysts, and Managers

- Production Controllers

- Material Flow Managers

- Business Process and Manufacturing Re-engineering Leaders

John R. Smith

401 E. Cranberry Street ♦ Englishtown, NJ 14410 ♦ Phone/Fax: (570) 492-9902
Cell Phone: (570) 837-7349 ♦ Email: JohnRSmith@clarisconnect.com

---

Career Profile

Results-driven and highly organized professional with significant experience and verifiable achievements in manufacturing operations. Strong qualifications in production processes for specialty products, components, and equipment. Solid organization and problem-solving skills. Interact successfully with diverse individuals and groups. Knowledge of computers: Fox Pro, Lotus 1-2-3, Microsoft Word and Excel. Specific areas of expertise include:

♦ Production Planning & Scheduling	♦ MRP & Inventory Control
♦ Team-Building & Leadership	♦ General Assembly Operations
♦ Quality Control & Improvement	♦ Staff Supervision & Training
♦ Customer Service & Support	♦ Project Management

PROFESSIONAL EXPERIENCE

R.F.B. ELECTRONICS, Gloucester, Berkshire   September 1978 to May 2001
Senior Production Controller
Rapidly promoted throughout career with this manufacturer of specialized electronic and mechanical equipment in an ISO-9001 facility. Advanced from Fitter/Assembler to Supervisor of Mechanical Assembly, Supervisor of New Production, Production Controller, and Senior Production Controller.

- Controlled master production schedule, including forecasting and performance, and supervised two Production Controllers.
- Oversaw development and manufacture of a new product line (part of Trident Missile Guidance System) within six months.
- Reduced inventory by 90% and achieved 98% on-time delivery through capacity planning and make-to-order policy. Evaluation team member (MRP).
- Recruited by management to troubleshoot and resolve difficult problems with units.
- Served as Acting Plant Manager and Production Manager as required.
- Worked directly with customers regarding specifications and systems repair.
- Interviewed and selected new hires. Trained staff in processes and system operations.
- Developed and implemented shop floor data collection system in Fox Pro, significantly reducing time and costs.
- Wrote comprehensive computer program in Fox Pro on new production processes.

PRIOR EMPLOYMENT HISTORY:
Bench Fitter — Precision Engineering, Gloucester, Berkshire ▪ 7/78 to 9/78
Lawn Mower Assembler — B.F. Engineering, Gloucester, Berkshire ▪ 3/76 to 7/78
Manager Trainee — W&JR Smith Associates, Reading, Berkshire ▪ 7/75 to 3/76

EDUCATION

Graduate, Gloucester Green School, Gloucester, Berkshire

Professional Development/Continuing Education:
   Microsoft Office/Microsoft Excel — Gloucester College
   Lotus 1-2-3 — Thames Training
   Production Control Intensive Program (Pera) — CPIM Equivalent
   Abrasive Wheels Regulations
   Safety in the Workshop — Henley College

Note the extensive space devoted to recent, related experience and accomplishments, with only a brief mention of prior positions.

Calvin J. Feltman

(408) 332-2279 ▪ 1775 Butler Rd., Milpitas, CA 95035 ▪ cjfeltman@sol.net

Professional Objective

Production Control / Operations Planning Analyst, Logistics Coordinator, or Logistics Supervisor within a high-technology corporation.

Career Summary

Eleven years' experience in materials handling — consistently assumed higher levels of responsibility, rising from shipping and receiving duties to technology industry logistics and production control. Multi-industry experience, always focused on maintaining balanced inventory, accurate tracking of material and inventory numbers — including WIP and FIFO, LIFO and JIT stock plans, resulting in highly accurate physical inventory. Proficient in several of today's top automated production tracking / costing systems. ISO 9000 trained. Strong work ethic, scrupulous attention to detail, and easy to work with.

Achievements

- Standardized Flomag's worldwide materials identifiers and part numbers. *Results:* 50% reduction in existing part numbers and ability to clear 20% additional warehouse space.

- Defined, documented, and trained 2 departments on specific procedures compliant with ISO-9000 standards for issuing, maintaining, and tracking part numbers. *Results:* Reduced duplications and minimized incorrect identifiers for material part numbers at Flomag's distribution sites worldwide.

- Created and implemented a process to maintain bill of materials systems utilizing Eflow on-line documentation. *Results:* Facilitated management's ability to identify production flow efficiency.

- Assisted in development of the improved Special Manufacturing Order (SMO) numbering system. Results: Avoided running out of numbers (as occurred with previous system) and created immediately recognizable code identifiers.

Employment History

Production Control Analyst ▪ *Flomag Inc.*, San Jose, CA   1998 – Present

Issued and maintained part number system for world's largest supplier of thin-film media for computer hard disk drives. Updated process documents with bill of materials data. Defined MESA flows of current finished goods; set up consumables, raw materials, and finished goods in Lawson Midrange System and Bin structure in MESA. Trained personnel to be accountable for maintaining inventory and performing transactions on the Lawson Midrange System.

The achievement summary briefly yet powerfully describes activities and—importantly—the results of those activities. This resume is particularly well formatted and easy to read.

Calvin J. Feltman

(408) 332-2279 ▪ 1775 Butler Rd., Milpitas, CA 95035 ▪ cjfeltman@sol.net

Page 2

Logistics Associate (Lead) ▪ *Flomag Inc.*, San Jose, CA   1992 – 1998

Lead associate responsibility for inventory control of raw materials and consumable supplies for 4 production sites plus main distribution center. Maintained accurate daily, monthly, quarterly, and year-end counts on physical inventory of 200 raw materials and 400 consumable supplies. Filled daily materials requirements and received incoming materials from vendors utilizing JIT, FIFO, and LIFO stock plans, as required. ISO 9000 trained.

Shipping Coordinator ▪ *Remark Tool & Supply*, San Jose, CA   1990 – 1992

Shipped orders for local store, catalog orders, and stock transfers of 5 store locations. Processed credit cards, expedited "pick and pack" orders, and shipped using UPS and other common carriers. Supervised one.

Shipping & Receiving ▪ *General R/C Distribution*, Dublin, CA   1988 – 1990

Maintained stockroom, managed inventory control, expedited shipping and receiving, and delivered superior customer service to vendors, to internal customers, and at trade shows.

Skills

Computer / Data Processing

Proficient in Windows NT, MS Word, Excel, Access '97, Visio, Lawson Midrange System (inventory control software), Camstar MESA (WIP lot tracking software), NGS New Generation Software (query interface), Eflow (Inbox) On-line Document Control

Training

ISO 9000, Forklift Certification, Contamination Control (Haz Mat)

Safety Committee — 5 years

Education

- Central County Occupational Center — Diesel Mechanic Training Program — 2 years
- Zinger Miller Working I and Working II Training System (interpersonal skills)
- Statistical Processing Control (SPC) training

SANDRA JENSINK

❖❖❖

4231 North River Road
River Hills, Wisconsin 53027

sjensink25@aol.com
Residence: 414-963-1448

PRODUCTION PLANNING & MANUFACTURING MANAGEMENT
Material Flow, Production Processes, & Inventory Management

A highly organized and analytical professional with 9+ years of experience working with world-class manufacturing and metal fabricating companies. Excellent planning, organizing, and controlling skills coupled with strong interpersonal communication and leadership abilities. An innovative problem-solver with demonstrated competency in the following areas:

- Master Production Scheduling (MPS)
- MRP, MRP II, ERP
- Purchasing & Inventory Control
- Risk Assessment & Cost Analysis
- ISO 9000/9001 Quality Standards

- Strategic & Tactical Business Planning
- Cell Manufacturing/Group Technology
- Vendor Contract Negotiations
- Continuous Process Improvement
- OSHA & State Safety Compliance

PROFESSIONAL EXPERIENCE

GH MACHINES—DIVISION OF GLOBAL INDUSTRIES
Milwaukee, Wisconsin

September 1995 to Present

A world-class manufacturer and distributor of capital machinery and components.

PLANNER SUPERVISOR (December 1998 to Present)
Prioritize production schedules based on capacity requirements planning (CRP) and communicate delivery schedules to Sales, Manufacturing, and Suppliers. Monitor production performance using statistical process control (SPC) methods, investigate discrepancies, and communicate to senior management. Analyze and implement engineering releases. Create and maintain process sheets. Procure and manage steel inventory—2 storerooms with $5 million combined value. Provide purchasing specialist with strategic information to negotiate favorable vendor contracts. Oversee production planner and industrial engineering staff.

Selected Accomplishments
- Re-introduced steel plate processing (process is at the beginning of production cycle) and achieved desired business plan objectives including:
  ✓ On-time deliveries maintained at 90%.
  ✓ Lead time for processed parts reduced from 4 ½ months to 2 weeks.
  ✓ Scrap maintained at a negligible (zero) level.
  ✓ Staffing and overtime levels maintained within budget.
  ✓ Inventory maintained at previous levels.
- Developed strategies to improve on-time performance to original promise dates.
- Implemented plate-nesting techniques to increase yield and maintain 85% burning efficiency.
- Achieved 95+% inventory accuracy resulting from internal and external auditing (2000).

Key areas of expertise are highlighted in a list format at the top of the resume, followed by a traditional chronological format with emphasis on strong achievements.

RESUME 35, CONTINUED

PROFESSIONAL EXPERIENCE (continued)

SUPERVISOR/GROUP LEADER—SMALL WELD (June 1998 to December 1998)
Directly accountable for maintaining on-time production schedule while ensuring cost efficiencies. Coordinated production priorities with staff and production managers. Expedited purchasing with internal and external suppliers. Managed 12 welding employees.

Selected Accomplishments
- Improved on-time deliveries to 90%.
- Selected to chair Safety Committee and ensure compliance with local, state, and OSHA guidelines.
- Nominated by management to serve on the Quality Team and review scrap, rework, and detail drawings for inaccuracies.

PLANNER/SCHEDULER II (September 1995 to June 1998)
Directly accountable for production control and inventory control of 9/16" to 15" steel. Maintained and adhered to ISO 9001 quality plan. Monitored and evaluated time and attendance for piecework employees.

Selected Accomplishments
- Reduced inventory costs (JIT) by 62% within 6 months.
- Achieved 100% inventory accuracy for 4 years.
- Assisted in the implementation of SAP system.

MILWAUKEE FOUNDRY, Milwaukee, Wisconsin   October 1992 to September 1995
International manufacturer of metal castings for government and aerospace contractors.

PRODUCTION CONTROL COORDINATOR
Directly accountable for maintaining master production schedule (molding, pouring, and upgrading of stainless steel components) to meet delivery commitments. Expedited upgrade functions (grinding, welding, heat-treating, and machining) and coordinated outside supplier production and MRO orders. Ensured accurate labor time records. Chaired production meetings.

Selected Accomplishments
- Participated on team to implement system to enable accurate business forecasting and inventory tracking. This resulted in reduced lead times (60 days) and increased sales of $500,000 annually.

EDUCATION

BS in Operations Management—Marquette University, Milwaukee, Wisconsin

TECHNOLOGY SKILLS

Advanced User of Microsoft Word, Excel, SAP, and BMS

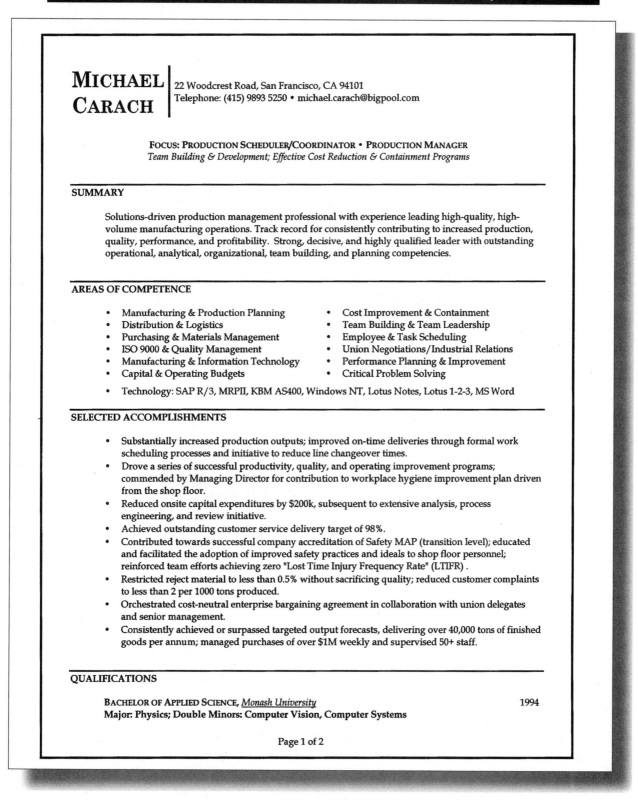

MICHAEL CARACH

22 Woodcrest Road, San Francisco, CA 94101
Telephone: (415) 9893 5250 • michael.carach@bigpool.com

FOCUS: PRODUCTION SCHEDULER/COORDINATOR • PRODUCTION MANAGER
Team Building & Development; Effective Cost Reduction & Containment Programs

SUMMARY

Solutions-driven production management professional with experience leading high-quality, high-volume manufacturing operations. Track record for consistently contributing to increased production, quality, performance, and profitability. Strong, decisive, and highly qualified leader with outstanding operational, analytical, organizational, team building, and planning competencies.

AREAS OF COMPETENCE

- Manufacturing & Production Planning
- Distribution & Logistics
- Purchasing & Materials Management
- ISO 9000 & Quality Management
- Manufacturing & Information Technology
- Capital & Operating Budgets

- Cost Improvement & Containment
- Team Building & Team Leadership
- Employee & Task Scheduling
- Union Negotiations/Industrial Relations
- Performance Planning & Improvement
- Critical Problem Solving

- Technology: SAP R/3, MRPII, KBM AS400, Windows NT, Lotus Notes, Lotus 1-2-3, MS Word

SELECTED ACCOMPLISHMENTS

- Substantially increased production outputs; improved on-time deliveries through formal work scheduling processes and initiative to reduce line changeover times.
- Drove a series of successful productivity, quality, and operating improvement programs; commended by Managing Director for contribution to workplace hygiene improvement plan driven from the shop floor.
- Reduced onsite capital expenditures by $200k, subsequent to extensive analysis, process engineering, and review initiative.
- Achieved outstanding customer service delivery target of 98%.
- Contributed towards successful company accreditation of Safety MAP (transition level); educated and facilitated the adoption of improved safety practices and ideals to shop floor personnel; reinforced team efforts achieving zero "Lost Time Injury Frequency Rate" (LTIFR) .
- Restricted reject material to less than 0.5% without sacrificing quality; reduced customer complaints to less than 2 per 1000 tons produced.
- Orchestrated cost-neutral enterprise bargaining agreement in collaboration with union delegates and senior management.
- Consistently achieved or surpassed targeted output forecasts, delivering over 40,000 tons of finished goods per annum; managed purchases of over $1M weekly and supervised 50+ staff.

QUALIFICATIONS

BACHELOR OF APPLIED SCIENCE, *Monash University*   1994
Major: Physics; Double Minors: Computer Vision, Computer Systems

Page 1 of 2

Similar to the previous example, this resume includes a list of important competencies (key words), followed by an achievement summary, and finally a chronological work history focusing on results attained for the organization.

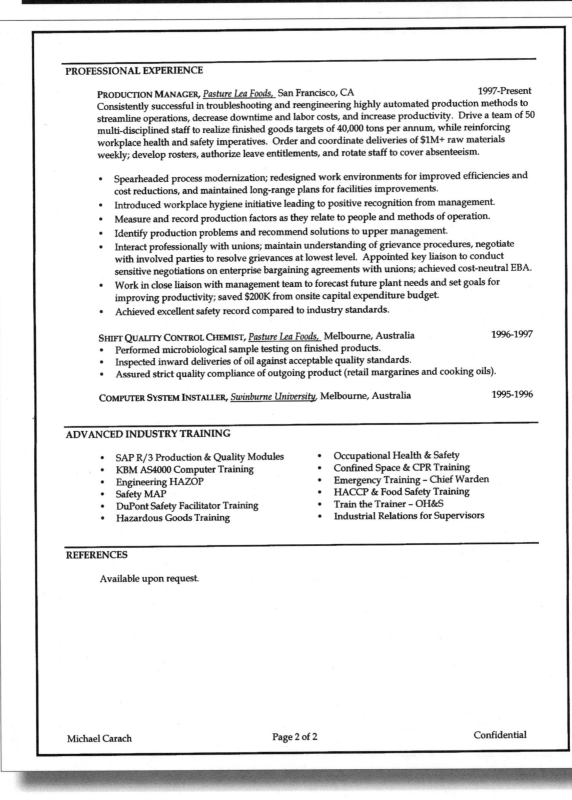

PROFESSIONAL EXPERIENCE

PRODUCTION MANAGER, *Pasture Lea Foods,* San Francisco, CA   1997-Present
Consistently successful in troubleshooting and reengineering highly automated production methods to streamline operations, decrease downtime and labor costs, and increase productivity. Drive a team of 50 multi-disciplined staff to realize finished goods targets of 40,000 tons per annum, while reinforcing workplace health and safety imperatives. Order and coordinate deliveries of $1M+ raw materials weekly; develop rosters, authorize leave entitlements, and rotate staff to cover absenteeism.

- Spearheaded process modernization; redesigned work environments for improved efficiencies and cost reductions, and maintained long-range plans for facilities improvements.
- Introduced workplace hygiene initiative leading to positive recognition from management.
- Measure and record production factors as they relate to people and methods of operation.
- Identify production problems and recommend solutions to upper management.
- Interact professionally with unions; maintain understanding of grievance procedures, negotiate with involved parties to resolve grievances at lowest level. Appointed key liaison to conduct sensitive negotiations on enterprise bargaining agreements with unions; achieved cost-neutral EBA.
- Work in close liaison with management team to forecast future plant needs and set goals for improving productivity; saved $200K from onsite capital expenditure budget.
- Achieved excellent safety record compared to industry standards.

SHIFT QUALITY CONTROL CHEMIST, *Pasture Lea Foods,* Melbourne, Australia   1996-1997
- Performed microbiological sample testing on finished products.
- Inspected inward deliveries of oil against acceptable quality standards.
- Assured strict quality compliance of outgoing product (retail margarines and cooking oils).

COMPUTER SYSTEM INSTALLER, *Swinburne University*, Melbourne, Australia   1995-1996

ADVANCED INDUSTRY TRAINING

- SAP R/3 Production & Quality Modules
- KBM AS4000 Computer Training
- Engineering HAZOP
- Safety MAP
- DuPont Safety Facilitator Training
- Hazardous Goods Training

- Occupational Health & Safety
- Confined Space & CPR Training
- Emergency Training – Chief Warden
- HACCP & Food Safety Training
- Train the Trainer – OH&S
- Industrial Relations for Supervisors

REFERENCES

Available upon request.

Michael Carach   Page 2 of 2   Confidential

CHAPTER 7

Resumes for Materials, Supply Chain, Distribution, and Logistics Personnel

- Buyers and Purchasing, Procurement, and Sourcing Agents

- Materials Handlers and Managers

- Inventory Planning and Control Personnel

- Inventory, Supply, and Stores Managers

- Logistics Engineers

- Integrated Logistics and Supply Chain Managers

- Warehousing, Dispatching, and Distribution Personnel

- Transportation Planners, Engineers, and Managers

- Truck Drivers, Mechanics, and Fleet Maintenance Personnel

HERMAN KEYNES

5488 Sherman Drive
Toluca Lake, CA 91455

Home (818) 555-9880
Mobile (818) 555-8777

PURCHASING

Buyer/Planner Skilled in Sourcing, Negotiations, and Inventory Management

- Expertise in purchasing, inventory planning/control, warehouse operations, and customer service.
- Skilled in sourcing and selecting suppliers, with a track record of consistently negotiating highest-quality merchandise at favorable prices and terms.
- Accurate in monitoring inventory levels to minimize lead times, ensure accuracy, and contribute to efficient, cost-effective operations.
- Analytical, with excellent decision-making strengths, team-building and leadership qualities.
- Highly computer literate, with experience on mainframes and PCs. Systems/applications include AS-400; CAPRMS; BPCS; COPS; UPS Online; Simbill; Microsoft Word, Excel and Outlook; Internet; e-mail.

EXPERTISE

MRP • JIT • TQM • ISO 9001 • KanBan Inventory • Vendor Sourcing, Selection & Negotiations
Raw Material & Inventory Planning/Control • Spreadsheets & Report Design/Preparation

PROFESSIONAL EXPERIENCE

HARRISON HEALTH PRODUCTS, Thousand Oaks, CA • 1985 to Present
$54 million international manufacturer and distributor of medical devices. Division of Fortune 100 company with 350 employees. Previously Moebius Controls and Stilton Industries.

Buyer / Planner (1997 to Present)

Oversee material planning, inventory management, vendor sourcing/selection, and negotiation of pricing and delivery terms for components required for custom surgical kits, injection-molded products, foam positioning products, and surgical kits. Work closely with cross-functional teams including marketing, R&D, and product development. Process material rejections and replacements; resolve quality and vendor problems; maintain inter-company transfers. Hold authorization for purchase orders up to $50,000.

- Served as key member of team in charge of transferring product line to Mexican manufacturing facility, implementing closure of Tennessee facility, transferring inventory to Thousand Oaks facility, and integrating new product line into facility — all within 10-month period.
- Reduced costs by $500,000 annually through new vendor sourcing and purchase negotiations.
- Identified and selected local vendors, reducing lead time by 50%.
- Implemented KanBan inventory management system.

Shipping Lead Man — Moebius Controls / Stilton Industries (1985 to 1996)

Supervised staff of 20 including warehousemen, fork-lift drivers, order pullers, and office staff. Diverse responsibilities encompassed overseeing order processing and shipment at 66,000-sq.-ft. warehouse.

- Maintained inventory transaction accuracy of 99%.
- Established procedures for on-line receipts of inventory to create live inventory transactions.
- Assisted management in closing and opening out-of-state distribution facilities.

EDUCATION / WORKSHOPS / SEMINARS

TQM (including problem solving, team skills, and conflict resolution) — 1999
ISO 9001, GMP Overviews & Practices, Kaizen Blitz Training — 1998

This resume presents strong qualifications in a broad range of purchasing-related functions and technologies, concisely captured in the Expertise section.

ARNOLD B. DONALDSON

5202 Redbud Trail
Houston, Texas 77901

Residence (703) 752-9788
Business (703) 644-9884

SENIOR PURCHASING AGENT

Results-driven professional with more than 15 years' experience in bidding, evaluation, and procurement of materials, commodities, and capital equipment for construction, manufacturing, and plant requirements.

Proactive manager with strong track record of reducing net purchasing costs and lowering inventory volumes while maintaining adequate stock on hand to meet daily production flow. Keen negotiation and vendor/subcontractor management skills. Maintain long-term vendor relationships built on trust, exceptional service, and responsiveness.

Liaison to engineering, project management, sales, and executive teams — serve both internal and external customers to achieve project completion, product development/redesign, and problem resolution. Highly articulate and effective communicator; work well with individuals on all levels.

PC proficient with expertise in MRO/MRP purchasing software, Microsoft Word, and Excel.

Areas of Expertise

• MRO/Capital Equipment Purchasing	• Acquisition Management	• Materials Management
• Contract Negotiation/Administration	• Price Negotiations	• Sourcing
• Government Contracting (FAR/DAR)	• Competitive Bidding	• Change Orders
• Request for Proposal/Quote (RFP/RFQ)	• Fixed Price Contracts	• Vendor Partnerships
• Worldwide Purchasing	• Bid Review	• Multi-Site Operations
• Supplier Management/Quality	• Terms and Conditions	• Warehousing
• Inventory Planning/Control	• JIT Inventory Systems	• Expediting

SIGNIFICANT CAPABILITIES AND ACCOMPLISHMENTS

□ Experienced in all aspects of contract administration, including prime and subcontracting for construction, engineered/capital equipment, and material for production and maintenance.

□ Issued large-dollar contracts governed by FAR or DAR using cost/price analysis techniques.

□ Purchased materials and capital equipment for use in production, construction, research and development, and plant maintenance.

□ Worked with suppliers on high-volume, high-use commodities, drafting firm fixed-price contracts based on manufacturer's list price less fixed discount.

□ Negotiated and administered multimillion-dollar contracts for large-scale facilities expansion, new construction, engineered items, MRO material, commodities, and replacement parts.

□ Oversaw personnel management in various distribution, construction, and manufacturing settings, including staffing assignments, scheduling, training, reporting, performance evaluation, and motivation.

□ Developed budgets based on debt structure and incoming cash flow. Negotiated payment schedules and reduced overhead expenses.

This resume for a recently laid-off senior purchasing manager was well received because of the Areas of Expertise key-word list and the Significant Capabilities and Accomplishments section. The strong first page de-emphasizes the fact that he has held five jobs in the last ten years.

ARNOLD B. DONALDSON   Page Two

PROFESSIONAL EXPERIENCE

Buyer/Planner, Baker Process (EIMCO), Houston, Texas, 1997 to Present

Worldwide supplier of fabricated process equipment for mining industries and wastewater treatment plants — division of Baker Hughes. Purchase commodities, including fabricated plastics, injected moldings, gages, and instrumentation. Administer competitive bids for computer systems. Work closely with engineering on design, acquisition, and expediting of specialty equipment for use in production applications.

- Execute, administer, and maintain more than $10 million in annual purchasing contracts.
- Managed highest dollar volume in materials purchasing and second-highest volume in contract fabrication among 10-person purchasing group.

Purchasing Manager, Turner Electric, Katy, Texas, 1995 to 1996

Largest building-automation contractor in the U.S. Directed materials management, purchasing all equipment and gear used by Turner in construction of new Compaq facility in Houston.

- Quickly assembled capable staff, experienced in managing purchasing, warehousing, and receiving responsibilities for large dollar construction projects.
- Located materials, moved them to site, and authorized payments. Set up warehouse, including receiving and authorization standards.

Project Administrator, Kennecott Copper, Salt Lake City, Utah, 1994 to 1995

Multi-national open-pit mining company. Purchased engineering gear for jobs utilizing FAR buying, P3 scheduling, and Sure Track.

- Strengthened vendor relationships and coordinated expediting to bring materials in as needed — pivotal in getting major project for Newmont Gold back on schedule. Saved company thousands of dollars in freight and expedited shipping charges.
- Guided sales and management team in getting on government contract list.

Procurement Specialist, Flour Daniel, Inc., Houston, Texas, 1992 to 1993

Leading international engineering, construction, and diversified services firm for the pharmaceutical, biotechnology, and fine chemicals industries. Directed purchasing, worldwide sourcing, and warehouse operations for fast-track construction projects, including the Chevron refinery and Kennecott smelter projects in the Salt Lake valley.

Subcontract Administrator, Hercules Aerospace, Inc., Clearlake, Texas, 1984 to 1991

Defense industry contractor for missile systems. Managed multi-million dollar inventory and purchasing for MRO, electrical gear, instrumentation, and computer hardware/software used in construction of sites for Poseidon, Polaris, Trident, and Peace Keeper missile systems.

EDUCATION

Bachelor of Arts in History, *cum laude*, Southern Methodist University, Dallas, Texas

JAN ROWE

1111 West Miner Road, #110 ▪ Tucson, AZ 85745
520.555.1212 ▪ rowjan@hotmail.com

CAREER PROFILE...

Proactive, results-oriented visionary with more than 8 years' demonstrated success in **operations, procurement, materials, and supply chain management.** Experienced and proven team member during **corporate reengineering** that addressed such areas as **strategic planning, organizational efficiency,** and **systems development.** Effective, quality-driven leader with consistent focus on building **strong, cohesive teams,** ensuring **customer retention, decreasing costs,** and **generating revenues.**

HIGHLIGHTS OF ADDED VALUE ....

- ❑ Demonstrated success in **Offshore Procurement,** contact negotiations, values leading, vendor sourcing, and inventory control.
- ❑ Expert in transitioning systems to **SAP,** including integration with other software.
- ❑ Comprehensive knowledge and experience in **e-commerce,** computer mainframes, the Internet, and **B2B development.**
- ❑ Proven ability to establish and maintain **positive interaction and rapport** within departments, with outside contractors and vendors, and with executive management.
- ❑ Expertise in implementing new technologies that translate into **cost savings** through focused inventory management and customer needs assessments.
- ❑ Thorough knowledge and hands-on experience with **NAFTA Certificates of Origin.**

PROFESSIONAL EXPERIENCE ....

Buyer/Planner, Mexico Division

JKG, Inc., Tucson, AZ   2000 – Present
Design, manufacture, and testing of ultra-miniature microelectronic devices used in the industrial, medical, and communications industries. Operations in 4 locations including Mexico with high-speed, automated SMT assembly line. Annual purchasing volume of $2 million.

- ■ Determined new vendor sources, conducted evaluations, and implemented relationship with management to solidify vendor alliances. **RESULT: Decreased annual purchasing costs by approximately 15% while increasing customer retention.**
- ■ Campaigned for and received executive management support to implement usage of the SAP R/3 computer system to run MRP for use in materials planning and production. **RESULT: Improved long-term planning/projections and maintained accurate inventory control.**
- ■ Collaborated with Production and Engineering to solve customer issues such as acceptable crosses for components, production capacity, lead times, and shipping schedules of finished goods. **RESULT: Decreased production errors and scheduling misrepresentations.**
- ■ Negotiated and purchased more than 500 components at a value of $1.6 million from domestic and offshore suppliers in Europe, Taiwan, Hong Kong, Mexico, and Canada.
- ■ Established international vendor sources for commodities such as custom-molded plastics, passive and active electronics, sub-contracted assemblies, metal products, printed circuit boards, and custom-made paper and metal products.
- ■ Developed strategies and executed delivery systems for global shipments.

The most notable feature of this resume is the Highlights of Added Value section, which points out experience, knowledge, and qualities that set this candidate apart from the competition.

JAN ROWE

Page 2

Contract Positions

TNT, Tucson, AZ   1999 – 2000
*Purchased and administered contracts of computer software and hardware courses offered by the
Education Department for employee technical-training programs.*

- Consulted with technical management to identify current and future skills needed to increase
  employee competencies.
- Determined internal markets, planned classroom curricula, drafted contracts with instructors, and
  outsourced technical trainers nationwide.
- Monitored trainer performance and oversaw implementation of company policies and procedures.

LAS VEGAS VALLEY DISTRICT, Las Vegas, NV   1998 – 2000

- Submitted Requests for Proposals (RFPs), created bid documents, and monitored contract
  performance and changes.
- Negotiated with internal and external parties, consulted with legal department, and ensured
  contract requirements and transactions were understood by both parties.

Practicum/Graduate Student

ADLER SCHOOL OF PROFESSIONAL PSYCHOLOGY, Chicago, IL   1996 – 1998
Specialized in teambuilding and business applications of the Myers-Briggs Type Indicator (MBTI).

Information Analyst

LIQUID CARBONIC, Oak Brook, IL   1992 – 1996
*Corporate Purchasing representative on reengineering team assembled to convert mainframe
computer system to SAP client-server system.*

- Assessed existing and future business requirements and recommended methods to accommodate.
- Liaison between senior management, Purchasing, and Information Technology.
- Successfully bridged diverse conversion approaches and maintained positive staff communications.
- Created measurement tools to track business improvement.

CONTINUING EDUCATION ....

CPIM Certification Review Courses: Master Planning of Resources ■ Detailed Scheduling and Planning
          APICS — Educational Society for Resource Management, Tucson, AZ   (ongoing)

Certified Contract Administration and Management
          National Association of Purchasing Management, Tucson, AZ   2001

Organizational Development Master Program, Adler School of Professional Psychology, Chicago, IL

EDUCATION ....

B.A., Science Education, Honors Graduate: Northwestern University, Evanston, IL

Nicholas Jameson

14 Pearl Harbor Road
Framingham, MA 01702

508/875-1668
nickj1@aol.com

MATERIALS MANAGEMENT

PROFILE

→ Comprehensive experience in materials planning, including responsibility for $2 million budget, inventory control, MRP, and Distribution Requirements Planning (DRP).
→ Proven ability to coordinate and continue normal daily production during corporate mergers.
→ Skilled at effectively utilizing Internet to research, source, and purchase materials, resulting in reduced costs and improved delivery time.

RELEVANT SKILLS

Ten years' experience in Materials Management in a manufacturing environment. Inventory Control, MRP, Importing and Exporting, Distribution, Licensing, Planning, Cost Analysis, Scheduling, Research, Shipping, Warehousing, Vendor Negotiation, Hiring, Training, BOM (Bill of Materials), OEM.

EXPERIENCE

Graphics Plus, Newton, MA (1991–Present)
Start-up equipment manufacturer for the print industry.
Materials Manager
Manage and control $1.5 million inventories. Reporting to the VP of Sales, successfully established purchasing, inventory control, and shipping/receiving departments, implementing efficient customer-returns process, export licensing procedure, and European shipping procurement policies.

• Liaison with engineering, manufacturing and service departments to ensure compliance with procedures and timely, accurate dispersal of corporate-wide informational correspondence.

• Brainstormed with engineers and vendors to implement a cost-effective customer service system, realizing savings of $100,000 annually.

• Streamlined system to process customer returns and export licenses through an automated tracking program.

• Negotiate vendor contracts.

• Hire, train, and supervise staff. Devised a promote-from-within program that maximized employee retention and improved productivity.

Note that the Relevant Skills section is an easily located key-word section supported by the experience and accomplishments detailed in the resume.

Nicholas Jameson
508/875-1668
Page Two

EXPERIENCE, continued

Original Copy, Inc., Hopkinton, MA — formerly Print Systems, Inc. (1988–1991)
Manufacturer of printing equipment.
Materials Controls Supervisor (1989–1991)
Promoted from Buyer
Designed and implemented cost-effective stockroom and quarterly inventory control system.

- Supervised all shipping and receiving personnel and managed stockroom operations including requisition of export licenses.

- Interacted with purchasing department to evaluate materials status and define efficient stock-ordering procedure.

- Assisted with conversion of inventory control system from manual to automated IBM system 36.

Print Systems, Inc., Ashland, MA
Buyer (1983–1988)
Responsible for 5,000-square-foot warehouse and stockroom.

- Planned, purchased, and expedited all electro-mechanical items, realizing significant cost reduction through effective vendor sourcing and negotiation. Interfaced with Manufacturing and Engineering departments as needed.

EDUCATION
Northeastern University, Boston, MA
Bachelor of Science, Business Management

CERTIFICATES
Human Behavior within the Organization
MRP — Inventory Control

John M. Kerr, CPM, CIRM

1455 Wisteria Drive
Philadelphia, PA 19222

Phone: 610-334-0112
E-mail: jmkerr@msn.com

SUMMARY

Senior Materials Management Manager (procurement, inventory control, fleet, facilities, travel services, outsourcing) with extensive global experience in applying innovative, state-of-the-art concepts to reduce costs and increase efficiency. Articulate, results-oriented professional experienced in leading diverse multi-functional project teams. Strategic planning focus with ability to develop long-term partnerships with key suppliers. Excellent interpersonal and task skills. Adept at developing motivated staff and enhancing performance and profit.

EXPERIENCE

BERKLEY MANUFACTURING, INC., Philadelphia, PA   1998–Present
(Major provider of medical devices and contract rehabilitation services)
Vice President, Materials Management
Provide change-management leadership to achieve strategic cost-control objectives.

Key Achievements:
- Negotiated national sourcing agreements.
- Designed and implemented multi-site perpetual inventory system.
- Created and implemented procurement strategies, policies, and procedures.
- Established world-class supplier performance standards.
- Devised and implemented staff development plans.
- Consolidated supplier base and rationalized product lines.
- Established cost-saving and process-improvement initiatives.

VISTA TECHNOLOGIES, INC., Charlotte, NC   1995–98
Senior Director, Corporate Sourcing
Initiated and led organizational and business process reengineering projects to achieve "world-class" standards. Developed and implemented global sourcing agreements. Implemented staff career development plan and achieved 80% NAPM/APICS certification.

Key Achievements:
- Increased cost savings/avoidance 400%.
- Implemented Automated Purchasing System (AP/PO).
- Established world-class supplier performance standards.
- Leveraged procurement with other corporate entities, reducing supplier base by 40%.
- Developed and implemented outsourcing plan, warehousing, fulfillment, and distribution.

P & K MANUFACTURING, Pittsburgh, PA   1989–95
Manager, Facilities Purchases

Key Achievements:
- Developed and implemented North American Coordinated Buying Strategy to maximize leverage, value, and efficiency.
- Created and implemented strategic planning in procurement, consolidating supplier base and establishing partnerships with key strategic suppliers.
- Developed global procurement sourcing strategy for all capital equipment, major construction projects, fleet maintenance, and all other operational products and services for all North American facilities (capital budget: $195MM in 1991).
- Implemented a cost-reduction/avoidance program.
- Initiated and oversaw implementation of numerous automation projects (purchasing system, online requisitioning, EDI, introduction of PCs).
- Directed various internal task forces (import/export business analysis; minority contributions; office automation; lease/buy analysis; partnerships).

With significant, measurable accomplishments nicely highlighted in the Key Achievements section, this resume paints an attractive picture of an individual who can add to the company's bottom line.

John M. Kerr, PAGE 2

1455 Wisteria Drive
Philadelphia, PA 19222

Phone: 610-334-0112
E-mail: jmkerr@msn.com

EXPERIENCE (cont.)

- Initiated national disadvantaged minority business-development program. Served as program director and external spokesperson.
- Introduced and established corporate-wide hazardous materials and recycling programs.

GRAHAM LOGISTICAL SYSTEMS, Philadelphia, PA   1983–89
Purchasing Manager (1987-89); **Purchasing Supervisor** (1985–87); **Buyer** (1983–85)

Key Achievements:
- Re-engineered procurement process to achieve best-in-class standards.
- Negotiated and executed systems contracts (plant stores operation).
- Instituted automated inventory-management system with direct order-entry replenishment.
- Negotiated and consolidated long-term leases and contracts, reducing purchase prices and administrative costs.

AMTECH MANUFACTURING COMPANY, Irwin, TN   1980–83
Buyer/Planner
Evaluated and selected suppliers for this manufacturer of diaphragm and ball valves. Responsible for expediting, forecasting, and production and inventory planning.

Key Achievements:
- Developed and implemented blanket orders/contracts for key production materials; consolidated supplier base.
- Exceeded cost reduction/avoidance objectives by 83% in 1982 and 30.4% in 1981.
- Established JIT replenishment plan with key suppliers.

SDM MANUFACTURERS, INC., Chattanooga, TN   1976–80
Buyer/Production Control Coordinator
Purchased and expedited steel/raw materials and building construction accessories. Maintained computerized-fabricated and purchased parts inventory in excess of $10MM. Performed MRP forecasting for primary steel structural components. Responsible for production planning and inventory control for the entire facility.

Key Achievements:
- Achieved #1 ranking in inventory management.
- Developed automated materials receiving system.

EDUCATION

Italian, French, & Japanese courses, Duke University

MBA, Philadelphia College of Textiles & Sciences

Materials Management Diploma, Elizabethtown College

BSBA and BA in English, Lebanon Valley College

CERTIFICATIONS

Certified Purchasing Manager (**CPM**), National Association of Purchasing Management
Certified Integrated Resource Manager (**CIRM**), American Production & Inventory Control Society

---

COMPUTERS

Proficient in Word, Excel, Internet, and various mainframe applications.

Donald P. Moraes

22 First Street
Fairfield, CA 55555

(707)444-8325
Email: @msn.com

EXECUTIVE SUMMARY

Eighteen years of progressive Purchasing, Materials, and Operations experience in high-tech and horticultural environments. Significant international contract and sourcing experience. Developed, negotiated, and managed multi-year supply agreements as large as $50MM. Have managed multi-facility organizations. Keen eye for improving efficiency while controlling costs. Demonstrated ability to identify problems and implement solutions. Utilize team approach to speed products to market, while decreasing costs and increasing manufacturability. Extensive MRP experience. Areas of expertise include:

- Contract Management
- Successful Outsourcing
- Project Management
- NPI Management

- Cost-Reduction Programs
- Cycle-Time and Lead-Time Reduction Programs
- Zero Defect Programs

Technical Expertise

Various manufacturing models, outsourcing. Industry experience includes ATE (Automated Test Equipment), Computer Manufacturing, operation of Audio and Video equipment, and Horticulture.

Extensive MRP-II environment experience, including SAP, ASK ManMan, 4th Shift, Expandable, ESI Solomon, and Real World Accounting programs.

Strong PC skills include 1-2-3, Excel, WordPerfect, Word, Access, PowerPoint, and Project Manager.

PROFESSIONAL EXPERIENCE

VP, Purchasing and Materials, Nurseries, Inc., Pleasant Hill, CA   1998–2001

Managed all purchasing, materials, and distribution elements of largest horticultural company in the world. Company had 19 plants. Launched first hard-goods line by a horticultural company. Provided website support and training. Established JIT programs with all major suppliers in first year.

- Reduced raw-material inventory in first year from $8.4MM to $2.3MM with no write-downs while eliminating virtually all stock-outs.
- First year costs reduced by 15%, second year by an additional 6%.
- Successfully co-branded products — an industry first.
- Improved Average Days Payable by over 20% to achieve unprecedented cash-management goals.
- Initiated and/or chaired major strategic committees, including Marketing, Strategic Planning, New Product Steering Team, and Quality Improvement Team.
- Managed fleet of over 500 trucks (800+ tractor/trailer units).

Materials Director, Nova Solutions, Novato, CA   1996–1998

Managed Materials, Purchasing, Order Fulfillment, and Shipping and Receiving departments. Outsourced most complex electronic systems assemblies within nine months. Developed significant cost-reduction programs and negotiated contracts with senior management of key suppliers.

- Significantly reduced lead times for components, subs, and assemblies
- Established inventory protection programs for components, subs, and FGI.

- continued -

Living in a state with an extensive agricultural industry, this executive made a point to highlight horticultural experience in his summary.

Donald P. Moraes
Page 2

PROFESSIONAL EXPERIENCE, *continued:*

- Partnered with senior engineering management on new development.
- Achieved significant first-year cost reductions (material and burdened); second-year cost reductions ranged from 5% to 18%.
- Reduced average backorder from 60 days to 3.
- Decreased inventory by 40% while company increased sales by 25%.
- Manufacturing expense decreased from 10.3% to 4% in nine months.

Contract Administrator, <u>Menard Corporation</u>, San Jose, CA   1992–1996

Contract management and administration of various commodities. Successfully outsourced many complex electro-mechanical assemblies. Implemented pull programs, blanket agreements, and dock-to-stock with key suppliers. NPI Engineering Representative.
- Reduced shortages in commodity group from 20% to less than 1% in 6 months.
- Mentored fabrication buyers through formal training programs.
- Chaired and developed corporate Supplier Performance and Analysis Program.
- Chaired Corporate Outsourcing Committee.
- Chaired Corporate Dock-to-Stock Program.

Purchasing Manager, <u>General Technical Corporation</u>, Berkeley, CA   1988–1992

Heavy presence in integrated circuit marketplace. Extensive engineering involvement on new products and ASIC contract development.
- Achieved first-year material cost savings of 39%, second year of 28%.
- Reduced first-year shortages from 15% to 1%.
- Reduced inventory levels by over 25% in 18 months.

Additional Highlights
- Appointed to Premier Purchasing Council, Cleveland, OH. Created and implemented purchasing guidelines for 19 divisions. Drafted teaching guidelines for major universities on purchasing theory and techniques.
- Appointed by U.S. Government and People-to-People program to travel to Russia in 1991 to instruct and assist Russian firms with international purchasing techniques.
- Advised Clark University on major research program that investigated the feasibility of American Just-In-Time Programs.

EDUCATION
B.S., Business Administration, University of San Francisco, 1983. Additional emphasis on law, contracts and UCC regulations.

PROFESSIONAL DEVELOPMENT
Extensive continuing education in contracts, negotiation, purchasing theory, quality programs, demand flow, and team-building programs. Management training includes Zenger Miller, Total Quality Management, and QIM training.

Jason Harrington

1012 South Street
Newton, Massachusetts 02465
617-969-1813 • jason_h@gis.net

LOGISTICS / ASSET MANAGEMENT / PRODUCTION CONTROL

✓ Business administrator adept at leading by example, marshaling resources, and creating teams to accomplish objectives. Natural communicator with strong motivational skills and the ability to train, build, produce, and succeed.

✓ Highly responsive to organization objectives and customer needs. Self-motivated to work independently; equally competent as a team player/leader with personal commitment to success. Create and maintain solid business/customer relationships.

✓ Combine experience, effort, and vision for total quality management to improve operational effectiveness and impact the bottom line per Six Sigma methodologies.

✓ Computer proficiency on Windows platform includes MS Word, Excel, PowerPoint.

PROFESSIONAL EXPERIENCE

Computer Equipment Company — Maynard, Massachusetts   1986 – Present
MATERIAL SERVICES SECTION MANAGER (1995 – Present)

- Organize and schedule daily operations of 32-person inventory control division with both union labor and support personnel. Foster cooperative relations with labor union leadership; ensure adherence to labor union contracts.

- Manage revolving $68 million inventory of contract material and in-house engineering development hardware. Track "need date" per computer database networked with project management to ensure timely delivery of items to production floor. Implemented bar coding system to streamline operation.

- Challenged to reduce obsolete inventory and recapture warehouse space. Systematically identified unused/old items and reduced inventory from peak of $140 million to $70 million within 18 months.

- Assist in overhead budget development, analysis, and implementation; adjust line items as needed in response to changes in projects.

MATERIAL CONTROL SUPERVISOR (1990 – 1995)

- Directed 16-person inventory control stockroom, coordinating procurement activities to support ongoing Max/Min inventories for commonly used material. Initiated monthly reports to management detailing volume and cycle time data.

- Oversaw logistics management of tooling; efficiently and expeditiously directed flow of inventory throughout numerous U.S. facilities.

- Trained personnel in efficient techniques and procedures, boosting productivity.

PRODUCTION CONTROL SPECIALIST (1986 – 1990)

- Coordinated all fabrication and procurement activities for multiple engineering projects. Negotiated with suppliers to secure timely delivery schedules on all purchase orders.

- Provided manufacturing floor support to resolve any production issues that arose. Monitored program materials requirements to ensure schedule targets were achieved.

EDUCATION

B.S., Business Administration, 1986, Suffolk University — Boston, Massachusetts

---

This candidate wanted to position himself as a superb manager who takes the initiative to identify areas to reduce costs and improve efficiency. His relevant accomplishments are emphasized in the summary as well as in the bulleted list under each position description.

RESUME 44: VIVIAN BELEN, NCRW, CPRW, JCTC; FAIR LAWN, NJ

DAVID PATTERSON
77 Elmwood Avenue ▪ Glen Rock, NJ 07410 ▪ (201) 688-2255 ▪ dp1@aol.com

MANAGEMENT TEAM
Distribution — Warehousing — Traffic — Import/Export

Proactive manager offers record of implementing change that achieves savings in productivity, distribution, and operations.... Proven ability to traffic supplies/finished products between US, Mexico, and the Far East.... Fully versed in supply chain management.

—— *Selected Accomplishments* ——

❑ Turned around operations at plant in Mexico, achieving $3 million in savings over two years.

❑ Successfully reduced transit time on deliveries from Mexico to United States by 70%.

❑ Selected to start up first Northeast distribution center, serving 14 states.

—— *Areas of Expertise* ——

Transportation / Custom Regulations / Inventory Control
JIT / FIFO / TQM
Safety and OSHA Implementation / Training / Facility Management

CAREER EXPERIENCE
PLASTICS, INC., Englewood, NJ   1999-Present
Assistant Director of Operations

Manage plant operations for this manufacturer of plastic containers using blow/vacuum molding and radio frequency sealing processes. Oversee 550 direct-labor personnel in manufacturing and warehousing, working over three shifts.

• Revamped warehouse, introducing FIFO and locations systems. Reduced forklift staff by 50%.

ELECTRIC APPLIANCE CORP.   1989-1999
Advanced to more responsible management positions for this manufacturer of small household appliances using digital technology. Promoted three times before facility closed.

Logistic Distribution Manager — Mexico City

Recruited to restructure traffic, distribution, and import/export operations out of Mexico for major plant, shipping/receiving approximately $2 million of goods daily. Coordinated border-crossing transit, including custom brokers and carriers. Supervised five department heads and over 150 direct-labor staff.

• Gained control of operating expenses through more efficient management. Saved $350,000 monthly on charge-backs within first three months.

• Implemented JIT delivery system for incoming supplies. Saved $35,000 per day in first six months of operation. Positively impacted supply chain of three other facilities.

• Instituted special security arrangements for shipping finished products to US. Reduced transit time from 17 to 4.5 days. Consistently met delivery dates.

• Reduced shipping costs to Far East by utilizing ocean instead of air transportation. Saved $700,000 in six-month period and met all delivery commitments.

Regional Distribution Manager — Englewood, NJ

Selected to start up Northeast distribution center (150,000 square feet), serving 14 states, while supervising Woodridge facility. Shipped $350 million annually in finished products.

• Negotiated contracts with third-party facility to increase storage capabilities by 20%.

• Secured more competitive rates from carriers, saving $300,000 in first six months.

Continued....

Despite the fact that this candidate had to take a step down in his most recent position, the resume promotes his exemplary experience managing operations in Mexico for his former employer.

DAVID PATTERSON   Page 2

(201) 688-2255

CAREER EXPERIENCE (continued)

ELECTRIC APPLIANCE CORP.

Traffic, Warehouse, Distribution Manager — Newark, NJ

Managed warehousing, shipping, and receiving functions at this 50,000-square-foot facility with staff of two supervisors and 28 direct-labor personnel. Shipped $145 million annually and controlled $25 million in raw material, WIP, and finished goods inventory.

- Improved efficiency of operation by implementing several new computerized systems, including pick location sequencing, bar code location, and UPS/FedEx/RPS automatic shipping.
- Installed a vigorous pallet-exchange program with freight carriers that resulted in $6,000 annual savings.
- Negotiated all LTL, TL, ocean, and small-parcel freight rates. Achieved $3.5 million annual savings.

SPECIALTY FOOTWEAR, Carlstadt, NJ   1988-1989

Assistant Plant Manager

Recruited to come on board to improve quality of leather products for this manufacturer of footwear and slippers. Oversaw direct-labor staff of 400 performing cutting, sewing, and laminating functions.

- Planned and coordinated production schedule in conjunction with inventory control. Oversaw stockroom operations.

QUALITY SHOES, Clifton, NJ   1985-1988

General Manager/Partner

Successfully restarted production for this bankrupt manufacturer of leather shoe bottoms and synthetic products with zero base sales. Managed production and distribution as well as sales/marketing.

- Achieved sales of $800,000 in year one and regained profitability in year two.
- Redesigned equipment to accommodate new manufacturing requirements.
- Handled documentation for domestic and international purchases of raw materials.

PREVIOUS EXPERIENCE includes management position with manufacturer of vinyl and aluminum windows.

EDUCATION/PROFESSIONAL PROFILE

BA Degree	Rutgers University, Newark, NJ
Certifications	JIT; MRP I and II; Forklift Training
Affiliations	American Production and Inventory Control Society (APICS)/NJ Chapter
	Material Handling Society of New Jersey
Languages	Fluent in Italian and Spanish. Working knowledge of French and Portuguese.

TECHNICAL

Mainframe System	AS/400
Software	JD Edwards / SAP
PC Applications	MS Excel / Access / Word

Phyllis A. Boutin

1211 Richard Street - Unit #45
Charlotte, Maine 04240

Telephone: (207) 555-5555

Email: Jolinegad@aol.com

PROFILE

Well-seasoned **LOGISTICS and CUSTOMER SERVICE MANAGER** with excellent skills developed while working with varied domestic and international client bases. Diversified hands-on work experience has contributed to a thorough understanding of manufacturing processes from monitoring and expediting orders, to meeting deadlines, and the proper selection and total processing of shipments to clients. Extensive interaction with marketing and sales departments. Ability to work very effectively independently through the utilization of excellent support skills — related business/clerical and technical/computer applications — and bilingual skills (English and French).

EXPERIENCE

Albany International, Inc., Auburn, ME   **1988-Present**
Manufacturer of molded automobile interiors (with two off-site locations) for major automobile manufacturers including GM, Toyota, Ford, Nissan, and Chrysler. Clients are domestic and international and also include approximately 100 suppliers in the molded interior car manufacturing industry.

Customer Service Manager
• Position reports directly to the President. Oversee a staff of 4 in coordinating all outbound freight logistics including land, sea, and air shipments. On call 24/7 (3 shifts). Work closely with VP of Manufacturing in handling problem calls to the Customer Service Department. Monitor customer orders and shipments to ensure best possible pricing while meeting deadlines for deliveries. Use English and French communication skills on a regular basis.

Accomplishments:
• Instrumental in the conceptualization, establishment, and set-up of overseas freight forwarding for the company's first overseas shipments including all related document preparation, processing, pricing, and the research and determination of freight forwarders (brokers) to be utilized; set up all procedures and trained the entire department. Researched and set up all licensing requirements.

• Assisted in the design and implementation of the Electronic Data Interchange software currently being used to record all customer orders on a daily and weekly basis; instrumental in weekly planning and scheduling; maintained daily for vital information. System is still in operation.

• Successfully worked within budgeted freight dollars, making necessary decisions to establish and maintain an excellent overall record of substantial savings for the company. Received Awards for Excellence in recognition for the significant dollar savings in the department each year from 1990-2000.

EDUCATION

Bachelor's Degree — Business Management   1993
Husson College, Lewiston, ME

University of Maine   Business Management
Central Maine Technical College, Auburn, ME   Business Management and dBASE III
Valcom, Portland, ME   Microsoft Works / Windows, Word, Excel, and Access
Albany International Inc., Auburn, ME   Radley Computer Software, EDI

Notice how the accomplishments demonstrate initiative and emphasize measurable contributions in logistics management.

John S. Lang

1068 Lewis Mountain Road, Charlottesville, VA 23801
(804) 268-1020

TRUCKING / SHIPPING / RECEIVING MANAGER

Recruiting / Hiring / Training / Scheduling

Cost-conscious, team-oriented, and dependable trucking professional with a history of promotions to positions of increasing responsibility. Self-starter energized by fast-paced environments. Quick learner. Comfortable with Microsoft Word and Excel. Qualification highlights:

- **Solutions-oriented manager with a hands-on management style.** Set high expectations and treat employees fairly and firmly.
- **In-depth knowledge of trucking industry operations and a solid understanding of the bottom line.**
- **Ability to recruit, train, motivate, and develop productive employees.** Excellent employee retention record; many have been promoted to management positions.
- **Thorough knowledge of DOT rules and regulations** including HazMat, hours of service, and OSHA safety regulations.
- **Ability to communicate effectively with people** from diverse backgrounds and employment levels. Experience dealing successfully with difficult people.

EXPERIENCE

BLUE TRANSPORTATION, INC., Charlottesville, VA   **1972-present**

Supervisor of Central Dispatch (1992-present)
Transferred to consolidate and manage freight movement between terminals. Directed 31 supervisors scheduling 8800 truck drivers.

- Led centralization of dispatch to Charlottesville, which slashed costs by 30%.
- Hired 30 new supervisors; trained and evaluated newly hired and existing supervisors and trimmed number from 38 to 31.
- Trained all supervisors on new computer program.

Terminal Manager, Charlotte, NC (1988-1992)
Promoted to open first facility in state. Recruited and hired employees for non-union company in a union state. Trained and managed 18 employees: dock workers, drivers, office manager, and sales staff.

- Managed all aspects of opening from recruiting, hiring, and training of employees to purchase of supplies.
- Successfully reached 80% operating ratio within eight months.
- Secured major national account through networking contacts.

Assistant Manager, Columbia, SC (1980-1988)
Managed terminal operations, hiring, scheduling, and safety.

- Played key role in building terminal from a city terminal to a major company break-bulk center.
- Hired and trained all new employees; staff increased from 50 to 650 employees.
- Set up and opened four satellites in Alabama and Kentucky.
- Kept operating ratio under 80%.

Central Dispatcher, Charlottesville, VA (1973-1980)
One of eight dispatchers in new 24 / 7 facility. Coordinated freight and worked directly with terminal managers. Was promoted through ranks to day supervisor with three direct reports.

- Earned respect of subordinates in a difficult environment.

Part-time Dock Worker (summers during college), Charlottesville, VA (1972-1973)

TRAINING / EDUCATION

Seminars completed include: Department of Transportation Rules and Regulations — Hazardous Materials — Dale Carnegie — Management

University of North Carolina, Chapel Hill, NC: Completed two years toward a political science degree.

With strong career progression from dockworker to supervisor of central dispatch, this individual has proved himself on the job. This resume emphasizes his deep expertise in transportation.

BROOKE G. MACLAREN

46645 Jarden de Flores Court
Fountain Hills, Arizona 85268
(W) 480-898-5446 — (H) 480-898-3254
brookemaclaren@tucson.rr.com

GLOBAL SENIOR LEVEL EXECUTIVE
Lean Manufacturing / Logistics / Supply Chain Management

Profit-driven top performer with over 17 years of executive-level achievements in international operations management, customer service and strategic development. Expert leadership skills combine with solid organizational, teambuilding and production management strengths to consistently lead production-manufacturing organizations in productivity improvement, cost containment and increased profitability.

AREAS OF EXPERTISE

- **Strategic Business Planning**
- **Training & Development**
- **Multi-Facilities Management**
- **Process & Productivity Improvement**
- **ERP Systems Integration**
- **Operations & Project Planning**

- **Large-Volume Inventory Control**
- **Global Distribution & Logistics**
- **Asset Utilization**
- **Materials Management**
- **Product Management**

EXECUTIVE HIGHLIGHTS

- Achieved a **50% improvement in direct material cost productivity** through reshaping of sourcing organization structure to facilitate globalization and rationalization of supply base.
- Piloted introduction of e-commerce-based tools for all direct/indirect procurement activities, **improving productivity by 50% and reducing census by 60%.**
- **Boosted customer satisfaction index by 50%** by installing innovative integrated supply chain process for all customers, products, and services.
- Spearheaded strategic business plans to achieve **$150M inventory reduction** and improve **customer on-time delivery from 80% to 92%.**

CAREER PROGRESSION

MASTERSON AEROSPACE — Tucson, Arizona   1998 to Present

Vice President, Supply Chain Management (1999)
- Selected to streamline integration of 2 business units into 1 newly formed strategic business unit with $5.2B in revenue. Supervise customer demand management, master production scheduling, asset management, sourcing, logistics, and e-commerce for the global production of aerospace systems and components. Responsible for 5 core product lines, 12 worldwide production facilities, and 2 repair centers.
- Credited with achieving $76M of direct material cost productivity and reducing days' supply from 106 to 86.
- Pioneered and managed Integrated Sales, Inventory Planning, and Operations (SIPO) process for all products and sites. Initiated logistical outsourcing to third-party service provider.
- Strengthened priority and action plans through close collaboration with suppliers and customers; established partnerships with internal customers through joint customer visits and CSI ownership.

Containing attention-grabbing numbers, the Executive Highlights section "hooks" the reader and gains his commitment to reading the tightly packed presentation.

BROOKE G. MACLAREN

Resume, Page Two
(W) 480-898-5446 — (H) 480-898-3254
brookemaclaren@tucson.rr.com

Vice President, Supply Chain Operations (1998)

- Oversaw site operations, customer demand forecasts, master scheduling, asset management, procurement, and logistics. Held full accountability for 16 production facilities, 3 repair centers, and 9,300 employees. Charted business plan with internal/external customers and aligned goals and metrics with customer requirements.
- Trimmed site operations' internal cycle time by 15%; defined and initiated Six Sigma/Lean Enterprises global deployment program for all operation sites.
- Increased on-time delivery performance by 25% and reduced inventory levels by 20%.
- Integrated supply/demand planning by establishing innovative sales forecasting model with corresponding capacity-planning model.
- Pioneered formal career development training program to accelerate existing talent and skills and to attract targeted SCM recruits.
- Directed strategic sourcing program that significantly reduced supply base by 30% and slashed annual total costs by 8%.

STONE CORPORATION   1989 to 1998

Director, Supply Chain Management (1996 to 1998) — Paris, France

- Oversaw customer demand forecasting, production scheduling, logistics, and asset management process for the $3.5B Europe, Africa, Middle East, and Central Asia region. Responsible for optimization of $1.2B of total assets, 9 production facilities, 3 after-sales support centers, and 7,200 employees.
- Significantly improved long delivery cycle for key products by establishing e-commerce links with North American plants.
- Facilitated globalization of SCM team by developing cross-geographical rotation policy for North American and EAFME regional SCM personnel.
- Doubled annual turnover rate, reducing assets deployed by $400M and slashing customer delivery cycle time from 15 weeks to 5 weeks.
- Successfully penetrated emerging markets of former CIS and Africa, resulting in an incremental $350M of annual sales through establishment of a distribution channel network.

Director, Corporate Transportation Logistics (1989 to 1996) — Racine, Wisconsin

- Directed global transportation and logistics functions required to support production and sales in 102 countries. Oversaw full management of storage and physical movement of all finished goods and components required to support $5.2B of total sales; managed 200-unit private fleet operation in North America.
- Defined strategic business plan that reflected a global outsource of logistics, leveraging the company with a strong competitive advantage.
- Reduced annual logistics costs by 5%, generating additional $22M in operating margin. Improved operating margins by $8M by reducing company fleet operating cost by 2%.
- Negotiated an alliance partner's 5-year contract, positioning company for annual 5% logistical operating cost reduction over term of contract and adding $20M in operating margins.

EDUCATIONAL ACHIEVEMENTS

Master of Business Administration (Finance) — Cornell University — 1995
Bachelor of Science (Materials Management) — Miami University — 1994

KENNETH DONALDSON

55 Leonard Avenue, Windborough, New York 11697 • (631) 988-5003

Transportation / Logistics Management

— Program Development — Crisis Management — Strategic Planning
— Route Management — Budget Forecasting — Logistics Planning
— Vendor/Client Relations — Contract Negotiations — Staff Management

Professional Experience

Vice President, 1982–2000
R.R. RAIL TRANSPORT CO., INC., Southworth, New York — *volume $250 million*

Successfully realigned company to achieve its current market position as a leading distributor of whole grain products including corn, wheat, and soybeans. Held positions of increased responsibility including Distribution & Logistics Coordinator and Merchandiser.

Business Management

- Directed the complexities of day-to-day business operations in areas of freight scheduling, expediting, procurement, inventory control, invoicing, billing, and contract negotiations through management of a Freight Controller and a Transportation Expeditor.

- Held full P&L accountability, overseeing sales analysis, forecasting, and reporting activities.

- Built a private fleet from ground zero, assuming full control of 500 long- and 100 short-term equipment leases. Realized a steady decline of nearly 35% in operational expenditures and an increased sales volume of $87.5 million for 1999–2000.

- Strategically planned the forward leasing of equipment based on current/historical market trends.

- Negotiated and managed contracts for the purchase of equipment (railcars) to ensure the cost-effective availability of transportation tools while maximizing profitability and service levels.

- Co-established a vendor base of 300 and company portfolio of 400 nationally recognized clients that partially include General Mills, Nabisco, Perdue, Tyson, and Ralston/Purina throughout Northeastern sales territories.

- Tracked nationwide distribution operations to identify and resolve unplanned constraints adversely impacting the transport of 100 million bushels of product by 28,000 railcars.

- Collaborated with key representatives throughout the railroad industry to expedite the timely shipment of grain from the point of origin to final destination, addressing critical issues in areas of derailments, union strikes, embargoes, and extreme weather conditions.

— continued —

Functional headings separate key areas of activity and accomplishment over an 18-year career with the same company.

KENNETH DONALDSON

Page 2 of 2

Business Management — continued

- Interfaced extensively with clients concerning unforeseen delays, quality control issues, freight discrepancies, and implementation of corrective action plans.

- Managed personnel issues in areas of interviewing, hiring, performance evaluations and promotions, and the development of job descriptions and salary structures.

- Conducted bimonthly corporate meetings to address business functions and improvements, financial activities, and critical issues at the inter- and intra-department levels including New York and Pennsylvania locations.

Program Development

- In 1999, captured cost savings of $300,000 by successfully negotiating modifications to industry standards restricting the allowable time period for loading/unloading private equipment.

- Pioneered an equipment sub-leasing program in 1995 in response to projected market demands, realizing average profit margins of $360,000 per year.

- Spearheaded a 1991 manual-to-computerized systems conversion, directing technical teams in the development of a LAN-based module designed to support an ever-increasing demand for additional equipment; achieved a 100% increase by 1997.

- In 1986, conceptualized and directed all phases of new business development, allowing for penetration into Southeastern markets; proposed the strategic utilization of inactive railroad yards due to cost cutting measures, leveraged by volume projection, realizing savings of $300,000.

Education

SYRACUSE UNIVERSITY
B.A., Business Management

Computer Skills

Windows 98/DOS; Word, Excel, Lotus, Access

RESUME 49: PIERRE G. DAUNIC, PH.D., CCM; LANCASTER, OH

TERRENCE A. HAWLEY

251 Arrow Wood Drive, Chillicothe, OH 43130   Home 740-281-2542

OBJECTIVE and QUALIFICATIONS

**A career in General Management and Continuous Improvement
utilizing a comprehensive background in Distribution, Manufacturing, and Sales.**

Seasoned Logistics and Distribution Manager with over two decades of experience in leading organizations to greater quality and productivity. Areas of expertise include cost containment, quality management, customer service, team building, and strategic planning. Strong background in distribution, manufacturing, and plant management. Recognized for attention to detail, sensitivity to employee needs, and calmness under stress.

PROFESSIONAL EXPERIENCE

<u>AGP Industries, Inc., Wheeling, WV</u>
[A Fortune 500 global producer of glass and chemical products and coatings with 2000 sales in excess of $7.5 billion.]
Market Manager, Branch Distribution North America (2/99–present). Manage the sales, warehousing, inventory, and distribution of aviation glass and sundry products throughout the region. Also plan, organize, control, and direct several branch operations in addition to aiding in the development of annual marketing, sales, and profit plans. Other responsibilities include management of key accounts, fixed assets, fleet, and fleet maintenance service operations.

Manager, PIG Distribution (1/92–2/99). Directed the operation of the Protective Insulated Glass Distribution Center including all aspects of ordering, receiving, storing, inventory control, repacking, loading, and shipping to customers worldwide. Responsible for cost control and customer satisfaction. Supervised 16 exempt employees and a workforce of up to 270.
Selected Achievements:
➢ Reduced safety Recordable Case Rate to 3.5 in 1998, a 96% improvement in seven years, and now a PIG benchmark.
➢ Saved over $21.1 million in inventory while reducing service days to only two by introducing in our distribution center one of the best bar-coding systems in the industry.
➢ Cut plant packaging costs by implementing a returnable steel rack program, a first in the PIG industry. The program was two years in the making but netted savings of over $2 million annually.
➢ Won the President's Award for Superior Pollution Prevention from the West Virginia EPA.

Director, Distribution and Customer Service (1989–91). Directed all architectural finished glass field distribution operations in North America. Also responsible for transportation service and cost analysis, selection of commercial transportation suppliers, production planning, inventory control, and customer service through each division's managers.
Selected Achievement:
➢ Reduced cost per ton for distribution by 18.3%.

Manager, Manufacturing, Residential Products (1986–89). Selected to provide more aggressive leadership in developing a new product that would meet stringent specifications required by AGP's largest residential customer. Responsible for planning, coordinating, and directing the functions of 2 penultimate glass manufacturing plants, each employing approximately 200 and located 650 miles apart.
Selected Achievements:
➢ Exceeded optimistic performance goals for a new high-performance penultimate glass unit by 10% and within two-thirds of the time designated.
➢ Reduced customer rejection rate from 0.22% to 0.15% on an annual basis.
➢ Instituted teamwork philosophy that reduced overhead in excess of 10% and improved overall quality.

This resume for a senior logistics and distribution manager includes many quantifiable accomplishments that communicate the value he will bring to his next employer.

TERRENCE A. HAWLEY   **PAGE TWO**

PROFESSIONAL EXPERIENCE, continued

Manager, Plastic Fabrication, Topeka, KS, and Pierre, SD (1981–86). Promoted because of proven ability to reduce costs and improve safety performance in an organization that required a strong leadership role. Responsible for managing glass fabrication operations employing 60 in Topeka and 250 in Pierre.
➤ Cut losses in operating budget by over $1 million by focus on overhead and standard variable cost reduction.
➤ Reduced away-from-work cases from 6 to 1 occurrence per year with an 85% improvement in safety.

Senior Sales Engineer, Atlanta, GA (1979–81). Chosen to broaden overall management experience because of demonstrated successes in the manufacturing arena. Responsible for sales and technical support of aircraft windows to the general aviation market. Reported to Sales Manager, Naval Products.
➤ Negotiated the highest one-year price increase of 12% to the largest and oldest AGP naval account.

Superintendent of Plastolite, Cheybogg, LA (1974-79). Responsible for a 200-employee department manufacturing plastic lights, tempered glass, touch-control panels, and other heat-treated products. Directly supervised 20 production supervisors.

Assistant Superintendent, Cheybogg, LA (1967–74). Hired as management trainee and advanced through Process Engineer, Shift Process Supervisor, and Quality Control Engineer to Assistant Superintendent.

EDUCATION

BS Math, St. Mathieu College, Baton Rouge, LA, 1967
MBA [28 credits toward degree], Harvard University, Cambridge, MA, 1973

Continuing Education has included courses and workshops in Teamwork, Gunneson Group International Quality Training, Rapid Improvement, Warehousing, Covey's "Putting First Things First," Benchmarking, Diversity, Interpersonal Relationships, Negotiating, Supply Chain Management, and related topics. Computer classes have included Microsoft Word and Excel. Have attended the Council of Logistics Management's annual conferences and other industry-related meetings.

AFFILIATIONS

- Treasurer, City Belle Health System Board of Trustees, 1993–98
- Board of Directors, Logan County, 1993–97
- Rotary Club of Wheeling, 1993–present
- Parish Council Member, St. Mark's Church; Lay Minister, Men's Prayer Group, 1992–98
- Board of Directors, Wyandotte Chamber of Commerce, 1988–89
- Co-Chair, Economic Development Committee, Cheybogg, LA, Chamber of Commerce

References Furnished upon Request

WILLIAM FRANKLIN

2700 Martha Drive
Yakima, Washington 98922
Phone: 509-882-4956
Cell: 509-342-6666
wfranklin55@yahoo.com

LOGISTICS MANAGER / CONSULTANT

Systems Development / Time & Labor Analysis / Mentoring and Motivation

A fast-track record of project management and accomplishment for major manufacturing and distribution companies punctuated with commendations and accolades from the CEO and divisional director level.

Excellent credentials in defining objectives, conducting financial and logistic analysis, training management and staff while mentoring in communications, motivation, and employment issues. Adept at modifying corporate culture, improving efficiencies, and enhancing revenues.

Certified Project Director   **Bachelor's in Logistics Management**

WORK HISTORY

6/99 to
Present

MANAGEMENT SYSTEM CONSULTANTS — Portland, Oregon
Consultants in Management Training and Operating Efficiencies
Senior Project Director
Consult to Fortune 100 Supervisors and divisional directors in management, cost control, and operational efficiencies in distribution and manufacturing environments. Profit and Loss responsibility for the implementation, and execution of multimillion-dollar contracts designed to improve total business performance for clients.

➢ Analyze operating procedures, manpower allocations and resource utilization to determine optimal levels.
➢ Review management procedures and operating systems; determine and, at times, reposition corporate culture.
➢ Conduct training programs in communications, team building, motivation, and management techniques throughout the enterprise.
➢ Design improved operating procedures to improve the output-to-labor ratio (throughput) and improve space and equipment utilization.

PROJECT MANAGEMENT HIGHLIGHTS

(Large Textile Manufacturer)
Successfully established the first operating benchmarks in corporate history, defining products, goals, and employee expectations and creating an issue-resolution index.
➢ Established basic maintenance schedules, operational chains of command, and emergency response criteria.

(Canadian Seafood Processing Corporation)
Delivered 35% reduction in labor and 27% increase in productivity over an 18-month period, resulting in $2.5 million in additional revenues for the company. Successfully implemented maintenance and work order systems, re-allocated personnel for increased efficiency, and improved work-day operations.
➢ Commended at contract completion by the CEO for exceptional performance of duties and results to the client.

(Continued on page two...)

William Franklin is a fast-track consultant who wants to get off the road. The Project Management Highlights section spotlights his consulting jobs, but the overall duties are presented in a block under the general job description to avoid repeating the same information for each project.

WILLIAM FRANKLIN – **page two**

(Major Overnight Delivery Service)
Generated over $14 million in cost savings to the client for its electronic services division (a co-location facility at Motorola Electronics). Accomplishments included redesign of the warehouse and inventory schematic and 20% reduction in workforce.
➢ Selected for accelerated admission to Project Director School based upon performance of this assignment.

1998   BOEING INDUSTRIES — Seattle, Washington
Logistics Intern
Managed various portions of the company's conversion from IBM to SAP management software.
➢ Received extensive training from Certified SAP Installers with special emphasis on Manugistics distribution and time-management software.
➢ Assisted with allocation of recourses to supply chains; gained expertise in balancing inventories among various warehouses.
➢ Personally conducted inventory audits and made corrections in software discrepancies.

1992 to   LUCENT TECHNOLOGIES — Richardson, Texas
1995   **Team Lead – Cellular Manufacturing**
Provided leadership for a 25-person line assembly section for Motorola's cellular phone division. Adhered to manufacturing procedures and processes while mentoring and coaching in quality control and machine operations.
➢ Completed in-house certification for Six Sigma Quality Control and maintained Six Sigma standards throughout employment.

EDUCATION

Bachelor of Business Administration — Logistics Management
UNIVERSITY OF WASHINGTON — Seattle, Washington
Financed 100% of educational costs

Certified Project Director - July, 2001
ASSOCIATION OF PRODUCTIVITY SPECIALISTS – New York, New York

TECHNICAL

Operating Systems	Windows 3.x, 9.x/00	CICS/CICS2	AS400 SPSS
Applications	SAP Lotus Suite * *Designates all applications within the suite	Manugistics Corel Suite*	MS Office*
Internet	MS Explorer	Netscape	

AFFILIATIONS

Member
ASSOCIATION OF PRODUCTIVITY SPECIALISTS — New York, New York

References Upon Request

CHAPTER 8

Resumes for Equipment and Facilities Design, Construction, and Maintenance Personnel

- Facilities Design Engineers

- Maintenance Technicians

- Maintenance Engineers

- Maintenance Operations Managers

- Security Officers

- Security Operations Managers

- Construction Managers and Directors

Edward L. Johnson

P.O. Box 1100
Raleigh, NC 27602
(919) 873-7537

SUMMARY

Over 18 years of experience in installation, operations, maintenance, and repair of high-speed, precision machinery and equipment used in pharmaceutical manufacturing environment.

✓ More than 5 years' experience in diesel engine maintenance and repair.
✓ Thorough knowledge of GMPs, SOPs, and ISO.
✓ Consistently met production goals and quality standards.
✓ Hardworking, dependable, and creative; always look for methods to improve efficiency and quality.
✓ Work well in team environment and independently.

EXPERIENCE

BIO-PHARM TECHNOLOGY, INC., Clayton, NC
High-speed Mechanic, Processing (1998)
High-speed Mechanic, Packaging (1980-98)

✓ Set up machines to manufacture pharmaceutical products.
✓ Ordered parts and maintained inventory.
✓ Scheduled and performed preventive maintenance.
✓ Maintained production line machinery at peak efficiency to meet production goals.
✓ Trained new employees in machine operations and production processes.
✓ Installed and operated machinery.

Selected Achievements:

— Selected to lead team responsible for installing new production line machinery for manufacturing plant in Canada.
— Served on SMED Task Force to examine machinery and find ways to improve changeover processes.
— Initiated process improvement to eliminate leaflet insertion errors by installing electric eyes into cartoners. Saved company $50,000/year.

DICKINSON TRANSPORTATION COMPANY, Cary, NC
Diesel Mechanic (1985-90)

✓ Promoted to Shop Foreman, supervising 2 mechanics.
✓ Scheduled work orders.
✓ Repaired diesel engines.

EQUIPMENT

Trained in and worked on different brands of the following equipment, including R.A. Jones, Hoppmann, Syntron, Lakso, Scandia, Westbrook, Wexxar, and Consolidated Edison:

Leaflet Inserters	Cappers	Bottle Cleaners
Fillers	Labelers	Bottle Elevators
Heat Tunnels	Hoppers	Neckbanders
Case Packers & Sealers	Carousels	Cartoners
Sorters	Cottoners	Bundlers

In addition to listing the candidate's expertise in procedures and equipment, this resume emphasizes important accomplishments that contribute to the bottom line.

Troy P. Burton

15288 Lake Villa Drive   Belleville, MI 48111   734-555-1928

Profile
▸ Accomplished machine repair/machinist experienced with wide range of automation and production equipment.
▸ Reputation for expertise in creating and fabricating machinery without engineering designs.
▸ Knack for quickly and efficiently assessing problems and instituting repairs; able to zero in on causes and determine solutions.
▸ Leadership and mentoring experience; respected by coworkers.

Relevant Skills & Experience
▸ Vast experience in setting up, maintaining, troubleshooting, and repairing:
- mechanical machinery   - hydraulic equipment   - stamping presses
- pneumatic equipment   - robotic machinery   - drawing presses
▸ Trained in and experience operating:
- metalworking equipment   - mills   - lathes
- fabricating equipment   - drill presses   - saws
▸ Skilled in tearing down and rebuilding machinery to identify and resolve operational problems.
▸ Ability to design, lay out, and build fixtures, mechanical handling devices, transfers and other automation equipment based on engineering designs; interact with engineers during fabrication.
▸ Skilled in using wide range of fabricating material including:
- sheet metal   - steel   - aluminum
▸ Participated in plant-wide preventative maintenance programs.
▸ Possess drafting, schematic, and blueprint reading skills.
▸ Served as Group Leader for Maintenance and Repair team.

Professional Experience
VISTEON CHASSIS SYSTEMS (formerly a division of Ford Motor Co.) • Dearborn, Michigan
Machine Repair/Machinist Journeyman   1965-Present
• Provide troubleshooting, repair, and preventative maintenance support for wide range of production equipment in as many as seven plants building automotive components.
• Serve as resource person for coworkers and supervision regarding equipment operation.

Education
WASHTENAW COMMUNITY COLLEGE • Ypsilanti, Michigan
Ford Motor Company Apprentice Program
• Earned Journeyman card in 1968

Ongoing training through employer and equipment manufacturers.

Related Information
▸ Extensive personal experience in home building, remodeling, and repair.

References available on request

This individual was getting ready to retire and used the resume to demonstrate his versatility so that he could look for similar work outside the automotive industry.

SCOTT MILLER

321 James Boulevard, Iselin, New Jersey 08820
Home: (732) 634-5431

INDUSTRIAL MAINTENANCE MANAGER / SUPERVISOR

- Background includes 8 years' experience as industrial maintenance manager and 1 year as a supervisor.
- Managed and trained skilled technicians, utilizing extensive personal experience troubleshooting, repairing, and rebuilding a variety of industrial equipment.
- Working knowledge of hydraulic, pneumatic, mechanical, and electrical prints as well as schematics.
- Hands-on experience with Barber Colman Maco VI, 8000, and 6500 series programmable controllers along with Omeron, Siemans, and GE controllers.
- Skilled in all aspects of industrial maintenance and servicing. Industrial Class A Mechanic Certified.

PROFESSIONAL EXPERIENCE

EAST COAST PLASTICS, INC. • Newark, New Jersey • 1998 - 2001

Maintenance Manager
- Oversaw and maintained 12 blow-molding machines as well as downline equipment.
- Set up and oversaw outside contractors including electricians, plumbers, and service technicians.
- Searched out and negotiated with new vendors for the best price on spare parts and equipment.
- Worked closely with production department to schedule machine service during usage downtimes.

NATIONWIDE CONTAINERS • West Orange, New Jersey • 1989 - 1998

Maintenance Manager • 1993 - 1998
- Successfully reduced costs in machine downtime, unscheduled overtime, and spare parts by 15-25%.
- Supervised 3-7 maintenance mechanics and 2 porters.
- Maintained and conducted preventative maintenance on 17 blow molders and related equipment.
- Managed a well-stocked spare parts department.
- Worked closely with engineering department to implement and oversee in-house projects.

Maintenance Supervisor • 1992 - 1993
Lead Mechanic • 1990 - 1992 // **Class A Mechanic** • 1989 - 1990

Career includes additional experience with a major food manufacturer/distributor as a Class A Maintenance Mechanic, Machine Operator, and Maintenance Stock Clerk.

EDUCATION & TRAINING

Advanced Blowmolding School, West Orange, New Jersey • 1999
Industrial Class A Mechanic Certification • MPR Technical School, Woodbridge, New Jersey • 1986
Computer Science Courses • Middlesex County College, Union, New Jersey • 1975

As is often the case with maintenance professionals, this candidate's education, certification, and training are important job qualifications that complement his relevant work experience.

RONALD MEYERS

5014 Main Street • Clearlake, California 95422 • ronmey@saber.net • (707) 554-7111

PROJECT MANAGER — FACILITIES / MANUFACTURING / MAINTENANCE ENGINEER

SUMMARY OF QUALIFICATIONS

More than 15 years' demonstrated experience on large capital and expense projects. Proficient with complex pump and piping systems, boilers, metallurgy, hydraulics, structured design, and welding processes. Work well under pressure of long hours and demanding deadlines. Solid communication skills with diverse disciplines of construction contractors.

- Project Manager
- Facilities Engineering
- Maintenance and Manufacturing
- Engineering
- Cost Control
- Supervision and Training

PROFESSIONAL EXPERIENCE & ACCOMPLISHMENTS

Senior Project Engineer, MASONITE CORPORATION, Clearlake, California   1992 to Present

Upgraded and redesigned piping in worn boiler steam-generating system during annual shut downs. Revised and optimized overall process flow of conveyor systems.

Project Management/Design
- ☑ Evaluated and replaced more than 150 pumping systems and redesigned water supply line.
- ☑ Replaced 100,000-gallon ASME-coded pressure vessels, de-aerator, and zeolite softeners.
- ☑ Shut down 85% of sawmill operation—sold and disposed of all wood-finishing machinery.
- ☑ Designed and installed variety of structural steel and reinforced concrete structures.

Maintenance and Repair
- ☑ Developed scope and cost packages for steam-generation maintenance operation.
- ☑ Reduced process-flow-limiting bottleneck and enhanced operation of pumping systems.
- ☑ Raised quality of equipment for effluent treatment and river disposal of clarified waste water.

Cost Control
- ☑ Devised safety device to prevent accidents in die press operation; reduced accident rate 30%.
- ☑ Improved heat distribution in die press platens to reduce moisture variation in final product.
- ☑ Designed fiberglass-reinforced plastic for pipe systems and overlays for corrosion protection.
- ☑ Saved $1 million by applying thorough knowledge of resin application.
- ☑ Evaluated, justified, and supervised installation of anodic protection system to eliminate high corrosion rates, resulting in over $200,000 annual savings.

Supervision/Training
- ☑ Mentored 3 engineers and 1 plant engineer in structural facilities and process application.
- ☑ Taught corrosion awareness and selection methods for metal alloys and synthetics. Reduced component failures and system shutdowns.
- ☑ Sought out, interviewed, and hired more than 30 project consultants.

Senior Maintenance Engineer, SIMPSON PAPER COMPANY, Anderson, California   1987 to 1992

Directed repair, refinement, and upgrade of machinery throughout mill operation. Troubleshot and remedied problems in all phases of pulping operation. Supervised two project engineers; oversaw construction crew, labor pool, and rail system maintenance.

EDUCATION

Bachelor of Science, Mechanical Engineering / University of California, Berkeley, California

---

Note how the lengthy list of accomplishments is broken down into relevant subheadings that improve the readability and impact of this one-page resume.

RANDY T. CARSON

609 Daisy Terrace
Beverly Hills, CA 90212   randytcarson@intcomm.com   311-541-1646
     311-541-0091

PROFILE

Senior-level facilities and operations manager with a proven track record of achievements planning and executing real estate and construction projects to support rapid company growth while achieving significant cost savings. Background includes establishing nationwide telecommunications and IT infrastructure. *Expertise:*

- Real Estate Site Reviews & Selections
- Tenant Improvement Designs & Construction
- Lease Negotiations
- Budget Administration

- Space Planning
- Growth Projections
- Security Systems Design
- Vendor Contracting

EXPERIENCE

FACILITIES MANAGER   **2000 to Present**
International Communications, Inc.   **Los Angeles, CA**

Direct facilities, real estate, space planning, and telecommunications for this national manufacturer of RF tranceivers for cable modems. Administer a $1M+ facilities budget. Manage all internal building maintenance: general facilities repairs, HVAC, plumbing, and electrical work. Lead all real estate site reviews, selections, and lease negotiations. Execute all tenant improvement design and construction projects. Designed and implemented security systems for all sites.

- Reduced rent 50% through subleasing 9,500 sq. ft. Reviewed executive management's original three-year lease proposal, then analyzed the headcount forecast and growth projections, ultimately determining that a two-year plan was more appropriate. Negotiated the lease and obtained a six-month security deposit.

- Saved a projected $10K by performing all space planning and furniture layouts in house. Located a firm that was going out of business and purchased $30K of near-new office furniture for just $3K.

- Negotiate all vendor contracts. Achieved a $5K cost savings in network cabling in one of the initial buildouts by maximizing professional contacts among the vendors.

SENIOR MANAGER, OPERATIONS SUPPORT   **2000**
Autosonline.com   **Los Angeles, CA**

Oversaw facilities management projects for online automobile retailer, pertaining to maintenance and upgrades, real estate, construction, remodeling, expansion, security, and space planning, which included preparing company growth projections. Structured and closed all vendor contracts. Administered facilities and telecommunications budgets totaling $12M. Managed telecommunications, network infrastructure, help desk, and a 300-seat call center. Supervised network engineers, system administrators, help desk, facilities supervisor, telecommunication supervisor, and administrative support.

- Expedited the move from a temporary facility in Pleasanton to a new site, twin 30,000-sq.-ft. buildings in Los Angeles. Evaluated and selected the site, administered the construction budget, directed furniture and fixture installation, and supervised the move. The 90-day timeline to complete construction in the cold shells was repeatedly revised, which required updating the time frames for each component of the project.

The resume writer's goal was to present this candidate as an integral contributor to the upper-management team. The resume repeatedly demonstrates how his collaborations with management and his suggestions and proposals positively impacted the "big picture."

RANDY T. CARSON

311-541-1646   randytcarson@intcomm.com   311-541-0091

- Directed the installation of a complete IT infrastructure at the new site. Designed and laid out the data center, including racking for the components, air conditioning, power, backup power, distribution, controlled-access security, and furniture. Managed the two-day move in phases with zero interruption in customer support.

SENIOR MANAGER, FACILITIES   **1996 to 2000**
PC Global Corporation   **Los Angeles, CA, and Osaka, Japan**

Managed nationwide IT infrastructure, data communications, networking, and facilities for this high-growth laptop computer manufacturer. Focused on space planning and real estate site selection. Initially managed a $2.5M budget, which grew to a $7M budget over the course of four years; administered the budget within 1% every year. Managed PBX and call center activities. Established a corporate helpdesk system. Supervised employees in three different office locations.

- Supported rapid growth by opening multiple offices in Los Angeles and Memphis, TN, from cold shells, including establishing national telecommunications and network infrastructures, in an 18-month period. Developed and managed project and operating budgets for these three sites.

- Relocated the call center from Los Angeles to Memphis. Collaborated with the local redevelopment agency in negotiating with the city and county to secure $300K in tax credits. Also implemented an interactive voice response unit and contracted to utilize the AT&T network, saving $60K in telecommunications expenses in just one year.

- Directed the opening of a second location in Memphis to transfer the manufacturing operation from Japan to the U.S. Located suitable space directly behind the original location and negotiated with the landlord to install a $14K conduit, at the landlord's expense, in order to route the existing infrastructure to the second location.

- Finalized lease negotiations for the Memphis site. Avoided presenting a letter of credit to the landlord, which counters Japanese business culture, by structuring a deal whereby PC Global paid $300K for capital improvements in exchange for nine months' free rent, an arrangement that resulted in a more financially favorable P&L position to the Japan HQ.

- Implemented a computer-aided facility management tool to integrate and store lease, space, employee and asset data such as facility drawings and an equipment database, thus facilitating space analyses, vacancy analyses, asset analyses, and move reports. Provided key support in developing a web-based help desk application utilizing this information, then incorporated the employee database and online employee telephone directory.

EDUCATION & PROFESSIONAL TRAINING

B. S., FACILITIES MANAGEMENT   1995
University of California   Los Angeles, CA

FACILITIES MANAGERS MASTER'S LEVEL CERTIFICATION CANDIDATE   2002
The University of Philadelphia Virtual Education Program

DEREK THOMAS

4024 South 2100 Street, Salt Lake City, UT 84117 • Tel: (801) 277-6299 • Mobile: (801) 550-5555
Email: dthomas@lighthouse.net

SENIOR FACILITIES MANAGER

• Strategic Planning • Capacity Planning • Construction Projects • Productivity/Efficiency Gain
• Financial Management/Budget Controls • P & L • Quality & Resource Maximization • Team Building

EXECUTIVE PROFILE

RESULTS-ORIENTED FACILITIES MANAGER with hands-on experience in all facets of maintenance management and production for high-volume plant manufacturing and off-site warehouse including machine shop functions. Combine exceptional technical, analytical, and engineering qualifications with outstanding business development, project planning, and project management. Expertise includes EPS, Plastics, and FDA Food Plant with transferable skills to direct any area of production/engineering. Superb written and oral communication skills combined with an outstanding team approach to troubleshooting and problem resolution in a production environment. Adept at mechanical/electrical and machine problems. Enjoy fast-paced environment to utilize team leadership skills and effective training strategies. Strong organizational skills with emphasis on preventative and predictive maintenance and Quality Assurance. Solid background of achievement delivering strong and sustainable cost reductions. Able to ensure safety practices: OSHA and Environmental Compliance including Wastewater, FDA, and GMP practices. Superior track record of creating and implementing innovative cost-saving procedures to effect energy and floor production that result in notable company profits. Willing to relocate internationally.

MAJOR STRENGTHS

Project Planning & Management	Materials Planning & Management
Production & Assembly Operations	Reliability & Performance Analysis
Product Cost & Production Scheduling	Maintenance Management
SPC Statistical Process Control	Advance Blueprint Drawing
AutoCAD LT / Syteline MRP Ordering	MP2 Maintenance Tracking
Technical Modifications & Upgrades	Subcontractor Negotiations

ACCOMPLISHMENTS

- Directed and managed $1.1 million annual budget and up to $6 million for construction projects including new equipment.
- Implemented segregation of incoming water flows by diverting to domestic water and steam boilers that **reduced sewer water return bill by $41,000 per year.**
- Spearheaded installation of summer/winter control switch for cooling towers, **saving over $9,000.**
- Utilized innovative bulb exchange that resulted in $19,706 electric rebate and **savings of over $24,000 annually.**
- Modified production machines to utilize thermal imaging in electrical trouble spots, dramatically reducing machine downtime and raising machine usage from 84% to 88%.
- Pioneered introduction of in-line motor testing to eliminate catastrophic motor failures and enable smooth motor change-outs.
- **Achieved Most Organized Person Award** for excellence in budgeting, presentations, and planning.

A lengthy executive profile, a list of major strengths, and a summary of accomplishments paint a strong picture of a well-qualified facilities manager... even before the experience summary appears on page 2.

DEREK THOMAS   Page 2

PROFESSIONAL EXPERIENCE

ABC Manufacturing, Orem, UT   1997–present
—*$47 million manufacturer and distributor of electrical components.*
FACILITIES MANAGER / MANUFACTURING ENGINEER

- Full responsibility for strategic planning, staffing, budgeting and technical performance of all phases of maintenance, engineering projects, and production to affect bottom-line profitability.
- Lead team of professional engineers and manufacturing personnel; supervise, train, and develop staff to produce phenomenal team performance results.
- Coordinate production planning, scheduling, purchasing, and subcontracting as well as provide engineering expertise.

Omnitech, Provo, UT   1995–1997
—*$20 million manufacturer of technical products and components.*
PLANT ENGINEER / MANUFACTURING ENGINEER

- Recruited as Team Leader of Product Research and Development.
- Coordinated production with maintenance and production schedule while implementing Quality Assurance process with documentation and MRP schedules.
- Managed and directed cost-reduction programs to produce significant savings of over $45,000.
- Executed all phases of facility maintenance.
- Acted as effective customer vendor and interdepartmental liaison.

Sleet Engineering, Salt Lake City, UT   1993–1995
—*$37 million engineering firm with two plant operations in Utah.*
MANUFACTURING SUPERVISOR

- Directed and oversaw all aspects of daily operation for CNC machining area.
- Devised and coordinated scheduling route sheets to ensure efficient material flow from stock room to machining area, deburring, and assembly.
- Proficiently use Accutrack system to estimate job cost, create and design fixtures, and manufacture finished product.
- Pioneered and implemented ISO 9000 start-up.
- Instrumental in conception and development of CAT scan machine design for Analogic systems and debugged production problems.

EDUCATION

Associate's degree (Manufacturing Engineering), Salt Lake Community College, 1995
Certified Lynn Tech Machinist

AFFILIATIONS

Board Member, Society of Manufacturing Engineers

Keywords: Facilities Manager, Director of Staff, Program Manager, Senior Facilities Manager, Senior Administrator, Engineering Manager, Project Manager, Project Director, Vice President of Development

Marlon S. Sloan

55 Park Lane, Apartment C   Montgomery, Alabama 36100   ✆ [334] 555-5555

❖ ❖ ❖ ❖ ❖ ❖ ❖ ❖ ❖ ❖

What I bring to Madison Oslin: As your **plant maintenance manager,** maximize productivity by providing comprehensive support for all production fixed assets.

❖ ❖ ❖ ❖ ❖ ❖ ❖ ❖ ❖ ❖

CAPABILITIES YOU CAN USE NOW

- ❖ Broad, deep **experience** that finds, fixes and prevents costly problems
- ❖ Focus on **quality** supported with "bulletproof" logic and hard numbers
- ❖ **Leadership** to help people excel

WORK EXPERIENCE WITH SELECTED EXAMPLES OF SUCCESS

Plant Maintenance Supervisor, Standard Publishers, Montgomery, Alabama, 1992–1996

Third-largest reference book producer in America with a 2.6-acre production floor and $217,000,000 annual sales.

- ❖ Supervised 4 multi-craft maintenance technicians directly and 25 machine operators indirectly.

- ❖ Designed and built machines myself when vendor set replacement costs at $111,000. *Payoffs:* Done for $5,000. Machines **10% faster,** operating **around the clock** for 2,160 days **without a minute downtime.**

- ❖ Sold leadership on my suggestion when 20-year-old equipment began to fail. Company was ready to spend $70,000 in repairs. *Payoffs:* Bought and installed new equipment with **better capability** and **much longer life** — no extra cost.

- ❖ Built, tested and installed critical workstations vendors couldn't provide. *Payoffs:* In two weeks, **tripled capacity** in the same floor space for $135 per station.

Field Representative, Aurora Life Insurance Company, Montgomery, Alabama, 1991-1992

- ❖ **Topped 100 others** to be best in sales, June 1991.

Maintenance Coordinator, Georgia Industrial Development Training, Athens, Georgia, 1988-1990

Georgia's organization that trains quality craftsmen of all kinds for companies relocating to the state. Operates on a $25,000,000 budget.

- ❖ Guided 25 training programs in almost every industrial skill. *Payoffs:* Graduation rate **at or above standards** in programs that normally washed out 50% of all students.

- ❖ Supervised entire warehouse operations that matched $2,000,000 inventory with training needs. *Payoffs:* Scheduling **efficiency up; costs down.**

The "payoffs" highlighted in each accomplishment statement are specific, measurable, and highly beneficial to the company. Thus, they make a strong impact.

Marlon S. Sloan	**Plant Maintenance Manager**	✆ [334] 555-5555

WORK EXPERIENCE, CONTINUED

Maintenance Mechanic, Bryant Manufacturing, Montgomery, Alabama, 1985-1988

Industry leader in bulletproof doors and windows. Operates 50,000-sq.-ft. plant with 100 employees. $7,000,000 in annual sales.

- ❖ Overhauled, on my own initiative, entire preventive maintenance program for 25 unique machines. *Payoffs:* **First-time capability** to see condition of entire production line at a glance.

Maintenance Mechanic, Transi-Corp, Evergreen, Alabama, 1984-1985

Builds small buses and delivery trucks in a 200,000-sq.-ft. plant.

- ❖ Installed, repaired, and inspected all plant equipment from production tools to electrical and heating systems. Produced parts available nowhere else. *Payoffs:* **Mastered every skill** needed to support industrial operations.

Emergency Medical Technician, Johnson Memorial Hospital, Brewton, Alabama, 1981-1984

Maintenance Mechanic, LTP Southern, Evergreen Alabama, 1979-1981

CERTIFICATIONS

- ❖ Type I Refrigerant Technician
- ❖ Adult CPR and Standard First Aid (American Red Cross)

TRAINING

- ❖ "Reliability Based Maintenance Workshop," CSI, 1 day, 1996
- ❖ "Today's OSHA: A Compliance Update," American Management Association, 1 day, 1996
- ❖ "Management Development," 3 days, 1995
- ❖ "Refrigerant Transition and Recovery," Alabama Power, 40 hours, 1995
- ❖ "Motors and Motor Controls," The Electrification Council, 40 hours, 1995

COMPUTER LITERACY

- ❖ Working knowledge of WordPerfect 5.0 for MAC, CAD for MAC (3.0).
- ❖ Full proficiency in proprietary financial needs analysis software.

KENNETH BARNS

227 Indiana Avenue, #C 202
Lubbock, Texas 79415

806.763.2201
kbarns@ODSY.NET

CONSTRUCTION ENGINEER

PROFESSIONAL QUALIFICATIONS

Over 4 years' experience in the construction and technical areas. Proven ability to complete projects safely, within budget, and on time. Excellent leadership, supervisory, and scheduling skills. Dedicated, hard-working professional. Projected to complete **Bachelor of Science** in **Construction Engineering**. Experience and skills include:

Problem Resolution	**Customer Relationships**
Teambuilding & Leadership	**Quality & Productivity Improvement**
Hands-on Leadership	**Engineering & Project Management**

Computer proficient in MS Word, Excel, PowerPoint; P-3; and Micro Station.

EDUCATION

B.S. in Construction Engineering, Texas Tech University, Lubbock, Texas   2002

- Maintained full-time (often over 55 hours weekly) and part-time employment throughout university career to finance education.

- Specialty courses included:

Construction Management	Masonry Structures
Contracts & Specifications	Surveying
Structural Design I & II	Cost Estimating
Strength of Materials	Structural Analysis
Cost & Profit Analysis	Foundations & Earthwork
Steel & Concrete Design	

EXPERIENCE

Time Concrete Construction, Lubbock, Texas   08/1998 to Present
Foreman (Internship)
Surveyed, created forms, graded, poured, and finished concrete. Supervised effectively and efficiently a 5-man crew. Held complete hiring and firing authority.

- Poured foundation slab for a quarter-million-dollar piece of machinery.

The clear, highly readable format of this resume makes it inviting, and the listings of expertise and accomplishments do a good job of selling this candidate.

KENNETH BARNS   kbarns@ODSY.NET
806.763.3201   page two

Gould's Pumps, an ITT Industries Company, Lubbock, Texas   1996 to 1998
Construction Supervisor
Removed asphalt and replaced with 5" thick reinforced concrete slab to create 62,850-sq.-ft. concrete and poured-concrete docking area for 18-wheeler shipments.

- Completed jobs on time and to specifications.
- Scheduling efficiency saved company money on project by changing work schedule to 3AM to 3PM.
- Increased morale and improved quality of crew; awarded crew $100 weekly incentives.

Universe Contracting, Lubbock, Texas   1995 to 1996
Crew Leader
Remodeled outer features of homes; removed and replaced shingles, decking, and felt.

- At age 19, effectively supervised crew of 9 mature men.
- Increased business by estimating and obtaining new jobs while supervising crew.
- Raised crew efficiency; completed more projects weekly than others; provided bonuses to crews that finished the most projects safely and correctly.

Keith's Body and Paint, Boerne, Texas   Summers 1995 to 1998
Auto Body Repair Technician
Removed and repaired damaged parts and installed new parts; sanded and prepared autos.

- Learned good work habits and provided excellent service for repeat business.

Service Master, Boerne, Texas   1992 to 1994
Carpet Cleaning Technician
Cleaned, removed, and installed carpet.

- As a high school, work-program student, received raises after 6 months and assumed more management responsibilities after the death of the owner/operator.

PROFESSIONAL ASSOCIATION AND CERTIFICATION

- Member, Association of General Contractors
- Health and Safety Certified (OSHA)

COMMUNITY / INTERESTS

- Volunteered at holiday seasons packaging and distributing food to those less fortunate; arranged caroling trips to retirement homes.
- Interests include working on engines, fishing, hunting, raising cattle, and horse training.

JOHN RUTGERS

111 Samson Way
Bronxville, NY 17702
631-599-2404

CONSTRUCTION ENGINEER / PROJECT MANAGER

Bring qualified training in civil engineering and professional construction management experience acquired over a 15+ year career track in industry-related positions of increased responsibility.

Core competencies encompass:

— Project Management	— Contract Negotiations	— Contractor / Client Relations
— Budget Control	— Regulatory Compliance	— Site / Facade Inspection
— Crew Management	— Proposal Development	— Progress Reports

PROFESSIONAL EXPERIENCE

On-site Engineer, Quality Assurance/Quality Control Inspector   10/99 - present
R.G. CONSTRUCTION, P.C., South Bendington, NY

Charged with ensuring the integrity of construction site operations encompassing site inspections, estimates, budget analysis and control, crew scheduling and supervision, regulatory compliance, and contractor/client/vendor relations, ensuring project completion on time and within budget.

- Review and assess project plans and specifications to ensure regulatory compliance with Department of Environmental Conservation (DEC) and Department of Environmental Protection (DEP) agencies, HAZMAT, and OSHA, concerning earthwork, electrical, concrete, environmental drainage systems, geo-synthetic material installation, waste management, and workforce safety issues.

- Inspect load-testing procedures at Mercer Mason Industries laboratories to approve the quality of structural support systems through elimination of stress and vibrations.

- Prepare progress reports for management review reflecting labor, material, machinery, and equipment requirements; track and control construction costs to avoid budget overruns.

- Interface on-site and in weekly meetings with contractors, engineers, electricians, DEC/DEP, vendors, inspectors, and environmental energy specialists to review project status.

- Direct in excess of 50 crew members in areas of scheduling, delegation, supervision, pay certifications, and performance evaluation from project inception to completion.

- Perform ground-up facade inspections in accordance with Local Law 11 inspection guidelines, and follow through with the preparation of status reports and Repair Plan Proposals, with supporting photographs and diagrams depicting potential public safety hazards.

Project Highlights

SMITHGATE MUNICIPAL PLAZA, Landfill Cap and Closure
NEW YORK PLACE HOTEL, Local Law 11 Inspection
WALDING ASTRAL HOTEL, Local Law 11 Inspection

— continued —

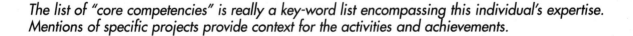

The list of "core competencies" is really a key-word list encompassing this individual's expertise. Mentions of specific projects provide context for the activities and achievements.

JOHN RUTGERS

— Page 2 —

COMPUTER / TECHNICAL SKILLS

Windows 95; MS PowerPoint; AutoCAD

Construction Site and Ground-up Façade Inspections; Blueprint Reading and Development;
Soil Pressures and Properties; Foundations; Testing Procedures

ADDITIONAL WORK HISTORY

Construction Materials Driver, WISCO NEW YORK CORP., Massapequa, NY	5/94 - 12/95
Construction Materials Driver, AIRODYNAMIC, INC., Bronx, NY	7/88 - 5/94
Independent Contractor, Huntington, NY	6/86 - 6/88
Mason's Assistant, M.L. CONSTRUCTION, Huntington, NY	9/85 - 6/86
Electrician's Apprentice, CUNNINGHAM SPARKS, Lindenhurst, NY	6/84 - 9/85

EDUCATION

SINGLETON COMMUNITY COLLEGE, Singleton, NY
Undertaking coursework toward A.A.S. in Civil Engineering, 2002
Computer Aided Drawing (AutoCAD); Land Surveying

POLYTECH COLLEGE, Farmingdale, NY
Coursework in Civil Engineering, 1997 - 1998
Attended lectures given by Civil Engineers in various fields that partially include:
Transportation; GeoTechnical, Structural, and Environmental
Land Surveying Methods and Materials; Drafting; Soil Properties

JORGE M. LEO

2261 South Mesa Drive
San Miguel, California 92334
jmleo@hotmail.com

Mobile: (714) 646-2626
Residence: (714) 687-4329
Fax: (714) 687-4330

DIRECTOR OF CONSTRUCTION
Growth Oriented . . . Profit Building . . . Business Development

A highly creative, profit-oriented construction management professional with 10+ years of experience directing regional and national retail store expansion efforts. Cross-functional abilities and excellent interpersonal and written communication skills. A strong leader with the ability to seek "out of the box" solutions to common construction issues. Demonstrated expertise in the following areas:

- Multi-store Expansion
- Building Codes—Local, State & National
- Outside Professional Services Management

- On-site Supervision
- Cost & Risk Analysis
- Bidding, Review & Contract Negotiations
- Quality Control Standards

- Staffing & Team Building
- Training & Development
- Lease Review
- Master Production Schedule

PROFESSIONAL EXPERIENCE

RETAIL CONSTRUCTION, INC., San Miguel, California
Privately held construction firm specializing in mini-mall and build-out projects.

1998 to Present

DIRECTOR OF CONSTRUCTION
Challenged to develop construction department capable of sustaining expansion efforts of 25 new mini-mall construction projects with tenant build-out and coordination. Develop and implement policies/procedures to ensure compliance with budgets and strict time schedules. Implement communication methods to allow frequent project updates to executive management. Monitor and supervise construction schedules, architectural bidding, contractor bidding, approvals, permits, construction, and quality control. Conduct extensive contract negotiations and lease reviews. Direct activities of outside professionals including developers, architects, structural and electrical engineers, contractors, and superintendents. Oversee 2 project managers and 1 assistant.

Accomplishments
- ✓ Built 22 stores in 1999-2000. Co-tenants included well known retail vendors including Subway, Burger King, and McDonald's.
- ✓ Constructed 10 Blockbuster Video franchises in 1999-2000.
- ✓ Negotiated national accounts with vendors, reducing per-store costs by $12,000 (avg.).
- ✓ Reduced per-square-foot costs from $95 to $77 while increasing quality of construction.
- ✓ Created prototype plan for store that allowed for brand compliance yet incorporated small details to retain tenant customers, including people-friendly furnishings, games, and devices for children. Developed quality-control methods for ensuring tenant satisfaction.
- ✓ Recognized by CEO for developing results-oriented staff that could manage multiple projects simultaneously.

Highlights of this resume include its attractive format, clear emphasis on accomplishments, and strong summary.

JORGE LEO RÉSUMÉ	(714) 646-2626	jmleo@hotmail.com	Page 2 of 2

PROFESSIONAL EXPERIENCE (continued)

SPECIALTY FOODS, San Diego, California   1992 to 1998
Gourmet cooking supplies and services corporation with 400 stores nationally and $800 million in annual sales.

SENIOR PROJECT MANAGER

Challenged to direct and manage expansion program of 70 retail stores nationwide per year. Prepared cumulative construction for executive management. Reviewed construction bids and conducted contract negotiations. Identified and implemented cost-saving measures and time efficiencies. Defined and carried out procedures for uniform department site surveys, compliance with building codes/permit requirements, and state safety requirements applicable throughout the U.S. Oversaw 6 construction managers, project managers, and administrative personnel.

Accomplishments
- ✓ Built department from ground floor and conducted recruitment and staffing activities.
- ✓ Configured store prototype and devised new concepts to control costs as company continued to expand its scope of operations and added new services, effectively doubling floor space (10,000 to 28,000 square feet) and construction requirements for each store.
- ✓ Created 4 nationwide project regions and assembled project managers and real estate staffs according to region, thereby facilitating communication and economies of scale.
- ✓ Established "New Store Team" consisting of representatives from each department who met weekly to resolve issues. Resulted in much smoother store openings.

R.C. PERLMUTTER & ASSOCIATES, San Diego, California   1989 to 1992
Architectural firm specializing in commercial and custom homes.

PROJECT MANAGER

Managed the Specialty Foods account with responsibility for drafting store plans and monitoring billing. Oversaw the construction of Quik Lube facilities. Created plans and supervised the construction of custom homes.

EDUCATION

Bachelor of Arts in Architecture—University of Southern California
Architect Registration Examination—Currently Enrolled—Successfully completed several architectural examination modules

<u>Continuing Education</u>
Microsoft Network Administration Certification Course—Currently enrolled

BUSINESS TECHNOLOGY SKILLS

Microsoft Word, Microsoft Excel, Microsoft Project, and Microsoft Outlook

Professional References Available

CHAPTER 9

Resumes for Manufacturing "Business Support" Personnel

- Training and Development Specialists and Consultants
- Human Resources and Organizational Development Personnel
- Program and Contract Managers
- Marketing, Business Development, and E-Business Professionals
- Labor Relations Specialists and Attorneys
- Industrial Safety, Health, Hygiene, and Risk-Management Professionals
- Safety Engineers and Analysts
- OSHA and Regulatory Compliance Personnel
- Accounting Managers/Project Accountants
- Technical Project Managers
- Cost Accountants/Cost Analysts/Cost Planners
- Plant Controllers

JOYCE WISE

2882 LEBOST • NOVI, MI 48375 • 248/555-5555 • GETJOBS@AOL.COM

CORPORATE TRAINER / FACILITATOR

A highly knowledgeable and dedicated professional with 15 years of manufacturing experience delivering impressive contributions to ensure organizational goals and objectives are attained ▪ Skilled at learning new concepts quickly, working well under pressure, and communicating ideas clearly and effectively ▪ Strong background in education and project management ▪ Improved methods and profitability by analyzing, prioritizing, creating, implementing, tracking, and evaluating effective plans of action.

PROFESSIONAL EXPERIENCE

INDEPENDENT CONTRACTOR
Facilitator / Trainer / Consultant

CREATE YOUR CAREER, Novi, MI, 1998 – Present

Recruit, interview, coach, and train corporate and private clients in designing a career by guiding them through self-assessment exercises, job search techniques, and interviewing and salary negotiation skills. Also assist with career marketing needs such as resumes and cover letters.

> ➤ Designed, developed, and deliver a workshop on "Acing the Interview" for corporate employees and private clients, providing the skills to better prepare them for an interview.
> ➤ In-depth knowledge of issues facing employees and employers in a changing work environment, and of the skills needed in various employment fields. Cognizant of current business trends and future industry needs.
> ➤ Established an Internet web site: www.careerist.com.
> ➤ Credentialed Career Master. Certified Job and Career Transition Coach. Certified Professional Resume Writer.

FORD MOTOR COMPANY, Dearborn, MI, 1996 – 1998

Hired to manage a three-year project of implementing Best Practices for 33 Ford Plant Vehicle Teams, located internationally, while accommodating the needs of the diverse teams.

> ➤ Implemented all phases of six separate Best Practices, enabling the assembly plants to maximize quality and reduce costs, which resulted in a 35% improvement in productivity for Product Development.
> ➤ Facilitated, coordinated, and trained North American Plant Vehicle Teams in Engineering Change Management. This process allowed for the inclusion of remote teams in changes and accelerated the implementation of warranty fixes and cost reductions into the product, effectively contributing to the bottom line.
> ➤ Analyzed, designed, and developed implementation training material for all Plant Vehicle Teams for Best Practices, with the assistance of subject matter experts. Also tracked and evaluated project results.

CHRYSLER CORPORATION, Auburn Hills, MI, 1994 – 1996

Recruited to facilitate Chrysler employees, at various assembly plants throughout the United States, through three-day Kepner-Tregoe / Global 8D workshops, training them on Problem Solving and Decision Making processes. Assignment was a two-year project.

> ➤ Guided various work teams through assigned projects and complicated problems. The many positive results attained through these efforts greatly contributed to Dodge Neon being named to the J. D. Powers "most improved" car list in 1996.

The challenge here was presenting the candidate as someone who blends effectively into different environments and de-emphasizing the long-time self-employment, which might not be viewed positively by hiring managers.

JOYCE WISE   PAGE TWO

ACADEMY OF COURT REPORTING, Southfield, MI, 1992 – 1994

Dean of Education. **Oversaw a staff of twenty and a student body of approximately 300 to ensure all aspects of the educational processes were properly accomplished.**

> ➢ Achieved an 89% student retention rate for four consecutive quarters, greatly enhancing company profits.
> ➢ Counseled students for academic progress and career choices, enabling them to take an active role in determining their future.
> ➢ Coordinated a project to involve the school and the community in mentoring and internship programs, strengthening the understanding and cooperation between the students and the business community.

MICHIGAN EDUCATION COMMISSION, Southgate, MI, 1990 – 1992

Trainer/Facilitator. **Managed a Learning Resource Center for Chrysler Corporation. Charted programs to help employees with career development and self-assessment needs.**

> ➢ Designed, developed, and delivered courses on Diversity, Team Building, Empowerment, Communication, etc., to corporate employees, enabling them to be more creative, competent, professional, and productive. Presented workshops on financial planning and time management to aid employees in learning these skills.
> ➢ Designed, developed, and delivered a career development course so employees would have the needed tools to guide them on the career path of their choice.

GENERAL MOTORS CORPORATION, Ypsilanti, MI, 1986 – 1990

Trainer/Human Resource Liaison. **Administered various training and human resource functions such as interviewing, needs analysis, training, and employee benefits for a five-plant division.**

> ➢ Managed a project that designed, developed, administered, and analyzed a Needs Analysis for a 65-person department. Then designed and developed a training program based on the results of the Needs Analysis. As a result, department efficiency was increased by 28%.
> ➢ Designed, developed, conducted, and evaluated a customer survey. Utilized results of survey to implement improved service standards. Received a recognition award for accomplishments.

EDUCATION

M.S.A. – *Business Administration* – Central Michigan University
B.S. – *Education* – Wayne State University
Certified – Global 8D/Kepner-Tregoe – *Problem Solving*
Certified – Development Dimensions International (DDI) – *Empowered Workforce*
Proficient in Windows software including MS Word, PowerPoint, and Excel.

PROFESSIONAL ASSOCIATIONS

American Society for Training and Development
Career Masters Institute
Professional Association of Resume Writers
National Association of Female Executives

Melanie P. Brownlee

1829 Valley Ridge Drive
Shoreview, MN 55126

www.mpbconsult.com

651-555-5672
melanie@mpbconsult.com

Human Development Trainer and Consultant
Specializing in Operations Turnaround,
Organizational Development, and Team Building

Innovative and creative transformational leader reshaping organizations from the industrial age to the knowledge age. Expert in developing team-building strategies and other tools needed by the workforce to internally facilitate successful change. Highly developed communication and people skills. Strong strategic planning background working with many diverse companies.

Highlights of Experience

Training, Consulting & Coaching

- ▸▸ Counseled businesses in strategic planning, visioning, brainstorming and implementation. Over 30 companies transformed (complete list available on request).
- ▸▸ Designed and developed workshops and seminars. Topics included:
  - — Team-Based Strategic Planning
  - — Empowerment
  - — Time Management
  - — Transformational Leadership
  - — Customer Service
- ▸▸ Created a learning community of 400 people of all ages and backgrounds. Taught families, individuals, and businesses empowerment and leadership skills.
- ▸▸ Delivered presentations to audiences of 300+ as keynote speaker.
- ▸▸ Conducted workshops for not-for-profit organizations including:
  - — Easter Seals
  - — Habitat for Humanity
  - — Minnetonka Focus Council
  - — American Red Cross
  - — Learning Team for Y2K & Beyond

Engineering, Manufacturing & Project Management

- ▸▸ Supervised construction, plant design, and other activities to coordinate model change and implement lean manufacturing assembly concepts and facilities.
- ▸▸ Engineered and designed manufacturing plants incorporating best practices and ergonomic features.
- ▸▸ Conducted product-line reviews for 5 distinct business units with the goal of identifying and implementing cost-saving opportunities.
- ▸▸ Utilized quality procedures and statistical methods in generating and evaluating laboratory tests.
- ▸▸ Acted as liaison and coordinated joint activities between UAW and Ford management.

Selected Accomplishments

- ▸▸ Managed Ford Motor Company Luxury Car Group Fuel System through program release and launch as a Tier 1 supplier. Drove team approach to turn around "at risk" supplier. Generated teams consisting of two Tier 1 competitors and common supplier to solve major design, performance, and quality issues. All companies involved realized significant cost savings.
- ▸▸ Developed and wrote project for multimillion-dollar offshore circuit-board assembly facility. Developed manufacturing philosophy and defined the facility and capital investment, developed business center, and performed competitive analysis.
- ▸▸ Managed industrial engineering project for Chrysler's 3-mode cruise assembly lines. Generated $10 million project for burn-in chambers and completed ergonomic design for loading and unloading.
- ▸▸ Refurbished and consolidated Ford's Inver 500,000-square-foot manufacturing facility as part of a 5-year project. Work was completed on time and within budget, facilitating an additional $2 million in plant cost savings.
- ▸▸ Led the generation and implementation of cost-saving ideas in manufacturing facility, resulting in average annual savings of $1.5 million.
- ▸▸ Successfully resolved 2 problematic processing issues using Shainin problem-solving methods and team approach.
- ▸▸ Hired as first female sales representative for American Motors with responsibility for coordinating automotive replacement part sales in Twin Cities region.

This individual wanted to establish her credibility as a self-employed consultant. A strong track record of accomplishments helps sell her expertise.

Melanie P. Brownlee   651-555-5672

Skills Inventory

Technical

- Lean manufacturing and industrial engineering
- Strategic planning
- Program management
- Project development and authorship
- Value management
- Knowledge management
- Training and facilitation
- Implementation planning
- Quality management and problem-solving

Human Relations

- Team management and development
- Communication and interpersonal relationships
- Coaching and mentoring
- Transformational leadership
- Organizational development
- Conflict resolution
- Understanding cultures
- Sensitivity to political issues

Career History

MPB Consultants & Associates • Shoreview, Minnesota   1991-Present
Founder/Consultant

- Provide strategic and problem-solving consulting for 30+ businesses. Clients include ADP, 3M, and Northstar Bank.
- Completed year-long, full-time assignment with Fast Track Systems as Program Manager-Fuel Systems Supplier Development (1999-2000).
- Collaborated with Mayflower Builders to develop strategic plan for business expansion and to develop 100 home subdivision as part of that expansion (1993-1994).

General Motors Service Parts Operations • Edina, Minnesota   1986-1992
Quality Network Coordinator/Internal Consultant
Project Manager/Industrial Systems Planner

Inver Grove Assembly Plant • Inver Grove Heights, Minnesota   1972-1986
Industrial Engineer
Value Engineer
Quality Control Supervisor/Laboratory Test Specialist
Manufacturing Supervisor
Dealer Merchandiser

Education

Macalister College • St. Paul, Minnesota
Bachelor of Arts — Human Resource Management   1986

Timberwoods Community College • Duluth, Minnesota
Associate Degree — Chemical Laboratory Technician   1970

Professional Training

- ▸▸ **Leadership Development** and **The Curriculum for Living** — Landmark Education [completed extensive year-long Team Leadership and Management Program in addition to 400+ hours of experiential and classroom training in topics including communication, excellence, and accomplishment] (1996-2000)
- ▸▸ **Empowerment Series** — Empowerment for Leadership, Value Management, Inc. [comprising 1,000 hours of training in empowerment, team building, relationship building, and coaching; completed community project] (1990-1996)
- ▸▸ **Internal Consultant Certificate** — Ford Motor Human Resource Center [6-week program] (1993)
- ▸▸ **Shainin Practitioner** — Dorian Shainin's Statistical Engineering Seminar (1992)
- ▸▸ **The President's Club** — Sandler Sales Training (Life Member)

Dennis Wander

140 Horning Drive
Clifton, VA 20124

(703) 222-4848
DWander@msn.com

SENIOR EXECUTIVE / TRAINING & DEVELOPMENT
ORGANIZATION DEVELOPMENT / HUMAN RESOURCES

- **Proactive, senior-level executive with 12 years' experience** leading training and organizational development initiatives in the U.S., Australia, Europe, Latin America, Africa, and the Far East.

- **Skilled at directing startups** and managing business functions in addition to training and development. Proven ability at streamlining organizations, reducing operating costs, and adding millions of dollars to the bottom line.

- **Managed corporate training for both exempt and non-exempt employees** in the areas of health and safety, franchisee operations, manufacturing and production operations, technical products and services, customer service call centers, consultative sales, marketing management, interpersonal skill development, diversity, sexual harassment, team development and management, and leadership development.

- **Designed and delivered programs** on team building, conflict management, management and leadership, coaching, performance management systems, change management, Myers-Briggs, marketing management, consultative selling, and train-the-trainer, among others.

- **Senior Professional in Human Resources (SPHR)** certification expected June 2002. Certified to deliver programs for MBTI, Zenger-Miller, Blanchard, Achieve Global, Prichet Rumler-Brache, Huthwaite, and Personnel Decisions International.

AREAS OF EXPERTISE

- Change Management
- 360-degree Feedback
- Team Building
- Conflict Management
- Organization Design
- Action Learning
- Leadership and Management Development

- Benchmarking
- Instructional Design
- Needs Analysis
- Measurement & Evaluation
- Competency Models
- E-learning
- Coaching
- Performance Management

- Appraisal Systems
- Succession Planning
- Individual Development Plans
- Career Development
- Compensation & Benefits
- Recruiting
- Employee Relations

CAREER HIGHLIGHTS

NATIONAL OIL *(formerly U.S. Petroleum)* — Fairfax, VA, and Irving, TX
GLOBAL TRAINING AND DEVELOPMENT MANAGER, 1998 to Present
Selected to lead transition, establish, and integrate training functions for 1999 National and U.S. Petroleum corporate merger. Prior to merger, directed training for 8,000 exempt and non-exempt worldwide employees, oversaw team of 16 international training managers and performance improvement specialists, and administered $7.8 million global operating budget. Managed global e-learning initiatives and organizational learning best-practice transfer initiative.
Key Accomplishments:
- Developed and launched worldwide brand management program for newly formed business unit within first 90 days.
- Created and staffed integrated global and regional training organization within 120 days.
- Formulated regional people-development strategy for 17 Asia-Pacific countries based on three-month training and needs study.
- Saved $1.1 million by centralizing resource library.
- Produced and implemented global competency template.

To showcase more than a decade of experience in training and development, organizational development, and human resources, this resume leads off with five very comprehensive achievement statements.

Dennis Wander
Résumé - Page Two

CAREER HIGHLIGHTS

EUROPEAN TRAINING AND DEVELOPMENT MANAGER, Brussels, Belgium, 1996 to 1998
Accountable for training and development programs to support U.S. Petroleum and British Petroleum European Joint Venture. Designed and set up Learning and Development Center, which provided product and technical, IT, interpersonal skills, business, manufacturing, health and safety, customer service call center, management, and marketing training for 4,000 employees in 18 countries. Administered $5.1 million operating budget, established internal communication channels, and facilitated executive leadership conferences. ***Key Accomplishments:***

- Negotiated global vendor agreement, which resulted in $650 million in annual savings.
- Implemented corporate university approach for training and development.
- Introduced self-learning programs that saved $500,000 within first year.
- Led cross-functional team that developed and introduced performance management system for 18 European affiliates.

MARKETING TRAINING MANAGER, London, UK, 1993 to 1996
Directed training function for U.S. Petroleum Europe, Ltd., and managed $3.4 million budget and staff of eight professionals. Developed and coordinated training for 3,200 employees in sales, marketing, customer service, and operations and 3,500 franchisee operators in 15 European countries. ***Key Accomplishments:***

- Increased productivity 25% and reduced operating and manpower expenses by $650,000 by creating external training consultant network and streamlining operations.
- Created matrix T&D organization and piloted shared-service approach that became best-practice company wide.
- Initiated, designed, and led leadership development program for 350 management personnel.
- Team awarded special stock option grants as recognition for contributions to organization.

Professional progression prior to 1993, Mobil Corporation:
REAL ESTATE AND ENGINEERING MANAGER, Tokyo, Japan, 1991 to 1993
FUELS MARKETING BUSINESS TRAINING MANAGER, Melbourne, Australia, 1989 to 1991
MOBIL MIDWEST BUSINESS SUPPORT MANAGER, Chicago, IL, 1987 to 1989
AREA MARKETING SALES MANAGER, Dallas, TX, and Portland, OR, 1984 to 1986
MARKETING EMPLOYEE RELATIONS ADVISOR, Los Angeles, CA, 1983 to 1984
FIELD MARKETING REPRESENTATIVE, Rapid City, SD, 1980 to 1983

EDUCATION

UNIVERSITY OF MARYLAND — College Park, MD
MS, HUMAN RESOURCES MANAGEMENT *(in progress),* May 2000 to Present
GRADUATE CERTIFICATE IN DISTANCE EDUCATION, E-TECHNOLOGY (December 2001)

UNIVERSITY OF MICHIGAN — Ann Arbor, MI
BA, ECONOMICS, 1979

EXECUTIVE EDUCATION PROGRAMS

ORGANIZATIONAL DEVELOPMENT	DePaul University, Chicago, IL	2000
ORGANIZATIONAL BEHAVIOR	Boston University, Brussels, Belgium	1998
MANAGING THE TRAINING FUNCTION	Management Centre Europe, Brussels, Belgium	1994
LEADERSHIP AND CHANGE	Monash University, Melbourne, Australia	1991
HUMAN RESOURCE MANAGEMENT	University of Michigan Business School	1988
MANAGEMENT DEVELOPMENT	University of Michigan Business School	1985

140 Horning Drive ▪ Clifton, VA 20124 ▪ (703) 222-4848 ▪ DWander@msn.com

Donald H. Devine
3227 Fayette Lane
Lexington, KY 40505

Message: 270.389.2808
Work: 270.418.4767
Alternate: 270.234.0135

Human Resources Professional: Manufacturing Industries

Education

NORTHERN KENTUCKY UNIVERSITY
Highland Heights, KY
Master of Arts in Industrial and Labor Relations
GPA: 3.85 / 4.0

GEORGETOWN COLLEGE
Georgetown, PA
Bachelor of Arts in Psychology

JOHN HONDROS REAL ESTATE SCHOOL
Cincinnati, OH
Real Estate Licensing

KENTUCKY STATE UNIVERSITY
Frankfort, KY
Business Administration (prerequisite for MBA)

Computer Proficiency
Continuously update knowledge of mainstream and industry-specific software:
Windows OS / Excel / PowerPoint / Outlook / Professional Write / Internet Proficient
Bureau of National Affairs HR & Safety / BLR Smart Jobs & Smart Policies / CCH HR Management Series
Simply OSHA 2.0 / ADP HR Perspective / Lawgic

Overview of Qualifications
**Versatile Human Relations professional with track record of quality and professionalism.
Provide competent and efficient management of HR departments, processes, and procedures.**

Human Resources Management

- Provide detailed reports on HR issues to highest corporate executives.
- Update / monitor policies and procedures.
- Administer salaried flex plans, payroll, contracts, management training.
- Comply with Federal / State regulations.
- Hire both exempt & non-exempt staff.
- Ensure proactive employee relations; adept with remedial programs and minority affairs.
- Administer Compensation and Benefits programs.
- Oversee the risk management function.

Total Quality Management

- Direct ISO & QS-9000 Certification processes.
- Conduct EPA and OSHA safety training.
- Provide management training in quality issues.
- Oversee metallurgical analysis and chemistry.
- Possess extensive program development experience.

Labor Relations

- Union / management relations.
- Contract negotiations.
- Labor / management dispute resolution.
- Grievance resolution and arbitration hearings.

Personal Strengths
Statements of strengths in the workplace as determined by professional personality profiling and
commentary solicited from colleagues

~Thrive on challenge~
~Efficient, seek logical solutions, organized~
~Place high value on time; focus on results~
~Join organizations to represent the company~
~Phenomenal attention to detail~

~Loyal, dedicated~
~Conscientious~
~Team player~
~Energetic~
~Discerning~

CONTINUED ON PAGE 2

All of page 1 serves as an introduction to the strong career history detailed on page 2. Note the Personal Strengths section culled from colleagues and assessment tools.

Donald H. Devine

PAGE 2

Highlights of Career Achievements

THOMPSON STEEL STRIP COMPANY 2000-Present   **Policies and Procedures Consultant**
Lexington, KY
- Effective departmental collaboration resulting in development of machinery procedures: Annealing, Normalizer, Continuous Coil, Tempering, Reduction and Reversing Mills, Slitters, Plating /Coating / Packaging Processes, Water Treatment Processes, and other equipment specific to steel manufacturing.
- Upgraded to OSHA compliance standards: HAZ-COM, LO/TO, Confined Space Entry, Fall Protection, Contingency Programs. Developed written plant-wide safety programs and operations procedures.
- Developed new plant policies and procedures, manuals, and evaluation, with simultaneous continuous generation of relevant productive training programs.

MURRAY STEEL COMPANY 1998-99   **Human Resources Manager**
Frankfort, KY
- Saved thousands of dollars via modified employee severance package.
- Assisted in restructuring sales and marketing department and in selecting new sales VP.
- Revamped maintenance department compensation package.
- Implemented early retirement incentives.
- Coordinated liquidation of corporate assets and retained entire salaried staff through transition.

DILLARD MANUFACTURING COMPANY 1997-98   **H.R. Director / Safety Department Advisor /**
Frankfort, KY   **QS 9000 Steering Committee**
- Provided HR support and direction for three plants.
- Initiated and organized QS 9000 effort, increasing overall marketability of the company and products.
- Inspired creation of centralized materials management department.
- Dramatically reduced absenteeism through "no fault" absentee policy.
- Implemented a production strategy that increased output by 25%-30%.
- Coordinated transfer of benefits and insurance during transition of corporate ownership to ensure uninterrupted coverage.

THE PHOTOMETRIC MACHINE COMPANY 1995-97   **H.R., Safety, and Maintenance Director**
Montclair, KY
- Added $50,000 to monthly profits with no additional labor costs.
- Directed successful transfer of all records to computer files.
- Restructured and upgraded departments to enhance marketability and promote sale of both facilities.

THERMABLAST: PLASTICS DIVISION 1992-93   **Human Resources Manager**
Sandersville, KY
- Reversed adverse labor relations with the UE via in-house settlement of grievances and labor disputes.
- Achieved 50% reduction in worker's compensation claims by implementing comprehensive safety program and aggressive case management of such claims.
- Acquired equipment for disabled employee accommodation.

MAGNATHERMAL CORPORATION 1989-92   **Employee Relations Director**
Ashland Park, KY
- Conducted effective and expeditious contract negotiations with the bargaining unit.
- Implemented Drugfree Workplace, EAP, and Lockout / Tagout Programs.
- Saved thousands of dollars through effective and efficient hazardous materials processing, shipping, and abatement projects.

VARIETY MOLD COMPANY 1980-89   **Industrial Relations Manager**
Kingston, KY
- Negotiated labor relations, contracts, and plant liability insurance coverage.
- Provided initial staffing and training assistance during start-up of new melt facility.
- Updated and improved plant safety programs.
- Reduced fraudulent compensation claims via effective claims management.

DONNA S. FOLEY

29 Meadow Road
Brockport, NY 14420

716.609.6828   dsfoley@att.net

PROFILE	**Senior Executive: Project Leadership • Account Management • Marketing**
	Alliance Building • Strategic Planning • Coaching

EXPERTISE   Proven ability to lead management teams to optimize operations — to devise and implement solutions to a wide range of business, technology, and marketing challenges — to create competitive value. Able to drive change, achieve objectives, and effectively manage simultaneous projects in rapidly changing, technologically demanding markets.

STRENGTHS
- Expert coaching ability; consistently effective leadership and development of both teams and individuals … ability to create consensus and encourage self-motivation.
- Skilled in strategic planning, team leadership, project management, and program implementation; effective and experienced in leading teams and individuals in a matrix organization as well as traditional line/staff structure.
- Track record of contributing innovative ideas … successfully developing, communicating, and executing vision.
- Technologically savvy; accomplished PowerPoint/Word/Excel/Internet user.

PROFESSIONAL EXPERIENCE

1991–Present   AMERICAN AEROSPACE, INC. • Rochester, NY
Marketing Account Manager *(1999–Present; promotion)*
Directed comprehensive initiatives to extend AAI's global market share through deeper penetration of #1 corporate account. Conceived and launched aggressive plans for immediately creating strategic alliances at highest levels within customer's management tier. Simultaneously defined tactical plan for enhancing day-to-day relationships with buyers. Overall accountability for creating new product identity for division, positioning company as the fully integrated source for a broad range of materials.

- Defined and laid foundation for comprehensive strategy selling entire scope of AAI products/services into account, positioning AAI as a fully integrated vendor across multiple channels; identified $150 million in incremental business opportunities.
- Effectively analyzed and developed plan to maintain production levels, ensuring quality, on-time delivery, and cost containment.
- Closely interfaced with CEOs/General Managers of 5 AAI Divisions to ensure support for partnership with #1 corporate account.

Managing Director, Sikorsky Programs *(1997–98; promotion)*
Managed large customer account totaling $20 million in annual sales; provided direction to cross-functional organization to ensure financial, quality, and schedule commitments for the company and customer were met/exceeded.

- Increased annual sales by 33% through dedicated customer interface/team building.
- Successfully completed transition of over 200 different parts from customer into Mississippi facility with no production interruption.
- Led cross-functional team that reduced scrap of critical part family by 20%.
- Initiated senior engineering quarterly meetings with the customer to exhibit technical advances and promote company capabilities.   *… continued*

This resume was designed for an individual who wanted to pursue several different types of leadership positions within a manufacturing company. The Profile statement encompasses key areas of expertise where she can play a role.

DONNA S. FOLEY   Page Two

PROFESSIONAL EXPERIENCE

AMERICAN AEROSPACE, INC.
Managing Director, Sikorsky Programs *(cont'd.)*

- Effectively managed production and development programs in multiple locations simultaneously.
- Successfully managed the implementation of EDI transmission of purchase order requirements directly into the company's MRP system.

Program Manager, New Business Programs *(1993–97; promotion)*
Key project implementation and management responsibility included customer satisfaction, proposals and estimates, contract negotiation, cost and schedule reporting, program schedule, and quality performance; in addition, managed annual business plans, emphasizing monthly sales and margin performance.

- Successfully managed production and delivery of 75 composite satellite structures ahead of delivery requirements, resulting in over $2 million in delivery incentives.
- Based on positive customer relations and program performance, negotiated a unit price increase of 50% on all option phases of the IRIDIUM satellite program, yielding a potential sales increase of $1.5 million through the option period.
- Managed the cost-reduction activities of a complex airframe part, resulting in margin performance of 50% on a fixed-price production program.

Senior Contract Negotiator *(1991–93)*
Oversaw government contract management/administration, preparation, and negotiation. Led contract organization training and directed staff of 4 contract administrators.

- Effectively negotiated terms and conditions package with largest customer to reduce repetitive proposal and negotiation for each purchase order.

1984–91   PRATT & WHITNEY DIVISION OF UTC • North Haven, CT
Senior Contract Administrator *(1987–91);* **Contract Administrator** *(1984–87)*
Managed departmental budgets, organized training programs for all department staff, and represented department on all cross-functional initiatives within the division.

- Designed, developed, and implemented a computer-based, division-wide contracts-tracking system that yielded significant productivity and cost-savings benefits.
- Organized training seminar for 100+ employees on key contractual issues; substantially improved understanding and compliance.

1983–84   DIGITAL EQUIPMENT CORPORATION • Burlington, MA
General Accountant

EDUCATION   RENSSELAER POLYTECHNIC INSTITUTE • Troy, NY
- **M.B.A., Management** *(1989)*

BRANDEIS UNIVERSITY • Waltham, MA
- **Bachelor of Science, Business** *(1983)*

Ongoing continuing professional education and personal development programs.

MICHAEL C. LOWES

1209 Red Barn Way * Laurel, MD 21045
410.555.1234 * mlowes@hotmail.com

OPERATIONS MANAGEMENT
- Worldwide Brand Recognition - International Marketing & Distribution Training

EXECUTIVE MANAGEMENT PROFILE

- Program Management	- Production Development	- Financials
- Contract Negotiations	- Multi-channel Distribution	- Marketing
- Strategic Planner	- Budget Allocation	- P&L

Polished professional with a consistent career track of upward progression. Conduct international negotiations. Significantly increase visibility, improve overall operations, and enhance profitability. Assemble, motivate, and inspire teams to excel. Apply strong leadership skills and capitalize on all available resources. Speak fluent Spanish and basic French.

PROFESSIONAL EXPERIENCE

Premier, Inc., Baltimore, Maryland   **1991 to Present**
* Premier, Inc. is a nonprofit educational organization that produces, markets, and administers classroom and Internet-based training courses with annual revenue of $20M. Classroom-based courses are conducted off-site throughout the U.S. and in 10 countries.

DIRECTOR OF INTERNATIONAL MARKETING & DISTRIBUTION   **1993 to Present**

- Report directly to the President & CEO. Supervise two marketing partners and 10 country managers. Negotiate licensing and distribution agreements with host country representatives and contracts with vendors for outsourced projects. Develop the annual budget for international operations. Generate, implement, and manage international growth strategies. Analyze trends in the financial services industry to assist in product development and marketing strategies.
- Serve as staff liaison to the International Committee of the Board of Trustees; advise the Board on the development of international and domestic policies that affect international operations.
- Provide technical marketing assistance to local distributors in 18 countries and the U.S. to increase enrollment in classroom-based training programs. Control and monitor company sales.

Specific Achievements
- Successfully developed a strategic plan and terminated unprofitable sponsorship relationships, reduced expenses, completed the development of international curriculum, finalized and placed online five international courses, re-branded Premier as an organization with multiple training modes, conducted market research on the viability for Internet-based training, and developed a new sponsoring licensing agreement— all in two years. Reduced year-on-year operational costs by 60%.

- Established an agreement for a partnership resulting in the restructuring of international operations and the expansion of the distribution from a single channel to a multi-channel approach.

- Evaluated and modified Premier's branding strategy, tailoring the perspective to global availability, flexibility in training options, and a collaborative approach in working with companies to develop integrated company-based training programs.

In this information-packed resume, setting apart notable achievements in a separate list with its own subtitle is an effective way to communicate the candidate's value.

MICHAEL C. LOWES, PAGE 2

REGIONAL MARKETING DIRECTOR   1991 to 1993

- Supervised four country managers. Analyzed business practices, cultures, and regulatory environments. Advised staff of product modification requirements. Guided local distributors in the region in developing marketing and sales strategies.
- Conducted press interviews. Created and delivered sales presentations to company executives and industry leaders.
- Collaborated with insurance regulators in establishing continuing education and more stringent licensing requirements.

Radio Shack, Inc., Baltimore, Maryland   1989 to 1991
* Radio Shack, Inc., manufacturers and distributes electronics worldwide.

WAREHOUSE MANAGER, CENTRAL DISTRIBUTION FACILITY (NORTH AMERICA)

- Effectively managed requirements for multiple service components. Supervised a staff of 45 warehouse specialists and monitored hundreds of transportation specialists. Controlled receipt for products from six manufacturing facilities and coordinated inventory and distribution to 415 retail outlets throughout North America.
- Managed and executed an operational budget of $1.6M annually.
- Monitored internal controls and introduced new processing procedures and streamlined forms, greatly increasing receipt, storage, and issue procedures— resulting in a 26% decrease in backlogged items. Reduced stockpiling of various items by conducting regular and spot inventories.
- Successfully tackled complex logistical issues.

EDUCATION & PROFESSIONAL DEVELOPMENT

- **Bachelor of Arts in Business, Minor in Economics, University of Maryland, 1988**

- **Associate's Degree in Spanish, Howard Community College, 1986**

- Operations Institute, Caracas, Venezuela, June 1988 to April 1989

- Completed various continuing education courses and seminars in business, contracting, logistics, distribution, and leadership

STUART G. MITCHELL

490 10th Avenue • San Francisco, California 94118
Residence (415) 308-2621 • Business (415) 465-2647
SGMitchell@att.net

SENIOR BUSINESS DEVELOPMENT EXECUTIVE
Aerospace – Satellite Communications

Procurement ■ Large Scale Contract Management ■ Contract Formation
Proposal Development ■ Multinational Strategic Partnerships ■ Corporate Development
Project Planning & Management ■ Operations Management

SUMMARY OF QUALIFICATIONS

✓ Delivered over $100 million in total cost savings throughout career through expertise in strategic planning, large-scale contract development, contract negotiations, strategic partnerships, work sharing, and specialized purchasing programs.

✓ Executive presentation skills with experience negotiating multibillion-dollar contracts for US military and major commercial contracts around the world.

✓ Successful in identifying and negotiating critical strategic partnerships and investor funding agreements for international telecommunications start-up and personally securing $100 million of initial seed capital.

✓ Managed $1 billion of annual procurement expenditures; expert in all aspects of procurement, including proposal development, contract management, material planning, and inventory management.

PROFESSIONAL EXPERIENCE

WorldCom LP; London, England   **1999 – Present**
Senior Vice President Strategic Alliances
Deputy Vice President Corporate Development
WorldCom is a global telecommunications start-up positioning to provide broadband access via satellites to telecommunications carriers worldwide. Recruited as part of the executive start-up team and charged with directing the corporate development activities, including oversight of the finance and legal organizations, budget development and expenditures, identifying and negotiating capital funding partnerships, identifying and negotiating strategic alliances, and establishing fixed pricing and contractual framework for potential new business exceeding $5 billion.

Corporate Development – Strategic Alliances – Contact Management

■ Led collaborative efforts to build the technical performance requirements, financial features, project deployment strategies, risk and liability terms, and elements of the contractual agreements to position WorldCom as a viable entity in compliance with all mandates needed to secure investment relationships with major telecom operators around the world.

■ Efforts resulted in winning WorldCom key industrial partnerships worldwide and capital investments in excess of $100 million. Successfully negotiated $5+ billion contracts for products and services, and defined fixed pricing, project development strategy, integration, tests and deployment, payment planning, and vendor financing agreements.

This is an attractive, well-organized presentation for a senior executive. The checkmark bullet points subtly confirm his qualifications.

STUART G. MITCHELL
Page Two

PROFESSIONAL EXPERIENCE
continued

Boeing Aerospace; Seattle, WA   1986 – 1999
Director Procurement (1994 – 1999)
Manager Contracts and Subcontracts (1991 – 1994)
Division provides satellite systems, ground networks, and related products to the government and commercial markets worldwide. Directed a team of 80+ professionals with 8 management reports and a $1 billion procurement budget supporting $4 billion annual revenue. Successfully developed critical strategic partnerships with key corporations, which led to attractive new business opportunities and independent development projects exceeding $1 billion.

Strategic Partnerships – Contract Management – Operations Management
- Participated in proposal development strategies and structured the contract and subcontract agreements to maximize corporate profitability goals and objectives. Managed a team of 50+ contract and procurement personnel; responsible for contracts and subcontract agreements for large military satellite programs exceeding $4 billion.

- Established the division's organizational structure including staffing, strategic planning, and budget development to support multiple projects in a highly matrixed operation. Cost-cutting initiatives and improved efficiency systems resulted in an increase in bid approval, development of dedicated partnerships with state-of-the art technologies, and significantly lower equipment costs and pricing.

Early Management Career with Boeing Aerospace Corporation (1986 – 1991)
Managed team of 20 responsible for the material requirements, planning, and procurement for a major satellite project.

EDUCATION

California State University; Chico, CA
Bachelor of Science – Business Management
May 1980

DARRELL BLANKENSHIP

587 North Elm • Kansas City, Missouri 64111
816-555-1259 • Cell: 816-555-3592 • dblankenship@hotmail.com

CAREER PROFILE

Strategic Partner / Change Agent / Solutions Manager

Strong managerial, human relations and quantitative skills. Increasing responsibility in a multi-site, multi-product global manufacturing business. Experienced in establishing and modifying operational methods and processes by recommending changes in procedures, communications and information systems. Organized approach to accelerating the recognition of revenue. Develop and execute business and financial management strategies utilizing progressive technologies to increase profit margins. Function effectively in a matrix environment. Comfortable executing the tough decisions. Familiar with several operating systems, platforms and databases. APICS; CPIM (Certified in Production and Inventory Management). MBA - Keller Graduate School of Management.

PROFESSIONAL EXPERIENCE

BD INDUSTRIES   1997 – Present
Highly leveraged worldwide specialty steel manufacturer, headquartered in Kansas City, Missouri. Revenues of $1.5 billion+.
Manager of E-Business, Kansas City, Missouri (1999 – Present)
Promoted to Manager of E-Business after demonstrating abilities in strategic technology utilization. Charged with establishing a B2B strategy to bridge information systems between key operating divisions and customers. Collaborated closely with software consultants / providers to strategize methods to link dual information systems (self-educating on software and hardware requirements).

- Innovated format authorizing customers to "peer inside" manufacturing facility and enhance inventory management / forecasting, while alerting BD Industries to potential internal problems.
  - ➢ Armed with more information, customers grew dependent on BD Industries' reliability and delivery of product and, consequently, more loyal.
- Designed a centralized (intranet-based) purchasing function for all operations to exploit volume purchasing and discounting opportunities with global vendors.
- Spearheaded Internet-based reverse auction from concept to launch.
  - ➢ Goal was to obtain best price without negatively impacting quality or delivery.
  - ➢ **Immediate result: $425,000 savings** (10% per pound), 4th quarter.
- Directed consolidation of two geographically separate customer service groups.
  - ➢ Originated information system providing seamless view / single contact point to customer.
  - ➢ **Result:** Unified and reduced competition between manufacturing facilities.
- Instrumentally involved in organizational restructure, specifically the complete shutdown of $350MM Des Moines facility.
  - ➢ Interfaced closely with information technology, planning, and corporate sales groups.
  - ➢ **Objectives:** Convert all raw, semi-finished and finished goods inventories into cash; pinpoint lucrative business sourced from Des Moines and transfer to Kansas City, Missouri, facility; and establish a bare-essentials workforce.

Continued...

Bold type is used effectively throughout the resume to emphasize the really important information, the hard numbers.

DARRELL BLANKENSHIP

Page Two

PROFESSIONAL EXPERIENCE, *continued...*

Manager of Marketing, BD STEEL COMPANY, Des Moines, Iowa (1998–1999)
Customer Service Manager, BD COMPANY, Des Moines, Iowa (1997–1998)
Recruited to BD Steel to manage and increase shipments and reduce a 25,000-ton inventory. Maintained fiscal responsibility for a $1 million cost center. Directly supervised six employees on customer account team and held dotted-line responsibility over sales and production. Liaison between production planning, customer service and quality assurance, troubleshooting and resolving problems and streamlining procedures.

- **Reduced** on-hand finished goods **inventory from $6.5MM to $2.5MM** (25,000 tons to 8,500 tons) in 10 months. **Improved on-time delivery** performance **from 60% to 85%:**
  - ➤ Pioneered communications system involving daily sales and production reports; improved communications between customer account representatives and production planning.
  - ➤ Emplaced strict controls on order input side, including daily measurements.
    Result: Eliminated over-production.
  - ➤ Designed and implemented a decision tree to prioritize order fulfillment.
  - ➤ Created monthly shipping target for each customer.
  - ➤ Slashed workforce by 33% by improving automation / information systems processes.
- Instituted performance appraisal system reinforced by substantive rewards and accountability.
- Orchestrated 24 hour/7 day remote sales group access to guarantee answerability.
- Maximized monthly profit margin: Strategically scheduled 63,000 tons per month in customer orders; analyzed product mix and recommended improvements.
- Represented wire rod sales group in daily operational meetings with other department heads.

MAJOR STEEL SERVICE, Memphis, Tennessee   1996
$200MM in sales
Project Manager
- Led 13-week operations analysis from raw material through shipment at Chicago processing center (Chicago is accountable for shipping 60% of company's sales). **Result:** Recommended improvements to **reduce** non-value-added activities by **$600,000 per year.**
  - ➤ Conducted over 26 hours of face-to-face interviews with 35 corporate and production employees representing multiple functions; gathered and analyzed financial data.
  - ➤ Presented results to CEO and Executive Committee, identifying process-improvement areas.
    Recommendation: Implement a structured production scheduling system to reduce machine downtime, eliminate bottlenecks and reduce over-production.

BENSINGTON FINANCIAL CORPORATION, Chicago, Illinois   1992 – 1995
Investment Counselor (1993 – 1995) • **Residential Loan Officer** (1992 – 1993)
- Implemented sales and marketing strategy, offering a comprehensive investment product line and consultative services to individuals and small companies; formulated competitive advantages.

EDUCATION

KELLER GRADUATE SCHOOL OF MANAGEMENT, Northwestern University, Chicago, Illinois
Master of Business Administration, 1997

BALL STATE UNIVERSITY, Muncie, Indiana
Bachelor of Arts in Political Science, 1992

Albert D. Beck

6482 E. Thoroughbred Drive
Tempe, Arizona 85284
(480) 735-2336 ● Albeck@uswest.net

CONTRACT MANAGEMENT

- Contract Manager with MBA and 20+ years of experience managing complex contracts, licenses, and agreements for DOD and OEM customers.
- Lead and conduct negotiations for cost-plus, fixed-price, and incentive contracts.
- Demonstrated leadership and ability to obtain optimum performance from professionals at all levels.
- Expertise in leading multi-functional teams.
- Excellent interpersonal, analytical, and problem-solving abilities.
- Completed Six Sigma Green Belt Certification — 11/99.
- Computer skills include Microsoft Word, Excel, and PowerPoint.

PROFESSIONAL EXPERIENCE

SPERRY-RAND, INC., Mesa, Arizona — 1984 to Present
Contract Manager, Systems Division — 1998 to Present
Manage 25 cost-plus engineering and technology contracts. Report to Director—Contracts.

- Proposal team leader for AGT1500 tank engine proposal, including offsets, for international customer.
- Project leader coordinating technical support for U.S. Army's tank engine depot overhaul program.
- Negotiated restructure of $20 million UNIJASU contract with U.S. Navy to resolve technical problems and complete development phase.
- Developed procedure that simplified and improved efficiency of standard closeout process.
- Chosen for special team charged with improving closeout of completed contracts. Met current goal 60 days before target date.

Business Manager, Engines / Auxiliary Power — 1993 to 1998
- Managed all business activities related to engine development and production.
- Hands-on experience in proposal preparation, contract administration, pricing activity, and development of acquisition strategies.
- Acted on behalf of Program Manager, as required, in day-to-day business dealings with customers, including U.S. government and airframe manufacturers.
- Department lead for several major programs including F/A-18 aircraft and AH-64 Apache/Longbow helicopters.

Senior Contract Manager, Crown Auxiliary Power Division — 1988 to 1993
- Managed contracts for both R&D and production of auxiliary power units for Government programs.
- Developed unique financial terms for J-Stars contract for development of APU that included complex cost-sharing contract terms.
- Team leader for five contracting professionals.

Needing a resume to apply for a promotion, this individual decided to test the waters at other aerospace companies as well. His old resume dealt primarily with duties and responsibilities, ignoring his contributions and his recent, desirable Six Sigma certification.

Albert D. Beck

Page 2

PROFESSIONAL EXPERIENCE

continued

Contract Manager, Crown Turbine Engine Company — 1984 to 1988
- Managed multiple R&D contracts with U.S. Government and subcontracts with major airframe manufacturers.
- Led negotiation team during source selection of $32 million NASA ceramic component development contract.

GOVERNMENT EXPERIENCE — 1972 to 1984
U.S. Air Force, Davis-Monthan Air Force Base, Arizona
- Managed in-plant representatives of DOD, ensuring compliance with government contracts by major aerospace companies. Conducted "Should Cost" reviews, schedule and performance reviews, and surveillance of quality assurance, subcontract management, and cost reporting.

U.S. Air Force, Bishop Engineering Development Center, Tennessee
- Contracted for and administered large cost-plus award-fee service contracts. Chief negotiator for source selection; contract value $125 million annually.

U.S. Air Force, Lackland Air Force Base, Texas
- Supported acquisition of B-1 development and initial production program. Led team of negotiators during restructure of B-1 contract. Planned and organized source selection of the concept definition phase for major missile program. Hands-on purchasing of services and sole source systems contracts.

EDUCATION / PROFESSIONAL DEVELOPMENT

Master of Business Administration, Pacific Coast University, San Francisco, California
Bachelor of Science, Business/Marketing, University of California, Los Angeles (UCLA)

Professional Development
- Sperry-Rand PM201 — Advanced Program Management Training
- NCMA One-Day Training Seminar, "The Contract Professional as a Business Manager"

MEMBERSHIPS

- National Contract Management Association
- Air Force Association

ARNOLD J. CRESSMAN, CSP

1717 Johnston Terrace Lane
Milwaukee, Wisconsin 55876
Phone: 414-449-9909
Email: ajc@rudder.net

SENIOR CORPORATE SAFETY & HEALTH EXECUTIVE
Occupational Medicine / Industrial Hygiene / Risk Management / Regulatory Compliance

Led development and implementation of advanced Safety, Health, and Risk Management programs for leaders in the manufacturing, aerospace, and hazardous waste industries. Credited with creating industry-leading programs that delivered multimillion-dollar cost savings while minimizing liability exposure.

Professional Credentials:

MBA Degree in Operations Management
MA Degree in Occupational Health & Safety
Certified Safety Professional (CSP)

PROFESSIONAL EXPERIENCE:

Director – Safety, Health & Risk Management   1992 to Present
ELSONI ENVIRONMENTAL, INC., Newark, Delaware

Senior Safety, Industrial Hygiene, Occupational Medicine & Risk Management Executive for the largest full-service hazardous waste treatment and disposal company in the U.S. Scope of responsibility includes 13 wholly owned companies operating 45 sites in 18 states nationwide, a professional staff of 15, and an $8 million annual operating budget.

Credited with the conceptualization, design, development, implementation, and leadership of the most effective and cost-efficient approach to total regulatory compliance and safety excellence. Concurrent responsibility for management oversight of DOT compliance and technical training programs nationwide.

- Formally recognized by Elsoni Environmental president and CEO for outstanding achievements.

- Revitalized the entire safety and health organization, restaffed with talented professionals, and reduced cost of non-compliance (property loss, EPA/OSHA fines, legal expenses, and worker's compensation) from a high of $4.1 million in 1992 to less than $350,000 in 1998.

- Reduced serious injuries and decreased lost workday cases by 70% and total worker's compensation costs by $550,000.

- Standardized national safety, health, and risk management policy, operating procedures, and practices for incineration, site remediation, hazardous waste landfill, and chemical treatment operations.

- Created/directed an annual safety and health systems audit program to assess legislative compliance, operations controls, and site compliance with corporate safety and health policy.

- Directed process safety and occupational health risk assessments for mergers and acquisitions.

Division Manager – Safety, Health & Environmental Compliance   1983 to 1992
WESTINGHOUSE AEROSPACE CORPORATION, Pittsburgh, Pennsylvania

Senior Safety & Health Manager for the $800 million Aerospace Division. Directed a staff of 7 safety, process engineering, and industrial hygiene professionals and 2 occupational health physicians. Managed annual operating and capital budgets in excess of $2 million.

This is a classic executive resume for an experienced safety and health professional. Experience is summarized relatively briefly, with most attention being given to valuable accomplishments.

ARNOLD J. CRESSMAN, CSP   *Page Two*

Challenged to expand and strengthen systems safety, hazards analysis, industrial hygiene, and regulatory compliance functions; reduce costs associated with workplace safety and employee health; and establish Westinghouse as the industry's safety leader. Concurrently, oversaw and audited safety and health process operations for assembly of solid rocket boosters to shuttle orbiter and post-launch retrieval.

- Delivered strong and sustainable improvements in the Division's safety organization. Implemented controls that reduced occupational injuries and illnesses by 40% within a 5-year period for a total cost savings of $1.5 million.

- Developed and implemented process safety, industrial hygiene, and environmental compliance protocols for handling, manufacturing, and disposal of high-hazard explosives and pyrotechnic materials. Expert knowledge of Department of Defense statutes, rules, and regulations.

- Designed procedures and standardized techniques for the review and evaluation of health, physical, and environmental hazards associated with the design, production, and static testing of solid rocket-propulsion systems for space and tactical applications.

- Performed detailed risk analysis studies to evaluate the effects of over pressures and fragmentation from detonation events. Studies were utilized to develop corporate-wide construction specifications, locate adjacent facilities, and establish operational limits and controls.

- Provided expert testimony on legal issues involving chemical exposures, detonation characteristics, and occupational injuries and illnesses.

- Honored with the 1991 Department of Defense Total Quality Safety Award and 1992 President's Award for Safety Excellence from the National Safety Council.

Regional Safety & Industrial Hygiene Manager   1979 to 1983
MERCK, SHARP & DOHME, Dallas, Texas

Management oversight for planning, development, and operations of Safety and Industrial Hygiene for 16 diversified industrial chemcial manufacturing facilities throughout U.S. Directed a professional staff of 12.

Research Industrial Hygienist   1977 to 1979
U.S. DEPARTMENT OF ENERGY, Sky Cliff, New Jersey

Appointed by U.S. Department of Energy to serve on 18-month task force to develop instrumentation criteria for accessing the health and environmental hazards associated with the emerging synthetic fuels industry.

EDUCATION:

MBA (Operations Management), 1995
WILMINGTON COLLEGE – GRADUATE SCHOOL OF BUSINESS ADMINISTRATION

MA (Occupational Safety & Health), 1979
RUTGERS UNIVERSITY – GRADUATE SCHOOL OF PUBLIC HEALTH

BS, NEW YORK UNIVERSITY, 1977

PROFESSIONAL PROFILE:

Certifications   • Certified Safety Professional (Board of Certified Safety Professionals)
                            • Radiation Safety Officer – University of Michigan

Affiliations   • American Society of Safety Engineers
                            • International Pyrotechnics Society
                            • American Industrial Hygiene Association

MALCOLM P. NOONAN

624 Avenue "F"
Salt Lake City, Utah 84103

Home (801) 555-6487
Mobile (801) 555-6688

Pager (888) 555-4477
mpnoonan@qwest.net

OPERATING & MANAGEMENT PROFESSIONAL

Expert in Organizational Effectiveness ▪ Operations Management
Corporate Training & Development ▪ Productivity/Performance Improvement

Results-driven professional with 10 years' experience providing senior-level business management consulting. Excellent problem-solving skills and a strong orientation in customer service/satisfaction. Able to work under pressure in fast-paced, time-sensitive environments. Experienced in identifying and streamlining safety/production bottlenecks, performing statistical analysis to distinguish trends, and devising strategic/tactical plans. Proven ability to motivate, empower, and lead cross-functional teams. Effective public speaker and training facilitator. MBA degree.

- Turnaround Management
- Statistical Process Control
- Cost Reduction/Control
- Workforce Management
- Business & Leadership Development
- Organizational & Policy Development
- Corporate Vision & Planning
- Occupational Health & Safety
- Total Quality Management
- Participative Management
- Corporate Culture Change
- Team Building & Leadership

PROFESSIONAL EXPERIENCE

ACCLAIM INSURANCE COMPANY, Salt Lake City, Utah   1994-Present
Worker's compensation specialty carrier writing insurance in 38 states; $400 million in annual revenues.

Senior Safety & Health Consultant
Evaluate risk to determine loss potential and management interest, support, and degree of commitment. Manage 80+ technically demanding accounts, including multimillion-dollar organizations, across the country in manufacturing, contracting, printing/publishing, farming, and ski resorts.

Consult with all levels of management to analyze loss trends, make recommendations, set goals, and follow up to ensure success. Counsel upper level management in worker's compensation issues, including experience modification factors, claims frequency/severity, loss ratios, and profit margin impact. Train and direct safety and health staff, underwriters, claims processors, and producers.

➢ Instrumental in developing and marketing new branch, helping to generate premiums of $3.7 million over 4 years in highly competitive mono-line insurance market and making Salt Lake City the company's most profitable branch and Acclaim the third largest worker's compensation provider in Utah.

➢ Assisted branch manager in expanding business to Idaho, Colorado, Arizona, and Nevada by building relationships with insurance agents and agencies.

➢ Key contributor to cost/benefit analysis of Acclaim's Safety & Health Services, helping to prevent 177 indemnity claims valued at more than $2.8 million.

➢ Developed safety and incentive programs, including Ergonomic, Drug Testing, Hazard Communication, LockOut/TagOut, Respiratory Protection, Confined Space, Forklift, and Safety Awareness.

➢ Streamlined consulting process by devising and implementing a Safety Program Evaluation procedure to identify methods to reduce workplace injuries.

This individual was seeking an operations management/organizational effectiveness position with a major manufacturer.

MALCOLM P. NOONAN   Page Two

> Motivated clients to adopt improved safety and health programs through focus on costs, profits, and benefits of employee education rather than emphasizing technical knowledge and OSHA standards.

> Improved inter-office employee efficiency, equaling $448,000 in-force premiums per employee, almost double the rate of Acclaim's closest market competitor.

> Prepared and presented financial data on workers' compensation costs and operating/profit margins to union management and steering committees on behalf of Browning Winchester Arms Company.

> Wrote, directed, and produced English/Spanish farm safety video, *Harvesting Lives Through Safety*, for Idaho potato growers, focusing on farming equipment, machine guarding, and related hazards.

> Analyzed safety concerns and past trends, set goals for improvement, and motivated insured clients to take corrective actions. Achieved notable success with Sundance Catalogue Company, improving experience modification factor to achieve worker's compensation premium decrease of 84%.

WALLACE CAMPBELL, Salt Lake City, Utah   1992-1994
International multi-line insurance brokerage company.

Director of Safety & Loss Control Services

> Developed national guidelines to oversee insurance carrier/client interactions. Organized client/carrier action plans, including inspections, training, and claim reviews.

> Created and presented standard-setting national program to train loss control representatives in ergonomics, detailing medical terminology, repetitive motion injuries, risk factors, and control measures.

WORKER'S COMPENSATION FUND, Salt Lake City, Utah   1989-1992
Safety and Loss Prevention Representative

UNIVERSITY OF TEXAS, Austin, Texas   1988-1989
Assistant Safety Trainer

EDUCATION

Master of Business Administration
Westminster College, Salt Lake City, Utah, 1998

Bachelor of Science in Occupational Safety & Health
University of Texas, Austin, Texas, 1988

CERTIFICATIONS

Occupational Ergonomics Certificate, University of Michigan, 1997
Advanced Safety Certificate, National Safety Council, 1994
Certified First Aid/CPR Instructor, National Safety Council, current

AFFILIATIONS

American Society of Safety Engineers, 1993-Present
Coalition for Utah Traffic Safety (CUTS), 1994-Present
Utah Highway Safety Office, 1994-Present

JANICE A. SORENSEN

709 Eastern Drive ▪ Grandview, Missouri 64134

JAS432@email.com   (816) 555-1212

MANAGEMENT PROFILE

Risk Management / Certified Safety Instructor

Customer Retention ▪ Staff Training ▪ Loss Control ▪ Customer Service ▪ Mediation

Proactive **Manager** driving customer loyalty initiatives with creative and pragmatic problem-solving. Proven results in identifying, controlling, and managing risk. Effective mediator between management and labor union personnel. Skilled in development and delivery of high-impact training programs in diverse learning environments. Expertise in worker's compensation issues. PC proficient in MS Office.

PROFESSIONAL EXPERIENCE

HARRIS DISTRIBUTION, INC., Lenexa, Kansas   July 1978 to Present
National $15 billion wholesale grocery distributor operating in 40 states

⊟ Loss Control / Security Manager, 1993 to Present

Supervise salvage operation including the disposal and/or sale of products, plus setting prices and interfacing with salvage dealers. Oversee handling of security issues and guard activities. Establish and administer policies regarding credits, shrink losses, product and damage controls. Resolve customer complaints referred from service department. Maintain communication with retailers, vendors, drivers, and merchants. Assist with presenting driver-training programs. Ensure customer satisfaction by performing store site visits, as needed. Coordinate facility safety issues with local fire department as part of company Emergency Response Plan. Interact and cooperate with drug enforcement agencies for facility inspections. Represent department in union disputes concerning security, theft, and past worker's compensation cases. Supervise three staff and direct billing department activities of seven. Act as Facilities Manager in absence of department head.

- Increased recoup salvage dollars by $150 thousand in 1999.
- Reduced truck short losses $25 thousand over company plan in 1998 ($51 thousand more than previous year) by establishing strict accountability programs.
- Decreased worker compensation claims from 300 lost days to only 50 in 18-month period.
- Developed HAACP (Hazard Analysis and Critical Control Points) program in direct response to FDA-imposed food safety requirement.
- Achieved employee approval ranking in 90th percentile with corporate-sponsored peer review survey completed by all company employees.
- Successfully mediated major worker's compensation cases with labor union representatives.

⊟ Customer Service Coordinator, 1991 to 1993

Assisted customers through entire service delivery process. Solved problems, wrote credits, and visited client sites. Informed new customers of credit policies. Advised managers of critical and recurring problems. Worked closely with transportation and warehouse managers. Maintained 99% customer satisfaction rate.

Continued on Page 2

This individual had worked for only one employer her entire life. Due to an unexpected layoff, she had to learn quickly how to sell her potential. The resume helped boost her confidence.

Page 2, Janice A. Sorensen   (816) 555-1212

Merchandising Secretary, 1986 to 1991

Supported department manager in activities related to merchandising, ad plans, and customer service. Handled confidential information for retailers. Participated in planning retail trips.

Planning Secretary, 1984 to 1986

Contributed to planning of new store openings and store resets. Ordered equipment, shelving units, and supplies. Processed initial product orders and returned overstock.

Department Secretary, 1979 to 1984

Tracked product orders and wrote credit memos. Received telemarketing orders from customers. Performed general clerical duties including routing clerical assignments and scheduling training.

Merchandising Clerk, 1978 to 1979

Provided clerical support to office personnel by filing, answering phones, and telemarketing.

EDUCATION

Bachelor of Science, Business Administration, Washburn University, Topeka, Kansas

CONTINUING PROFESSIONAL DEVELOPMENT

Certified Safety Instructor

Introduction to OSHA Standards, Acorn Community College, Lenexa, Kansas

Leadership Management for Women, Fred Pryor Seminars, Lenexa, Kansas

Process Safety Management (PSM), study course completed through correspondence

Company-paid training courses: *Leadership Management Styles, Management Principles, Excellence in Customer Service,* and *Safety Courses I, II, III, IV*

COMMUNITY INVOLVEMENT

Volunteer & Participant, Multiple Sclerosis Walk-A-Thon, 3 years

Volunteer & Participant, March of Dimes Walk-A-Thon, 3 years

Volunteer Youth Leader, Boy Scouts of America, 5 years

PAUL JAMES

374 WILLOW WAY ◆ KALAMAZOO, MI 49007
HOME: 616.320.6667 ◆ MOBILE: 616.321.7957 ◆ E-MAIL: pjames@aol.com

SENIOR COST PLANNER

Solutions-driven, high-performance industrial cost planner with 6 years' experience interpreting design feasibility and performing strategic cost analysis for a Fortune 500 automobile component manufacturer that supplies major automakers in the United States, Canada, and Japan. Demonstrated achievement in completing projects accurately and on time. Recognized for results-oriented approaches to improve the accuracy of existing cost systems or facilitate the development of new cost systems in support of company goals. Respected advisor to executive operating, management, and financial teams. Proven proficiency in teambuilding, productivity/efficiency gain, quality, and resource maximization. Experienced in training and developing a strong, cohesive cost-planning staff. Expert organizational, leadership, and communication skills. Recognized for high degree of self-confidence, integrity, and strong commitment to excellence. Complete knowledge of foreign currency exchange rates. Bilingual English/Spanish. Highly proficient with Microsoft Office Suite. Specific areas of expertise include:

◆ Cost Analyses	◆ VA/VE Activities	◆ Kaizen Activity
◆ Standard Costs	◆ Sales Expansion	◆ Strategic Analysis
◆ Profitability Improvement	◆ Quality Performance & Improvement	◆ Cost & Profit Management

PROFESSIONAL EXPERIENCE

AMES Manufacturing Michigan, Inc., Grand Rapids, Michigan   **1994 – Present**
(Subsidiary of AMES Corp., Ltd., one of the world's largest tier-one manufacturers of automotive heating and cooling systems with $8 billion in total annual sales.)

Advanced Cost Specialist with full responsibility for performing strategic cost analysis for the manufacture of automotive components from start up of initial prototypes to time of mass production. Successfully conduct price negotiations with the company's sales office leading to agreement on optimum sales price for products. Estimate costs of design changes in product components, providing essential information to executives involved in the decision-making process. Effectively negotiate import/export fees between AMES Michigan and AMES' overseas affiliates. Research and analyze design specifications and, based on results, recommend ways to minimize costs in the manufacturing process and subsequently reduce the cost of the finished product. Assist the business-planning department in the development of annual, revised annual, and long-term profit plans to reach company goals.

Notable Achievements:

◆ Worked closely with engineering and sales departments during major sales expansion initiative that increased company sales from approximately $500 million in 1994 to over $1 billion in 2000. Superior cost-planning expertise was credited with bringing four topflight customer contracts (Ford Motor Company, Dodge, Toyota of America, and Toyota of Canada) to AMES Michigan, generating $150 million in additional sales over the past two years.

◆ Effectively directed a company-wide Profit Improvement Activity (PIA) for products with low profitability margins. Presented specific targets to the related PIA groups and tracked each product achievement target until start of mass production. Efforts resulted in a cost savings of $5 million per year.

This straightforward, information-packed presentation for an experienced cost planner clearly identifies notable achievements. The formatting is crisp and attractive.

PAUL JAMES   PAGE 2

PROFESSIONAL EXPERIENCE (CONT.)

AMES Manufacturing Michigan, Inc. (cont.)

Notable Achievements:

♦ Assisted Information Systems in conceptualizing and ultimately creating a Preliminary Information Request (PIR) program (a PC-based online approval system). This automated operational form allowed for efficient and rapid communication between design, engineering, purchasing, and business planning departments and significantly improved service levels and efficiency (processing time was reduced from 10 to 3 days, a 300% increase in efficiency).

♦ Co-directed a project to improve fixed-asset accounting that ultimately led to the development of a new policy and procedure manual and enhanced communications among purchasing, engineering, production, and maintenance departments. This project produced fixed-asset reports that contained more accurate and useful information.

♦ Created innovative, user-friendly financial reports that concisely outlined the profitability of each product, model, and total system package. These enhanced reports made it possible for Japanese and American auto executives to have a better understanding of each product's profitability results and financial position.

CorpBank Computer Services, Lansing, Michigan
(A Midwest-based financial holding company with assets approaching $90 billion.)

Credit Analyst in charge of providing commercial customers with proven understanding of credit operations to help them meet their credit objectives. Demonstrated understanding of all commercial credit functions including the preparation of written analysis of commercial credits and the identification of potential credit risks as revealed on customer applications.

Notable Achievements:

♦ Recognized as an expert in analyzing and processing commercial credit applications. Exceptional skills resulted in a 15% increase in application approval rates.

♦ Specially selected to assess a state-of-the-art, Windows-based computer system for use in the credit department. Opinions and recommendations led to the eventual replacement of the outdated system with the improved Windows system. Implementation of the new system significantly improved the ability of the department to manage and process information and reduced staffing requirements.

EDUCATION

B.S., Business Administration (Finance and General Business), 1993
GRAND VALLEY STATE UNIVERSITY, Grand Rapids, Michigan

Continuing Professional Education in cost estimation, Nagoya, Japan, 1999
Intensive 3-week–long, company-sponsored program that included training in new product introduction methods (sales expansion), advanced cost table development and usage, and cost estimation and design of next-generation automotive components.

RESUME 74: MEG MONTFORD, CCM, CPRW; KANSAS CITY, MO

CARMEN L. ANDERSON

4536 Maple Lane, Kansas City, Missouri 64111
CLAnder48@kc.rr.com
(816) 555-1212

ACCOUNTING MANAGER / CONTROLLER / OFFICE MANAGER

Financial Reporting ... Job Costing ... Payroll ... Analysis ... Cash Flow ... Accounting Software

Dedicated **Accounting Manager** promoting internal culture change initiatives to enhance profitability. Creative and pragmatic problem-solver with proven ability to meet deadlines while working in high stress situations. Trainer, coach, and mentor of staff. Computer proficient in Tech Gap (UNIX-based accounting solutions software), Quattro Pro, and Excel. Conscientious and loyal self-starter who consistently produces results.

CAREER HIGHLIGHTS

- Chosen Employee of the Month for outstanding customer service and expert staff training methods.
- Received annual Achievement Award for exemplary service and dedication.
- Researched, advocated, and coordinated installation of phone/voice mail system providing improved technical support and customer service.
- Recommended and supervised computer conversion that simplified software solutions for processes in manufacturing, construction, and distribution.
- Trained staff on use of new equipment introduced into work environment.
- Met special deadline of closing year-end books and providing preliminary schedule within two days.

PROFESSIONAL EXPERIENCE

CAPITAL COUNTERS, INC., Kansas City, Missouri   1973 to Present
Kansas City-based manufacturer and installer of kitchen counter tops.

Controller 1999 to Present	Direct staff in daily, monthly, and annual accounting operations. Prepare all journal entries and financial statements. Organize year-end audit schedules, coordinating with audit firm. Analyze general ledger accounts. Process W-2s, quarterly commissions, and quarterly payroll reports. Provide informational reports and make recommendations to management.
Challenge......................	Analyze and resolve discrepancies identified from three-year audit of all purchases, sales, and payroll.
Action.........................	Reviewed each audit item by scrutinizing purchases, jobs, and tax exemption certificates. Researched problem areas, defending rationales to auditor and negotiating solutions.
Result	Reduced company tax liability, partly due to longstanding relationship with audit tax bureau. Commended by management for tenacity and thorough handling of situation.

Continued on page 2

To avoid repetition of accounting job duties, the resume writer approached this project from the CAR (challenge-action-result) perspective and included career highlights up front so they wouldn't be overlooked.

Page 2, Carmen L. Anderson   (816) 555-1212

Accounting / Office Manager   Supervised staff in preparing financial statements, year-end
1980 to 1999   audits, collections, payroll, bank reconciliation, account analysis,
                                  sales tax audits, and office equipment purchases. Served as
                                  computer administrator.

Challenge......................   Implement direct-deposit payroll system, despite employee
                                  resistance, when company was chosen as test site for new
                                  software.

Action..........................   Coordinated system installation with software vendor and bank,
                                  consulting state on legal requirements. Conducted employee
                                  meetings to communicate facts and justification for new system.

Result ....   *Resolved concerns of* initially *non-supportive hourly employees,
                                  paving way for smooth transition. Identified and recommended
                                  system improvements to software vendor that were accepted and
                                  instituted for all users.*

General Accounting Manager   Supervised staff of four in handling accounting processes.
1978 to 1980   Assisted with financial statements. Prepared journal entries,
                                  payroll, bank reconciliations, year-end audit, and sales/use tax
                                  audits. Collected past-due accounts.

General Accounting Clerk   Processed accounts payable, accounts receivable, payroll,
1976 to 1978   fixed assets, prepaid expenses, insurance, and worker's
                                  compensation claims reports.

Accounts Payable Clerk   Prepared voucher packets and processed checks.
1973 to 1976

EDUCATION

Park College, Kansas City, Missouri
Bachelor's degree program, 39 credit hours completed in upper-level accounting courses

Maplewoods Community College, Kansas City, Missouri
Associate in Applied Science, Certificate in Accounting

CONTINUING PROFESSIONAL DEVELOPMENT

- Fred Pryor Seminars on leadership, sales, management, presentation, and effective
  communication
- Computer training through computer vendor

COMMUNITY INVOLVEMENT

Harding High School Booster Club, Kansas City, Missouri, Treasurer, 3 years
Harding School Board Liaison, Audit and Scholarship Committees, Member, 2 years
Boy Scouts of America, Troop 123 Mothers Club, Member, 10 years

- Recipient of Silver Acorn, highest award for any non-scout, 1999
- Social Chair, Eagle Award Receptions

RESUME 75: JANE ROQUEPLOT, CBC; SHARON, PA

DENISE HAMILTON

304.555.7815

9703 Johnsonville Road • Alderson, West Virginia 24910

CAREER PROFILE: OFFICE MANAGEMENT SPECIALIST

➤ Accomplished leader and manager with exceptional organizational skills; project oriented; work effectively under pressure and stress. Identify problems/needs and initiate effective solutions. Thrive on challenges.

➤ Promote working environment/procedures conducive to improving productivity, increasing efficiency, enhancing quality, and strengthening financial results. Knowledgeable in certification process of ISO 9001:2000 standards.

➤ Motivated to work efficiently without direct supervision in busy environment, handling many tasks simultaneously; able to prioritize workload and multi-task. Consistently "get the job done" and exceed expectations.

➤ Dynamic communication/interpersonal skills and a team player; interact positively with a wide range of people and establish relationships based on respect. Generate spirit of enthusiasm in personnel, prompting ready implementation of recommended processes.

➤ Computer proficiency on Windows platforms (3.11, 95/98 and NT) includes Microsoft Word, Excel, Outlook Express, PowerPoint, Internet communications and research, File Manager. Also knowledgeable in operations of various e-mail and voice mail systems.

PROFESSIONAL EMPLOYMENT

Allied Tubular Division, Bethlehem Steel Corp. — Bethlehem, West Virginia   **1986 – Present**

MANAGER – CUSTOMER SERVICE, SCHEDULING, WAREHOUSE, SHIPPING *(1996 – Present)*

• Key player in certification process for ISO 9001:2000 Quality System. Documented customer service order entry and complaint procedures; ensured Quality Policy as detailed by management is understood by department staff. Spearhead plans for continuous improvement of processes in the short, medium, and long term.

• Designed and established a model, more efficient inventory system. Pioneered and implemented plan for maintaining proper inventory mix. Achieved 30% inventory reduction yet eliminated stock outs.

• Spearheaded development of an order-tracking system, enhancing on-time delivery performance from 80% to 99%.

• Implemented a "low value" complaint system. Improved complaint resolution by reducing cost of processing these claims, which resulted in improved customer service.

• Received written commendations from company president (2000) and vice president of sales/marketing (1998) for exceptional performance on special project teams.

CUSTOMER SERVICE SUPERVISOR *(1988 – 1996)*

• Streamlined order-entry system and improved accuracy of documentation, reducing shipping and order entry errors. Facilitated improved communication among departments.

• Restructured department and instituted training program to cross-train staff, improving efficiency and professionalism of entire department. Consistently received high praise from customers, vendors, and even competitors for being the best in the industry.

• Oversaw transition to computer-based access to workload, production, and shipping schedules. Significantly revitalized accuracy of schedules and documentation and reduced shipping-production errors.

• Scheduled regular training for staff to increase their product knowledge, thereby enabling them to better serve customers vendors. Other workshops covered topics such as effective listening/speaking skills, problem resolution, techniques in professional customer service, etc.

This resume is chock-full of significant accomplishments, measurable results, and contributions to the bottom line.

DENISE HAMILTON, 304.555.7815
Page 2

Allied Tubular Division, Bethlehem Steel Corp., *continued*
CUSTOMER SERVICE REPRESENTATIVE *(1986 – 1988)*

- Originated customized order intake process to meet customers' specific ordering needs, improving delivery performance and optimizing customer satisfaction.
- Recommended and implemented revisions to shipping documents to enhance accuracy and efficient utilization of documents.
- Competently handled complex quotations from customers and sales personnel.

Domino Tube Company — Griffith Creek, West Virginia   **1984 – 1986**
CUSTOMER SERVICE / INSIDE SALES REP / TRAFFIC SUPERVISOR

- Provided product information, pricing, quotations and delivery information to customers. Displayed professionalism and product knowledge, which contributed to an increase in inquiry-to-order capture rate.
- Expedited shipments to comply with special customer delivery remarks; dispatched carriers in manner to ensure on-time deliveries. Created goodwill and improved customer satisfaction.

Elkins Castings Division, Midvalley Steel Corp. — Clayton, West Virginia   **1973 – 1984**
TRAFFIC / INSIDE SALES / CUSTOMER SERVICE / PRODUCTION PLANNING

Trained and made significant contributions in numerous departments of organization: logistics, sales, customer support, production.

PROFESSIONAL ORGANIZATIONS

Association of Women in the Metal Industry (AWMI), Wheeling Chapter   **1987 – present**
- Membership Chairperson, 1993–1995
- Conference Committee, 1990
- Member, Founding Board of Directors National Organization — 12,000 members
- Fundraising Chairperson, 1990
- Board Member, 1987–1989

American Business Women's Association, Brighton Chapter   **1998 – present**
- Member of Scholarship Committee
- Co-chair of Business Associates of the Year Committee
- Member of Fundraising Committee

EDUCATION / CONTINUING EDUCATION

Certificate, Leadership and Supervisory Skills for Women — Bethany College

Certificate, Exceptional Customer Service Seminar — Fred Pryor Seminars

American Business Women's Association workshops:
- Microsoft Project
- Superior Service on the Telephone
- Effective Coaching
- Making Small Talk a Big Deal
- Managing E-mail
- Art of Facilitation
- Manage Multiple Projects and Meet Deadlines
- Constructive Criticism
- Everyday Business Etiquette

Certificate, Materials Processing
Steel Technology, 1989–1990, Marshall University — Huntington, West Virginia

Bachelor of Science Degree, with Honors
St. Francis University — Lorreto, Pennsylvania

Business Coursework
Seton Hill College — Greensburg, Pennsylvania

Thomas R. Street

914-991-2229
seniorexec@email.com

2238 Hanging Pine Avenue • Yonkers, NY 10543

SENIOR MANAGEMENT EXECUTIVE

**Project Management Methodology ... Cross-Functional Technology Teams ... Process Definition
Computer Architecture ... Software Development ... Telecommunications Technology**

Dynamic management professional skilled in utilizing cutting-edge technology in the design, budgeting, and delivery of advanced systems and applications. Successful in selecting and leading cross-functional teams working cohesively to develop and integrate technologies to support broad-ranging operating, financial, and organizational needs.

TECHNICAL EXPERTISE

Satellite-Delivered Broadband Systems
Object-Oriented Techniques
Accelerated Life Testing
Systems Integration and Testing

Real-Time Software Development
Cellular Communications Systems
Computer-Aided Design
Wireless Application Protocol (WAP)

CAREER EXPERIENCE

NOKIA, INC., New York, New York —Since 1985
(*A global leader providing integrated communications solutions and embedded electronic solutions*)

Software Development Manager — 1998 to Present
Custom Satellite Products (Ground Systems Division)

Selected to lead a 17-person team integrating Internet access and satellite wireless technology, with full P&L responsibility for a $3 million budget. Oversee strategic planning and implementation; develop technical designs, architecture, and general product definitions.

➤ Executed plans and forged external relationships. Team project is on schedule and within budget to meet company goals.

Manager, Iridium SV Factory Test — 1996 to 1998
Space Payload Integration and Test (Satellite Communications Division)

Spearheaded project developing and supporting testing of space satellites on a 24x7 basis. Created first-ever assembly-line process, which produced an unprecedented new satellite every 5 days.

➤ Saved the company an estimated $5 million annually by initiating and implementing an efficient testing process.

Manager, Software Development — 1993 to 1996
EPIDIGM™ Systems and Software / SATCOM (Government & Space Technology Division)

Personally selected members of the software team charged with developing a ground-based system-test environment for a space-based cellular communication system. Directed the original system control segment integration and test plan and implemented quality plans.

➤ Received team recognition by the company for completing the project on time and under budget.

➤ Selected to serve as a key member of the SEI evaluation team charged with measuring the maturity of its internal software organizations.

The Technical Expertise section is important on this resume for a senior technical manager. A chrono-logical work history follows, emphasizing strong achievements.

Thomas R. Street	Page 2	914-991-2229

CAREER EXPERIENCE (continued)

NOKIA COMPUTER SYSTEMS
Manager, Engineering Development Services — 1992 to 1993

Selected to oversee quality control and provide regulatory services for computer products; directed CAD functions for new product development. Full P&L responsibility for a $3 million budget.

➤ Ensured timely delivery of quality products and customer satisfaction and loyalty.

Manager, Specials Development — 1991 to 1992
Technical Systems Division

Conceived, created, and managed the development of non-standard computer systems for OEM and technical users, with a focus on software development, sales, product definition, customer satisfaction, and product quality.

➤ Realized a highly-profitable ROA of 2000 times the cost of production.

Senior Product Manager, Special Systems — 1986 to 1991
Manager, Communications Software Development — 1985

EDUCATION

Bachelor of Science, Computer Science
New York University, New York, NY

PROFESSIONAL DEVELOPMENT

40 hours annually including …
Negotiating for a Positive Outcome
Software Process Management
Six Sigma Development
Nokia Management Institute
Team Leadership Topics
Project Management
Managing for Reality: Accountable Leadership
Developing Quality Software
Various technical classes from "Object-Oriented Development Methods" to "ATM Concepts"

COMMUNITY ACTIVITIES

Board of Directors, Yonkers League for the Arts
Chairman, Yonkers Culinary Festival

CHARLES REGAN
MANUFACTURING EXECUTIVE

FINANCE • NETWORK ADMINISTRATION • OPERATIONS • MARKETING

Over 15 years of executive and core management team experience in manufacturing and distribution with
Mohawk Industries, Inc., and Linux Cable Corp.

Skilled in multi-company/multi-division manufacturing oversight of fiscal, credit, information management, human resources, risk management, marketing, and warehouse/distribution operations. Manage LAN and WAN infrastructures. Early pioneer in practical applications of mainframe and PC systems.

In all positions, have held broad responsibilities ranging far beyond job title. Extremely resourceful and committed to excellence. Adapt to change without interruption, assessing needs and devising detailed solutions. Have been described as a well-respected and high-achieving leader, technician, troubleshooter, negotiator, educator, and listener — proactive, quick learning, energetic, humorous, and honest. Possess outstanding across-the-board communication and presentation abilities.

MANUFACTURING-RELATED EXPERTISE

Computer Operations • Software Design • LAN and WAN Network Administration
System Implementations • System Conversions and Migrations • Data Center Processing and Overhauls
First Class Machinist • Computer Assisted Machinery

Management Reporting • Strategic Planning • Budget Preparation • Forms Management
General Accounting • Purchasing • Credit and Collections • Banking Relationship Development
Project Management • Materials and Capital Expenditures • Security and Facilities Oversight

Comprehensive Marketing • Advertising Strategies • Vendor Negotiation • Inventory Control
Resource and Risk Management • Insurance • Benefits and Pension Administration • Notary Public
Compensation Planning and Management • Hiring and Training • Federal/State Labor Law Compliance

CAREER DEVELOPMENT

MOHAWK INDUSTRIES, INC., LONG ISLAND CITY, NY   1996 to present
Corporate Controller and Operations Specialist / Senior Member Core Management Team

● Overview
Mohawk Industries is a multi-company wholesale and private-label die casting manufacturer with $16.5 million in sales and 100 employees. Mohawk produces custom die castings and manufactures America's number-one-selling bicycle kickstand as well as a proprietary line of outdoor electrical weatherproof boxes and covers. Customers include Schwinn, Raleigh, Trek, Diamondback, Intermatic, Pass & Seymour, Thomas & Betts, RAB, and Stonco, among others. Mohawk's private-label products can be found in Home Depot, Sears, and Menards.

Directly responsible for all day-to-day general operations including administrative, financial, information management, marketing, and human resource areas, reporting to the President. Control multimillion-dollar budgets. Oversee company's LAN infrastructures. Share responsibility for warehouse and distribution. Liaise with outside legal counsel on all corporate matters. Handle heavy resource management and coordination with internal departments and vendors to define scopes of work, required components, schedules, and price/contract negotiation. Prepare comprehensive management reports. Hire, schedule, and review employees. Handle UL and CSA product approvals.

● Representative Achievements
Saved company $300,000 annually by reducing overloaded inventory, freeing up dollars, and negotiating with vendors.
Strategically lowered component costs by 24.5%, saving the company $283,986 in one year alone; reduced component inventory on the shelves by 17.3% without being out of stock; decreased shipping supplies 16.1%, saving $22,660; and lowered inbound freight expenses by 11.1%. (All FYE 09/30/97 to FYE 09/30/98) Analyzed inventory and converted excess to available cash, relieving pressure on cash flow and floor space. Negotiated with vendors for monthly releases, cash discounts, FOB destination freight terms, and savings on component costs. Savings continue to be secured.

42 –37 165 Street, Flushing, NY 11353 • 718-555-5555 • fax 718-000-0000 • cregan@aol.com

This accomplished technology pioneer had worked with manufacturers his whole career. He wanted to move to another employer that would allow him the hands-on, cross-functional freedom to "tinker" with systems and processes to create change and enhance profits, as described in his track record.

CHARLES REGAN   page 2

CAREER DEVELOPMENT continued

MOHAWK INDUSTRIES, INC.
- **Representative Achievements, continued**

Updated computer system to provide complete and accurate management tracking and reporting to every workstation.
Carefully invested over $100,000 for new, ground-up computer project to replace Mohawk's outdated, non-networked, non-Y2K compliant system that did not provide any form of accurate management reporting.

Installed a server, networked all workstations, and personally designed major customized modifications to a proven, off-the-shelf, Y2K-compliant accounting package. Provided a one-entry system for values and integrated all system components. Tested and debugged software. Imported all data from the old system into the new and trained staff. Company is now ready for the 21st century.

Provided an automated and streamlined payroll process that totally eliminated human error.
Identified that company was running payroll system multiple times to correct bookkeeping mistakes because bookkeeper was manually adding, verifying, entering, and processing net earnings.

Replaced company's manual system with a computerized time clock system and developed an export program that would automatically take hourly data, transfer it into the payroll system, and then on to direct deposit via an ACH (Automated Clearing House) program.

LINUX CABLE CORP., YONKERS, NY   1984 to 1995
Corporate Controller / Operations Manager / Senior Member of Management Team
- **Overview**

Linux Cable Corp. is an electrical and electronic wire and cable distributor (wholesaler) with $8 million in sales. Linux Cable distributes to electrical supply houses and the entertainment industry including The Disney Company, Broadway theatres, and the motion picture industry.

Senior Member of management team, reporting directly to the President. Within one year of joining firm, fast-tracked to Controller's position. Managed operations of all departments including general accounting, collections, data processing/information systems, inventory, purchasing, warehouse/distribution, human resources, security, and facilities management. Oversaw sales department profitability. Negotiated and purchased 80% of inventory to be resold; office/warehouse supplies; capital, office, and warehouse equipment; printed materials; and building and maintenance contracts. Designed and maintained entire computer network and computer software including all application software.

- **Representative Achievements**

Increased company's sales 35% the first year by modifying and successfully operating company's unused computerized inventory system, providing sales department with instant access to availability and pricing.

Prior to conversion, inventory tracking was done manually using an outdated, error-filled Cardex system, viewable at only one desk. Salespersons had to keep customers on hold or call them back, go to inventory clerk's desk, and manually thumb through Cardex system or piles of paper to check availability, then go to management for pricing.

With new system, inventory was securely available from every workstation, with costing at a lot level, specs, and catalog reference numbers. Customers could be helped in a matter of minutes—essential in a highly competitive market. Saved substantial dollars on toll-free phone costs.

Developed a new catalog that allowed company to increase sales and regain the respect of the industry as a first-rate electrical and electronic wire and cable distributor.

Company had a badly outdated, 62-page catalog that no longer served its customers. Sales department was spending a great deal of time gathering product specs from manufacturers and re-faxing them to customers. Customers were not sure what items company carried.

Personally created, from the ground up, a 154-page catalog with very detailed specifications and creative four-color cover. Utilized services of typesetter for production and marketing professional to design cover. Personally designed layout and wrote all copy, complete with specs. Customers were able to order by item number and were ordering items they had not ordered in the past. Sales department was freed from copying and faxing specs to customers.

42 – 37 165 Street, Flushing, NY 11353 ● 718-555-5555 ● fax 718-000-0000 ● cregan@aol.com

CHARLES REGAN page 3

EARLY EMPLOYMENT

EAGLE ELECTRIC, INC., LONG ISLAND CITY, NY 1983 to 1984
Office Manager and Credit Analyst, reporting directly to President

CASE PAPER COMPANY, INC., LONG ISLAND CITY, NY 1980 to 1983
Computer Operations Manager and Office Manager, reporting directly to President

METRO MANUFACTURING CORP., PITTSBURGH, PA 1978 to 1980
Assistant Foreman, supervising large department and functioning as machine troubleshooter

TECHNOLOGY ACHIEVEMENTS

Blend excellent management and technical abilities, consistently meeting the challenges presented by rapidly changing technology. Have been building and working with computers since the mid-70s, learning continuously.

Thoroughly hands-on. Can run anything and can build a PC, with components, from the ground up. Have conceived, designed, and written software at every company worked for, on many varied platforms, creating programs that greatly enhanced productivity and accuracy and are operable with very little, if any, training. Acted as an Alpha and Beta test site for many hardware and software packages from names such as MSI (Mustang Software) and US Robotics. Extremely Internet savvy.

Use and understand a wide variety of hardware, operating systems, languages, and software including: DEC PDP-10, DEC PDP-11, IBM Series 1, PC, DG Aviion, Macro, Fortran, COBOL, BASIC, DOS, UNIX, PICK, Windows v3.x-9x, MS Word and Excel, Corel WordPerfect, and all associated components such as monitors, printers, CD drives, and TBUs.

- **Coordinated and supervised the creation of a Novell NetWare v4.x network.** (Mohawk)

- **Spec'd, ordered, and migrated a new high-speed dual processor RISC-based UNIX box** that ran company's same application software so that transition required no retraining. Personally set up on a Friday night, migrated over the weekend, and started system Monday with no hitch. System provided 50 times more processing speed. (Linux Cable)

- **Learned the program language PICK and heavily modified application software** to provide true gross-profit reporting on a lot-level basis. Modifications enabled company to review productivity and profitability figures daily. Work saved company $150 per hour on programming consultant. (Linux Cable)

- **Spec'd and ordered a dedicated line to link New York mainframe with Massachusetts satellite office.** Installed a multiplexer at each end and wired/configured the Massachusetts workstations to connect to New York mainframe. Gave both offices instant access to inventories, creating efficiencies and reducing costs. (Linux Cable)

- **Brought systems to Y2K compliance by conceiving and designing modifications for off-the-shelf accounting software** (MAS 90). New software streamlined data entry and supplied unlimited full management reporting. (Mohawk)

- **Successfully operated a hobbyist, multi-line BBS (Bulletin Board System)** for nine years.

- **Commended by Digital Equipment,** while working with Board of Cooperative Educational Services, for the identification of an obscure computer bug in school's digital mainframe computer that would have crashed Orange County Schools' entire system. Was a visiting student technical liaison at the time.

- **Took two years of college computer courses while still in high school.** Was the only student in school's history to receive a "sysop" computer account and keys to the building. Operated large mainframe computer network. Acted as assistant teacher and liaison between school and Orange County's Computer Sciences Departments. Founded county's school user group.

EDUCATION

New York Polytechnic Institute, Farmingdale, NY 1976 to 1978 • Major: Computer Science; Minor: Accounting

42 –37 165 Street, Flushing, NY 11353 • 718-555-5555 • fax 718-000-0000 • cregan@aol.com

CHAPTER 10

Resumes for Plant Management and Operations Management Personnel

- Plant Managers

- Operations Managers

- Directors of Manufacturing

- Manufacturing Managers/Supervisors

- Production Managers/Superintendents

- Project Managers

- Manufacturing Engineer Managers

BARRY LOGAN, B.Sc

4124 Schoolmaster Lane
Oakville, Ontario
L6M 4V3

Home: (905) 912-2377
Cell: (905) 916-4200
Email: blogan@earthlink.net

PROFILE

Proactive, creative, and dedicated professional with an extensive background in paint processing, plant operations, and product development.

Industrious, tenacious, work diligently to achieve optimum results efficiently and effectively. Recognised as a team builder, exercise strong leadership and motivation skills, deal patiently with contentious issues. Loyal, ethical, flexible, work well with all levels, thrive in a challenging, fast-paced environment. Resourceful, goal oriented, strong business acumen, fiscally responsible, highly organized multi-tasker. Considered an excellent communicator and negotiator, cost conscious; possess a strong understanding of business goals and practices. Sound knowledge of legislative regulations relating to plant operations and handling dangerous goods.

PROFESSIONAL EXPERIENCE

Royal Chemicals   **1997 – 2000**
Held the following progressively responsible positions:
PLANT MANAGER, Hamilton, Ontario   **1999 – 2000**
  Accomplishments
  - Initiated a production and process review recommending process changes. *Result:* Production yielded a 21% growth after implementation of adjustments.
  - Created the infrastructure and procedures to reduce inventory levels, while realising 95% JIT delivery, reducing costs significantly.
  - Selected by senior management to prepare a forecast and business plan combined with overseeing the preparations for an 8,000-square-foot plant extension. Process involved extensive work with architects and engineers; liaised with local municipal officials.
  - Developed a reputation with clients for operating a production unit that permitted the inclusion of last-minute rush orders.
  Responsibilities
  - Controlled all plant and production operations for two-shift manufacturing facility employing 30 in the production of 165,000 gallons per month of industrial paint products.
  - Prepared and monitored annual $1.5 million operating budget.
  - Accountable for recruitment, appraisals, training, and other human resource issues; staff scheduling, facility management, and production schedules.

PRODUCTION CHEMIST, Winston-Salem, North Carolina   **1998 – 1999**
  Accomplishments
  - Assigned to install and integrate the Gretag MacBeth machine that reduced the number of colour hits from 5 to 3 per batch, yielding a significant manpower and production saving.
  - Reduced a $750,000 rework inventory to $500,000 by evaluating the inventory, destroying old stock, and gradually integrating other material back into the manufacturing process.
  Responsibilities
  - Devised production-friendly, cost-efficient chemical formulas and processes for implementation in metal- and wood-coating products.

INVENTORY COORDINATOR, Winston-Salem, North Carolina   **1997 – 1998**
  - Scheduled production for plant producing 100,000 US gallons per month.
  - Designed, built, and installed MRP and MRPII systems that enabled more efficient organization.
  - Managed a $3.6 million inventory.

This resume reverses the traditional order of responsibilities and accomplishments, leading first with strong achievements, then following up with a summary of job activities.

BARRY LOGAN, B.Sc   **PAGE 2**

Regal Paint Limited, Barrie, Ontario   **1984 – 1997**
GENERAL MANAGER/OWNER
- Controlled all facets of business producing 250,000 gallons of paint per year, primarily anti-corrosive paint for the retail sector.
- Devised business plan, negotiated financing, created and implemented marketing strategy and operating budgets.
- Recruited 25 staff; oversaw all human resources issues.

Northern Paint and Varnish Ltd., Brampton, Ontario   **1981 – 1984**
PLANT MANAGER
- Directed the daily operations required to keep production lines active and profitable.
- Plant produced 20,000 gallons of paint per month.

EDUCATION

Wilfred Laurier University, Waterloo, Ontario   **Enrolled**
   Economics/Business

University of Toronto, Toronto, Ontario   **Enrolled**
   Engineering Management/Chemical Engineering

Wilfrid Laurier University, Waterloo, Ontario   **1981**
   BACHELOR OF SCIENCE

CONTINUING EDUCATION

Saint Paul University, Florida   **2000**
   C++ Programming
   Visual Basic Programming

American Production and Inventory Control Society   **1999**
   CPIM — Basics of Supply Chain Management

Advanced Microsoft Access 97   **1998**

Gretag-MacBeth Color Theory   **1998**

Lotus 1-2-3, COBOL Programming, BASIC Programming   **1981 – 1989**

PRESENTATIONS

Won *FIRST* place in the "Great Canadian Paint Challenge"   **1995**
Selected to participate in this challenge for 150 inventors of recycled paint

---

MEMBERSHIPS & AFFILIATIONS

National Paint & Coating Association   **1980 – Present**

American Production and Inventory Control Society (APICS)   **1996 – Present**

Jack W. Moore
2105 Pinetop Court Montgomery, AL 36100   [334] 555-4197

Objective

As a **plant manager**, to delight the customers of a leading manufacturing firm by ensuring end-to-end quality at the lowest possible cost.

Profile

- Hands-on **results-oriented experience** at every level of plant operations from machine operator to area manager.

- Gifted problem-solver in **serving the customer.** Can separate the important from the urgent, the symptoms from the problems.

- Established track record in leading employees to **produce more high-quality goods** at **lower costs.**

Selected Examples of Success

SERVING THE CUSTOMER

Made time to help key customer — a leading truck builder — improve quality and reliability while cutting costs. In face-to-face visits, offered profitable, cost-saving alternatives to their production plan.

> **Results:** Customer adopted my suggestions. Our company, our suppliers, and the customer avoided significant costs in tooling, delays in manufacturing, slower shipping. Quality remained high. Customer's pricing remained competitive.

LEADING PEOPLE TO QUALITY

Inherited line with long history of breaking tools and generating too much waste. Engineers unable to solve the problem despite the lure of bonuses. Quickly traced the problem to missing critical measurements and lack of input from operators. Sold senior management on fix I designed.

> **Results:** Rework rate and scrap fell fast. System costs quickly offset by savings. Old machinery made more efficient; newer machinery used more effectively.

CUTTING COSTS WHILE RAISING QUALITY

Helped an inexperienced quality manager make the SPC program work for the customer. Trained machine operators not only to gather data but use them as a quality tool. Replaced quantity production goals with quality targets.

> **Results:** Production capability rose; $300,000 in shipping costs cut dramatically.

The Selected Examples of Success in three critical areas serve as a very effective introduction to the traditional chronological summary that follows on page 2.

Jack W. Moore   [334] 555-4197

Experience

More than 20 years with the Dana Corporation:

Area Manager	1991 – Present Spicer Heavy Axle and Brake Division, Montgomery, AL Supervise production, engineering, maintenance, purchasing.
Shift Superintendent	1983 – 1991 Spicer Light Axle Division, Syracuse, IN Supervised production and assembly foremen, maintenance technicians, shipping and receiving personnel, quality control workers.
Department Foreman	1981 – 1983 Spicer Transmission Division, Toledo, OH Responsible for assembling heavy-duty 5- to 20-speed transmissions.
Production Foreman	1979 – 1980 Spicer Universal Joint Division, Pottstown, PA Supervised machining on several lines producing automotive components.
Management Trainee (Purchasing)	1978 Spicer Universal Joint Division, Purchasing Office, Pottstown, PA Matched purchases of forgings, casting, and bar stock to production needs using an MRP system.
Machine Operator	1972 – 1978 Spicer Universal Joint Division, Pottstown, PA Set up and operated lathes, milling machines, broaches, drills, balancers, and the like.

Education

- A.A., **Manufacturing Technology,** Oakland Community College, Auburn Hills, Michigan. **4.0 GPA.** Degree anticipated 2001.

- **M.B.A.,** Bowling Green State University, Bowling Green, Ohio, 1990

- B.S., Psychology, Ursinus College, Collegeville, Pennsylvania, 1975

Training

- MRP II

- Extensive training in systems and quality both here and abroad.

CALHOUN A. BENTNOR

54 Larchmont Avenue, Lakewood, New Jersey 08721
(732) 901-6922 ❑ calhoun@aol.com

OPERATIONS MANAGEMENT PROFESSIONAL
Production Efficiency / Industrial Engineering / Preventative Maintenance
Quality Assurance / Customer Service

❑ **Strategic Planning:** Transformed strategic planning into tactical action for plant-wide quality improvements.

❑ **Continuous Process Improvements:** Performed layout reengineering and implemented continuous process improvements that accelerated production output and strengthened quality performance.

❑ **Cost Containment:** Captured revenues through streamlining operations and reducing waste, as well as cost-effective purchasing via vendor sourcing, comparison shopping, and re-negotiation of vendor contracts

❑ **Technology Integration:** Spearheaded automation into manufacturing operations.

❑ **Leadership by Example:** Empowered employees by holding them to a benchmark, promoting camaraderie, and allowing them the freedom to achieve success.

❑ **Computer Skills:** Microsoft Word business applications, Internet experience, light troubleshooting skills, Allen Bradley PLC2 and PLC5 operating software.

CAREER HISTORY

COCA-COLA COMPANY, Hightstown, NJ   1980-99
Quality, Service, and Cost Manager, 1994-99
Full P&L and budget responsibility for leading manufacturing operation comprising 300 production and warehouse employees, encompassing two city blocks, and located in the hub of central Jersey's business district on the outskirts of Princeton.

❑ Transitioned facility from a labor-intensive production operation into a state-of-the art automated manufacturing facility, resulting in both waste and manpower reductions as well as increased quality.

❑ Accelerated production from 8 million cases per year in 1980 to 26 million cases a year in 1999. Captured 15% operating budget reductions annually through expanded vendor sourcing and by addressing critical productivity, efficiency, and quality issues negatively impacting production yields and customer satisfaction. Achieved cost-effective procurement of computers, touch screens, processors, metering valves, and blending tanks.

❑ Initiated and implemented the company's premier preventative maintenance program by contacting vendors directly, learning equipment preventative maintenance techniques, and training staff on preventative maintenance procedures.

❑ Revitalized production competencies by revamping plant layout, saving $120,000 a year and driving a 12% manpower reduction. Instrumental in the successful completion of a $33 million capital improvement project, with accountability for determining line layout that propelled the operating efficiency of filters, casers, and palletizers.

❑ Hired and directed the activities of a staff of 82, comprising machine operators, mechanics, quality assurance technicians, and a supervisor. Provided on-the-job training, produced top-achieving managers, and served as a resource to engineering personnel.

Production Supervisor, 1985-94 — **Group Leader,** 1981-85 — **Quality Assurance Technician,** 1980-81

TD FINANCIAL SERVICES, Browns Mills, NJ (1988-Present)
President
Built consulting firm from start-up into solid revenue generator with 500+ corporate and individual customer accounts.

EDUCATION / PROFESSIONAL TRAINING

Business Management and Accounting Curriculum at Bucks County Community College and Burlington County College, Computer Training at Allen Bradley School, MRP Training, Union-Company Relations Training, Supervisor as a Leader Training, Effective Discipline As A Supervisor Training, Quality Training, Diversity Training

Six key management capabilities are highlighted in the introduction. Note how the education section downplays the candidate's lack of a formal degree.

SUMCHAI ALI
EMAIL: S-ALI@EARTHLINK.NET

[650] 595-2514 (Day)
[650] 594-3102 (Eve)

1601 El Camino Real
Belmont, CA 94002

Versatile **Operations Management** professional with expertise in general management, accounting, and marketing.
- Intuitive problem solving, strong customer service skills, versatility, and integrity.
- Action and results orientation; dedicated to following through to completion.
- Commitment to reducing costs and improving profitability.
- Ability to prioritize, delegate, and motivate.
- Excellent verbal and written communications skills; interact and work well with people.
- Speak and write English, German, Farsi, and Turkish; some Spanish.
- Organized • Flexible • Dedicated • Ethical

PROFESSIONAL EXPERIENCE

Operations Manager   1987 to Present
Sees Candy, San Bruno, CA
Successful production and distribution facility with 20 retail stores, over 500 wholesale accounts, and a full-time staff of 38. Oversee purchasing, marketing, production, and accounting.
- Cut production costs by 25%.
- Increased sales by 70% within two years.
- Built excellent rapport with vendors, customers, and staff.

Manager, Accounting Department   1983 to 1987
NextCom Corporation, San Jose, CA
Accounts receivable, accounts payable, payroll, cost accounting. Supervised 10 full-time employees.
- Promoted to accounting department for a subsidiary company based on outstanding performance.

Associated Buyer   1974 to 1983
ConoCorp, London, England
Managed all communications between international buyers and facilitated bids from global vendors.
- Ensured accurate bids, competitive prices, and excellent customer service.

EDUCATION

MBA Candidate, Information Systems Management (anticipate completion 2002)
University of San Francisco, San Francisco, CA

B.S., Business - emphasis: Accounting and Organizational Behavior
San Jose State University, San Jose, CA

INTERESTS
Economics, music, art, basketball, gardening

This concise presentation of a 27-year career focuses on capabilities and a few highlighted achievements.

David J. Reynolds

21 Canal Pointe Boulevard, Princeton, NJ 08540
609-452-5555 ▪ davreynol@aol.com

SENIOR MANUFACTURING & PLANT OPERATIONS MANAGEMENT
Specialty Consumer Products and Components Manufacturing

Senior manufacturing-industry manager with 20+ years of experience in high-quality plant operations, labor relations, quality control, safety, and engineering. Proven track record of consistent contributions to increased production, quality, cost effectiveness, and profitability. A persuasive leader and team builder skilled in cross-functional team collaboration with all operating departments. Key player in strategic planning. Expertise in:

✓ Manufacturing / Production Planning	✓ Performance Improvement	✓ IT / ERP Initiatives
✓ Inventory / Materials Management, MRP	✓ Cost Reductions / Controls	✓ Team Leadership
✓ Process Redesign / Reengineering	✓ Quality Management / TQM	✓ GMP / JIT
✓ Cell Manufacturing Operations	✓ Vendor Negotiations	✓ Safety / OSHA

Delivered performance improvements through cost reductions, production efficiency, statistical process controls (SPC), and company culture of continuous improvement. Proven problem-solving and decision-making skills. Promoted through a series of increasingly responsible production, quality, and plant management positions.

PROFESSIONAL EXPERIENCE

SKILLMAN MEASURES, INC., Skillman, NJ   1979 – 2001
Market leader in design, manufacturing, sales, and distribution of industrial measurement devices for the mass wholesale distribution market. Privately held company with annual revenues of $24 million.

Plant Manager (1998 – 2001)
Directed production, planning, inventory control, quality, maintenance, and engineering for 160,000-square-foot manufacturing facility. Managed 4 direct reports, 13 indirect reports, and 150 to 220 unionized employees.

- **Production Improvements.** Increased production efficiency from 85% to 98% within 2 years through ongoing employee training, good manufacturing practices (GMP), and cell manufacturing. Developed and maintained performance measurements for key cost elements to ensure annual performance improvements.

- **Capital Expansion.** Key player in transition of manufacturing to offshore facility in Mexico. Conducted on-site evaluation of Mexican vendor capabilities, land selection, new facility design, and budget development.

- **Technology Implementation.** Championed active use of ERP (Enterprise Resource Planning) software for manufacturing enterprises, integrating manufacturing into cross-departmental functions. Initiated computer-generated reporting for improved inventory control and customer service.

- **Operations Management.** Pioneered streamlined processes and standardized operating procedures. Reduced components and finished goods inventories by 12% in 2000 (cost reduction of $480K), 60% in the caliper category. Maintained a secure facility by instituting new procedures that reduced false alarms by 50%.

- **Relationship Management.** Maintained positive relations with union leaders, employees, outside vendors and suppliers, executive management, customers, and industry colleagues. Revitalized customer service by upgrading customer return responsiveness from a low of 20 days to a consistent response time of 3–5 days.

- **Safety Management.** Led all safety programs as Director of the Safety Committee (8-member team). In 1998, company won "Elite Award" from the State of New Jersey for the effectiveness of safety programs.

- **Human Resources & Training.** Managed and trained more than 120 hourly employees, focusing on safety, GMP, and quality. Held monthly meetings for supervisors and group leaders, including on-site visits to vendors, as well as wholesale distributor checks. Saved $57K in labor costs in 2000 through these initiatives.

continued

Under the most recent position, measurable results are noted in seven important areas that are emphasized with bold-type introductions.

David J. Reynolds
609-452-5555 ▪ davreynol@aol.com   Page 2

PROFESSIONAL EXPERIENCE

Quality Control Manager (1993 – 1998)
▪ Directed competitive product testing, new design testing, and training and development of production staff in best calibration procedures for accurate products. Monitored product accuracy and reliability by reviewing daily production audit records, SPC charts, and warranty returns. Oversaw UL and CSA factory inspections.

▪ Chosen to lead project management of new sales catalog, in collaboration with new CEO, cross-functional departments, and outside vendors; produced a comprehensive, top-quality sales collateral tool.

▪ Initiated systematic quality inspection procedures, which led to 20% reduction of quality department staff without any reduction in quality output. Initiated close communications with suppliers and a corrective action system, which contributed to continuous improvement of quality issues.

▪ Utilized self-directed work teams to problem-solve highest cost scrap items, reducing cost of top 5 by 22%.

▪ Selected to begin corporate initiative for ISO 9002 certification. Achieved most advanced ranking (out of 6 divisions) — just months short of certification — before initiative was abandoned due to cost constraints.

Engineering Assistant (1992 – 1993)
▪ Conducted research and testing on new product design and development, and prepared product variation samples for sales and marketing departments. Supervised tooling inventory update, in-house and at vendor.

▪ Tracked cost-reduction proposals and assisted in cost-reduction implementation. Maintained accurate bill of materials and product archives in database.

Shipping Manager (1991 – 1992)
▪ Directed product shipments through cross-functional collaborations with manufacturing, sales, and customer service departments. Attained consistent record of on-time deliveries at lowest possible cost.

▪ Saved $100K of annual costs for freight carrier services by researching all carriers' rate schedules and negotiating first-ever, low-cost corporate contract with major carrier.

General Production Foreman (1990 – 1991)
▪ Held complete responsibility for all industrial measurement lines and sub-assembly operations including production, safety, and quality, ensuring cost-effective delivery of quality products on schedule.

R & D Assistant (1980 – 1990), **Production Line Repairs** (1979 – 1980)
▪ Collaborated with Engineering in product development phase of multimillion-dollar new product line. Chosen to head pilot run and subsequent production run on semi-automatic assembly line.

▪ Key player in department start-up for magnetic film measurement. Assisted Engineering in incorporating new technology. Managed project for 9 months before transferring product to manufacturing department.

EDUCATION & PROFESSIONAL DEVELOPMENT
Ongoing Professional Development through professional seminars and classes in:
  ✓ Introduction to Industrial Engineering   ✓ Problem Solving   ✓ JIT / MRP II
  ✓ Achieving Results Through Teams   ✓ Inventory Management   ✓ ISO 9000
  ✓ Best Practices for Process Improvement   ✓ Systems and Technologies   ✓ Master Planning

A.A.S. Program, Electrical Power Technology — 95 credits earned (GPA 3.96)   1994 – Present
Middle County Community College, Trenton, NJ

COMPUTER SKILLS
Windows 98 / 95; MS Office 97 — Word, Excel; MAPIC (ERP software); Internet Explorer

PROFESSIONAL ASSOCIATION
American Production and Inventory Control Society — APICS

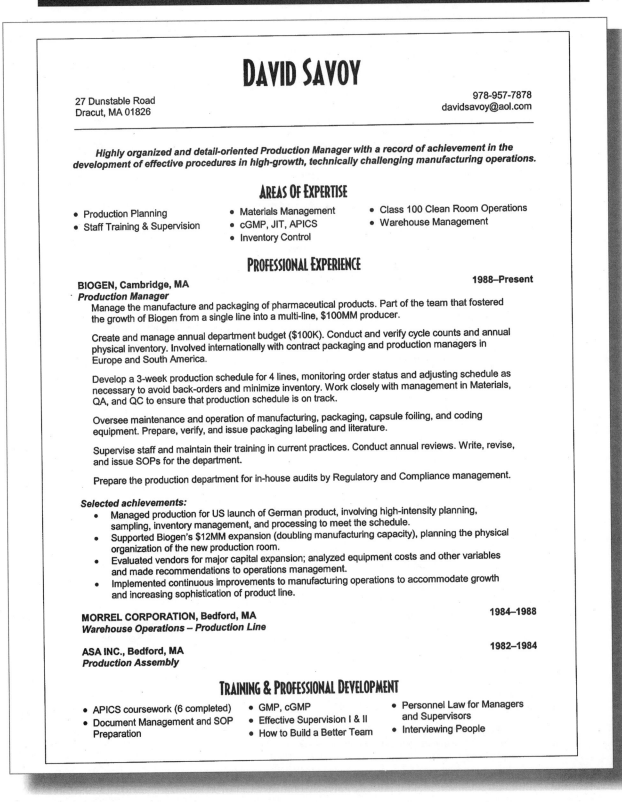

DAVID SAVOY

27 Dunstable Road
Dracut, MA 01826

978-957-7878
davidsavoy@aol.com

Highly organized and detail-oriented Production Manager with a record of achievement in the development of effective procedures in high-growth, technically challenging manufacturing operations.

AREAS OF EXPERTISE

- Production Planning
- Staff Training & Supervision
- Materials Management
- cGMP, JIT, APICS
- Inventory Control
- Class 100 Clean Room Operations
- Warehouse Management

PROFESSIONAL EXPERIENCE

BIOGEN, Cambridge, MA
Production Manager

1988–Present

Manage the manufacture and packaging of pharmaceutical products. Part of the team that fostered the growth of Biogen from a single line into a multi-line, $100MM producer.

Create and manage annual department budget ($100K). Conduct and verify cycle counts and annual physical inventory. Involved internationally with contract packaging and production managers in Europe and South America.

Develop a 3-week production schedule for 4 lines, monitoring order status and adjusting schedule as necessary to avoid back-orders and minimize inventory. Work closely with management in Materials, QA, and QC to ensure that production schedule is on track.

Oversee maintenance and operation of manufacturing, packaging, capsule foiling, and coding equipment. Prepare, verify, and issue packaging labeling and literature.

Supervise staff and maintain their training in current practices. Conduct annual reviews. Write, revise, and issue SOPs for the department.

Prepare the production department for in-house audits by Regulatory and Compliance management.

Selected achievements:
- Managed production for US launch of German product, involving high-intensity planning, sampling, inventory management, and processing to meet the schedule.
- Supported Biogen's $12MM expansion (doubling manufacturing capacity), planning the physical organization of the new production room.
- Evaluated vendors for major capital expansion; analyzed equipment costs and other variables and made recommendations to operations management.
- Implemented continuous improvements to manufacturing operations to accommodate growth and increasing sophistication of product line.

MORREL CORPORATION, Bedford, MA
Warehouse Operations – Production Line

1984–1988

ASA INC., Bedford, MA
Production Assembly

1982–1984

TRAINING & PROFESSIONAL DEVELOPMENT

- APICS coursework (6 completed)
- Document Management and SOP Preparation
- GMP, cGMP
- Effective Supervision I & II
- How to Build a Better Team
- Personnel Law for Managers and Supervisors
- Interviewing People

Eliminating details on earlier positions keeps the resume to one page, while providing ample information on the most recent, relevant position.

GLENDA HOLMES

736 Clover Lane

Grosse Pointe, MI 66589

666.123.8899

siusmtk@aol.com

MANUFACTURING SUPERVISOR

Highly competent manufacturing professional recognized for taking a leadership role in support of top management. Accustomed to handling diverse responsibilities resourcefully. A proven and verifiable record for utilizing strong technical and interpersonal skills to enhance organizational efficiencies and profits. A team player who is energetic, organized, reliable, and known for getting the job done. Adapt easily to many work environments. Fluent in Spanish.

SKILLS

Personal: Excellent problem-solving and decision-making skills.
Proven ability to prioritize and complete tasks while meeting deadlines.
Work well (and competently) under stress while taking the pressure off superiors.
Dynamic listener who creates an environment for optimal work performance for employees.
Communicate effectively with superiors, peers, and subordinates.

Computer: Microsoft Office: Word, Excel, PowerPoint, Internet

SELECTED ACCOMPLISHMENTS

Analytical: Analyzed operations on the plant floor to evaluate if organizational objectives would be met and if the changes would be cost effective. Updated the contingency plan for the area, enabling employees to be aware of modifications on the plant floor; this resulted in less down time.

Organized: Compiled plan to match the skills of 30 employees working in an assigned section with the required job needs. By cross-training and matching employee skills to jobs, was able to eliminate down time, build morale, and lower absenteeism. Prioritized work to accommodate employer needs.

Self-starter: Initiated monthly team meetings with subordinates to answer questions and give feedback regarding problems and concerns of the workers. These meetings were held after work hours, and were not mandatory, yet had over 66% attendance.

Risk-taker: Assigned employees to different jobs based on their skill level and potential. Switching manpower around led to increased production and avoided worker monotony. Delegated two employees to work on ISO compliance projects.

Presentation/
Training: Designed and delivered a training program for all interns and new employees that gave an overview of a typical "Day in the Life of a Supervisor," giving them a realistic idea of what to expect once they begin working. Some new employees were asked to shadow daily routine to learn skills and were assigned tasks to assess their skill level.

This resume combines a functional format on page 1 with a chronological structure on page 2. This allows room for the high-impact Selected Accomplishments that take up most of the first page.

GLENDA HOLMES – PAGE TWO

PROFESSIONAL EXPERIENCE

GENERAL MOTORS CORPORATION — PONTIAC EAST ASSEMBLY PLANT, Pontiac, MI
Automobile Manufacturing Plant

Floor Supervisor/Special Assignment (Training Coordinator), 1999–Present

Supervise 30 employees in the Engine/Chassis/Final Line section of the production line, to assure quality standards and production schedules are met. Act as a resource person, conflict intermediary, and counselor, effectively handling any situations that might arise during the shift.

➢ Implemented change of the 2001 build-out, conducting meetings and submitting work orders to relocate the engine line. This change decreases transit time, reduces total employee movement, and increases handling of commodities by employees. Headcount reduced once change was in place.
➢ Wrote new procedures and activated better ways to schedule departmental overtime.
➢ Received the "Perfect Attendance Award" for 1999.
➢ Designed a monthly newsletter to make employees aware of upcoming plant changes.
➢ Handled employee time/pay discrepancies and resolved problems promptly.

FLAGSTAR BANK, Bloomfield Hills, MI
A Full-service Financial Institution

Loan Analyst, 1998

Processed loans for mortgages and maintained production logs on the status of mortgages, in order to maintain quota. Initiated a marketing newsletter to increase employee awareness of changing trends.

DTN MANAGEMENT COMPANY, East Lansing, MI
Company Leases Apartments to College Students

Leasing Agent, 1997

Guided prospective students on a hunt for apartments, increasing their awareness of what the different apartment complexes offered.
➢ Received a sales award for selling the most apartments in a two-month time. Used communication skills to listen to student needs and pointed out amenities of the various complexes that best met those needs.

EDUCATION

BA, *Supply Chain Management*, 1998, MICHIGAN STATE UNIVERSITY, East Lansing, MI
Course work included: Purchasing; Manufacturing & Logistics; Negotiation, Marketing; Management
"Leadership Strategy Building" — General Motors University, Auburn Hills, MI
"Managing Conflict" — Generals Motors University, Auburn Hills, MI
"Seven Habits of Highly Effective People" — General Motors University, Auburn Hills, MI

AFFILIATIONS

American Cancer Society, Volunteer
Lansing Community Schools, Tutor — Math and Science (grades 4–12)

SUSAN D. BIERNAT

90 North Road
Lehi, UT 84043
(801) 543-1098 • sbiernat@aol.com

QUALIFICATIONS OVERVIEW

Results-oriented **Plant Manager/Chemical Engineer** with a career distinguished by consistent progression and a verifiable record of achievement in initiating and leading the improvements that have streamlined operations, optimized efficiency, and increased production. Multifaceted qualifications include:

- ❑ Six years of pharmaceutical and cGMP experience.
- ❑ Bachelor of Science degree in Chemical Engineering; currently pursuing P.E. designation.
- ❑ Motivational supervisor and team leader; strong training and development skills.
- ❑ Reputation for outstanding problem solving and troubleshooting abilities.
- ❑ Loyal and hard working; dedicated to achieving the highest standards.
- ❑ Advanced computer skills; experienced with Macintosh, IBM, and VAX systems.

PROFESSIONAL EXPERIENCE

Harrison Chemicals, Inc., Lehi, UT   **1994 – Present**
(Leading manufacturer of bulk pharmaceuticals and fine chemicals.)

BUILDING MANAGER (1999 – Present)
BUILDING MANAGER/PRODUCTION SUPERVISOR (1998 – 1999)
PRODUCTION SUPERVISOR/CHEMICAL ENGINEER (1994 – 1998)

Initially hired to direct production, supervising multi-product batch operations and special plant projects. Provided team leadership for 70 operators within a union environment. Reviewed batch log records, ensured proper documentation for the FDA and DEA. Managed work permitting (hot work, confined space, and line breaking). Troubleshot and coordinated raw materials, production, and maintenance. Oversaw QC and QA, inventory, and ordering.

Promoted to building manager in 1998 to manage 7x24 production operations of a 47-acre, 2-building plant. Continued supervisor functions and performed the work of 2 full-time equivalents for 11 months while hiring and training a replacement. Direct the activities of 4 shift supervisors/80 operators and manage a $20 million budget. Write, review, and revise Batch Log Records (BLRs) and coordinate with QA and shift supervisors to ensure production goals are met.

Key Results & Achievements:

- Led plant through a challenging transitional period following the receipt of a 483 warning from the FDA. Planned and directed all improvements and upgrades, achieving FDA approval on the qualification and validation of equipment, materials, and processes.
- Opened new lines of communication that substantially enhanced information flow between operators and management. Established an atmosphere that rewards proactive identification of areas for process efficiency and performance improvements.
- Drafted new standard operating procedures (SOPs) and initiated intensive retraining of operators to improve quality and production and to optimize compliance with GMPs, SOPs, OSHA regulations, and environmental requirements.
- Replaced and modernized antiquated and inefficient equipment; successfully streamlined production processes, decreased cycle times, and minimized downtime.
- Established reputation as a decisive, action-oriented leader, dedicated to achieving corporate goals. Consistently rated as a top performer and supervisor in annual reviews.
- Partnered in an international effort with parent company to create and implement an in-depth technical and hands-on operator training program.

Note how all the positions since 1994 are grouped together, thereby emphasizing career progression and allowing results and achievements to span the entire time frame. This strategy would be particularly helpful if there were few notable achievements in the most recent position.

SUSAN D. BIERNAT — Page 2

Harrison Chemicals, Inc., continued

- Developed and instituted rigorous training program that enhanced accuracy and production levels during a period of expansion that included 200% growth of the operator workforce.

- Spearheaded year-long study to determine accurate dryer times; authored guide that has significantly improved efficiency and was used in construction of a new $14MM dryer building.

- Collaborate on 8 committees and numerous sub-committees involving all plant operations from training to materials movement and regulatory compliance.

- Managed labor relations and served as a key participant in contract negotiations and the resolution of grievances.

- Recruited operators to serve on the emergency response team; revised safety training documentation to formalize and improve training procedures.

- Developed and implemented documentation for all shift change processes; measurably streamlined procedures and improved accuracy.

Industrial Insurers, Kimball, CA   1993 – 1994

FIELD ENGINEER/LOSS PREVENTION ASSOCIATE

Worked independently to inspect insured chemical plants and refineries for the second largest industrial insurer in the world. Checked adequacy and condition of fire-protection systems and equipment to ensure compliance with standards and codes. Key player in the development and implementation of management programs to reduce risk of fire or explosion resulting in lost production and damage to property.

PROFESSIONAL CREDENTIALS

EDUCATION:	**B.S., CHEMICAL ENGINEERING** (1992) Wilcox University, Lehi, UT
CERTIFICATIONS:	■ Pursuing Professional Engineer (P.E.), anticipated March 2000 ■ Utah State Red Seal Boiler License ■ Utah N2 Industrial Wastewater License, currently pursuing N3 ■ CPR/First Aid Red Cross Certified ■ Level A Technician/Incident Command System Certified

TRAINING:

■ Industrial Fire Control Concepts	■ High Reach Driver Training
■ Loss Prevention	■ Forktruck Driver Training
■ EHS Training	■ Confined Space Supervisor
■ Interpersonal Relationship Skills	■ Management Leadership Development

ASSOCIATIONS:
- American Institute of Engineers
- Cogeneration, Boiler Operation, and Refrigeration Association

EARLY CAREER

ACCOUNTANT, Biernat Auto Specialists, Lehi, UT, 1990 – 1993
INVENTORY COUNTER/COMPUTER OPERATOR, Tekon Inventories, Lehi, UT, 1986 – 1990

SCOTT G. MATTHEWS

5614 Fox Cove
Beaumont, TX 77713

E-mail: scottgm2@aol.com

Residence: (409) 232-5311
Cellular: (409) 432-0932

MANUFACTURING MANAGER
Greatest Strength: Production Management

Reputable, integrity-driven, and successful management professional offering 16 years of manufacturing experience. Sharpened talents in multiple business areas with concentration on production management, quality, on-time delivery, and personnel cross-training. Strong proponent of team-concept management, identifying staff's unique talents and providing them with necessary tools to achieve maximum potential.

Professional strengths include:

Capital Budget Management ... Capital Projects ... Computer-Integrated Manufacturing ...
Cost Reductions ... Cross-Functional Teams ... Expediting ... Inventory Control & Planning ...
Labor Relations ... Logistics & Supply Chain Management ... Manufacturing Technology ...
Process Improvements ... Production Scheduling ... On-time Delivery ...
Operations Reengineering ... Operations Start-up ... Plant Operations ... Procurement ...
Production Forecasting & Scheduling ... P&L Management ... Regulatory Compliance ...
QA/QC ... Yield Improvements ... Cell Manufacturing ... Just-In-Time Management

CAREER TRACK

Held series of management positions within pulp and paper industry and developed expertise in working with natural products and manufacturing processes.

EAST TEXAS PAPER CORPORATION – Beaumont, TX – 1998 to Present
Operations Manager, Finish Division

(Profitable company has 4 production facilities (24/7 operations) that manufacture 45 products. Company employs 625. Sales reached $125 million in 2000.)

Brought on board due to years of industry experience and record of success in production management, expediting, scheduling, and on-time delivery coupled with superior track record in developing departments.

Guide all aspects of Finish Operations Division with principal focus on **production operations, meeting production goals** as mandated by Board of Directors, and achieving **clients' production and quality objectives.**

Key activities include P&L management; direction of 10 supervisors and 160 line production employees; production management; development and execution of strategies to meet production goals and delivery schedules; identification and resolution of production problems; oversight of $3.5 million in state-of-the-art capital equipment; new equipment recommendations; building modifications and process change in conjunction with safety, quality assurance/quality control, scheduling, expediting, inventory control, regulatory compliance, training, and other activities. Control $8 million to $9.5 million budget.

Major Achievements:

- Member of team charged with streamlining facility and operations. Team designed new floor plans and presented remodeling idea to Board of Directors. $1.6 million facility addition earned approval and was instrumental in eliminating 5 personnel (saving $125,000 annually), speeding up production process 20%, and contributing to overall productivity improvements.
- Played role in improving on-time delivery from 85% to 93% and lowering reject rate to less than 1%.
- Co-developed new personnel pay system based on certification process. System encourages personnel to produce quality products and is based on "learn more to earn more" principle. Drastically aided in production scheduling and prioritizing initiatives.
- Concentrated on cross-training employees, enabling company to maintain same level of productivity with 25% fewer personnel. Downsizing effort saved approximately $3 million annually.
- Involved in creating special cell to manufacture most profitable and delicate product.
- Appointed to Expediting & Flow Committee formed to research production-flow and late-delivery problems.

The list of Professional Strengths in the introduction serves as an effective key-word list that is supported by detailed accomplishments in the rest of the resume.

SCOTT G. MATTHEWS   **Page 2**

ADAMS PAPER CORPORATION – Beaumont, TX – 1997 to 1998
Director of Operations

Remained on board after investment group purchased Conroe Paper Corporation (former employer) to launch new start-up venture. Challenging role included spearheading facility operations, staffing new facility, instituting company policies and procedures, managing human resource activities, overseeing production operations, managing workforce, directing production scheduling/planning and work flow processes, and managing inventory in concert with all associated manufacturing/production activities.

Led 9 departmental supervisors and 65 employees. Held additional roles as **Production Control Director, Customer Service Manager,** and **Human Resource Director.** Company generated $2 million in sales.

Major accomplishments:

- Delivered $225,000 in payroll savings via cross-training program. Launched cross-training and streamlining program to enable company to operate with 25% less personnel than predecessor while maintaining higher production levels.
- Introduced program that slashed problem absenteeism 50%.

CONROE PAPER CORPORATION – Conroe, TX – 1991 to 1997
Vice President and Director of Operations, 2 years

Advanced to high-level management position and led operations for 225,000-sq.-ft. facility employing as many as 105 union employees. Annual sales averaged $5 million. **Activities were parallel to above mentioned.**

- Represented company in several union contract renegotiations, language disputes, and wage re-open sessions. Successfully negotiated new contract in 1996.
- Created team-oriented environment to motivate and empower employees. Introduced techniques to improve communications between departmental supervisors and upper management. On-time delivery improved 25%, and reworks decreased 10% due to strengthened communication.
- Directed continuous movement of unionized, piece-rate personnel from job to job while adhering to strict union contract that restricted employee movement options.

Director, Bleach Division, 4 years

Managed 65 employees in division that produced 70% of annual company sales.

- Instilled strict quality control procedures in 4 departments to ensure high-quality products.
- Created and/or improved existing manufacturing methods for new and current products.
- Chaired grievance hearings among management, employee(s), and union officials. No unfair labor practices were filed with union.

NEWBURY PAPER, INC. – Jasper, TX – 1984 to 1991
Sales and Operations Manager, 3 years
West Coast Sales Representative, 4 years

Directed productivity operations and related activities for 2 factories. Led 22 national and international sales team members. Conducted market research and product development activities. Established internal methods for order processing.

EDUCATION

Bachelor of Science, Business Administration
Sam Houston State University — Huntsville, TX

Dale Carnegie Institute
Zenger Miller Management Training

Computer literate ... Traveled to Canada, Mexico, Europe, Africa, and the Orient.

Clyde P. Johnson

4645 Harris Road
Marysville, Ohio 43040
(937) 555-8546 ▪ clydejohnson@aol.com

ENGINEERING AND PROJECT MANAGER: MANUFACTURING INDUSTRIES

Delivering strong and sustainable improvements in efficiency, productivity, and reliability through technical innovations, process improvements, automation, and creation of integrated manufacturing environments.

- Recognized expertise in automation systems, PLCs, control systems, microprocessor-based applications, and knowledge-based systems.

- Proven ability to lead a team of professional engineers, manage at the department level, and direct major capital improvement projects from concept to completion.

- Strategic vision; ability to conceive and execute concepts that provide solid solutions to present-day problems while providing building blocks for long-range strategic goal achievement.

- Strong communication, technical writing, and interaction skills at all levels... effective in interactions with senior management, technical colleagues, and factory-floor personnel.

PROFESSIONAL EXPERIENCE

HONDA CORPORATION, Marysville, Ohio   1994 to Present
Facilities Electrical Engineering Supervisor, 1998–Present

Promoted to newly created position as director of all Electrical Engineering activities for 2000-employee automotive plant supplying parts to Honda assembly plants worldwide. Direct and coordinate the activities of 7 engineers responsible for all plant electrical and control systems.

Manage average $150 million in capital projects annually, directing all phases from proposal and budget development through planning, installation, and long-range support. Work collaboratively with Mechanical Engineering counterpart and cross-functional engineering teams to execute joint projects and corporate purchasing directives.

- Initiated process improvements with a focus on waste reduction and production increases; **generated cost savings averaging $1.1 million per year.**

- Managed $86 million project — initiation of purchasing process, installation, programming, testing, and start-up of new equipment in preparation for **new vehicle launch.**

- Implemented a cutting-edge interconnected communications network, creating an integrated manufacturing environment that **reduces machine downtime, improves reliability, and enables full-system monitoring and troubleshooting.**

- Directed installation of a new automated process incorporating a high-speed blanking line with an ASRS (automatic storage and retrieval system); one of the first fully operational applications of this technology by this vendor, **benchmarked by other automotive manufacturers and showcased by OEM** as a highly successful application of equipment capability.

- Built a top-performing electrical engineering team with the **strongest technical qualifications** among all Honda plants in North America.

- Directed deployment and full utilization of an **online documentation library** (blueprints, OEM manuals, component locators/indicators, SWIs, BOM, general layouts, reference material) for all machinery in plant.

- Drove **team-building initiatives** among formerly fragmented staff; formalized reporting structures and improved day-to-day communication, resulting in a highly cohesive team that works collaboratively to achieve organizational goals.

This resume was written for an engineering manager who wished to consider opportunities both within and outside the automotive industry. Thus, the summary describes more generic expertise in manufacturing industries. Bold type helps strong accomplishments stand out.

Clyde P. Johnson Page 2

HONDA CORPORATION, continued
Electrical Engineer, 1996–1998

- Drove the development of a standardized automation control system capable of application to all automation equipment, regardless of manufacturer. **Achieved savings of $672K in direct production costs, $300K in increased equipment uptime, and $350K in reduced training.**

- Managed a comprehensive project to monitor, analyze, and correlate press tonnage. **Improved quality and equipment up-time; created process documentation for QS 9000 certification.**

- Created automated press-setup routine through interface of press subsystems, **capturing $258K in production savings** and promoting quality through tight manufacturing processes.

Project Supervisor / Automation Supervisor, 1994–1996

Led capital equipment projects, managing staff and coordinating activities with external suppliers. Supervised UAW skilled trades and the installation of capital equipment.

- Directed the electrical installation, I/O verification, and start-up of 'C' size transfer presses and automatic destacking equipment. Each installation represented a **$9 million capital investment and was integral to a new vehicle launch.**

- Upgraded blanking press equipment to integrate digital controls and enhance safety features.

COLUMBUS STEEL PRODUCTS, Columbus, Ohio   1991 to 1994
Electrical Engineer / Process Manager

Led a team of 16 electricians in implementing a comprehensive mill modernization program; also supervised team in ongoing machine maintenance activities. Employed PLCs, Integrated Solutions, Distributed Control Systems, and a diverse set of design and planning processes. Controlled department expenditures.

- Introduced the plant's first PLCs to automate product handling processes. Improved production, reduced downtime, and lowered ongoing maintenance costs by stabilizing the process.

- Programmatically enhanced the Reliance DCS to reduce process waste and substantially increase yield, **saving upwards of $100,000 per month.**

- Utilized GE Fanuc PLC, computer-based MMI, and intelligent decision capabilities to upgrade and enhance productivity of a material conveyor system.

- Headed project team that assessed the plant's inspection process and improved quality control, reduced scrap, and decreased associated labor costs.

- Established training program to improve staff analytical troubleshooting/repair skills and increase equipment up-time.

EDUCATION AND TRAINING

Bachelor of Science in Electrical Engineering, 1991: University of Michigan, Ann Arbor, Michigan

Technical Training / Programming: Reliance Electric DCS — Symax PLC Programming — AutoCAD — Reliance Electric Non-Driven Program — Allen Bradley PLC 5 Programming & System Design — GE Fanuc PLC Programming

Leadership / Management Training: Ongoing professional development through Honda, including management courses at Kellogg Graduate School of Management, Northwestern University: Management of Technical Professionals — Global Competition: The Role of Technology — Stimulating and Managing Creativity and Innovation

Languages: C, C++, BASIC, Visual Basic, dBASE

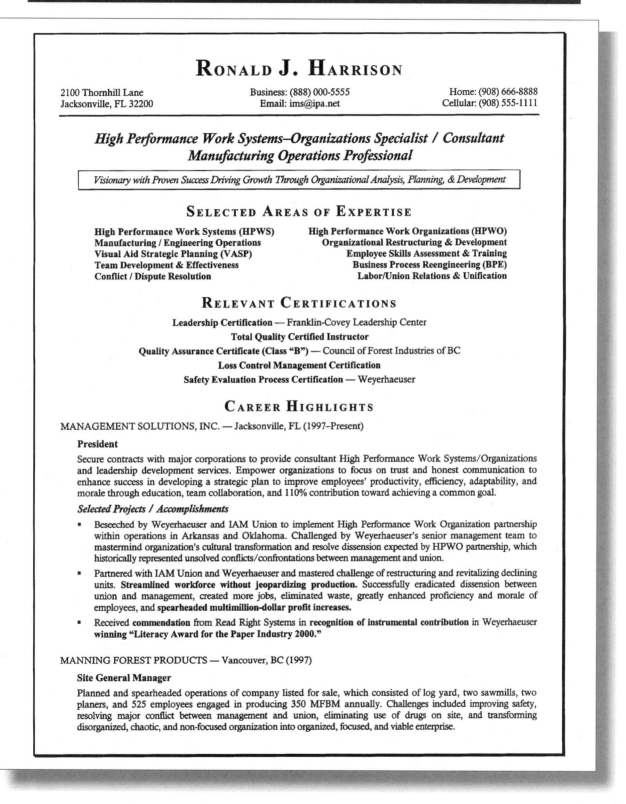

RONALD J. HARRISON

2100 Thornhill Lane Business: (888) 000-5555 Home: (908) 666-8888
Jacksonville, FL 32200 Email: ims@ipa.net Cellular: (908) 555-1111

High Performance Work Systems–Organizations Specialist / Consultant
Manufacturing Operations Professional

Visionary with Proven Success Driving Growth Through Organizational Analysis, Planning, & Development

SELECTED AREAS OF EXPERTISE

High Performance Work Systems (HPWS) High Performance Work Organizations (HPWO)
Manufacturing / Engineering Operations Organizational Restructuring & Development
Visual Aid Strategic Planning (VASP) Employee Skills Assessment & Training
Team Development & Effectiveness Business Process Reengineering (BPE)
Conflict / Dispute Resolution Labor/Union Relations & Unification

RELEVANT CERTIFICATIONS

Leadership Certification — Franklin-Covey Leadership Center

Total Quality Certified Instructor

Quality Assurance Certificate (Class "B") — Council of Forest Industries of BC

Loss Control Management Certification

Safety Evaluation Process Certification — Weyerhaeuser

CAREER HIGHLIGHTS

MANAGEMENT SOLUTIONS, INC. — Jacksonville, FL (1997–Present)

President

Secure contracts with major corporations to provide consultant High Performance Work Systems/Organizations and leadership development services. Empower organizations to focus on trust and honest communication to enhance success in developing a strategic plan to improve employees' productivity, efficiency, adaptability, and morale through education, team collaboration, and 110% contribution toward achieving a common goal.

Selected Projects / Accomplishments

- Beseeched by Weyerhaeuser and IAM Union to implement High Performance Work Organization partnership within operations in Arkansas and Oklahoma. Challenged by Weyerhaeuser's senior management team to mastermind organization's cultural transformation and resolve dissension expected by HPWO partnership, which historically represented unsolved conflicts/confrontations between management and union.

- Partnered with IAM Union and Weyerhaeuser and mastered challenge of restructuring and revitalizing declining units. **Streamlined workforce without jeopardizing production.** Successfully eradicated dissension between union and management, created more jobs, eliminated waste, greatly enhanced proficiency and morale of employees, and **spearheaded multimillion-dollar profit increases.**

- Received **commendation** from Read Right Systems in **recognition of instrumental contribution** in Weyerhaeuser winning "Literacy Award for the Paper Industry 2000."

MANNING FOREST PRODUCTS — Vancouver, BC (1997)

Site General Manager

Planned and spearheaded operations of company listed for sale, which consisted of log yard, two sawmills, two planers, and 525 employees engaged in producing 350 MFBM annually. Challenges included improving safety, resolving major conflict between management and union, eliminating use of drugs on site, and transforming disorganized, chaotic, and non-focused organization into organized, focused, and viable enterprise.

This three-page resume uses a project/accomplishment format to convey how the candidate has helped organizations be more profitable and productive. Page 3 provides details of consulting projects.

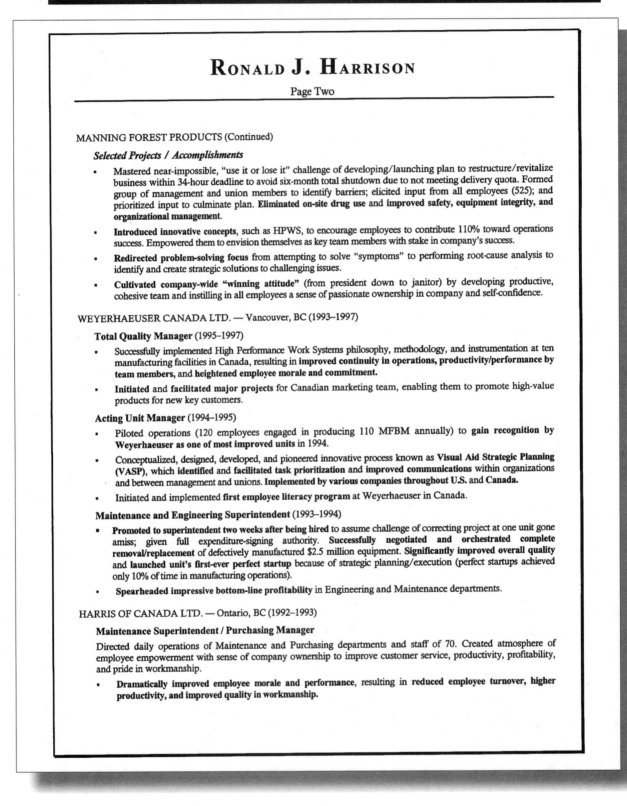

RONALD J. HARRISON

Page Two

MANNING FOREST PRODUCTS (Continued)

Selected Projects / Accomplishments

- Mastered near-impossible, "use it or lose it" challenge of developing/launching plan to restructure/revitalize business within 34-hour deadline to avoid six-month total shutdown due to not meeting delivery quota. Formed group of management and union members to identify barriers; elicited input from all employees (525); and prioritized input to culminate plan. **Eliminated on-site drug use** and **improved safety, equipment integrity, and organizational management.**

- **Introduced innovative concepts,** such as HPWS, to encourage employees to contribute 110% toward operations success. Empowered them to envision themselves as key team members with stake in company's success.

- **Redirected problem-solving focus** from attempting to solve "symptoms" to performing root-cause analysis to identify and create strategic solutions to challenging issues.

- **Cultivated company-wide "winning attitude"** (from president down to janitor) by developing productive, cohesive team and instilling in all employees a sense of passionate ownership in company and self-confidence.

WEYERHAEUSER CANADA LTD. — Vancouver, BC (1993–1997)

Total Quality Manager (1995–1997)

- Successfully implemented High Performance Work Systems philosophy, methodology, and instrumentation at ten manufacturing facilities in Canada, resulting in **improved continuity in operations, productivity/performance by team members, and heightened employee morale and commitment.**

- **Initiated and facilitated major projects** for Canadian marketing team, enabling them to promote high-value products for new key customers.

Acting Unit Manager (1994–1995)

- Piloted operations (120 employees engaged in producing 110 MFBM annually) to **gain recognition by Weyerhaeuser as one of most improved units in 1994.**

- Conceptualized, designed, developed, and pioneered innovative process known as **Visual Aid Strategic Planning (VASP),** which **identified and facilitated task prioritization** and **improved communications** within organizations and between management and unions. Implemented by **various companies throughout U.S. and Canada.**

- Initiated and implemented **first employee literacy program** at Weyerhaeuser in Canada.

Maintenance and Engineering Superintendent (1993–1994)

- **Promoted to superintendent two weeks after being hired** to assume challenge of correcting project at one unit gone amiss; given full expenditure-signing authority. **Successfully negotiated and orchestrated complete removal/replacement** of defectively manufactured $2.5 million equipment. **Significantly improved overall quality and launched unit's first-ever perfect startup** because of strategic planning/execution (perfect startups achieved only 10% of time in manufacturing operations).

- **Spearheaded impressive bottom-line profitability** in Engineering and Maintenance departments.

HARRIS OF CANADA LTD. — Ontario, BC (1992–1993)

Maintenance Superintendent / Purchasing Manager

Directed daily operations of Maintenance and Purchasing departments and staff of 70. Created atmosphere of employee empowerment with sense of company ownership to improve customer service, productivity, profitability, and pride in workmanship.

- **Dramatically improved employee morale and performance,** resulting in **reduced employee turnover, higher productivity, and improved quality in workmanship.**

RONALD J. HARRISON

Page Three

MADISON FOREST PRODUCTS — Ontario, BC (1979–1992)

Superintendent of Maintenance and Engineering (1989–1992)
Head Millwright (1982–1989)
Millwright (1981–1982)
Maintenance Millwright (1979–1981)

CONSULTING PROJECTS

WEYERHAEUSER — NORTHERN HPWO PARTNERSHIP (Currently)
Contracted by Weyerhaeuser and IAM Union to resolve past dissension and
create new foundation based on principles, trust, and maturity.

MASON TRUCKING — Vancouver, BC (1998)
As labor relations consultant, unified management and union employees.
Empowered employees to get on track for positive, collective, and strategic purpose for the future.

UNIVERSITY COLLEGE OF HIGHLANDS — Vancouver, BC (1995)
Educated management on strategic customer service techniques.
Immense improvement in customer relations elicited first-ever compliment by Omega.

UNIVERSITY COLLEGE OF HIGHLANDS — Vancouver, BC (1996–1997)
Created, implemented, and facilitated strategic planning program that enhanced
and further developed working atmosphere for team environment.

REGIONAL CORRECTIONAL CENTER (RCC) — MacKenzie, BC
Established atmosphere of respect between the Union and Management at RCC.
Created and presented workshop on "Building Communication and Trust" (1997).
Developed and presented workshop on "Building Relationships and Conflict Resolutions" (1996).

PROFESSIONAL DEVELOPMENT

Management and Training Systems for Industry

AMERICAN MANAGEMENT ASSOCIATION
Basic Project Management (Calgary)
Successfully Managing People (San Francisco)

CERRITOS COLLEGE — Norwalk, California
Psychology and General Education

BRITISH COLUMBIA SAFETY COUNCIL
Industrial Safety

B.F. GOODRICH
Analytic Troubleshooting

B.J. TABERNER AND ASSOCIATES
Fluid Power Instruction — Industrial Hydraulics

KOCKUMS CANCAR INC.
Safety and Maintenance Procedures

■ ■ ■

CHAPTER 11

Resumes for General Management and Executive Management Personnel

- Vice Presidents of Manufacturing

- Vice Presidents of Production Operations

- Chief Financial Officers

- Executive Vice Presidents

- General Managers

- Chief Operating Officers

- Chief Executive Officers

- Presidents

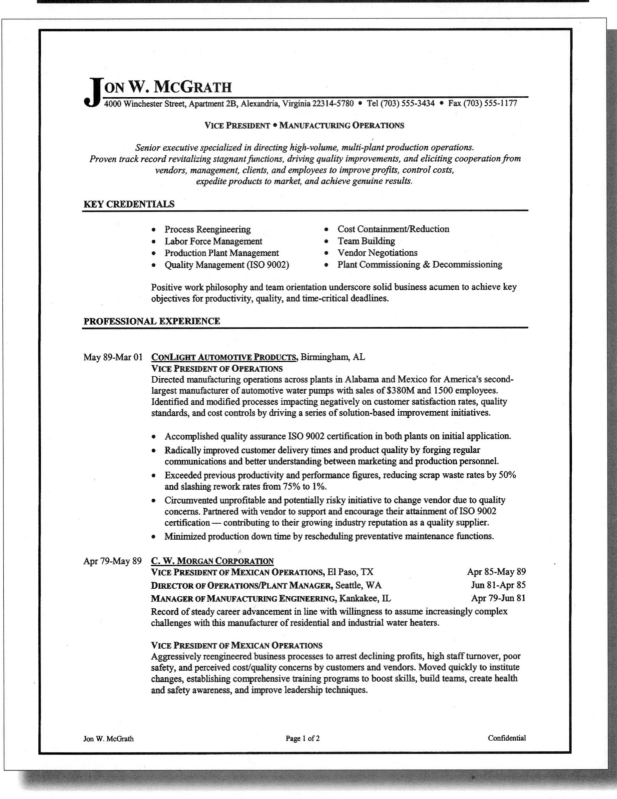

JON W. MCGRATH

4000 Winchester Street, Apartment 2B, Alexandria, Virginia 22314-5780 • Tel (703) 555-3434 • Fax (703) 555-1177

VICE PRESIDENT • MANUFACTURING OPERATIONS

Senior executive specialized in directing high-volume, multi-plant production operations.
Proven track record revitalizing stagnant functions, driving quality improvements, and eliciting cooperation from
vendors, management, clients, and employees to improve profits, control costs,
expedite products to market, and achieve genuine results.

KEY CREDENTIALS

- Process Reengineering
- Labor Force Management
- Production Plant Management
- Quality Management (ISO 9002)
- Cost Containment/Reduction
- Team Building
- Vendor Negotiations
- Plant Commissioning & Decommissioning

Positive work philosophy and team orientation underscore solid business acumen to achieve key
objectives for productivity, quality, and time-critical deadlines.

PROFESSIONAL EXPERIENCE

May 89-Mar 01   **CONLIGHT AUTOMOTIVE PRODUCTS,** Birmingham, AL
VICE PRESIDENT OF OPERATIONS
Directed manufacturing operations across plants in Alabama and Mexico for America's second-
largest manufacturer of automotive water pumps with sales of $380M and 1500 employees.
Identified and modified processes impacting negatively on customer satisfaction rates, quality
standards, and cost controls by driving a series of solution-based improvement initiatives.

- Accomplished quality assurance ISO 9002 certification in both plants on initial application.
- Radically improved customer delivery times and product quality by forging regular
  communications and better understanding between marketing and production personnel.
- Exceeded previous productivity and performance figures, reducing scrap waste rates by 50%
  and slashing rework rates from 75% to 1%.
- Circumvented unprofitable and potentially risky initiative to change vendor due to quality
  concerns. Partnered with vendor to support and encourage their attainment of ISO 9002
  certification — contributing to their growing industry reputation as a quality supplier.
- Minimized production down time by rescheduling preventative maintenance functions.

Apr 79-May 89   **C. W. MORGAN CORPORATION**

VICE PRESIDENT OF MEXICAN OPERATIONS, El Paso, TX	Apr 85-May 89
DIRECTOR OF OPERATIONS/PLANT MANAGER, Seattle, WA	Jun 81-Apr 85
MANAGER OF MANUFACTURING ENGINEERING, Kankakee, IL	Apr 79-Jun 81

Record of steady career advancement in line with willingness to assume increasingly complex
challenges with this manufacturer of residential and industrial water heaters.

VICE PRESIDENT OF MEXICAN OPERATIONS
Aggressively reengineered business processes to arrest declining profits, high staff turnover, poor
safety, and perceived cost/quality concerns by customers and vendors. Moved quickly to institute
changes, establishing comprehensive training programs to boost skills, build teams, create health
and safety awareness, and improve leadership techniques.

This clean, concise presentation for an experienced VP uses powerful language in the summary to stir
the reader's interest in this individual and his capabilities.

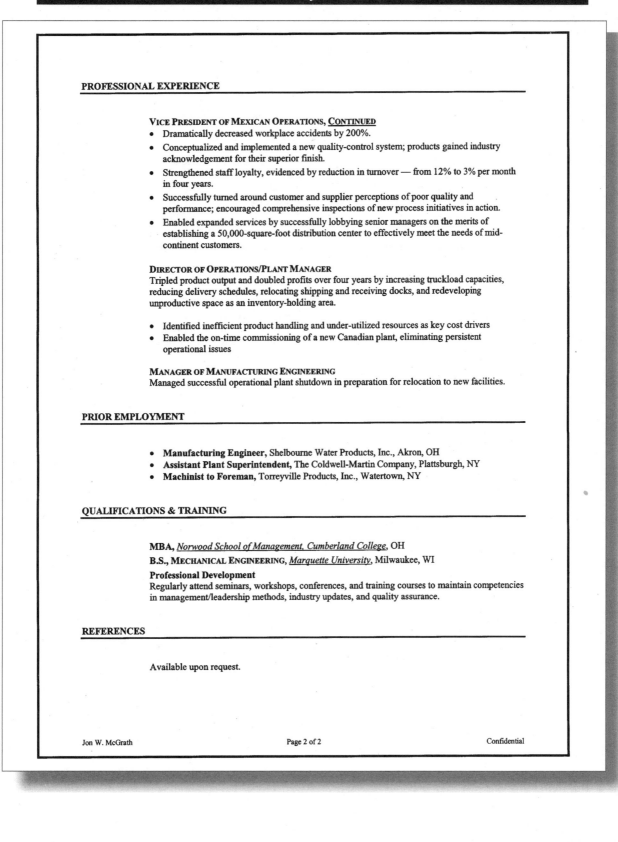

PROFESSIONAL EXPERIENCE

VICE PRESIDENT OF MEXICAN OPERATIONS, <u>CONTINUED</u>
- Dramatically decreased workplace accidents by 200%.
- Conceptualized and implemented a new quality-control system; products gained industry acknowledgement for their superior finish.
- Strengthened staff loyalty, evidenced by reduction in turnover — from 12% to 3% per month in four years.
- Successfully turned around customer and supplier perceptions of poor quality and performance; encouraged comprehensive inspections of new process initiatives in action.
- Enabled expanded services by successfully lobbying senior managers on the merits of establishing a 50,000-square-foot distribution center to effectively meet the needs of mid-continent customers.

DIRECTOR OF OPERATIONS/PLANT MANAGER
Tripled product output and doubled profits over four years by increasing truckload capacities, reducing delivery schedules, relocating shipping and receiving docks, and redeveloping unproductive space as an inventory-holding area.

- Identified inefficient product handling and under-utilized resources as key cost drivers
- Enabled the on-time commissioning of a new Canadian plant, eliminating persistent operational issues

MANAGER OF MANUFACTURING ENGINEERING
Managed successful operational plant shutdown in preparation for relocation to new facilities.

PRIOR EMPLOYMENT

- **Manufacturing Engineer**, Shelbourne Water Products, Inc., Akron, OH
- **Assistant Plant Superintendent**, The Coldwell-Martin Company, Plattsburgh, NY
- **Machinist to Foreman**, Torreyville Products, Inc., Watertown, NY

QUALIFICATIONS & TRAINING

MBA, *Norwood School of Management, Cumberland College*, OH

B.S., MECHANICAL ENGINEERING, *Marquette University*, Milwaukee, WI

Professional Development
Regularly attend seminars, workshops, conferences, and training courses to maintain competencies in management/leadership methods, industry updates, and quality assurance.

REFERENCES

Available upon request.

Jon W. McGrath   Page 2 of 2   Confidential

Michael W. Ackley

14855 South Avenue
Midvale, IL 82516
(708) 924-1472 ▸ AckleyMW@vwest.com

Management Executive — Manufacturing

Dynamic management career offering 20+ years of progressive experience and documented contributions in all areas of manufacturing operations across diverse industries. Track record of increased productivity, cost-effective systems, continuous process improvements, and positive employee relations. Instrumental in start-up success of industrial facilities and leading-edge technology and programs in three Fortune 100 companies.

Articulate communication skills for motivating personnel to personal bests in performance, resolving conflicts, and building strong relationships with staff, vendors, and customers at all levels. Goal-driven solutions provider, recognized for superb leadership and ability to achieve results in seeming impossible situations.

Areas of Expertise

- Operations Management
- Team Building & Leadership
- Policies & Procedures
- Project Lifecycle Management
- Inventory Control & Purchasing
- Quality Assurance

- P&L Control / Budgeting
- Recruitment, Training & Supervision
- Customer Relationship Management
- Health, Safety & Environmental Regulations
- Process Reengineering
- Labor Union Proceedings

Career Progression

R.J. Thomson, Inc., Midvale, IL   **May 2000 - Present**

AREA MANAGER

Full P&L control as area manager of 17 states and 2 Canadian provinces for $500 million global industrial chemical manufacturer. Oversee 20 direct reports in service portion of business.

- Turned around overspending budget situation, meeting expense budget and bringing capital budget in at 6.9% of sales compared to 8% budgeted.
- Reduced delivery times from 40 days to 10 days with new production line to accommodate JIT (Just-In-Time) manufacturing techniques.
- Catalyst for top-notch safety program resulting in more than 1 million accident-free man hours.
- Drove purchase and implementation of computerized maintenance system for plant equipment.
- Special Recognition Awards for JIT system and safety programs; Top Performer award for computerized maintenance system.

Waste Management International, San Diego, CA   **1995 - 2000**

PLANT MANAGER (1998 - 2000)

Achieved corporate goals through strategic planning, operations management, and resource development. Cultivated safe work environment, ensured compliance with government and corporate regulations, and coached personnel to maximum performance.

- Built lasting relationships with community, customers, vendors, and labor unions.
- Promoted to plant manager to lead multi-plant startup of world's largest, most aggressive Material Recovery and Recycling facility.
- Managed 9 direct reports to management level and 200 indirect reports.
- Orchestrated operational goals and budgets to maximize profit potential for shareholders.

The Areas of Expertise section includes important key words, and accomplishments are clearly distinguished from job responsibilities.

RESUME 90, CONTINUED

Michael W. Ackley - Page 2

DIVISION MAINTENANCE MANAGER (1995 - 1998)

Strategically positioned department goals and budgets for maximum profitability. Recruited and developed maintenance managers. Monitored compliance with safety and environmental regulations.

- ▸ Piloted success of maintenance system and operations for more than 400 pieces of process equipment, 100-truck fleet, and 4 plants totaling nearly 1 million square feet.
- ▸ Managed payroll, operating, and capital budgets in excess of $5 million.
- ▸ Supported start-up of new plants through tool, equipment, and supply procurement.
- ▸ Instituted computerized maintenance system (MP2, Datastream).

Paper Resources, Jonesburg, OK   1993 - 1995

PLANT SUPERVISOR

Led start-up and maintenance of new plant including purchasing, staff supervision, quality control, and environmental affairs for regulatory compliance issues.

- ▸ Change agent for systems development including maintenance system encompassing preventive scheduling, work order prioritizing, spare parts inventory, and inventory control system to set inventory levels, reorder points, and purchasing procedures.
- ▸ Recognized "Top Performer" for dynamic contributions and leadership of self-directed work team.
- ▸ Garnered "Superior" ratings from AIB (American Institute of Banking).

Steel Works, Inc., Coatings Service Division, Alsip, IL   1981 - 1993

HEALTH, SAFETY & ENVIRONMENTAL AFFAIRS COORDINATOR

Progressive experience to final position governing health, safety, and environmental activities at all plant levels. Administered local area network (LAN) and provided support for hardware and software applications. Directed employees and production operation of JIT manufacturing.

- ▸ Formulated production and resource plans on incoming orders with MRP system.
- ▸ Innovated and integrated world-class manufacturing concepts into multiple areas of operations to fulfill corporate goals by building group dynamics and employee empowerment.

Education & Professional Qualifications

B.S., Organization Management/Human Resources — 2000
San Diego State University, San Diego, CA

Certifications
Advanced Safety Certification – National Safety Council
Production and Inventory Control Management (CPIM) – American Production and Inventory Control
Society (APICS)

Computer Skills
Technical proficiencies spanning all popular business and manufacturing management software, SAP,
MRP systems, and LANs.

Professional & Community Involvement
American Production and Inventory Control Society (APICS) — Member
Association for Manufacturing Excellence - Member
St. Francis School Board - Chairperson for Building and Maintenance Committee (1992 – 1996) and
Vice-President (1994 – 1995)
Planned, organized, and hosted fund-raising event for Cystic Fibrosis Foundation. Actively involved in
coaching youth sports.

C R

CONSTANCE S. ROSE
58391 Herrick Road, Mooers, NY 12958
Phone: (518) 623-3468 ▪ E-mail: crose@myhome.com

PROFESSIONAL PROFILE	**BUSINESS MANAGEMENT PROFESSIONAL**

Reengineer — Facility, Operations, and Administrative Procedures

Strategic Corporate Planning / Workflow Optimization / Ergonomic Efficiency

Professional business manager, a "results producer," documented for cutting costs through aggressive management tactics, administrative restructuring, and resource allocation / management. Recognized for accident rate and turnover reductions, workforce cutbacks, and business development.

HIGHLIGHTS

Business Development —
- Proven track record of increased productivity through high-level networking and personnel management.
- Significantly improved workmanship quality and safety standards by initiating random drug testing; sending the message, "drugs have no place within a successful business."
- Responsible for implementing ISO9000 and ISO9002 certification.

Operations / Management —
- Analyzed each department — implemented floor plan adjustments, space optimization, and waste reduction.
- Network amongst cross-functional teams enabling quick problem resolution.
- Instituted new computer system supplying necessary technical support.
- Reduced the number of employees "performing duplicate functions."
- Keen ability to locate inefficiencies within business or employees day-to-day functions.

Cost Control —
- Saved the company $500K yearly through administrative restructuring, eliminating redundant tasks, and improving efficiency.
- Cut staffing requirements by 15% and saved $150K per year in unnecessary salaries and benefits.
- Reduced accident rate by 200% within the third quarter.
- Imposed new training programs, provoking a 9% turnover rate decrease.

AT A GLANCE

Operations Systems	Strategic Planning	Cost Management	Facility Design
Offshore Production	Quality Control	Supplier Partnerships	Labor Relations
Facility Consolidation	Process Automation	Safety Management	Compliance

EXPERIENCE

PAPER AND ASSOCIATES, MOOERS, NY
Outsource company, supplier of forms and stationery, including postal and presort mailing services.

This resume was written for an individual who had to act quickly after an unexpected layoff. She had inadvertently worked herself out of a position due to her success in restructuring the company's business processes.

CONSTANCE S. ROSE   **Page Two**

EXPERIENCE
continued

Manager   **2000 – 2001**
Hired to completely restructure existing processes and allow increased
revenues.
- Assisted with massive merchandising program implementation,
  including prominent companies — Graphics On-Line, Alliance
  Financial, and McMann — creating prestigious cross-
  promotional partnerships.

MEDIA ENTERPRISES, PLATTSBURGH, NY

Vice President of Operations   **1997 – 2000**
Oversaw all operations within this fast-paced multi-media business,
a provider of various types of services and products.

Completely restructured the business to operate efficiently and cost
effectively. Extensive redesign included floor plan layout, space
optimization, and detailed workstation analysis. Performed cost-cutting
tactics, staff consolidation / reduction, and restructuring bottleneck
processes within cross-functional teams.
- Implemented QC system that resulted in the highest quality in
  the company's history.
- Spearheaded outstanding issues, enabling the plant to open on
  schedule; received promotion to Vice President.
- Negotiated vendor commitments, producing a smooth JIT process.
- Promoted twice in six years.

Manager / Director of Operations   **1996 – 1997**
Manager   **1994 – 1996**

PLATTSBURGH PAPER AND STEEL, PERU, NY
Leading paper-product manufacturer with annual sales of $1 billion, employing
over 1,500 employees nationwide.

Manager   **1984 – 1994**
Managed multi-site facilities, supervising management teams,
overseeing training, and directing operational systems.
- Initiated and secured ISO9002 certification in two plants on the
  first application.
- Decreased preventive maintenance scheduling by 50% and
  eliminated rework.
- Improved sub-standard quality; achieved ISO9000 certification.

**CONTINUING
EDUCATION**

Strategic Planning Seminar	Understanding Border Culture
Leadership at the Park	MRPII Oliver Write
Herb Massillon Ergonomics	Hanks Manager / Supervisor Classes
The Employees Team Concept	Massasoit College Business / Computer
World Class Manufacturing &	
Process Capability Studies	

JACK JACKSON, CPA

555 St. James Court
Oakdale, Wisconsin 55555
(555) 555-5555
Email: Jackson@aol.com

EXECUTIVE PROFILE

- High achiever with strong leadership abilities. Communicate positively with people at all levels of organization.

- Analytical and perceptive. View problems from various perspectives and evaluate viability of alternative solutions.

- Entrepreneurial spirit complemented by ability to be innovative and creative.

- Strategic thinker with ability to perceive future needs. In response to changing technological needs, develop successful and innovative growth strategies to expand product offerings and diversify distribution channels to keep company profitable.

- In addition to strong manufacturing environment, attuned to marketing aspects of business and sensitive to needs of customers. Committed to providing top-quality products and the best customer service.

EMPLOYMENT

London Corporation, New York, NY
SENIOR VICE PRESIDENT – DIRECTOR OF OPERATIONS, 1999 – 2001
Manufacturer of coated papers and films for wide-format reproductions.

Directed all manufacturing and scheduling of 19 coating lines. Converted operations in 3 U.S. facilities that supply 200+ products in 30,000 configurations to customers, national and international distribution centers, and subsidiary company.

- Presided over R&D Department with goal of accelerating expansion of color ink-jet media product line. Promoted program for pre-trial and post-trial reviews to effectively utilize time on production equipment and control materials consumed for testing purposes. **Results:** Estimated annual savings of $80,000.

- Provided corporate management involvement in continued installation and de-bugging of MOVEX ERP system. Coordinated with others to define problems; isolated causes, defined solutions, and developed corrective actions. Identified capability within ERP to accommodate additional decimal places for pricing of bulk sales. **Results:** $300,000 in estimated revenues to be realized annually.

- Negotiated and secured commitments from vendors, obtaining best prices, delivery terms, and extended price guarantee periods. Brought fragmented purchasing activity under control of Central Purchasing and competitive bid process.

- Initiated program to install product-labeling capability in domestic distribution centers. **Results:** Reduced inventory requirements and allowed distribution centers to private-label products for multiple customers.

- Interfaced with marketing department to identify needs for new products and modify performance characteristics of existing products.

The highlighted word "Results" in each accomplishment statement draws the eye to this important information.

JACK JACKSON, CPA   Page 2 of 2

Midwest Paper Company, Stonegrove, IL
PRESIDENT, 1976 – 1999
Coated paper manufacturer for wide-format reproductions with annual sales of $6,500,000.
Reported to Board of Directors and oversaw 4 direct and 25 indirect staff.

Established company as progressive organization with high-quality products and reputation for excellent service. Became respected competitor in industry dominated by larger companies.

- Revamped plant layout, resulting in increased efficiency in material storage, movement, and order picking.

- Installed inventory control system with minimum stocking levels and reorder points. Negotiated with major paper mills and chemical suppliers to obtain pricing on par with larger-volume users within industry.

- Developed marketing and sales programs. Introduced new products such as specialty-coated papers for plotters and color ink jet printers/plotters to meet changing demands of reprographic industry.

- Pioneered industry use of photo-black opaque plastic for wrapping light-sensitive products. **Results:** Eliminated 2 operators, increased productivity, and saved approximately $40,000 annually in packaging costs.

- Spearheaded the use of computer-printed product labels—another first for industry. **Results:** Enabled this small company to have competitive advantage by offering private labeling as added service for customers.

- Started up sister company, Strom Computer Printing, Inc., when need arose for faster, cleaner, and more flexible means for printing variable information on product labels. Drew upon systems and programming background to develop software that fulfilled needs but would also be flexible enough to allow other companies to design, format, and print variable information on labels.

- Through capitalizing on its limited resources and continually improving efficiency and productivity, company remained profitable during most of tenure. Involved in all aspects of business and responded quickly with innovative products and services.

- Developed service-bureau operation to scan large-format documents. Marketed service to existing and new dealers as additional benefit they could offer to their clients without any capital investment.

- Established and maintained favorable banking relationships.

- Designed, specified, and installed UNIX-based system for order entry, billing, production reporting, sales analyses, and all accounting functions. Successfully upgraded and converted all applications for Y2K compliance.

EDUCATION

DePaul University, Chicago, IL
B.S. ACCOUNTING
Graduate coursework in accounting, finance, marketing, and management in MBA program.

PROFESSIONAL ORGANIZATIONS

Association of Engineering Graphic Imaging Systems (AEGIS), formerly Association of Reproduction Materials Manufacturers (ARMM) — **Treasurer and Director**, ARMM, 1984 —1999
American Institute of CPAs
Illinois Society of CPAs
International Reprographics Association (IRgA)

Harrison Torrance

11 Crator Court
Heavenly Beach, NJ 07750

732 – 363 – 7854
HarrisonT@home.com

PROFILE and CAPABILITIES

Senior Manager and Industry Pioneer in Global Manufacturing Operations:
Sourcing, Controls, and Forming Creative Marketing Alliances

Fast-tracked Operations/Manufacturing/International Manager for NYSE 500 corporations. Promoted for ability to develop new products, source raw materials, set up operations, control costs, increase productivity, and distribute efficiently. Pioneered trend to offshore manufacturing and international sourcing. Became an expert in manufacturing environment in most of the countries on 6 continents. Recently added skills in sales, marketing, forming alliances with resellers, and negotiating variety of large contracts with senior executives worldwide.

CORE COMPETENCIES

International dealmaker familiar with strategic factors worldwide including labor variables, raw-material sourcing, private-label contract manufacturing, import-export factors, etc. New business development, start-up, and turnaround. Establish foreign sales and operations offices. Form policy, establish systems, and manage IT projects. Evolve all aspects of company for rapid growth. Treasury functions, cost accounting, cash management, budgeting, and forecasting. Strategic plans and implementation. Production systems, union and non-union labor relations, materials management. Set quality and service level standards internally and externally.

EXPERTISE and EXPERIENCE

- P & L Responsibility
- Robust Profitability
- Cost Control
- Turnarounds

- Quality Service Levels
- Contract Negotiations
- Key Account Relations
- Brand Management

- Production / Distribution
- Sourcing
- Retail Strategies
- Catalog Outlets

PROFESSIONAL BACKGROUND

Partner, Reminisce Clothing/Baumton Apparel, 1995–Present
Clothing manufacturer formed in 1980, supplying both mid-line and top-tier retailers.
- Turnaround situation. Produced first profit in four years; increased sales by 70%
- As consultant, designed plan to exit the branded business and concentrate on selling private-label sweaters and knitwear to the existing customer base.
- Completely revamped the company — upgraded suppliers, personnel, and customers. Business increased significantly. Concurrently, cut costs by increasing productivity and eliminating many inventory requirements.
- Formed alliance with Hong Kong-China factory to produce sweaters in the Philippines. Avoided tariffs and duties without sacrificing legality, quality, or delivery.
- Discovered counter-trend niche for contract-manufactured product in the U.S. This market forms one-third of our current revenue.

To avoid stereotyping the candidate as part of the garment industry, where he had spent virtually his entire career, none of the introductory material in this resume mentions his industry expertise.

Harrison Torrance, page two

Senior Vice President, Rockwear Company, 1993–95
Marketing, Sourcing, Manufacturing, and International Operations.

Senior Vice President, Taal Beal Inc., 1989–93
Large NYSE manufacturer and distributor.
- Reduced costs by moving 60% of manufacturing offshore.
- Consolidated distribution. Established internal quality production methods and set supplier quality standards.
- Set up offices in Hong Kong and Taiwan to remove third-party agents from production process. Enjoyed 4 types of cost savings.

Senior Vice President, Mast Harbor Co., 1988–89
Marketing, Sourcing, Manufacturing, and International Operations.

Senior Vice President, The Companioner LTC Sportswear (NYSE CLTC), 1973–88
- Promoted through series of executive production-management positions while volume increased from $65MM to $150MM. Among youngest executives in the industry at this level.
- Pioneer in moving 70% of U.S. production offshore. Reduced per unit costs significantly.
- Manufacturing Systems Analyst for enterprise management software that reported real-time financial results. Integrated merchandising, sales, distribution, and customer service to propel delivery and shipping service levels to new heights.
- Among first U.S. companies to produce garments in Australia. Set up manufacture with good quality, price, and schedule factors while reducing quota constraints and price pressure.
- Among the first to develop garment production in Hungary and Portugal. Imported raw material from Italy and reaped favorable manufacturing cost advantages.
- Pioneered Mexico City as a manufacturing center 3½ years ahead of trend. Saved 30%–40% while enjoying quality, cost, and schedule advantages over border facilities. Reaped millions in significantly higher profits.

Manager, LTC Sportswear, Div. Major Morris, 1971–73
Management Development program in Production and Operations

EDUCATION, ASSOCIATIONS, and INTERESTS

B.S. Philadelphia University   A.A. Fashion Institute of Technology

President, 9 years, Fashion Apparel Manufacturing Association.
Chief Management Negotiator for labor agreements throughout Philadelphia and South Jersey

Enjoy boating, scuba diving, reading, and collecting antique automobiles

James B. Lindseth

28 River Drive
Bismarck, ND 58701

701-844-6666
jlindseth@aol.com

‣ **Veteran Manufacturing Manager** seeking opportunity to share years of experience with an employee-centered company. Experience ranges from family-run businesses to large corporations and cash-poor businesses to extremely profitable businesses.

‣ Demonstrated versatility and diversification in responsibilities.

‣ Ability to develop a productive, entry-level labor force from wide-ranging ethnic groups. Trained entry-level employees to become responsible managers.

‣ Employee supervision experience includes union, non-union, uneducated, highly educated, non-English speaking, on-site, off-site, production laborers, and top management.

‣ Strengths: team-driven leader; persistent, innovative, and progressive thinker.

Areas of expertise:

Operations	Integrating modern technology	Personnel management
Strategic planning	Customer service	Worker's Compensation
Cost containment	Sales techniques	OSHA regulations
Purchasing	Multicultural relations	Safety
Building remodeling/expansion	Problem resolution	Conflict resolution

Professional Experience

President / General Manager
Bismarck Manufacturing
Manufacturer of body frames for heavy-duty vehicle industry.

11/88–Present
Bismarck, ND

‣ Played leadership role in:
Increasing sales from $5 million to $30 million ...
Increasing manufacturing square footage from 26,000 to 110,000 ...
Increasing employees from 75 to 550+ ...
Expanding from one plant to seven.

‣ Interviewed, reviewed, counseled, and released entry-level to management-level employees.

‣ Researched and added state-of-the-art processing equipment, integrating robotics and automation.

‣ Renovated abandoned and underutilized buildings to expand operations to small rural communities.

‣ Replaced paper with custom-made computer programs and bar-code technology.

‣ Successfully completed three ISO-type audits; revised quality systems, procedures, and manuals in anticipation of ISO 9001 audit.

‣ Completed ND Worker's Compensation-Risk Management Program and reduced compensation costs 5%.

‣ Collaborated with Bismarck School System to establish on-site *English as a Second Language* program.

This particularly inviting and readable resume has a distinctive typeface, bold headings, and an effective boxed-table treatment of the candidate's areas of expertise.

James B. Lindseth
Page 2

Professional Experience cont.

Director of Manufacturing   3/88–11/88
Linton Manufacturing Company   Linton, ND
Manufacturer of agricultural products.

- ▸ Integrated three independent departments into one team, sharing responsibilities and inventory.
- ▸ Originated and set up central warehouse.
- ▸ Administered inbound/outbound freight activities for entire company.
- ▸ Implemented IBM MAPICS software.

Director of Manufacturing / General Manager   6/86–3/88
Bismarck Corporation   Bismarck, ND
Manufacturer of communication systems.

- ▸ Expanded production capacity and doubled employee population.
- ▸ Purchased and installed state-of-the-art Wave Soldering and Auto Wash equipment to automate circuit board production.
- ▸ Administered the design, manufacturing, and shipment of entire line of 900 MHz radio remotes for General Electric.
- ▸ Initiated a telemarketing department to sell private-label land-mobile equipment.
- ▸ Established a computer-based MRP inventory system.
- ▸ Restructured management style from one dominant leader into four independent departments functioning as a team.

Operator / Owner   4/77–6/86
Lindseth Hardware   Milnor, ND
Operated and managed two hardware stores.

- ▸ Merged two separate stores into one extremely profitable business.
- ▸ Purchased and remodeled an adjacent building for expansion purposes.
- ▸ Made strategic decisions to improve profit margins.

Education

Master of Business Administration
University of Mary, Bismarck, ND

Bachelor of Science – Electrical Engineering
North Dakota State University, Fargo, ND

WILLIAM T. PARKERSON

35 Sunderland Drive
Cedar Grove, NJ 07009

E-mail: parkersonw@compuserve.com

Home: (732) 599-6694
Fax: (732) 599-4481

PLANT / OPERATIONS / GENERAL MANAGEMENT EXECUTIVE

Multi-site manufacturing plant/general management career building and leading high-growth, transition, and start-up operations in domestic and international environments with annual revenues of up to $680 million.

Expertise: Organizational Development • Productivity & Cost Reduction Improvements • Supply Chain Management • Acquisitions & Divestitures • IPOs • Plant Rationalizations • Safety Performance • Customer Relations • Change Agent

CORE COMPETENCIES

Manufacturing Leadership—Strong P&L track record with functional management experience in all disciplines of manufacturing operations • Developing and managing operating budgets • Spearheading restructuring and rationalization of plants and contracted distribution facilities • Initiating lean manufacturing processes, utilizing SMED principles • Establishing performance metrics and supply chain management teams.

Continuous Improvement & Training—Designing and instituting leadership-enhancement training program for all key plant management • Instituting Total Quality System (TQS) process in domestic plants to promote the business culture of continuous improvement • Leading ISO 9001 certification process.

New Product Development—Initiating plant-based "New Product Development Think Tank" that developed 130 new products for marketing review, resulting in the successful launch of 5 new products in 2000.

Engineering Management—Oversight of corporate machine design and development teams • Developing 3-year operating plan • Directing the design, fabrication, and installation of several proprietary machines • Creating project cost tracking systems and introducing ROI accountability.

PROFESSIONAL EXPERIENCE

BEACON INDUSTRIES, INC., Maspeth, NY   **1994-Present**
Record of continuous promotions to executive-level position in manufacturing and operations management through periods of transition/acquisition at a $680 million Fortune 500 international manufacturing company. Career highlights include:

Vice President — Manufacturing (1997-Present)

Senior Operating Executive responsible for the performance of 7 manufacturing/distribution facilities for company that experienced rapid growth from 4 plants generating $350 million in annual revenues to 14 manufacturing facilities with revenues of $680 million. Charged with driving the organization to becoming a low-cost producer. Established performance indicators, operating goals, realignment initiatives, productivity improvements, and cost-reduction programs that consistently improved product output, product quality, and customer satisfaction.

Achievements:

- Selected to lead corporate team in developing and driving cost-reduction initiatives that will result in $21 million saved over the next 3 years through capital infusion, process automation, and additional rationalizations.

- Saved $13 million annually by reducing fixed spending 11% and variable overhead spending 18% through effective utilization of operating resources and cost-improvement initiatives.

- Cut worker's compensation costs 40% ($750,000 annually) by implementing effective health and safety plans, employee training, management accountability and equipment safeguarding. Led company to achieve recognition as "Best in Industry" in OSHA frequency and lost workday incident rates.

- Reduced waste generation 31%, saving $1 million in material usage by optimizing manufacturing processes as well as instituting controls and accountability.

- Enhanced customer-service satisfaction 3% annually during past year (measured by order fill and on-time delivery percentage) through supply chain management initiatives, inventory control, and flexible manufacturing practices.

- Trimmed manufacturing and shipping-related credits to customers from 1.04% to .5% of total sales in 1999, representing annual $1.8 million reduction.

- Decreased total inventories 43% from 1997 base through combination of supply chain management, purchasing, master scheduling, and global utilization initiatives.

- Rationalized 3 manufacturing plants and 6 distribution facilities, saving $6 million over 3 years.

Note the detail included under Core Competencies; these strong, value-added statements should pique readers' interest.

WILLIAM T. PARKERSON — (732) 599-6694 — Page 2

General Manager — Northeast (1994-1997)

Assumed full P&L responsibility of 2 manufacturing facilities and a $20 million annual operating budget. Directly supervised facility managers and 250 employees indirectly in a multi-line, multicultural manufacturing environment. Planned and realigned organizational structure and operations to position company for high growth as a result of acquiring a major account, 2 new product lines, and 800 additional SKUs.

Achievements:

- Reduced operating costs by $4.5 million through consolidation of 2 distribution locations without adverse impact on customer service.
- Accomplished the start-up of 2 new manufacturing operations, which encompassed a plant closing and the integration of acquired equipment into existing production lines for 2 new product lines without interruption to customer service; achieved 2 months ahead of target and $400,000 below budget.
- Increased operating performance by 15% while reducing labor costs by $540,000.
- Reduced frequency and severity of accidents by 50% in 3 years, contributing to a worker's compensation and cost-avoidance reduction of $1 million.
- Decreased operating waste by 2% for an annual cost savings of $800,000 in 2 manufacturing facilities.
- Negotiated turnkey contracts for 2 distribution warehouses to meet expanded volume requirements.
- Maintained general management and administrative cost (GMA) at a flat rate as sales grew by 25% annually over 3 years.

ROMELARD CORPORATION, Detroit, MI   **1980-1994**

Division Manufacturing Director (1989-1994)

Fast-track advancement in engineering, manufacturing, and operations management to division-level position. Retained by new corporate owners and promoted in 1994 based upon consistent contributions to revenue growth, profit improvements, and cost reductions. Scope of responsibility encompassed P&L for 3 manufacturing facilities and a distribution center with 500 employees in production, quality, distribution, inventory control, and maintenance.

Achievements:

- Delivered strong and sustainable operating gains: increased customer fill rate by 18%; improved operating performance by 20%; reduced operating waste by 15%; reduced inventory by $6 million.
- Justified, sourced, and directed the installation in $10 million of automated plant equipment.
- Implemented and managed a centralized master schedule for all manufacturing facilities.
- Reduced annual worker's compensation costs by $600,000.
- Created Customer Satisfaction Initiative program to identify areas of concern; implemented recommendations, significantly improving customer satisfaction.

Prior Positions: Manufacturing Manager (1987-1989); Plant Manager (1986-1987); Engineering Manager (1984-1986); Plant Industrial Engineer (1980-1984).

EDUCATION & PROFESSIONAL DEVELOPMENT

Bachelor of Science in Manufacturing Engineering
Syracuse University, Syracuse, NY

Continuing professional development programs in
Executive Management, Leadership, and Finance

RAYMOND SIMMONS

1002 Timber Creek Drive • Fort Wayne, Indiana 46818
(219) 596-1823 • Fax (219) 596-2794 • Mobile (219) 788-0202 • Email rsimmons@worldmail.com

EXECUTIVE PROFILE

BUSINESS STRATEGY DEVELOPMENT • GLOBAL SUPPLY CHAIN MANAGEMENT
MANUFACTURING REDESIGN • MERGER & ACQUISITION INTEGRATION
ORGANIZATIONAL LEADERSHIP • PROFIT & PROCESS IMPROVEMENT

SENIOR EXECUTIVE with over 20 years of experience and expertise in leading strategic initiatives, merger and acquisition integration, and P&L responsibility. Highly qualified and knowledgeable in general management and cultural change leadership, employee development, and leadership in turnaround efforts and process improvements. Proven ability to develop and implement highly effective global supply strategies and skill in identifying market potential for significant business growth. Fully computer and business systems literate. Conversant in French and German.

"Ray's positive influence has gone well beyond that of a Manufacturing Executive. Ray constantly challenges himself and his people, providing leadership and demonstrating excellence by example." – S. Montana, President – Chemical International

PROFESSIONAL EXPERIENCE

CHEM TECHNOLOGY (Formerly Chemical International, Inc.), Fort Wayne, Indiana
(Specialty Chemical Manufacturer)

Vice President / General Manager — Performance Markers / Organic Specialties / Primenes   **1997 – 2000**
Defined Term Appointment
    Managed and held P&L responsibility for this $100 million global unit with direct line report for all organizational functions. Defined business strategies and executed operating budgets and plans. Led management team of 9 overseeing 135 employees

NOTABLE ACCOMPLISHMENTS
- Restructured manufacturing operations and reduced yearly direct costs by $1.4 million in the United States, $1.5 million in the United Kingdom, $0.3 million in Europe, avoiding capital expense threat of $4.5 million.
- Recaptured 3% of market share — improved business outlook and broadened potential product lines and markets through detailed analysis of defined market, segmented potential product uses, and new technology to uphold marketplace.
- Consolidated and relocated targeted product lines to third-party toll manufacturing within the UK after investigating alternatives in India and People's Republic of China.
- Increased Pre-Tax Income (PTI) over 25% — leveraged suppliers, increased operating efficiencies, and controlled costs
- Increased RONA 3.2% — through controlled capital investment and aggressive management of working capital, exceeded company goal of 15%.
- Refocused business strategy from "product offered" to "market focused/customer driven," resulting in a culture change from "price based" selling to "value-added" relationships with the customer.
- Launched SpecMark Product Line — generated $1.5 million in additional sales within 24 months.

SPECIALTY CHEMICALS — Fort Wayne, Indiana
(Water Treatment Chemical Company)

Vice President — Customer Fulfillment   **1996 – 1997**
    Optimized all aspects of supply chain and rationalized all supply chain operations and customer support systems. Managed worldwide manufacturing, logistics, customer service, engineering, quality, corporate services, and facilities management. Led management team of 9, overseeing 180 employees.

This resume effectively highlights strong career progression and measurable results. A quote from the company president is a nice touch.

RESUME 96, CONTINUED

RAYMOND SIMMONS   (219) 596-1823 • Email rsimmons@worldmail.com • Page 2

SPECIALTY CHEMICALS — CONTINUED

NOTABLE ACCOMPLISHMENTS

- Saved corporation $5.2 million — successfully restructured plant site organizations, consolidated and leveraged suppliers, redefined raw material specifications, and restructured central engineering and corporate staff functions.
- Restructured manufacturing sites and submitted cost-saving proposals for an additional $1.8 million.

ELECTRONICS INTERNATIONAL, INC. — Dallas, Texas

Vice President — Manufacturing and Logistics	1992 – 1996
Director — Manufacturing Operations	1986 – 1992
Plant Manager	1983 – 1986
Office Manager	1978 – 1983
Warehouse Manager	1973 – 1977

Managed manufacturing, logistics, health and safety, and engineering/environmental affairs for this $200 million business unit. Logistics functions included customer service, purchasing, inventory management, production scheduling, distribution, and business systems. Led management team of 8 overseeing 200 employees.

NOTABLE ACCOMPLISHMENTS

- Avoided business unit foreclosure — reclaimed sufficient levels of pre-tax income, reduced direct manufacturing costs $3.4 million per year, improved chemical process throughput 50%, improved converting throughput 400%, and reduced manufacturing plant organizational structure from 7 to 3 layers.
- Configured traditional management style and organization structure to high performance work team environments — implemented TQM, JIT, and Kaizen management principles.
- Reduced company warehousing locations by 38%, decreasing operational costs 65%.
- Led the design and implementation of automated information systems — JIT delivery exceeded 99.5%, and obsolete inventory was reduced by 95%.
- Ensured organizational and cultural changes would result in favorable opportunities for high performing employees – marked positive impact on overall staff. Employees were recognized for their empowered participation and efforts pertaining to organizational turnaround.
- Implemented Supplier Certification Program — eliminated non-value-added costs in supply chain.
- Negotiated single-source tolling agreement — resulted in savings of over $6 million per year on a 10-year contract basis.
- Negotiated agreement to integrate Morton facility with third-party tolling operations — improved manufacturing efficiencies 80% and reduced rework over 90%.
- Led project team to complete a fully integrated MRP II System conversion.
- Launched the Logistics Integrated Systems Program — enabled future process improvement in working capital management and logistics performance/metrics.

PROFESSIONAL DEVELOPMENT

Business Turnaround/Acquisition — A.T. Kearney/McKinsey, 1996 – 2000
Every Business is a Growth Business — Chem Technology, 2000
Customer Certification Program Implementation — Course Facilitator, 1998

EDUCATION

MBA — Business / Operations Research
BS — Business
George Mason University — Fairfax, Virginia

JOHN D. ANDERSON

8 500 South Autumnwood Circle, #2002, Weddington, North Carolina 98075
(704) 336-3260

EXECUTIVE MANAGEMENT • GENERAL OPERATIONS
TRANSPORTATION • DISTRIBUTION • LOGISTICS • SUPPLY CHAIN MANAGEMENT

PROFILE

Over 15 years' success in increasing revenues, enhancing supply chain efficiency, and improving operational performance through a series of aggressive organizational revitalization, process simplification, and staff development initiatives. Experienced in turnaround and new division startups. Also open to equity position or consulting contract. MBA degreed. Competencies:

— Strategic and tactical planning — commodity management
— Performance and productivity improvement — contract negotiations
— Financial management / P & L responsibility — demand forecasting
— Expense / cost control / budget oversight   — order fulfillment
— Vendor sourcing / negotiations / procurement — inventory management
— Process design / benchmarking / improvement — quality assurance
— Six Sigma / ISO 9000, 14000 / TQM —facilities management
— Customer relationship management   — marketing and business plans

---

VALUE OFFERED

▶ Restore structure from chaos through process simplification / standardization
▶ Advance profit and revenue growth through strategic long-range planning
▶ Expand profit margins through negotiations with vendors / suppliers / buyers
▶ Improve asset productivity through cost reduction / removal
▶ Accelerate performance and productivity of employees through incentive
▶ Maximize human capital resources during post-layoff reduction
▶ Heighten operational efficiency / profitability through technology upgrade
▶ Revitalize customer loyalty through customer relationship management

---

SELECTED ACHIEVEMENTS

POST-ACQUISITION OPERATIONS CONSULTANT / CHIEF OPERATING OFFICER
DIRECTOR OF PURCHASING
HUMAN RESOURCE MANAGER

Danton Food Industries, Inc, Charlotte, North Carolina (1985-2001, until sale of company)

[A 130-employee, $60 million, 250,000-square-foot, wholesale grocery food / consumer products retailer-owned distribution center servicing 200+ regional stores in four states]

EXECUTIVE MANAGEMENT
- Orchestrated all post-sale activities of corporate acquisition: work force assimilation, process integration, customer conversion, and financial reporting to new owners.
- Led each phase of corporate sale including prospective buyer solicitation, strategic negotiations, investor relations, customer retention, and cash flow optimization.
- Spearheaded an aggressive productivity, quality, and performance management initiative that successfully revitalized a significantly under-performing operation seriously affected by market downturn conditions. Returned company to profitability by next calendar year with a $340,000 annual savings.

After the sale of the family-owned company (his only employer in 15+ years), this individual wanted to transition to a new industry. To help him, the resume writer eliminated industry jargon from his resume and emphasized his transferable skills, strong achievements, and "Value Offered."

JOHN D. ANDERSON

PAGE TWO

SELECTED ACHIEVEMENTS (continued)

Danton Food Industries, Inc. (continued)

EXECUTIVE MANAGEMENT (continued)

- Pioneered several key programs and projects that accelerated profit and revenue growth:
  - Captured a 60% increase in sales through introduction of new convenience-store program
  - Increased profit margins by .5% through changes in purchasing and inventory management practices, elimination of non-performing products, and process automation
  - Upgraded inventory-forecasting system, which tracked 15,000-item inventory more accurately
  - Reduced job-related injuries by 48% and Worker's Compensation premiums by $100,000 (23%) through enhanced employee training in safety and occupational health procedures

PURCHASING / MERCHANDISING

- Decreased inventory by $1.2 million with incrementally improved service levels through conversion to a Just-in-Time process and automation of inventory-forecasting tasks.
- Produced over $1 million in sales within six months through creation of a new private-label program, creative purchasing incentives, promotions and merchandising strategies, and cultivation of strategic relationships with national manufacturers, brokers, and their marketing representatives. Held total responsibility for over $40 million in annual sales.
- Elevated quality and production standards, which led to a 19% reduction in per-case handling costs and decreased product damage.

HUMAN RESOURCES / TRAINING & DEVELOPMENT

- Coached 130+ staff (primarily hourly workers) to greater productivity through pay-through-performance incentive and measurement, cross-functional training for skills upgrade, and management succession programs.
- As primary facilitator, directed and presented numerous safety training workshops and meetings for warehouse operations, truck fleet (company had fleet of 30 trucks, 8 automobiles, and 20 semi-tractor trailer rigs), field support representatives, and office personnel.

Prior experience as Buyer, Warehouse Manager

EDUCATION
- **Master of Business Administration**
  Clemson University — obtained MBA while working full time
- **Bachelor of Science — Business Administration**
  Clemson University

TECHNOLOGY
- MS Word, Excel, Lotus, Peachtree Accounting, dBASE III, Windows, DOS, A/S 400

KEITH SMITH

P.O. Box 1013
Greensboro, North Carolina 28036

(704) 899-4308
keithsmith@worldnet.att.net

GENERAL MANAGEMENT EXECUTIVE
Small & Midsize Manufacturing Organizations

Dynamic career with proven success in accelerating market expansion, increasing revenues, and improving profit contributions. Forward-thinking and decisive leader with the natural ability to anticipate customer requirements. Interactive and motivational management style. Patent holder; MBA degree.

- Corporate Strategy & Operations Leadership
- Team Building & Leadership
- Technology & Quality/Process Improvement

- New Product Launch & Business Development
- Sales, Marketing & Multichannel Distribution
- International Partnerships & Client Management

Create proactive business cultures rewarding innovation and commitment to customer service.

PROFESSIONAL EXPERIENCE:

GREENSBORO SCIENTIFIC CORPORATION, Greensboro, North Carolina   1985 to Present
($77 million product manufacturer/distributor of components and capital equipment with 500 employees)

General Manager – Resins Division (1998 to Present)
Vice President of Engineering & New Product Development (1996 to 1998)
Director of New Product Development (1992 to 1996)
Manager of Engineering (1989 to 1992) / **Manager of Product Development** (1985 to 1989)

Member of a six-person corporate management team and the #1 executive of a $5 million division. Played a key role in building a cohesive, customer-driven organization to compete in a rapidly changing marketplace, leading both entities through growth, revitalization, and organizational change.

Hold full P&L responsibility and focus on maintaining growth momentum through aggressive marketing tactics, product development strategies, and refinement of distribution channels. Provide hands-on leadership to a seven-person team.

- *Business Strategy & Team Leadership.* Integrated a "customer-focus" management philosophy with aggressive revitalization initiatives. Recruited and led top-caliber teams, drove forward a common vision, and established rapport across functional lines. Led fast-paced performance reengineering initiatives to keep pace with market expansion and customer growth.

  - Transitioned $2.4 million annual losses and $64 million in sales to $3.4 million in profits and $77 million in sales in six years.
  - Exceeded first-quarter goals, accelerating profits by 52% and production efficiency by 125%. Surpassed all performance objectives on a shoestring budget without increasing costs.

- *Cost Reduction & Process Redesign.* Revamped processes and introduced strict accountability measures that delivered improvements in cost control, quality, productivity, and cycle time.

  - Reduced overall costs by 30%.
  - Projected to continue increasing efficiencies by 20% during FY00 while continuing to accelerate sales growth and gross profits.

- *Product Development.* Linked product, R&D, and business development functions versus traditional order fulfillment to deliver high-quality, customer-focused products. Widely recognized for the highest quality product innovations.

  - Redesigned four major product categories and led complete development/commercialization cycles, from R&D through production/roll-out.
  - Doubled product portfolio and expanded into new market segments (education, healthcare, industrial, pharmaceutical, consumer goods, R&D firms).
  - Created a modular product line, leveraging CAD technology that facilitated product customization.

Subheadings set apart detailed accomplishments; numbers and results strengthen the candidate's record. Note the attention-getting Value Statement that concludes the summary.

KEITH SMITH **Page Two**

- *Sales & Marketing.* Patented new products/technologies, identified/capitalized on marketing channels, and established joint ventures to increase market presence throughout US and international arenas.
  - Expanded global market presence from 5% to 25% and distribution channels from 10 to 50+.
  - Solidified long-term business relationships with independent dealers, national representatives, and direct-sales dealers worldwide (Brazil, Singapore, UK, Hong Kong, Spain).

- *IT, Manufacturing & Service Delivery.* Introduced an "options rich" technology program and drove forward initiatives to expedite "go to market" strategies and expand scope, level, and caliber of customer service and delivery. Replaced outdated assembly systems governed by pre-staged parts and time-consuming specifications.
  - Designed a parametrically driven front-end system and created templates with cost-based product options. Streamlined order processes and introduced products at "breakneck" speed.
  - Accelerated turnaround delivery time by 60%, improved product reliability by 70%, and achieved outstanding ratings in customer satisfaction.
  - Currently leading negotiations with a Brazilian firm to launch start-up manufacturing/assembly operations projected to deliver $2 million in revenues.

ALLEN & SONS, Greensboro, North Carolina 1983 to 1984

Design Engineer

Recruited to this family-owned firm specializing in theatrical facility design with government and commercial clients worldwide. Gained extensive experience in product design, facilities engineering, and international customer relations. Recognized for unprecedented performance in achieving quality assurance, regulatory compliance, and customer specification requirements.

ASSOCIATIONS:

SCIENTIFIC FURNITURE ASSOCIATION (SFA) Greensboro, NC 1997 to Present
Chairman of Casework Committee (1997 to Present) / **Board of Directors** (1999)

Joined this high-profile organization to represent the interests, issues, and needs of designers, manufacturers, and installers of industry-related products. As Member of the Board of Directors, charged with all policy matters and the development of an annual strategic plan to support organizational goals. Selected by major casework manufacturers to serve as Committee Chairman.

- *Policy & Procedure Development.* Led the development, implementation, and regulation of the SFA Casework Recommended Practices & Procedures Manual. Outlined specific standards and criteria relating to design, fabrication, performance, and assessment for international manufacturers, installers, and casework operators.

EDUCATION:

MBA, University of North Carolina, Charlotte – 1991
BS in Mechanical Engineering Technology, Purdue University – 1982

Ellen M. Burrell

54 Sherwood Glen Lane
Carmel, NY 10512
Residence: (914) 625-7093 ▪ Office: (914) 625-2106 ▪ Email: eburrell@email.com

---

SENIOR OPERATIONS & BUSINESS DEVELOPMENT EXECUTIVE
20+ Years' Management Experience in Leading Consumer Goods/Industrial Manufacturing Corporations

Accomplished management executive offering expansive, cross-functional qualifications providing general management, sales, and marketing expertise to build corporate value for diverse manufacturing organizations. Broad-based background spanning a wide range of packaging, consumer, and industrial products. Proven corporate leader, defining and driving vision, strategies, and goal attainment. Exceptionally capable team builder and people manager, inspiring motivation, group cohesion, and cooperation to achieve common objectives.

Areas of Expertise

Strategic Vision & Mission Planning	General & Operations Management
Revenue & Sales Growth/Business Development	Organizational Reengineering/Change Management
Global Expansion & Market Growth	Team Building & Staff Leadership
Technology Innovation & Product Development	Merger & Acquisition Transactions & Strategies

Professional History

Poulin Solutions, Inc. – Carmel, NY   **1998 – Present**
Leading international manufacturer of decorative systems and performance chemicals, generating $766 million annual revenue. Spin-off of OmniCorp., Inc., as of October 1999.

GENERAL MANAGER, DECORATIVE LAMINATES

Senior executive, recruited as change agent to manage pivotal consolidation and integration of recent acquisition, build team cohesion, and open new markets through a broadened product portfolio. Hold full P&L responsibility for key $70 million business segment comprising 3 U.S.-based manufacturing plants. Lead a 24-person operations, sales, marketing, design, and product management team and provide cross-functional direction for all plant operations, R&D, quality, and financial accounting.

Key Results:

- Broadened product portfolio with 48 new designs and strengthened diversification, defining 7 key markets and circumventing potentially critical losses from decline of previous top target industry.
- Initiated and drove development of new topcoat technologies and processes that improved quality of paper and vinyl substrates while boosting new topcoat volume $2.6 million the first year.
- Pioneered new in-house design studio with state-of-the-art equipment that enhanced design quality, improved speed to market, and increased share against foreign-based competition.
- Expanded global presence into new European and Mexican markets; restructured the sales team to drive international growth and built the European product management/design team.
- Cultivated new domestic joint development partnerships and initiated Asian imports into key markets from offshore plants in Thailand and China.

Atlantic Corporation – Portsmouth, NH   **1994 – 1998**
Multinational manufacturer of plastic film and printed/converted film products. Acquired by Hayward Packaging in May 1998.

VICE PRESIDENT, MARKETING AND SALES (1995 – 1998)
DIRECTOR, ADVANCED AND INDUSTRIAL MARKETS (1994 – 1995)

Recruited by company President to lead complete reorganization and management of sales, marketing, and customer service functions for the $120 million Mercier Plastic Division.   (continued)

This particularly well-written resume paints a picture of a talented and successful executive ready for new challenges.

Ellen M. Burrell ▪ Page 2

Led a 20-person team and managed all strategic planning and department operations. Represented company as an officer, handling expanded P&L responsibilities and collaborating on the Acquisition Team to formulate M&A strategies and perform due diligence for potential buyers.

Key Results:

- Spearheaded transformation to a marketing-driven management philosophy, reengineering operations to enhance customer focus with new regional sales offices and national account coverage.
- Drove a 10% increase in sales and 36% increase in profit contributions during first full year as VP. Built new business $55 million over 4-year period, a figure representing 45% of 1997 total sales.
- Attained leading share in key markets and increased gross margin to 35%+ by rebalancing product mix to target higher-margin markets while optimizing profit capacity of 3 plants.
- Negotiated new strategic alliances for preferred vendor status with key accounts, including Kimberly-Clark, Kendall Healthcare, Johnson & Johnson, Molnlycke, Confab, and PaperPak. Garnered "Vendor of the Year" awards at Johnson & Johnson and PaperPak.
- Instrumental executive player in preparing company for sale, tripling stock price to $24, and structuring final acquisition of company by Huntsman Packaging for $250 million.

K.C. Corporation – Orlando, FL   **1987 – 1994**
Manufacturer of barrier shelf-stable plastic food packaging. Initially hired by Hayward Packaging, a wholly owned subsidiary of Thomas Chemical Co., and retained following acquisition by K.C.

DIRECTOR, MARKETING AND SALES – Hayward Products (1991 – 1994)
VICE PRESIDENT, MARKETING AND SALES – Hayward Packaging (1987 – 1991)

Executive team member tasked with driving new business development through strategic and tactical direction of all sales, marketing, technical marketing, customer service, advertising, and promotions. As company officer, contributed to long-range planning, business objectives, policies and procedures, human resource issues, operating budgets, capital expenditures, safety, and expansion/acquisition planning.

Key Results:

- Accelerated sales 300%, attaining 95% share of hot-fill business, dominant position in low-acid aseptic market, and reversing market-share decline of the struggling retort business. Strengthened competitive positioning in other key markets by driving SPC, GMP, and TQM programs.
- Created and executed account development programs that opened new key accounts with Lipton, Del Monte, Ocean Spray, Seneca, Gerber, Michigan Fruit, and Frito-Lay, among others.
- Achieved 100% share, valued at $5 million annually, with the company's 3 largest customers — Cadbury Schweppes, Lipton, and DelMonte. Generated 192% sales increase with #1 customer.
- Introduced technical advances that were a key factor in establishing long-term development programs with industry leaders, such as ConAgra, Nestlé, Campbell Soup, and Ross Labs.
- Captured 5 major supply contracts and delivered 38% increase in sales the first year with company.

Early career includes fast-track promotion through 8 positions in 11 years (1976 – 1987) at **General Electric Company. Progressed** rapidly from Sales to Manager of Marketing and Sales in the Plastics Business Group. Worked in progressive sales positions (1971 – 1975) at **Procter & Gamble Distributing Co.**

Education

B.S., MARKETING (1971)
New York University, New York, NY

Extensive continuing education and training in sales, marketing, management, and computer-related topics.

RICHARD BOYLSTON

SENIOR MANAGEMENT • MANUFACTURING • MARKETING • GLOBAL OPERATIONS

Fifteen-year strategic and analytical foundation in manufacturing management and business development.

Have developed products and systems responsible for over $28 million in sales increases and over $4 million in cost reductions.

Solidly experienced in the 24x7x365 oversight of global manufacturing operations and related core businesses.

AREAS OF ABILITY

Plant Management • Plant Turnarounds • Acquisitions • Market Expansion • Multimillion-Dollar Cost Reductions
Profit & Loss Oversight • Multimillion-Dollar Budget Creation • Capital & Operating Budgets
Systems Development • ISO 9001 • Capital Projects • Capital Equipment Purchasing
Quality Assurance • Regulatory Oversight • Client Relations • Team Building • Consensus Building
Microsoft Word • Microsoft Excel • Microsoft Access • Microsoft PowerPoint

EXECUTIVE PERFORMANCE MILESTONES

Innovative thinker with a cross-border knowledge of operations, core business practices, manufacturing, sales, and marketing.

Quickly analyze and determine key business drivers, developing strategies and tactics to grow the bottom line and to build strong teams that stay focused on organizational goals. Committed to doing whatever is necessary to achieve business objectives.

SALES GROWTH

- Instrumental in increasing 2000 annual sales by 11% to $37.2 million (with projected 2001 sales of $41 million) by developing and implementing productivity and cost-reduction improvements.

- Helped generate over $750,000 in annual sales through the development and implementation of an innovative "turn-key" container reconditioning / return service for blow-molded intermediate bulk containers.

- Added $4.5 million in sales by implementing ISO 9001 standards to meet the needs of business globalization and to enhance the focus of plant's customer satisfaction.

- Opened new market generating nearly $800,000 in annual sales by executing a new coextrusion blow-molding process that enabled containers to hold petrochemical products.

- Elevated revenues of an under-performing business from $15 million to $26 million, with a capital expansion of $4 million to add a second production machine to handle the increased demand.

COST REDUCTION

- Reduced costs by $400,000 by creating and initiating a formal *Kaizen* to attack key issues in the areas of productivity, waste, and overall quality.

- Developed a container-recycling program to salvage fiber drum business, creating annual revenues of $1 million.

- Decreased extraneous annual personnel costs by $88,400 by utilizing multi-functional teams, problem-solving techniques, and improved training programs.

- Produced $187,200 in annual savings by streamlining plant operations and reducing crew from nine to six employees.

- Gained $350,000 in annual price concessions by negotiating resin pricing through vendor consolidation.

- Spearheaded plant turnaround operations, achieving an estimated profit of over $2.5 million by the end of 2000 vs. negative $1.4 million in 1998 earnings.

- Grew the bottom line $560,000 by reducing waste from 14% to 9% through initiatives that included specification changes, new equipment, employee training, and superior maintenance.

- Reduced annual worker's compensation costs by $40,000 while lowering OSHA recordable rates from 16 to 4.2 by implementing a comprehensive safety program focused on raising employee awareness.

201-23 39th Avenue, Bayside, NY
phone: 718-000-0000 • cell: 212-555-5555 • fax: 718-555-5555 • e-mail: boylston.r@aol.com

Extremely accomplished across many areas of manufacturing operations, this individual handled multi-level responsibilities. He was very clear on one thing: He wanted to be "in the trenches." To reflect

RICHARD BOYLSTON

SELECTED ACCOMPLISHMENTS

Dramatically revived stagnant business, creating multimillion-dollar revenue gains.

Business needed to justify capital investment after wallowing in inactivity for years. To determine strategic direction, met with key stakeholders including employees, customers, and vendors. Built a "strategic development" staff team, then planned and implemented tactics based on five key success factors: business globalization, product / service innovation, technology improvements, cost reductions, and employee involvement. (Division General Manager, Charleston Containers)

Bottom Line

- Revenues grew from $15.2 million to $26.3 million in three years, or 20% per year on a compounded basis.
- Profits grew from $2.2 million to $4.2 million over the same timeframe, or 24% compounded.
- Division earned two corporate awards for producing the highest customer loyalty ratings in the company.

Returned a money-losing plant to multimillion-dollar profitability in under two years.

Plant purchased in 1995 was at negative $1.4 million by 1998, was threatened with closure, and would eliminate 160 jobs. Began reversal process by analyzing issues, examining data, and practicing "MBWA" (management by walking around). Defined key issues: procedural non-compliance, poor quality, waste, and a low margin business mix. Using staff as a "Corrective Action Team", implemented *Kaizen* or continuous improvement to set objectives for all key work centers. Developed and implemented Total Operating Management (TOM) and Operating Management System (OMS) to ensure procedural compliance. Collaborated with sales to either eliminate or raise prices at low margin customers. (Plant Manager, Parnell Packaging, Inc.)

Bottom Line

- Sales grew from $33 million to $41 million in 2000 and margins gained four percentage points.
- Profits grew from negative $1.4 million in 1998 to a positive $2.5 million projected for 2000.

Protected a $30 million business by developing an innovative container disposal method.

Business was being threatened with a $30 million loss (6% of total revenues), due to refusal of landfills to accept our customers' empty containers. Identified problem through market survey, visited customers to better define issue, developed a list of alternative disposal methods, and selected a method that used mobile recycling vehicles. Gained capital approval for the first truck, wrote a market plan, and introduced vehicle to customers and the market. (Market Manager, Charleston Containers)

Bottom Line

- Program saved the $30 million and generates over $1 million in new annual revenues from competitors' contracts.
- Recycling program has grown from initial truck to a nine-vehicle fleet.

Penetrated lucrative petrochemical market by developing a container to meet regulated products requirements.

Formed a multifunctional team with representatives from sales/marketing, engineering, R&D, and manufacturing. Developed an implementation including container specifications and obtained necessary corporate funding. Implemented the plan, monitored performance, and continued to adjust as required. Developed market introduction plan and visited all target accounts to familiarize them with new container. (Marketing Manager, Charleston Containers)

Bottom Line

- Penetrated the petrochemical market and generated $1.5 million annually in new sales.

Reduced container weight and associated manufacturing costs, making company more competitive.

Visited vendors in the US and Europe to study available technologies; identified state-of-the-art German technology called PWDS. Obtained capital approval, negotiated purchase, and managed system's implementation on four machines at a cost of $800,000. (General Manufacturing Manager, Charleston Drum)

Bottom Line

- Reduced individual drum weight by three pounds, creating annual savings of $600,000, or $1.2 million, during tenure.

201-23 39ᵗʰ Avenue, Bayside, NY
phone: 718-000-0000 • cell: 212-555-5555 • fax: 718-555-5555 • e-mail: boylston.r@aol.com

this, his resume positions him as a hands-on, senior manufacturing generalist, not a niche senior manager.

RICHARD BOYLSTON

RECENT EMPLOYMENT

PARNELL PACKAGING, INC., LONG ISLAND CITY, NY
1998 TO PRESENT

Company is a wholly owned subsidiary of Parnell Group specializing in manufacturing of plastic flexible packaging for the domestic and global meat, dairy, food, and healthcare markets. Annual revenues fall in the area of $900 million.

PLANT MANAGER   **1998 TO PRESENT**

- Maintain full Profit & Loss responsibility and accountability for safety, quality, productivity, and customer satisfaction. Develop and / or manage operating and capital budgets.
- Report directly to Vice President of Healthcare and Specialty Products. Supervise seven direct and 150 indirect reports.
- Developed and implemented numerous cutting-edge cost-reduction programs that have saved over $1.4 million annually.

CHARLESTON CONTAINERS, INC., BROOKLYN, NY
1986 TO 1998

Company is a division of Charleston Products Company, a $3 billion manufacturer of paper and plastic shipping containers, with 14 locations in the US, employing over 1,200 workers, and global operations in 32 countries / five continents, with over 17,500 workers.

DIVISION GENERAL MANAGER • CHARLESTON CONTAINERS   **1994 TO 1998**

- Oversaw manufacturing of blow-molded plastic containers for the chemical, food, and hazardous waste markets, with annual revenues of $26 million.
- Maintained both Profit & Loss and revenue growth responsibility.
- Developed and implemented strategies for business operations. Set and achieved financial and operating targets, as well as new business development efforts.

MARKET MANAGER • CHARLESTON CONTAINERS   **1989 TO 1994**

- Managed all marketing and business development activities for fiber and plastic drum markets including new product development, market planning and development, sales support, advertising/promotion, pricing, and competitive analysis.
- Reported to Vice President of Marketing and Sales. Supervised two Marketing Associates handling $250 million in revenue.
- Earned Innovator's Award for developing specialized recycling program in 1993.

GENERAL MANUFACTURING MANAGER • CHARLESTON DRUM   **1986 TO 1989**

- Implemented capital expansion plans, built and developed manufacturing team, and oversaw day-to-day activities of manufacturing plants, quality assurance, and engineering.
- Worked closely with the General Manager on this $30 million Charleston Drum division. Supervised six direct and 200 indirect reports.
- Oversaw full P&L responsibility for a three-plant multi-state manufacturer of blow-molded plastic drums.
- Established manufacturing strategy and developed financial / operations targets through the budgeting process.

EDUCATION AND DEVELOPMENT

MBA in Marketing and Logistics, New York University, New York, NY 1977

BA in History, Queens College, Flushing, NY 1970

RECENT SEMINARS AND WORKSHOPS
Supervisory Training • Value Creation • Strategic Selling
International Business Development • Center for Creative Leadership

201-23 39th Avenue, Bayside, NY
phone: 718-000-0000 • cell: 212-555-5555 • fax: 718-555-5555 • e-mail: boylston.r@aol.com

JAMES R. SOKOL

555 Country Road
Birmingham, AL 35645
256-756-0991 ▪ jsokol@bellsouth.net

CHIEF EXECUTIVE OFFICER ▪ CHIEF FINANCIAL OFFICER
Durable Goods Manufacturing, Textile Manufacturing, Distribution

PROFILE	**Solution-focused executive regarded as an expert** at formulating and executing financial strategic plans that support expansion, improve margins, and enhance profitability across all lines. Present depth of experience across industry lines, medium and large corporations, publicly and privately held corporations, start-up, turnaround, LBO, and IPO environments. Thorough understanding of entire manufacturing cycle contributes to ability to resolve existing and anticipated problems while moving business forward. Accustomed to dealing with high-profile clients, providing sales support, and formulating sales plans and forecasts.

AREAS OF EXPERTISE

- Fiscal / Capacity Planning
- P&L / Cash Management
- Financial Reporting / Analysis
- SEC Reporting
- Credit / Collections
- Accounts Payable
- Financial Management Systems
- MRP (Manufacturing Resource Planning)
- Lean Manufacturing
- Human Resources

- Outsourcing
- Vendor Relations
- JIT (Just in Time) Inventory
- Supply Chain Management
- Strategic Partners / Alliances
- Joint Venture
- Economy of Scale
- Production
- Asset-based Lending
- Capital Equipment Leasing
- Operating Leases

CAREER HIGHLIGHTS

CONCORD FABRICS, INC. — Birmingham, AL
VICE PRESIDENT / CHIEF FINANCIAL OFFICER, 1998 to present
($30 million specialty sportswear manufacturer providing custom products to clients including Nike, Disney, and Tommy Hilfiger. Employ 500 at U.S. and Mexican locations.)
Brought aboard to reverse poor financial performance and increasing losses with opportunity for ownership equity. Key member of senior management team and board of directors. Oversee budget preparation, internal and external auditing, financial planning, analysis and reporting, A/R and A/P, inventory control, capacity planning, cost accounting, capital and operating leases, and banking and investor relations. Manage manufacturing and finance software on AS400 system. Provide sales support at meetings with high-level clients. *Key Accomplishments:*

- Within two years, reversed $3 million loss to $2 million profit.
- Achieved $800,000 annual savings in payroll and operating costs by closing two plants and absorbing operations into other sites.
- Garnered additional $500,000 to bottom line through relocation of Mexican plant to site of newly established strategic partnership. Alliance resulted in reduction of foreign manufacturing costs by $3 per dozen and improved governmental and labor union relationships.
- Sourced, negotiated, and upgraded antiquated computers with state-of-the-art information systems, which, in past year alone, have identified costing shortfalls, an internal theft, and critical inventory issues.
- Acquired $500,000 in manufacturing equipment that increased capacity by 17% (125 lbs. to 150 lbs.) weekly, revenues 25% ($5 million) annually, and reduced irregulars 1% ($300,000).
- Investigated and negotiated new health insurance coverage, saving $400,000 annually.

This text-heavy resume remains very readable due to a clear typeface, excellent organization, and easily distinguished accomplishments.

RESUME 101, CONTINUED

JAMES R. SOKOL

Résumé - Page Two

CAREER HIGHLIGHTS

REGIS CORPORATION — Atlanta, GA
CORPORATE FINANCIAL MANAGER, 1989 to 1998
($160 million manufacturer of vacuum cleaners and floor care products.)
Member of senior management team during LBO from parent company and subsequent IPO. Developed systems, procedures, and training that supported increased capacity within sales and production. Directed and trained staff of 12 professional and clerical employees and oversaw all cash management activities.
Key Accomplishments:

- Brought company into profitability by improving cash flow $6 million through effective cash management strategies.
- Solidified relationships with key customers, including Wal-Mart, K-Mart, and Home Depot, and secured early payments on invoices, which contributed directly to increased cash flow, reduced interest payments, and favorable terms from vendors.
- Lauded by president in a speech at annual "key employee" meeting in Hawaii in May 1996: *"We all know that if it hadn't been for Jim we wouldn't have come this far...."*

GENERAL ELECTRIC SUPPLY COMPANY — Kansas City/Chicago/Atlanta
CUSTOMER FINANCIAL SERVICES MANAGER, 1980 to 1989
($1 billion distributor of electrical, construction, and manufacturing products.)
Maintained oversight for 10 regional credit offices in the eastern U.S. and 10 direct and 60 indirect reports, including regional credit managers and support staff. Managed budgets, forecasts, bad debts, monthly and annual closings, and audits. Developed training programs and worked with sales managers to resolve credit issues. *Key Accomplishments:*

- Reduced personnel by 30% by consolidating finance and credit functions and eliminating duplication. Consolidation plan adopted by divisions throughout the corporation.
- Conceived and implemented business-to-business telemarketing to facilitate sales and support to several thousand marginal customers, which resulted in $3 million in increased sales. Gross margins exploded, averaging 50% to 60% compared to 5% to 7% on traditional outside sales. Program adopted division-wide within four years.
- Sold City of Pittsburgh $1 million street-leasing programs during a period in which the concept of leasing was in its infancy.
- Took lead in offering clients leasing options rather than outright purchases, which added high-dollar deals ranging from $500,000 to several million.

EDUCATION

UNIVERSITY OF MISSOURI — Kansas City, MO
BS, ECONOMICS, 1972

PROFESSIONAL DEVELOPMENT
- **Human Resources Management,** University of Alabama, ongoing
- **Sales Management Program (SMP),** General Electric, 1984
- **Financial Management Program (FMP),** General Electric, 1981 to 1983

AFFILIATIONS
- Financial Executives Institute (FEI)
- Protective & Benevolent Order of the Elks

555 Country Road . Birmingham, AL 35645 . 256-756-0991 . jsokol@bellsouth.net

Jack Redvor

P.O. Box 3261
Columbia, Missouri 62499

(H) 931-773-0332
(O) 931-723-9134
E-mail: jackrvdr@aol.com

Global Management Executive / Chief Operations Officer

Manufacturing — Technology Design & Implementation — Product Development

Multi-disciplinary professional with over 20 years' experience in international business development with Fortune 100 manufacturing leader. Responsibilities included design of products, technological systems, equipment, and processes. Management responsibilities included 1.1M square feet of facility, 5M square feet of compound, 2300 employees, and P&L of annual budget of $40M within the framework of a $7B global organization. Scope of production included over 2000 high-demand flexible manufacturing pieces; delivery responsibility in excess of 12,000 part numbers.

Diplomatic skills were foundation to providing the physical needs of 8800 employees and family members within the social/governmental framework of Communist culture. A "work & live" demographic required development of projects including, but not limited to: foundry, machinery, schools, day care, medical clinic, restaurants, roads, fuel, electricity, water, waste management, and recreation/hospitality. Recognized by the Communist government as "the ideal model" for corporate provision within a communal system.

Professional Objective

I believe my **domestic and international** experiences, partnered with my **Bachelor of Science Degree in Mechanical Engineering,** would enable me to serve your organization in a variety of leadership capacities. These skills could be maximized as **Vice President of Manufacturing, Chief Operations Officer,** or **Director of Global Business Development.**

Functional Strengths

- Discerning business sense for organizational efficiency
- Initiator of change to increase profit, revenue, and productivity
- Orchestrated operational plans within numerous international environments
- Strong analytical skills; able to solve problems resourcefully
- Implementer of global information technological reengineering and leverage
- Engineered criteria for custom product development
- Manager of existing accounts/established new accounts
- Expert implementer of quality control and standardization of procedures
- Customer-driven executive with an intuitive sense for what will sell
- Seasoned professional with internal and external negotiations

Executive-level resumes frequently use the narrative tone and extensive summary seen in this resume. The entire first page summarizes strengths and capabilities before pages 2 and 3 address career history.

Redvor, Page Two

Career History

Executive Director, Midrange GIEA   **2000–present**
Harvester Industrial Engine Manufacturers, Inc.   **Columbia, MO**
- Implemented Oracle ERP program; set scope and directives for entire project.
- Hired, fired, and trained team of 74 employees; coordinated project assignments.
- Negotiated project supply needs with outside vendors.
- Advised all plant managers on systems modifications and impact.
- Interfaced with Human Resource/Program Office to establish appropriate project benchmarks.
- Successfully completed design review for three operating facilities.
- Resolved 167 data complications and brought project on line within 4 months.
- Wrote and implemented goals and procedures to save in excess of $25M in 2001.

Director, Y2K Readiness Program   **1999**
Harvester Industrial Engine Manufacturers, Inc.   **Multi-National Conversion**
- Developed a global systems validation/correction team of 150 people.
- Served as link between worldwide manufacturing, treasury, supply, and communications.
- Established web site to provide information to global locations regarding project goals.
- Set industry-leading standards for information-based intranet web site.
- Project completed on time and within budget parameters.
- 24 global facilities were functioning to full capacity January 1, 2000.
- Ensured protection of product and resources of $4B organization.

Directory, IT Planning and Finance   **1998**
Harvester and Sons Engine Company   **Columbia, MO**
- Managed company-wide project development and spending parameters worldwide.
- Facilitated the rationalization of shared services and brought order out of chaos.
- Led and delivered 15% cut in IT-related spending, saving $22M in 1999.
- Trained all Information Technology directors on Project Planning Methodologies.
- Highlighted overlaps in the roll-out of shared services, leading to additional $10M in savings.

General Manager   **1994–1998**
Shanghai Diesel Engine Company   **Shanghai, China**
- Served as CEO, COO, Planner, Manager of International Joint Venture Design and Manufacturing project for sale of diesel engines.
- Developed business plan, strategic plans, and product development scope and sequence.
- Interfaced with local and national government officials as Relationship/Community Manager.
- Supervised 2300 employees living on site with 8800 family members; managed all family services as well as employee services.
- Evaluated and implemented quality systems to reduce defects by 30% each year.
- Raw material waste diminished from +30% to less than 5%, order accuracy increased to 85%.
- Introduced 6 new products for marine markets to open new export opportunities.
- Overhauled all facilities on the compound, consolidated operations, and improved safety.
- Cut production cost by 40%, reduced staff by 10%, while profit margins grew from 25%–40%.

Career History (continued)

Plant I, Business Manager	**1990-1994**
Eagle Engines Incorporated	**Raleigh, NC**

- Supervised the manufacture of diesel engine components; responsible for 13 different production lines and 250 employees producing 80M products per year.
- Established specifications for flexible manufacturing systems to produce 12,000 part numbers, with 2000 unique products in production at all times.
- Increased machine utilization by 30% over 18 months; increased production to save $40M.
- Served as consultant to Eagle Plants nationwide in the areas of cost, delivery, and quality.
- Selected as Chairman of the North American Machine Utilization Improvement Team.
- Established benchmarks and standards for performance and reporting.
- Achieved 100% on-time delivery with profit margin growth to 40%.
- Recognized by Fortune 100 customer as world leader in quality, service, and productivity

Product Manager, Industrial Duty Parts	**1987-1989**
Eagle Engines Incorporated	**Raleigh, NC**

- Parts engineering manager for Heavy Duty Engines.
- Evaluated customer needs and introduced new custom products.
- Took initiatives to evaluate the market and establish competitive pricing criteria.
- Conducted competitive analysis, identified strategic plans for marketing, and revised forecasts.
- Developed cooperative efforts between production and sales to solve delivery problems and increased delivery ratio to 98%.
- Instituted new after-market fuel systems that sold in excess of $5M in 36 months.

Senior Engineer – Big Cam III	**1984-1987**
Shorters Engine Design Company	**Elizabethtown, KY**

- Served as product development specialist for company's largest division.
- Developed testing protocols for engine component validation.
- Supervised technical staff in test procedures of components under normal/extreme conditions.
- Reduced costs by 50% per unit while improving product efficiency; led to increase of North American market share by 10%, $300M in additional sales.

Group Manager/Technical Sales	**1980-1984**
Holderstands Engineering Company	**Madison, WI**

- Supervised manufacture of turbochargers; responsible for 60 engineers and operators.
- Led plant initiatives in cost, quality, and product development.
- Redesigned manufacturing bottleneck; redeployed 43 of 44 machines.
- Improved efficient use of floor space by 25% and reduced labor staff 30% while increasing production output by 60%.
- Served as primary liaison between turbocharger manufacturer with Fortune 500 clients, including John Deere, Detroit Diesel, Allison Engine, International Harvester, and Cummins.

References Provided upon Establishment of Mutual Interest.

APPENDIX

Internet Resources
for Manufacturing Careers

With the emergence of the Internet has come a huge collection of job search resources for manufacturing industry professionals. Here are just a few of our favorites.

Organizations for Manufacturing Professionals

American Institute of Chemical Engineers	www.aiche.org
American Society for Industrial Security	www.asisonline.org
American Society for Production and Inventory Control	www.apics.org
American Society for Quality	www.asq.org
American Society of Materials International	www.asm-intl.org
American Society of Mechanical Engineers	www.asme.org
American Society of Safety Engineers	www.asse.org
Institute for Supply Management	www.ism.ws
Institute of Electrical and Electronics Engineers	www.ieee.org
Institute of Industrial Engineers	www.iienet.org
National Association of Manufacturers	www.nam.org
National Society of Professional Engineers	www.nspe.org

Society of Automotive Engineers	www.sae.org
Society of Manufacturing Engineers	www.sme.org
Society of Plastics Engineers	www.4spe.org

Dictionaries and Glossaries

Outstanding information on key words and acronyms.

| Acronyms | http://acronymfinder.com |
| Key words | www.keywordcity.com |

Job Search Sites

You'll find thousands and thousands of current professional employment opportunities on these sites.

MANUFACTURING AND ENGINEERING SITES

Blue Collar Jobs	www.bluecollarjobs.com/
Engineering Jobs	www.engineeringjobs.com
HotJobs.com—Manufacturing Jobs	www.hotjobs.com/htdocs/channels/ manufacturing/
IEEE Job Site	http://jobs.ieee.org/recruiter.html
iHire Manufacturing Engineers	www.ihiremanufacturingengineers.com
iSixSigma JobShop	www.isixsigma.com/jobs/
JobServe: Engineering Jobs	www.engineering.jobserve.com/ jobserve/homepage.asp
Manufacturing.net	www.manufacturing.net
Manufacturing Jobs	www.manufacturing-jobs.net
Manufacturing Jobs from JobJunction	www.jobjunction.com/manufacturing.htm
NationJob Engineering and Manufacturing Jobs Page	www.nationjob.com/engineering/
Plant Automation	www.plantautomation.com

GENERAL SITES

4Work	www.4work.com
6FigureJobs	www.6figurejobs.com
America's Job Bank	www.ajb.dni.us
Best Jobs USA	www.bestjobsusa.com
Career Atlas for the Road	www.jobmag.com/guide/ c047/c047262.htm
CareerBuilder	www.careerbuilder.com
CareerCity	www.careercity.com
Career.com	www.career.com
CareerEngine	www.careerengine.com
CareerExchange	www.careerexchange.com
Career Exposure	www.careerexposure.com
Career Magazine	www.careermag.com
CareerShop	www.careershop.com
CareerSite	www.careersite.com
CareerWeb	www.careerweb.com
FlipDog	www.flipdog.com
Futurestep	www.futurestep.com
Headhunter.net	www.headhunter.net
HotJobs.com	www.hotjobs.com
Internet Job Locator	www.joblocator.com
Internet's Help Wanted	www.helpwanted.com
It's Your Job Now	www.ItsYourJobNow.com
JobBankUSA	www.jobbankusa.com
JOBNET.com	www.jobnet.com
JobOptions	www.joboptions.com
JobWeb	www.jobweb.com
Monster.com	www.monster.com
monsterTRAK	www.jobtrak.com
NationJob Network	www.nationjob.com
Net Temps	www.net-temps.com
Online-Jobs.Com	www.online-jobs.com
Shawn's Internet Resume Center	www.inpursuit.com/sirc

WorkTree   www.worktree.com

Yahoo! Careers   http://careers.yahoo.com

PROFESSIONAL CAREERS

Contract Employment Weekly   www.ceweekly.com

Vault.com   www.vault.com

GOVERNMENT CAREERS

Careers in Government   www.careersingovernment.com

Federal Jobs Central   www.fedjobs.com

CAREERS FOR SENIORS

MaturityWorks   www.maturityworks.org
(careers for seniors)

ENTRY-LEVEL CAREERS

CampusCareerCenter   www.campuscareercenter.com

College Grad Job Hunter   www.collegegrad.com

Jobsource   www.jobsource.com

monsterTRAK   www.jobtrak.com

Company Information

Outstanding resources for researching specific companies.

555-1212.com   www.555-1212.com
(directory information)

AllBusiness   www.comfind.com

Chambers of Commerce   www.uschamber.com/Chambers/
                                        Chamber+Directory/default.htm

Experience Network   www.experiencenetwork.com

Fortune 500 Companies   www.fortune.com/lists/F500/index.html

Hoover's Business Profiles   www.hoovers.com

mni/Guide to U.S.   mniguide.com/index.asp
Manufacturers

SuperPages.com   www.bigbook.com

Thomas Register of   www.thomasregister.com
American Manufacturers

Interviewing Tips and Techniques

Expert guidance to sharpen and strengthen your interviewing skills.

About.com Interviewing	jobsearch.about.com/business/ jobsearch/msubinterv.htm
Bradley CVs Introduction to Job Interviews	www.bradleycvs.demon.co.uk/ interview/index.htm
Dress for Success	www.dressforsuccess.org
Job-Interview.net	www.job-interview.net

Salary and Compensation Information

Learn from the experts to strengthen your negotiating skills and increase your salary.

Abbott, Langer & Associates	www.abbott-langer.com
America's Career InfoNet	www.acinet.org/acinet/default.htm
Bureau of Labor Statistics *Occupational Outlook Handbook*	www.bls.gov/oco
CareerJournal	www.careerjournal.com
Economic Research Institute	www.erieri.com
ESCAPE: Salaries of Engineers	https://engineering.purdue.edu/FrE/ ESCAPE
JobStar	jobstar.org/tools/salary/index.htm
Monster.com: The Negotiation Coach	midcareer.monster.com
Salary.com	www.salary.com
Wageweb	www.wageweb.com
WorldatWork (formerly American Compensation Association)	www.worldatwork.org/
Yahoo! Salaries	http://careers.yahoo.com/careers/ salaries.html

GEOGRAPHIC INDEX OF CONTRIBUTORS

The sample resumes in chapters 4 through 11 were written by professional resume and cover letter writers. If you need help with your resume and job search correspondence, you can use the following list to locate a career professional in your area.

A note about credentials: Nearly all of the contributing writers have earned one or more professional credentials. These credentials are highly regarded in the careers and employment industry and are indicative of the writer's expertise and commitment to professional development. Here is an explication of the most common resume writer credentials:

Credential	Awarded by	Recognizes
CBC: Certified Behavioral Consultant	The Institute for Motivational Living and Target Training International	
CCM: Credentialed Career Master	Career Masters Institute	Specific professional expertise, knowledge of current career trends, commitment to continuing education, and dedication through *pro bono* work
CEIP: Certified Employment Interview Professional	Professional Association of Resume Writers	Expertise in interview preparation strategy
CPC: Certified Personnel Consultant	National Association of Personnel Services	Expertise in staffing and placement
CIPC: Certified International Personnel Consultant		
CMP: Certified Career Management Practitioner	International Association of Career Management Professionals	
CPRW: Certified Professional Resume Writer	Professional Association of Resume Writers	Knowledge of resume strategy development and writing
CWDP: Certified Workforce Development Professional	National Association of Workforce Development Professionals	

continues

JCTC: Job and Career Transition Coach IJCTC: International Job and Career Transition Coach	Career Planning and Adult Development Network	Training and expertise in job and career coaching strategies
LPC: Licensed Professional Counselor	Individual states	Master's in counseling plus three years of supervised counseling experience
NCC: National Certified Counselor NCCC: National Certified Career Counselor	National Board for Certified Counselors (affiliated with the American Counseling Association and the American Psychological Association)	Qualification to provide career counseling
NCRW: Nationally Certified Resume Writer	National Resume Writers' Association	Knowledge of resume strategy development and writing

United States

ALABAMA

Don Orlando, MBA, CPRW, IJCTC, CCM
Executive Master Team—Career Masters Institute™
Owner, The McLean Group
640 S. McDonough St.
Montgomery, AL 36104
Phone: (334) 264-2020
Fax: (334) 264-9227
E-mail: yourcareercoach@aol.com

ARIZONA

Kathryn Bourne, CPRW, IJCTC
President, CareerConnections
5210 E. Pima St., Suite 130
Tucson, AZ 85712
Toll-free: (800) 895-4435
Phone: (520) 323-2964
Fax: (520) 795-3575
E-mail: CCmentor@aol.com
URL: www.bestfitresumes.com

Patricia S. Cash, CPRW, CEIP
President, Resumes For Results
P.O. Box 2806
Prescott, AZ 86302
Phone: (928) 778-1578
Fax: (928) 771-1229
E-mail: pscash@goodnet.com

Wanda McLaughlin, CPRW, CEIP
President, Execuwrite
314 N. Los Feliz Dr.
Chandler, AZ 85226
Phone: (480) 732-7966
Fax: (480) 855-5129

E-mail: wanda@execuwrite.com
URL: www.execuwrite.com

Joann Nix, CPRW, JCTC, CEIP
President, A Great Resume Service, Inc.
5704 McClure Rd.
Van Buren, AZ 72956
Toll-free: (800) 265-6901
Phone: (479) 410-3101
Fax: (501) 474-4013
E-mail: info@agreatresume.com
URL: www.agreatresume.com

CALIFORNIA

Leatha Jones, CPRW, CEIP
John F. Kennedy University
Career Development Center
12 Altarinda Rd.
Orinda, CA 94563
Phone: (925) 258-2568
E-mail: career@jfku.edu

Nancy Karvonen, CPRW, CEIP, IJCTC, CCM
Executive Director, A Better Word & Resume
4490 County Road HH
Orland, CA 95963
Toll-free: (877) 973-7863
Phone: (209) 745-5107
Fax: (209) 745-7114
E-mail: Careers@AResumeCoach.com
URL: www.aresumecoach.com

Myriam-Rose Kohn, CCM, JCTC, CPRW, CEIP
President, JEDA Enterprises
27201 Tourney Rd., Suite 201
Valencia, CA 91355-1857
Toll-free: (800) 600-JEDA
Phone: (661) 253-0801

Fax: (661) 253-0744
E-mail: myriam-rose@jedaenterprises.com
URL: www.jedaenterprises.com

Laura Lyon
President, Executive Image Resumes
San Jose, CA 95132
Toll-free: (800) 917-5100
Phone: (408) 254-2232
Fax: (888) 830-5930
E-mail: Laura@MyExecutiveImage.com
URL: www.MyExecutiveImage.com

Anita Radosevich, CPRW, JCTC, CEIP
President, Anita's Business & Career Services
315 W. Pine St., Suite 5
Lodi, CA 95240
Toll-free: (888) 247-3786
Phone: (209) 368-4444
Fax: (209) 368-2834
E-mail: anita@abcresumes.com
URL: www.ABCResumes.com

Makini Siwatu, CPRW, JCTC, CEIP
President, Accent on Words
405 El Camino Real, Suite 631
Menlo Park, CA 94025-5240
Phone: (650) 327-7935
Fax: (650) 323-2106
E-mail: accentwrds@aol.com

Vivian VanLier, CPRW, JCTC, CEIP
President, Advantage Career Services
6701 Murietta Ave.
Valley Glen (Los Angeles), CA 91405
Phone: (818) 994-6655
Fax: (818) 994-6620
E-mail: vivian@CuttingEdgeResumes.com
URL: www.CuttingEdgeResumes.com

CONNECTICUT

Louise Garver, MA, CMP, JCTC, CPRW
President, Career Directions, LLC
115 Elm St., Suite 203
Enfield, CT 06082
Toll-free: (888) 222-3731
Phone: (860) 623-9476
Fax: (860) 623-9473
E-mail: TheCareerPro@aol.com
URL: www.resumeimpact.com

Jan Melnik, CPRW, CCM
President, Absolute Advantage
P.O. Box 718
Durham, CT 06422
Phone: (860) 349-0256
Fax: (860) 349-1343
E-mail: CompSPJan@aol.com
URL: www.janmelnik.com

FLORIDA

Arthur I. Frank, MBA
President, Resumes "R" Us

334 Eastlake Rd., #200
Palm Harbor, FL 34685
Toll-free: (866) 600-4300
Phone: (727) 787-6885
Fax: (727) 786-9228
E-mail: info@powerresumesandcoaching.com
URL: www.powerresumesandcoaching.com

Cindy Kraft, CPRW, JCTC, CCM
President, Executive Essentials
P.O. Box 336
Valrico, FL 33595
Toll-free: (888) 221-0441
Phone: (813) 655-0658
Fax: (813) 685-4287
E-mail: careermaster@exec-essentials.com
URL: www.exec-essentials.com

Sherri Morgan
Career Resumes
1311 Keats St.
Inverness, FL 34450
Toll-free: (800) 284-7540
Toll-free fax: (888) 321-3738
E-mail: sa.morgan@att.net
URL: www.career-resumes.com

ILLINOIS

Sally McIntosh, NCRW, CPRW, JCTC
Advantage Resumes
35 Westfair Dr.
Jacksonville, IL 62650
Toll-free: (800) 485-9779
Phone: (217) 245-0752
Fax: (217) 243-4451
E-mail: sally@reswriter.com
URL: www.reswriter.com

INDIANA

Richard A. Lanham, CCM, MDiv, MA, MRE
General Manager/Senior Consultant,
R.L. Stevens & Associates, Inc.
8888 Keystone Crossing, Suite 950
Indianapolis, IN 46240
Toll-free: (888) 806-7313
Phone: (317) 846-8888
Fax: (317) 846-8949
E-mail: rlanham@rlstevens.com
URL: www.interviewing.com

IOWA

Marcy Johnson, CPRW, CEIP
President, First Impression Resume & Job Readiness
11805 U.S. Hwy. 69
Story City, IA 50248
Phone: (515) 733-4998
Fax: (515) 733-4681
E-mail: Firstimpression@prairieinet.net
URL: www.resume-job-readiness.com

KANSAS

Jacqui D. Barrett, CPRW, CEIP
President, Career Trend
7501 College Blvd., Suite 175
Overland Park, KS 66210
Phone: (913) 451-1313
Fax: (913) 451-3242
E-mail: jacqui@careertrend.net
URL: www.careertrend.net

KENTUCKY

Debbie Ellis, CPRW
President, Phoenix Career Group
103 Patrick Henry Ct.
Danville, KY 40422
Toll-free: (800) 876-5506
Phone: (859) 236-4001
Toll-free fax: (888) 329-5409
Fax: (859) 236-4001
E-mail: debbie@phoenixcareergroup.com
URL: www.phoenixcareergroup.com

MAINE

Rolande L. LaPointe, CPC, CIPC, CPRW, IJCTC, CCM
President, RO-LAN Associates, Inc.
725 Sabattus St.
Lewiston, ME 04240
Phone: (207) 784-1010
Fax: (207) 782-3446
E-mail: Rlapointe@aol.com

MARYLAND

Diane Burns, CPRW, IJCTC, CCM, CEIP
President, Career Marketing Techniques
5219 Thunder Hill Rd.
Columbia, MD 21045
Phone: (410) 884-0213
Fax: (410) 884-0213
E-mail: dianecprw@aol.com
URL: www.polishedresumes.com

MASSACHUSETTS

Bernice Antifonario, MA
President, Antion Associates, Inc.
885 Main St. #10A
Tewksbury, MA 01876
Phone: (978) 858-0637
Fax: (978) 851-4528
E-mail: Bernice@antion-associates.com
URL: www.antion-associates.com

Rosemarie Ginsberg, CPRW, CEIP
Employment Recruiter, Creative Staffing
Associates, Inc.
15 Michael Rd.
Framingham, MA 01701
Phone: (508) 877-5100

Fax: (508) 877-3511
E-mail: csadirecthire@aol.com
URL: www.CreativeResumesNJobs.com

Beate Hait, CPRW, NCRW
President, Word Processing Plus
80 Wingate Rd.
Holliston, MA 01746
Phone: (508) 429-1813
Fax: (508) 429-4299
E-mail: beateh1@aol.com
URL: www.resumesplus.net

MICHIGAN

Janet L. Beckstrom
President, Word Crafter
1717 Montclair Ave.
Flint, MI 48503
Toll-free: (800) 351-9818
Phone: (810) 232-9257
Fax: (810) 232-9257
E-mail: wordcrafter@voyager.net

Joyce L. Fortier, MBA, CPRW, JCTC, CCM
President, Create Your Career
23871 W. Lebost
Novi, MI 48375
Toll-free: (800) 793-9895
Phone: (248) 478-5662
Fax: (248) 426-9974
E-mail: careerist@aol.com
URL: www.careerist.com

Maria E. Hebda, CPRW
Managing Executive, Career Solutions, LLC
2216 Northfield
Trenton, MI 48183
Toll-free: (877) 777-7242
Phone: (734) 676-9170
Fax: (734) 676-9487
E-mail: careers@writingresumes.com
URL: www.writingresumes.com

Richard Porter
CareerWise Communications, LLC
332 Magellan Ct.
Portage, MI 49002-7000
Toll-free: (888) 565-7108
Phone: (616) 321-0183
Toll-free fax: (888) 565-7109
Fax: (616) 321-0191
E-mail: rtporter@worldnet.att.net

MINNESOTA

Barb Poole, CPRW, CRW
President, Hire Imaging
1812 Red Fox Rd.
St. Cloud, MN 56301
Phone: (320) 253-0975
Fax: (320) 253-1790
E-mail: eink@astound.net

Linda Wunner, CPRW, JCTC, CEIP
President, A+ Career & Resume Design
4516 Midway Rd.
Duluth, MN 55811
Toll-free: (877) 946-6377
Phone: (218) 729-4551
Fax: (218) 729-8277
E-mail: linda@successfulresumes.com
URL: www.successfulresumes.com

MISSOURI

Robert Jones, JCTC, CJST
College of Engineering Career Services
University of Missouri—Columbia
W1025 Eng. Bldg. East
Columbia, MO 65211
Phone: (573) 882-4487
Fax: (573) 882-2490
E-mail: JonesER@missouri.edu
URL: www.engineering.missouri.edu/ecs.htm

Meg Montford, CCM, CPRW
President, Abilities Enhanced
P.O. Box 9667
Kansas City, MO 64134
Phone: (816) 767-1196
Fax: (801) 650-8529
E-mail: Meg@abilitiesenhanced.com
URL: www.abilitiesenhanced.com

MONTANA

Lynn Andenoro, CCM, CPRW, JCTC
President, My Career Resource, LLC
264 White Pine
Kalispell, MT 59901
Phone: (406) 257-4035
Fax: (406) 257-4035
E-mail: Lynn@MyCareerResource.com
URL: www.MyCareerResource.com

Laura West, JCTC
President, Agape Career Services
634 N. Birch Creek Rd.
Corvallis, MT 59828
Toll-free: (888) 685-3507
Phone: (406) 961-8366
Fax: (208) 460-5804
E-mail: laura@agapecareerservices.com
URL: www.AgapeCareerServices.com

NEW HAMPSHIRE

Michelle Dumas, NCRW, CPRW, CCM, JCTC, CEIP
Executive Director, Distinctive Documents
Somersworth, NH 03878
Toll-free: (800) 644-9694
Phone: (603) 742-3983
Fax: (603) 947-2954
E-mail: resumes@distinctiveweb.com
URL: www.distinctiveweb.com

NEW JERSEY

Gary Ames
Merrill-Adams Associates
202 Carnegie Center, Suite 103
Princeton, NJ 08540
Phone: (609) 275-2992
Fax: (609) 275-1006
E-mail: garyames@Merrill-Adams.com
URL: www.Merrill-Adams.com

Vivian Belen, NCRW, CPRW, JCTC
Managing Director, The Job Search Specialist
1102 Bellair Ave.
Fair Lawn, NJ 07410
Phone: (201) 797-2883
Fax: (201) 797-5566
E-mail: vivian@jobsearchspecialist.com
URL: www.jobsearchspecialist.com

Nina K. Ebert, CPRW
President, A Word's Worth Resume & Writing Service
808 Lowell Ave.
Toms River, NJ 08753
Phone: (732) 349-2225
Fax: (609) 758-7799
E-mail: wrdswrth@gbsias.com
URL: www.keytosuccessresumes.com

Susan Guarneri, NCC, NCCC, LPC, CPRW, IJCTC, CEIP, CCM
President, Guarneri Associates/Resumagic
1101 Lawrence Rd.
Lawrenceville, NJ 08648
Phone: (609) 771-1669
Fax: (609) 637-0449
E-mail: Resumagic@aol.com
URL: www.resume-magic.com

Carol Rossi, CPRW
Computerized Documents
4 Baywood Blvd.
Brick, NJ 08723
Toll-free: (866) 477-5172
Phone: (732) 477-5172
Fax: (732) 477-5172
E-mail: info@powerfulresumes.com
URL: www.powerfulresumes.com

NEW YORK

Ann Baehr, CPRW
President, Best Resumes
Long Island, NY 11717
Phone: (631) 435-1879
Fax: (631) 435-3655
E-mail: resumesbest@earthlink.net
URL: www.e-bestresumes.com

Arnold G. Boldt, CPRW, JCTC
Arnold-Smith Associates
625 Panorama Trail, Building 2, Suite 200
Rochester, NY 14625
Phone: (585) 383-0350
Fax: (585) 387-0516
E-mail: Arnie@ResumeSOS.com
URL www.ResumeSOS.com

(Ms.) Freddie Cheek, CPRW, CWDP
Cheek & Cristantello Career Connections
4511 Harlem Rd., Suite 3
Amherst, NY 14226
Phone: (716) 839-3635
Fax: (716) 831-9320
E-mail: fscheek@adelphia.net
URL: www.CheekandCristantello.com

Deborah Wile Dib, CCM, NCRW, CPRW, CEIP, JCTC
President, Advantage Resumes of New York
77 Buffalo Ave.
Medford, NY 11763
Toll-free: (888) 272-8899
Phone: (631) 475-8513
Fax: (501) 421-7790
E-mail: 100kPLUS@advantageresumes.com
URL: www.advantageresumes.com

Judy Friedler, NCRW, CPRW, IJCTC, CCM
President, CareerPro New York
56 Barrow St., #G1
New York, NY 10014
Toll-free: (877) 626-3398
Phone: (212) 647-8726
Fax: (646) 349-1563
E-mail: Judy@rezcoach.com
URL: www.rezcoach.com

Betty Geller, NCRW, CPRW
President, Apple Resume and Career Services
456 W. Water St., Suite 1
Elmira, NY 14905
Phone: (607) 734-2090
Fax: (607) 734-2090
E-mail: appleresumesvc@stny.rr.com
URL: www.appleresumes.com

NORTH CAROLINA

Dayna Feist, CPRW, JCTC, CEIP
President, Gatehouse Business Services
265 Charlotte St.
Asheville, NC 28801
Phone: (828) 254-7893
Fax: (828) 254-7894
E-mail: gatehous@aol.com

Karen McMahan, JCTC
President, Do-It-Write, Inc.
2530 Meridian Pkwy., 2nd Floor
Durham, NC 27713
Phone: (919) 806-4690
Fax: (919) 806-4790

E-mail: kemcmahan@aol.com
URL: www.do-it-write.com

NORTH DAKOTA

Mary Laske, MS, CPRW
President, ExecPro
1713 Park Blvd.
Fargo, ND 58103
Phone: (701) 235-8007
Fax: (707) 760-3951
E-mail: execpro@att.net
URL: www.execproresumes.com

OHIO

Pierre G. Daunic, Ph.D., CCM
R.L. Stevens & Associates, Inc.
1674 Quail Meadows Dr.
Lancaster, OH 43130
Phone: (740) 689-8056
Fax: (740) 689-8056
E-mail: pdaunic@rlstevens.com
URL: www.interviewing.com

Deborah S. James, CPRW
Executive Director, Leading-Edge Resumes &
Career Services
1010 Schreier Rd.
Rossford, OH 43460
Toll-free: (800) 815-8780
Phone: (419) 666-4518
Fax: (419) 791-3567
E-mail: OhioResGal@aol.com
URL: www.leadingedgeresumes.com

Louise Kursmark, CPRW, JCTC, CCM, CEIP
Executive Master Team—Career Masters
Institute™
President, Best Impression Career Services, Inc.
9847 Catalpa Woods Ct.
Cincinnati, OH 45242
Phone: (513) 792-0030
Fax: (513) 792-0961
E-mail: LK@yourbestimpression.com
URL: www.yourbestimpression.com

Sue Montgomery, CPRW, IJCTC
President, Resume Plus
4130 Linden Ave., Suite 135
Dayton, OH 45432
Toll-free: (888) 792-0030
Phone: (937) 254-5627
Fax: (937) 253-3080
E-mail: resumeplus@siscom.net
URL: www.resumeplus.com

Teena Rose, CPRW, CEIP, CCM
President, Resume to Referral
P.O. Box 328
Dayton, OH 45322
Phone: (937) 264-3025
Fax: (937) 264-9930

E-mail: admin@resumetoreferral.com
URL: www.resumebycprw.com

Janice Worthington, MA, CPRW, JCTC, CEIP

President, Worthington Career Services
6636 Belleshire St.
Columbus, OH 43229
Toll-free: (877) 9RESUME (973-7863)
Phone: (614) 890-1645
Fax: (614) 523-3400
E-mail: janice@worthingtonresumes.com
URL: www.worthingtonresumes.com

PENNSYLVANIA

Barbaraanne Breithaupt, IJCTC, CPRW, CO

Barbaraanne's Lasting Impressions
3202 Holyoke Road
Philadelphia, PA 19114-3522
Phone: (215) 676-7742
Fax: (215) 676-5733
E-mail: Tiger4PARW@aol.com

Jewel Bracy DeMaio, CPRW, CEIP

President, A Perfect Resume.com
340 Main St.
Royersford, PA 19468
Toll-free: (800) 227-5131
Phone: (610) 327-8002
Fax: (610) 327-8014
E-mail: mail@aperfectresume.com
URL: www.aperfectresume.com

Jane Roqueplot, CBC

President, JaneCo's Sensible Solutions
194 N. Oakland Ave.
Sharon, PA 16146
Toll-free: (888) JANECOS (526-3267)
Phone: (724) 342-0100
Fax: (724) 346-5263
E-mail: info@janecos.com
URL: www.janecos.com

SOUTH CAROLINA

Karen Swann, CPRW

President, TypeRight
384-4 College Ave.
Clemson, SC 29631
Phone: (864) 653-7901
Fax: (864) 653-7701
E-mail: karzim@carol.net

TENNESSEE

Carolyn Braden, CPRW

President, Braden Resume Solutions
108 La Plaza Dr.
Hendersonville, TN 37075
Phone: (615) 822-3317
Fax: (615) 826-9611
E-mail: bradenresume@comcast.net

Marta L. Driesslein, CPRW, CCM

President, Cambridge Career Services, Inc.

300 Montvue Rd., Suite A
Knoxville, TN 37919
Phone: (865) 539-9538
Fax: (865) 453-3109
E-mail: careerhope@aol.com
URL: www.careerhope.com

TEXAS

Lynn Hughes, MA, CEIP

A Resume and Career Service, Inc.
P.O. Box 6911
Lubbock, TX 79493
Phone: (806) 785-9800
Fax: (806) 785-2711
E-mail: lynn@aresumeservice.com
URL: www.aresumeservice.com

Shanna Kemp, M.Ed., JCTC, CPRW, CCM

President, Kemp Career Services
3612 Hawk Ridge St.
Round Rock, TX 78664
Toll-free: (877) 367-5367
Fax: (512) 246-8353
E-mail: respro@aresumepro.com
URL: www.aresumepro.com

Ann Klint, NCRW, CPRW

Ann's Professional Resume Service
2130 Kennebunk Ln.
Tyler, TX 75703-0301
Phone: (903) 509-8333
Fax: (734) 448-1962
E-mail: Resumes-Ann@tyler.net

William G. Murdock, CPRW

President, The Employment Coach
7770 Meadow Rd., Suite 109
Dallas, TX 75230
Phone: (214) 750-4781
Fax: (214) 750-4781
E-mail: bmurdock@swbell.net

Kelley Smith, CPRW

President, Advantage Resume Services
P.O. Box 391
Sugar Land, TX 77487
Toll-free: (877) 478-4999
Phone: (281) 494-3330
Fax: (281) 494-0173
E-mail: info@100kresumes.com
URL: www.100kresumes.com

UTAH

Diana C. LeGere

President, Executive Final Copy
P.O. Box 171311
Salt Lake City, UT 84117
Toll-free: (866) 754-5465
Phone: (801) 550-5697
Fax: (626) 602-8715
E-mail: executiveresumes@yahoo.com
URL: www.executivefinalcopy.com

VIRGINIA

Wendy S. Enelow, CPRW, JCTC, CCM
President, Career Masters Institute™
119 Old Stable Rd.
Lynchburg, VA 24503
Toll-free: (800) 881-9972
Phone: (434) 386-3100
Fax: (434) 386-3200
E-mail: wendyenelow@cminstitute.com
URL: www.cminstitute.com

Jean Oscarson
3610 Plymouth Place
Lynchburg, VA 24503
Toll-free: (888) 808-6949
Phone: (434) 384-6124
Fax: (413) 294-7508
E-mail: JeanOscarson@aol.com
URL: www.career-resumes.com

Betty H. Williams, CPRW, NCRW
President, BW Custom Resumes
4531 Menokin Rd.
Richmond, VA 23225
Phone: (804) 359-1065
Fax: (804) 359-4150
E-mail: bwresumes@aol.com

WASHINGTON

Janice M. Shepherd, CPRW, JCTC
Write On Career Keys
2628 E. Crestline Dr.
Bellingham, WA 98226
Phone: (360) 738-7958
Fax: (360) 738-1189
E-mail: resumesbywriteon@earthlink.net
URL: www.resumesbywriteon.com

WISCONSIN

Michele Haffner, CPRW, JCTC
Advanced Resume Services
1314 W. Paradise Ct.
Glendale, WI 53209
Toll-free: (877) 247-1677
Phone: (414) 247-1677
Fax: (414) 247-1808
E-mail: mhaffner@resumeservices.com
URL: www.resumeservices.com

Australia

Gayle Howard, CPRW, CRW, CCM
Founder/Owner, Top Margin Resumes Online
7 Commerford Pl.
Chirnside Park, Melbourne 3116
Australia
Phone: +61 3 9726 6694
Fax: +61 3 9726 5316
E-mail: your.cv@bigpond.net.au
URL: www.topmargin.com

Canada

Martin Buckland, CPRW, JCTC, CEIP
President, Elite Resumes
1428 Stationmaster Ln.
Oakville, Ontario L6M 3A7
Canada
Toll-free: (866) 773-7863
Phone: (905) 825-0490
Fax: (905) 825-2966
E-mail: martin@aneliteresume.com
URL: www.AnEliteResume.com

George Dutch, Ph.D., JCTC, CCM
President, JobJoy, Inc.
750-130 Slater St.
Ottawa, Ontario K1P 6E2
Canada
Toll-free: (800) 798-2696 or (877) 2JOBJOY
Phone: (613) 563-0584
Fax: (613) 594-8705
E-mail: george@jobjoy.com
URL: www.jobjoy.com

Ross Macpherson, MA, CPRW, JCTC, CEIP, CJST
President, Career Quest
1586 Major Oaks Rd.
Pickering, Ontario L1X 2J6
Canada
Phone: (905) 426-8548
Fax: (905) 426-4274
E-mail: ross@yourcareerquest.com
URL: www.yourcareerquest.com

INDEX